Favorite Operas

BY ITALIAN AND FRENCH COMPOSERS

by Paul England

Dover Publications, Inc., New York

This Dover edition, first published in 1973, is an unabridged reprint of appropriate sections from *Fifty Favorite Operas,* by Paul England, second enlarged (1929) edition, London (George G. Harrap & Co., Ltd.) .

International Standard Book Number: 0-486-22932-7
Library of Congress Catalog Card Number: 72-96410

Manufactured in the United States of America
Dover Publications, Inc.
180 Varick Street
New York, N. Y. 10014

MUS

CONTENTS

IL BARBIERE DI SIVIGLIA

Music by ROSSINI. *Words by* STERBINI, *from* BEAUMARCHAIS
Rome, 1816; *London,* 1813; *New York,* 1819.

ALTHOUGH present-day opinion is sharply divided as to the value of Rossini's comic master-piece, and it would be rash to prophesy how long it may continue to hold its rather precarious place in the repertory, historically it must always be considered as of first-class interest. In *Il Barbiere* not only did Rossini introduce new effects both vocal and instrumental, surpassing in brilliance anything that had gone before, but he also finally abolished the method of the old *recitativo secco* (dry recitative), with its thin chords on the keyed instrument, in favour of a full orchestral accompaniment throughout. Moreover, for an opera which is well over its century, *Il Barbiere* is brought curiously close to our own times by reason of its connexion with a great line of singers whose actual personal influence still lingers among us. In 1906 there died in London, at the age of 101, Manuel Garcia, the world-famous teacher of singing, some of whose pupils are still carrying on the great tradition in our midst. This Garcia was the son of a still more famous father. Manuel del Popolo Vicente Garcia was the original Almaviva in the first production of *Il Barbiere* at Rome in 1816, and repeated his performance at the first New York performance in Italian in 1825, when his son, Manuel, aged 20, sang the part of Figaro, while the Rosina was his daughter Maria, who, as Mme Malibran, was destined in the few short years of her career to prove herself perhaps the greatest genius that ever appeared in opera. It is not easy to realize that a man who took a prominent part in this historic performance died in London not twenty years ago.

The first night of *Il Barbiere* (Rome, 5th January, 1816) was a fiasco of the loudest; the noise began with the Count's first solo and reached its climax with the second Act, very little of which got across the footlights. The opposition came chiefly from the partisans of the great Paisiello, a composer of the former generation, whose opera on the same subject had been immensely popular with the Italians for close on fifty years. Rossini had foreseen the difficulty; he had written a flattering letter to the aged *maestro*, and received a civil reply; moreover, he had named his work *Almaviva, ossia l'inutile precauzione* in order to disavow any idea of competition with the accepted masterpiece, Paisiello's *Barbiere di Siviglia*. But, ironically enough, his own precautions proved of no avail. Happily, the first-night failure did not greatly disturb the genial composer; he made a few prudent alterations in the score, and by the end of the week the new *Barbiere* had triumphed, and Rossini was the darling of the Roman public.

Apart from the prejudice in favour of Paisiello, one of the objections to the new opera was that the voices were overpowered by the instrumentation. The charge was no new one; it had been brought against Gluck more than half a century ago, and at the first performance of Haydn's *Creation* in 1797 did not the soprano complain that this was "the first time she had ever been asked to accompany an orchestra"? In Rossini's case the suggestion was ridiculous; he worshipped the voice as the loveliest of all instruments, and no composer has ever handled it more tenderly. At the same time, he was most exacting in his demands on the singers; he was the first to try to curb their excessive passion for ornamentation by writing out all florid passages in full, and insisting, as far as he was able, that they should sing nothing but what was set down. One would have thought that Rossini's original *fioriture* would suffice for the most exuberant of prima donnas, yet when Adelina Patti, soon after her *début*, sang *Una voce poco fa* to the aged *maestro*, she did so disguise the air in a network of new embroideries as to provoke his gentle sarcasm : " That's a very pretty song, my child ! Who composed it ? "

Il Barbiere is, in fact, the most persistently florid opera in existence ; should anyone suppose that *Una voce* is an exceptional show-piece, let him examine the music of Almaviva (tenor), Figaro (baritone), and Bartolo (bass) ; each of these parts abounds in florid passages demanding a quite exceptional agility—indeed, for sheer *bravura*, Almaviva eclipses Rosina, and is, musically, the dominant rôle in the opera. It is doubtful whether it would be possible at the present day, in any of the leading opera houses, to give a really worthy performance of *Il Barbiere* as Rossini wrote it.

The music for Rosina, it should be noted, was written originally for contralto, or low mezzo, a type of voice which Rossini was the first to bring into prominence ; the part, however, passed into the hands of the high soprano with results that can only be deplored ; *Il Barbiere* in our days is revived only occasionally, and for the sake of the popular prima donna of the hour, and in too many cases means little more than *Una voce* and the interpolated display in the Lesson Scene. This is a thousand pities ; for *Il Barbiere*, if properly given, is not only a feast of gay, delicious music, but manages also to convey a fair amount of the spirit of Beaumarchais' brilliant comedy from which it is derived.

The well-known overture has a queer history attached to it ; originally written for a serious opera on a classical subject (*Aureliano*), it had served, later, as an introduction to *Elizabeth, Queen of England* ; it would seem, however, to have found its proper place in *The Barber*, where its rather jiggety melodies are a fit preparation for the scenes of impossible gaiety which follow. The truth is that Rossini never troubled much about the dramatic propriety of his music—his creed seems to have been that a really good tune could be made to fit any situation.

To the present generation Mozart's *Marriage of Figaro* is probably better known than Rossini's *Barber of Seville* ; anyone familiar only with the first opera may feel slightly confused on making acquaintance with the second, as in both works we meet the same characters—Figaro, the Count Almaviva, Rosina (the Countess), Dr Bartolo, Basilio—under very different circumstances. We must bear in mind that the dramatic action of *The Barber* precedes that of *Figaro*. Rossini shows us the wooing and winning of Rosina, the ward of Bartolo, by the Count Almaviva with the assistance of Figaro the Barber ; in Mozart's opera, Figaro (now the Count's valet) is intriguing to secure his own matrimonial happiness, which his master is most ungratefully striving to destroy ; Rosina, now the Countess, plays the rôle of the neglected wife ; the characters of Bartolo and Basilio are much the same in both operas, though the old Doctor naturally looms larger in *The Barber* as the guardian and prospective husband of Rosina. The vocal differences are interesting ; Almaviva, the florid tenor of *The Barber*, appears as a baritone in *Figaro* ; Figaro, the volatile baritone of Rossini, is a *basso-cantante* with Mozart, who treats Basilio, another Rossinian baritone, as a light tenor.

Act I. *Scene* I. A street in Seville, flooded with early morning sunlight. Here lives old Doctor Bartolo with his pretty young ward Rosina, whom he intends soon to make his wife. Her room looks on the street, but the shutters are still closed when Count Almaviva appears with his band of music, to waken the lady with a gentle *aubade*. [This effective number, *Ecco ridente il cielo*, like the overture, had already done duty in two previous operas.] The Count dismisses the musicians, but with such a liberal reward that they refuse to go till they have sung a noisy chorus of gratitude ; finally the Count and his servant, Fiorello, have to drive them off the stage.

Now that all is quiet, Rosina appears on the balcony, only to be frightened back again by the thrumming of a guitar ; Almaviva too goes into hiding. Indeed, the empty stage is hardly big enough to hold the important personage who now advances—Figaro, the pride of Seville, the barber of quality, prince of all barbers, blood-letters, plotters and go-betweens. " Room for the city's fac-totum ! " (*Largo al factotum*) sings this agreeable rattle in a breathless patter-song which for sheer high spirits has no rival in opera.

The Count recognizes in Figaro an old acquaintance who had been useful to him in Madrid, their native city ; it was there that Almaviva had first seen the lady of the balcony, whom he had followed to Seville, and who is, as he supposes, old Bartolo's daughter. Figaro enlightens him—he happens to be intimate with that household, where he is " barber, perruquier, chirurgeon, botanist, and horse-doctor "—Rosina is not Bartolo's daughter, but his ward.

At this moment the young lady reappears on the bal-cony—oh, so modest and demure !—with the suspicious Doctor at her heels.

What is that paper she holds in her hand ? Merely a

ballad from the latest musical piece, *The Futile Precaution*; the Doctor knows it, of course ? The Doctor does not ; he disapproves of all poetry and playgoing, at any rate for young ladies. In her surprise at his ignorance Rosina lets the paper flutter from her hand to the street below—how careless !—and will the good Doctor kindly fetch it for her ?

As soon as his back is turned, the minx signals to the waiting Count (whom she knows well enough by sight) to pick up the dropped note. When Bartolo finds it already gone—" It must have been the wind ! " she says innocently. The old man is not so sure ; but his business calls him abroad, and he bustles off, after giving strict orders to admit no one in his absence, with the exception of Basilio, the music-master.

Rosina's note assures the Count that she is not indifferent to him—if only she knew his name and his station ! Could he not manage to convey such information in a little ballad sung beneath her window ? Taking Figaro's guitar, the Count replies in the air *Se il mio nome saper voi bramate* ; his name, he tells her, is Lindoro ; he has no riches, nothing but a faithful heart, on fire for her alone. This greatly delights Rosina, who, at the end of the second stanza, begins a reply, when the loud slamming of a door alarms her, and she is seen no more.

[Rossini's music here is fresh and charming, but anyone who will take the trouble to look up the corresponding air (*Saper vorreste*) in Paisiello's superannuated *Barbiere* will have to confess that the older work loses nothing by comparison.]

Almaviva is now more on fire than ever, and gladly listens to Figaro's proposals for forwarding his suit : a company of soldiers has just come to town ; the Count must disguise himself as a trooper, and present himself at

Bartolo's house with a billeting order, which is bound to procure him a lodging in the house of his beloved. The Count at once recognizes a master-mind in Figaro, agrees to reward him liberally, and requires his address for future emergencies. Figaro gives it to him in several pages of music—his *Numero quindici* is the climax of the long and rollicking duet which ends the first Scene.

Scene II. Rosina's boudoir ; the embroidery frame, the music-stand, tell us of her accomplishments, while the stout jalousies of the balcony, securely locked, suggest old Bartolo's opinion of her true character. Further, on a little writing-table, please notice that there are only five sheets of paper ! The sixth, written and folded, is in the hands of Rosina, as she enters for her opening air. *Una voce poco fa*, like *Ombra leggiera*, and the Mad Scene from *Lucia*, is one of the half-dozen examples of old-fashioned florid Italian opera which every light soprano is still expected to have on her list, and is perhaps the one which produces the greatest effect with the least expenditure of energy. In it Rosina expresses her resolve to risk all for her dear ' Lindoro ' ; if her guardian tries to coerce her, let him look out !—" for," sings the charming rogue, " I can be a regular viper when I choose ! "

She seals the note she has written to her lover ; how shall she send it ? She thinks naturally of Figaro, who enters at this moment, but has to fly at the approach of Bartolo. The old man's tantrums fairly drive Rosina from the room, and, on Basilio's entry, he announces his resolve to marry his ward the very next day. Basilio quite approves, especially as he has just heard that Count Almaviva (whom Bartolo has long suspected) is now in Seville ; however, Basilio has a plan—he will spread such slanderous reports about him that the Count will have to fly the city. The singing-master is an adept in this art ;

in the famous " Calumny " song (*La Calonnia*) he pictures
the progress of a slander from a tiny whispering breeze
that grows and grows in force until at last it bursts in a
furious tempest that brings the victim down in ruin.

Figaro and Rosina now have the stage once more to
themselves ; he tells her of her guardian's determination
to marry her on the morrow, and, at the same time,
assures her of Lindoro's devotion.   There is no time to
be lost ; Figaro undertakes to deliver Rosina's letter and
assures her that he will contrive a meeting between the
lovers without delay.   Bartolo returns to find Rosina with
her fingers inky, the pen ruined, and one sheet of paper
missing ; to his angry questions she returns such fantastic
answers that he flies into a passion, and ends the scene
with such an elaborate specimen of florid patter, *A un
dottor della mia sorte*, as is frankly beyond the skill of our
modern basses.

Now begins the amazing *finale*, dramatically not too
well constructed, but musically a sustained effort of
mingled humour and brilliancy hard to parallel.

The Count, disguised as a trooper rather the worse for
drink, forces his way noisily into Bartolo's presence, and
waves his billeting-order in his face ; their angry alterca-
tion brings Rosina quickly on the scene, with whom the
Count at once manages to establish an understanding,
and drops a note for her, which she conceals under her
handkerchief.   The Doctor, who has been searching for
a paper which exempts him from all billeting, turns just
in time to see the manœuvre, and, in a fury, orders the
trooper out of the house.   Figaro now enters and endeavours to prevent an actual struggle, for the Count is
rather carried away by the part he is playing, and is inclined to overdo it.   Just as the turmoil is at its height a
knocking is heard, and the Civil Guard enters, to inquire

the reason of the row ; Bartolo orders them to arrest the
trooper, which they are about to do, when the latter,
managing to take the officer aside, shows him the insignia
of his nobility. The effect is magical; instead of arresting him, the officer steps back and salutes; the rest are
struck dumb with amazement. Old Bartolo, in particular,
seems turned to stone, and the fine *largo* which follows,
Freddo ed immobile, is of the same duration as the Doctor's
stupefaction, which ends in a violent sneeze, the result of
some snuff considerately administered by Figaro. In spite
of this incident, ' cold and immovable ' they all remain
through eighty more pages of closely constructed *ensemble*, of which a noticeable feature is a broad melody of
thirty bars (*Mi par d'esser colla testa*) sung by all the
voices in unison or in octaves, and repeated later on in a
higher key. The musical interest is well sustained to the
end, but the whole *finale* is of such interminable length
that it is doubtful if it will ever be heard again in its
entirety.

Act II. The farther we proceed in this opera the more
must we regret that Rossini's original title, *Almaviva, or
the Useless Precaution*, has not been retained, for, whether
as Lindoro, the drunken soldier, or the singing-master of
the coming scene, Count Almaviva is by far the most
prominent personage in the play : Barber Figaro may be
the inspirer of the complicated intrigue, but the Count
is always the protagonist. His music, too, naturally out-
shines all the rest, written as it was for Manuel Popolo del
Vicente Garcia, one of the most remarkable tenors of that
or any other period ; if we examine, for instance, the
close of the present Act, we shall find it little more than
a series of florid solos for Almaviva, of an almost incredible
brilliance, while Rosina's vocal claims are practically
ignored. However, for more than half a century their

positions have been reversed—the Count has dwindled, and Rosina has demanded all the limelight ; people go to *Il Barbiere* to hear Mme Melbazzini in the Lesson Scene.

The Doctor is alone in Rosina's boudoir, when Almaviva appears, this time in the dress of a cathedral chorister ; Alonzo is his name, he says, and he is Basilio's pupil ; his master is ill, and has sent him in his place to give Rosina her singing-lesson. Bartolo is at first not too ready to agree to this, but ' Alonzo ' has hit on a cunning device for persuading him—he has found, he says, a letter from Rosina to ' Lindoro ' ; in the course of the lesson he proposes to inform her of his discovery in such a way as to arouse her suspicions of her lover's honour. Bartolo approves the idea, pockets the letter, and brings Rosina into the room to have her lesson.

As everyone knows, this scene is the prima donna's playground ; at her master's request for a song she sings what she likes, with no regard for dramatic propriety, and adds just as many encores as she feels inclined to. We do not propose to trace the origin and development of the custom ; it would be tedious to compile a list of the " airs with variations," the " vocal waltzes," in which different prima donnas have ' fancied themselves,' or to note that Mme A. always finishes with " Robin Adair," while Mme B. prefers " Home, sweet home ! " A prima donna, as experience teaches us, if once given her head, is *capable de tout*. Catalani, for instance, might well have introduced *Non più andrai*, the bass air from *Figaro*, into this scene—it was one of her favourite *tours de force* ; and was there not a favourite ' Marguerite ' in the last century who made a point of singing " Nearer, my God, to Thee ! " in the Church Scene in Gounod's *Faust* ?

Rosina having sung herself out at last, it is old Bartolo's turn ; after obliging with an old-fashioned love-song, he follows it up with an old-fashioned fling, but stops short on finding that Figaro is mimicking his absurd capers behind his back. The Barber has come to shave the Doctor, who bids him fetch the soap-dish, and hands him his bunch of keys for the purpose ; Figaro takes the opportunity to detach the key of the balcony shutters—(" 'Tis the newest one ! " whispers Rosina). His search for the soap-dish results in a loud crash of falling china, which sends old Bartolo hurrying to the spot, leaving the lovers time for the long-wished-for *tête-à-tête*, in which they have just time to plan an elopement for that night. Bartolo and Figaro return, and the shaving is about to begin when all are amazed by the entrance of Basilio, apparently in perfect health, and with no knowledge of any pupil by the name of Alonzo ! Figaro rises to the occasion ; with his practised eye he sees at once that Basilio is undoubtedly very ill—in fact he is suffering from scarlet fever ! Old Bartolo takes alarm at this, Basilio's protests are useless, and he is hustled from the room. The shaving at last begins in earnest, and the two lovers are thereby enabled to carry on a conversation in a low voice ; but the Count, forgetting the situation, raises his voice too high, and some remarks to Rosina about ' disguises ' serve to kindle the old man's worst suspicions. In a towering passion he drives ' Alonzo ' and Figaro from the house, and proceeds to show Rosina her own letter to ' Lindoro,' with a scandalous account of how it came into his possession ; indignant at what she considers proof of her lover's faithlessness, she volunteers to marry her guardian the next morning, and leaves the room in tears.

Act III. Midnight was the hour appointed for Rosina's elopement with her ' Lindoro ' ; well, she will be ready, but only to load him with reproaches, to show him " what a regular viper she can be when she chooses ! "

To prepare us for a stormy scene Rossini has written an orchestral *tempesta* which, if not very convincing, makes an effective background for the entrance of the two conspirators, the Count and Figaro. Hardly have the balcony-shutters been thrown back, and the pair stept softly into the room, when Rosina confronts them in a blaze of indignation. ' Lindoro,' however, has little difficulty in clearing up the misunderstanding ; he throws off his cloak, and reveals himself as that glittering personage the Count Almaviva. Their mutual rapture is expressed in a duet, *Ah quel colpo!* of so excessively florid a character that even Figaro, who himself is no stranger to such vagaries, is compelled to cut in with a mocking imitation. But, looking from the window, he sees two figures with lanterns approaching the house— there is no time to be lost—the three prepare to descend from the balcony.

[Here comes the famous trio, *Zitti, zitti!*—a trivial little tune, but so daintily handled that it rarely fails of its encore.]

Alas ! there is no escape that way—someone has removed the ladder ! The arrival of Basilio and the Notary with the marriage-contract for Bartolo and his ward Rosina seems to threaten complete disaster—but Figaro's assurance carries all before it. He takes instant possession of the Notary, introducing himself as the uncle of Rosina, who is about to be married to the Count Almaviva. Is the contract sealed ? Very good ; then let us proceed to the signing. No use for the astonished Basilio to protest—the Count holds him up with a pistol in one hand and a valuable ring in the other—Basilio chooses the ring. Old Bartolo—it was he who discovered the tell-tale ladder !—now bursts into the room with an officer of the guard to arrest the burglars ; but as it is obviously impossible to arrest the Count Almaviva on such a charge, and as the marriage-contract between him and Rosina is already signed, there is nothing for it but a general reconciliation. The Doctor, while cheated of his Rosina, is somewhat consoled by her dowry, which the Count places in his hands, and is left to reflect on the singularly appropriate title of " the new opera, *The Useless Precaution*."

We have given the plot of this opera in all the detail of the original for the better information of the reader, but he must not expect to find it in exact correspondence with any present-day performance. Even more than Mozart's *Figaro*, Rossini's *Barber* is usually cut so clumsily as to make it almost unintelligible. The sad truth is that it is impossible to-day to find a full cast capable of doing justice to the exceedingly florid music ; we must wait for a great revival of the art of singing, and a corresponding change in public taste, before we can hope for a worthy performance of *Il Barbiere* in its entirety.

GUILLAUME TELL

Music by Rossini. *Words by* Jouy and Bis.
Paris, 1829; *London,* 1830; *New York,* 1857.

IT must be confessed that the interest of this opera
for our day is largely historical. If Rossini is to
maintain a place in the repertory, it will be through
the florid elegance and sparkling gaiety of *Il Barbiere,*
the most perfect expression of his peculiar talent and
purely Italian in style ; *Tell,* on the other hand, must be
classed with the French School, to which the composer
belonged by adoption only. In *La Gazza Ladra* and *La
Cenerentola* he had given us very suitable companions to
Il Barbiere, and although he had written serious operas
as well, *Tancredi, Otello,* and *Semiramide,* these were every
whit as Italian in conception and treatment as the lighter
works from his pen.

However, in the thirteen years that elapsed between
The Barber and *Tell,* Paris had become, or was rapidly
becoming, the centre of operatic activities ; Rossini seems
to have discerned the rising star of Meyerbeer upon the
horizon, and judged that the time was come for him to
compose a ' grand ' opera in the French manner. The
production of *Guillaume Tell* in 1829 served to raise the
composer higher than ever in public esteem, and he had
arranged to write four other works of a similar character,
when the revolution of 1830 and the subsequent change
in the French dynasty upset all his plans, and drove him
into exile.

During this period Rossini may possibly have come to
doubt whether he was quite the man to write the ' serious '

opera which the future seemed to demand. Whatever his reason, he composed no more for the stage—in fact during the thirty-two years of life that still remained to him his only important production was the completed version of the famous *Stabat Mater*, a work so little 'serious' in character that it was found possible in the eighteen-sixties to utilize it for an admirable set of quadrilles, where the luscious tunes seem less out of place than when forced into connexion with the grave Latin stanzas for which they were originally written.

But although *Tell* was brilliantly successful on its first performance, it was seen to be far too lengthy. Its five Acts were cut down to three, and finally left at four; nor was it long before it became the custom in Paris to present a single Act of the opera in conjunction with some other work. In England it was treated with greater reverence; till well into the sixties it was regarded as Rossini's masterpiece and, with the exception of *Fidelio*, the finest example of dramatic opera in existence. But not all its picturesque setting, nor even the novelty and brilliance of its orchestration, can convince us to-day that, as an opera, *Tell* is anything but a clumsy and long-winded affair.

The composer was unfortunate in his libretto. The rather colourless story of William Tell, undistinguished except for the incident of the perilous shot at the apple, hardly lends itself to operatic treatment. The practised hand of Scribe perhaps might have succeeded in pulling it together, but the two obscure librettists (MM. Jouy and Bis) to whom it was entrusted could make nothing of it—the plot, as we have it, is flat and amorphous.

The scenario has every advantage of the picturesque, in the lakes and mountains of Switzerland, with its fishers, herds, and hunters—the historical background, too, is of interest, showing the struggles of Helvetia in the 13th century to throw off the Austrian yoke. The opening Scene promises well ; we have the familiar figure of the young and ardent patriot, Arnold, opposed to the cruel tyrant, Gessler, yet in love with that tyrant's daughter, Mathilde, and we scent the inevitable conflict between love and duty. So far, so good. But the trouble is that Arnold, though the *primo tenore*, is not the real hero, and that William Tell, who of course occupies that position, is unfortunately prevented from marrying the heroine, being already provided with a shadowy wife, Hedwige, and a puppet son, Jemmy. The result is that our sympathies are divided and our minds confused. For a successful intrigue it would be necessary to make Tell a single man, and to marry him to Mathilde after shooting the apple from her head instead of Jemmy's. The purists, it is true, might possibly kick at such a variant of a time-honoured legend ; and there is the still graver objection that no prima donna would ever consent to marry a mere baritone, however heroic.

The overture to *William Tell* still holds an honoured place in the repertory of the concert-hall, but can only make its full effect when heard as an introduction to the opera. It is a beautiful example of descriptive music ; we see the placid waters of the lake, we breathe the pure mountain air, we hear the call of the shepherd on the heights, the sound of the sheep-bells ; then comes the storm, only to yield again to returning calm, and the rhythmic gallop of a hunting party ends the scene.

Act I offers but poor dramatic fare. The scene is by the lake of Lucerne ; such a chance for Swiss music was not to be missed, and Rossini has stuffed his score with choruses and dances of peasants, shepherds, and fisher-men, with the sounds of hunters in the distance. Much is made of a village festival at which several couples go through a ceremony of betrothal. Old Melcthal, the venerable patriarch of the village, who blesses the affianced pairs, is vexed that his son Arnold (also referred to as Melcthal, to our confusion) has not yet made up his mind to enter into the ' bonds of Hymen.' The unhappy tenor, who dares not let his secret be suspected, finds what consolation he may in acquainting the audience, in a series of asides, with his passion for Mathilde, the daughter of the hated tyrant Gessler. As the heroine does not appear at all in this Act, these asides are the only means Arnold has of informing us of the truth, and it is this necessity which accounts for the interminable duet between him and Tell, in which the future liberator of his country urges Arnold to join him in his effort to throw off the yoke of the oppressor. To Tell's fiery pleadings he gives but a lukewarm response—" all," as he is careful to keep us informed, " on account of Matilda," for Arnold, of course, is a sturdy patriot at heart.

We are half-way through the Act before anything happens. At last the stagnation is ended by the entrance of Leuthold, a shepherd, breathless and exhausted, his dagger still dripping with blood. His only daughter had been abducted by one of Gessler's soldiers—he has killed him, and is fleeing from the wrath of his pursuers. His only chance of escape is to reach the opposite shore of the lake: who will row him across ? No one, it seems, not even the most experienced boatman, will venture on so perilous a journey in the face of the storm that is gathering. Gessler's men are already heard approaching, when Tell himself arrives and at once offers to take the risk of the crossing. As he hurries the hunted man into the boat and rows swiftly away, the villagers sink on their knees in one of those stage prayers which Rossini had already done so much to popularize.

If this particular example is not quite so spell-binding as its famous predecessor in *Moses in Egypt*, it certainly makes an effective contribution to a picturesque and vigorous *finale*.

The fugitives are already out of reach when the soldiers arrive, led by Rudolph, furious at Leuthold's escape. He at once demands the name of the other man in the boat. Not only will no one give it him, but the venerable Melcthal comes boldly forward to denounce the blustering Rudolph to his face, and is immediately seized, to be led before Gessler, at whose hands he is little likely to find mercy.

Act II is also singularly devoid of dramatic interest. The scene is in the deep heart of a forest where Mathilde has come to await her lover. After an irrelevant huntsmen's chorus, our heroine sings the best-known solo in the opera, *Sombres forêts*, an air hardly distinguished, except for its comparative freedom from Rossini's usual florid ornamentation. On Arnold's arrival she joins him in a duet of tedious length, at the end of which she is driven into hiding by the sound of voices—it is Tell and his fellow-patriot Walter Furst, who have been witnesses to the lovers' hurried parting. They both upbraid Arnold for his want of patriotism in dallying with the tyrant's daughter at a time when his country needs his aid in the struggle for freedom. In the course of an interminable trio Tell informs Arnold that his father, the venerable Melcthal, has been put to death by Gessler's orders ; he is now thoroughly roused to a sense of his position— Mathilde is no more for him, he must live and die for Switzerland alone. All the patriots of the Three Cantons now assemble on the stage, and in what is known as the Conspirators' Chorus call heaven to witness that they will never cease to fight till Switzerland is delivered from the foreign yoke.

Act III. We now come to the famous incident of Tell and the apple, which so long passed for history, but has now been relegated to the category of sun-myths.

Before we get to action, however, we must have a farewell interview between Arnold and Mathilde. We cannot help feeling that up to this point the prima donna has been rather unhandsomely dealt with, but some compensation is now made her in the long solo, *Pour notre amour*, a vigorous affair with some bold flights of *coloratura*, enabling the lady to display a compass of two good octaves.

We now pass to the big scene of the opera. We are in the market-place of Altdorf, where Gessler has arranged to celebrate the centenary of the Austrian occupation of Switzerland, and so enable the natives to express their thankfulness for all the benefits derived from that happy event. This, of course, gives admirable opportunity for the inevitable ballet, with Tyrolese choruses, and military evolutions on the part of the Austrian soldiers. (It is worthy of note that on the first night of *Tell* the great Taglioni herself led the dancing.)

A prominent feature of the spectacle is a hat fixed on the top of a pole which Gessler has set up as a symbol of the imperial power, to which all are obliged to do homage. Tell alone refuses to make the required obeisance. He is at once arrested and condemned to imprisonment, together with the boy Jemmy. The tyrant, however, realizing that he can wound Tell still more grievously through his affection for his son, offers to release the latter on one condition—Tell, the famous archer, must give an exhibition of his skill by shooting at an apple placed on Jemmy's head. He is in honour bound to accept the challenge, and Gessler confidently expects to see the son's death brought about by his own father. After performing the perilous feat, Tell, in embracing his son, lets drop a second arrow to the ground ; on being questioned as to its purpose, he boldly confesses that it was intended for Gessler, in case the first one had done its deadly work. He is again arrested and doomed to end his days in the dungeons of Kussnach (" a prey to hungry reptiles," as Gessler pleasantly assures him). Jemmy is condemned to a similar fate, but on this point the tyrant yields to the unanimous pleadings of peasants and soldiers, and more especially to those of Mathilde, who takes the boy into her safe keeping until she can restore him to his mother.

Act IV. With the commanding figure of William Tell to dominate the opera, it is no easy matter to provide sufficient opportunities of vocal display for Arnold, who, if not the hero, is at least the *primo tenore*. However, now that Tell is safe in prison, the tenor is temporarily promoted to the place of First Patriot. We find him revisiting the deserted house on the shores of the lake, so rich in memories of childhood. The thought of his murdered father fills him with bitter grief, and in the andante *Asile héréditaire* he takes his last farewell—henceforth his life must be his country's, and revenge his only business. Cries of " Vengeance ! Vengeance ! " announce the arrival of a band of armed insurgents, who acquaint Arnold with Tell's arrest, and call on him to lead them at once against the tyrant ; he responds in the martial air *Amis ! Amis !* which as a show-piece for a really robust tenor is comparable only to *Di quella pira* in *Il Trovatore*.

Hedwige now enters, distracted at the fate of her husband, whom she looks upon as lost, but the unexpected return of their son Jemmy, accompanied by Mathilde, brings her some comfort, besides allowing for a trio for three sopranos : *Je rends à votre amour*. Tell, meanwhile, has managed somehow to escape from his chains, and is now seen on the lake in a boat struggling to reach the shore.

The voyage is a perilous one, for a hurricane is raging. However, after another of Rossini's celebrated prayers, and some pages of storm music, our hero gains the shore and stands once more among his own people, the determined liberator of his beloved land. Jemmy hands his father his bow and arrow, and Gessler the tyrant arrives on the scene only to receive the last convincing proof of Tell's unerring aim. The tyrant falls, Helvetia is freed from the foreign yoke, and all unite in a song of thanksgiving for the triumph of liberty.

Such is the story of the opera when extended over four Acts. There is fortunately a condensed version in which the Swiss insurgents pour on to the stage immediately after the incident of the apple, despatch the tyrant, and so bring matters to a conclusion at the end of Act III.

The last performance of *Guillaume Tell* at Covent Garden was in 1889; it is hardly likely that it will again find its way into the repertory. If in the future we are called upon to drink to "the immortal memory of Rossini," we shall surely couple it with the name of that enchanting opera *Il Barbiere di Siviglia*.

LA SONNAMBULA

Music by BELLINI. Words by ROMANI.
Milan, 1831 ; London, 1831 ; New York, 1835.

IT has long been a fashion, not altogether wise, to
sneer at *La Sonnambula,* that long-cherished idol of
the early Victorians ; it is doubtful if any opera
remained so long at the height of popularity to fall at
last so low in the general esteem. Yet this work has so
many excellent qualities that the modern attitude toward
it can only partially be justified. So great a man, so
opposite a genius as Wagner, was always ready to recognize Bellini's extraordinary gift of melody, and in *La
Sonnambula* we have that melody in rich abundance, sweet
and crystal-clear. The libretto, too, has conspicuous
merits ; a simple story is unfolded in a natural forthright
manner, with no unnecessary padding, and offering just
the right opportunities for Bellini's peculiar and limited
talents—in fact the whole has a definite artistic value,
although the conventions in which it was begotten have
long since passed away ; the opera of *La Sonnambula*
is just a pleasing pastoral, commendably free from the
customary operatic extravagance of incident.

Act I. *Scene* 1. A hamlet in a picturesque valley of
Italian Switzerland ; a handful of houses, a considerable
hostelry, an old water-mill, with mountains for the background. The villagers are excited over the approaching
nuptials of Amina, the popular village beauty, and Elvino,
a young farmer of the neighbourhood. [Bellini's choruses
are never his strong point, and these peasants do not get
beyond " Long live Amina ! Tra-la-la-la-la ! " to the

thinnest of accompaniments.] Lisa, the young hostess of the tavern, the only unsympathetic character in the piece, now enters, and in a showy but colourless air, *Tutto è gioja*, gives us to understand that Elvino's affections were once hers, and that, in consequence, she is not well-disposed toward Amina, his present *fiancée*. The attentions of Alessio, the young peasant to whom she is actually betrothed, merely irritate her, especially as he is the leader of the choral demonstration in honour of Amina, who now appears, in all the bloom of youth and innocence.

The history of opera is no bad guide to the changing psychology of the centuries. For the England of 1831, Amina, the spotless village maiden, established a type which exactly answered to the ' ideals ' of the coming Victorian epoch. It took a quarter of a century to prepare for the acceptance of the frail Violetta in Verdi's *Traviata*, and a complete revolution in the moral outlook was necessary before the morbid horror of *Salome* could become the rage of two continents. Enter, then, from the mill Amina, the guileless orphan, with Teresa, her foster-mother. With the very first notes she sings the charm of Bellini begins to work ; he has peculiarly the art of natural, graceful recitative, every phrase of which produces its effect. Amina's first air, *Come per me sereno*, and the following caballeta, *Sovra il sen*, expresses perfectly, within their own conventions, the innocent joy of a young girl in love, under the serene Italian sky. Moreover, no music that was ever written shows a more perfect knowledge of the capacities of the voice as a medium of æsthetic beauty ; so long as we have singers equal to the task, so long shall we listen gladly to the joys and sorrows of Amina as Bellini has conceived them in song.

Now comes the Notary, to draw up the contract of espousals ; Elvino follows with the ring for Amina's finger, and a posy of flowers which she slips into her bosom. Their flowing duet, *Prendi l'annel*, is followed by an 'ecstasy' solo for the soprano, *Ah, vorrei trovar parola*, which may have served Verdi as a model in more than one similar situation.

So far the soprano and tenor, supported by a feeble chorus, have managed to sustain the whole interest ; now with some bustle of importance enters the baritone, a distinguished stranger, who asks the way to the Castle— he is actually the Count Rodolfo, the long-absent lord. His air, *Vi ravviso*, for a long time perhaps the most popular number in the whole opera, has lost its savour for us to-day ; it seems to lack the true Bellinian glamour which still surrounds so much of Amina's music.

Evening is falling ; it is too late for the Count to proceed on his journey—indeed, it is better that all should retire to rest, for this is the hour when the dreaded spectre which haunts the valley is wont to appear. The credulous villagers tell us all about it in a chorus, *A fosco cielo*, which gave a new thrill of mystery to the audiences of that day.

The Count resolves to put up at the village inn ; before retiring, however, he finds time to show his admiration for the pretty Amina, so pointedly indeed as to arouse Elvino's jealousy, and the Scene ends with one of Bellini's most graceful duets, *Son geloso del zeffiro errante*, too often omitted in performance.

Act II. The bedroom in the inn perpared for the reception of the Count—a full moon shines in through a large wide-open window. Lisa, the comely and flirtatious hostess, enters to wish his lordship pleasant dreams, and is only too willing to prolong her stay, when a sudden noise drives her into hiding. Then at the window appears " a tall figure all in white "—is it the spectre ?

No, 'tis Amina, the spotless heroine, walking in her sleep. Her mind filled with the thought of her Elvino, she advances into the room, imagining, as her snatches of song confess, that she is even then approaching the altar with her lover at her side. She sinks in slumber on the bed, the picture of virginal purity. Lisa, rejoicing at what she construes as a scandal, now makes her escape, dropping a tell-tale handkerchief as she goes. The Count, awed by the presence of innocence, takes his departure, leaving Amina to sleep in peace.

The spiteful Lisa loses no time in seizing her opportunity; she goes in search of Elvino and Teresa, who, with a crowd of villagers, enter the room to find Amina in her unfortunate situation. Appearances are too strong for her; no one believes her protestations of innocence, least of all Elvino, who casts her from him, leaving her fainting in her mother's arms. The duet *D'un pensiero*, with the broad sweep of its phrases, makes excellent material for the well-wrought *finale*, and comes perhaps as near to passion as the conventionalities of the form will allow.

Act III. *Scene* i. On the way to the Castle, whither the villagers are going to intercede with the Count in favour of Amina. Enter Elvino, to pour forth his sorrows in the much extolled *Tutto è sciolto* which, as a contemporary critic writes, in the manner of his time, is " an effusion which nor can the audience hear nor the vocal histrionic express without being suffused in tears ! " Without going so far as that, we may allow that the melody is truly ' affecting,' in the Victorian idiom, and, given a tenor with the right *timbre*, could never fail to suggest a lover's melancholy. High praise, too, must be given to Elvino's second solo, the vigorous *Ah, perchè non posso odiarti* [literally, " Ah, why can I not hate thee ! " but

known, wherever English is spoken, by the idiotic title
" Still so gently o'er me stealing "]. It must be mentioned
that the latter air is called forth by Amina (supported, of
course, by her foster-mother Teresa), who pleads for
a reconciliation. Elvino, however, is still furious ; he
snatches the betrothal ring from her finger, and leaves her
once more to faint in Teresa's arms. This Scene is
Elvino's great opportunity ; no tenor who could do
justice to the two numbers alluded to could fail to have
the world at his feet in a very short time. Unfortunately,
the extraordinarily high *tessitura* employed, in which the
high B, C♯, and even D, are of constant recurrence,
makes the adventure an impossible one for all but quite
exceptional voices.

Scene II. The water-mill is here the chief feature of
the stage setting ; it must be old and dilapidated, with a
big wheel, a rushing torrent, stone steps, crumbling and
slippery, and a ' trick ' bridge of wood so rotten that one
of its planks is ready to give way any moment. Elvino
has returned to his old love Lisa, and they are actually
on their way to the church when the Count stops them.
He upbraids Elvino for his base suspicions of Amina,
which, he declares, are without the slightest foundation ;
Amina has never wavered in her love and truth.   He then
expounds the nature of somnambulism ; how its victims
are led to do the most extraordinary things while under
its influence, of which they have no recollection in their
waking hours ; Amina, he declares, is a somnambulist,
and, therefore, not responsible for her actions of the previous night. They are all incredulous, but convincing
proof of the Count's statements is immediately forth-
coming. From an upper chamber of the mill comes
Amina, robed in white, holding a lamp in her hand—the
unnatural fixity of her gaze shows that she is in the sleep-

walker's trance. To the horror of the onlookers she ventures on the crazy bridge that spans the foaming stream ; a plank gives way beneath her, the lamp falls from her hand ; miraculously guarded, as it seems, she continues her perilous course, down the uneven moss-grown stairway, until she stands safe among her neighbours, unconscious of their presence. Poor Amina ! why should her life be preserved ? What has she to live for now ? Elvino is gone for ever ; even the ring he placed on her finger is no longer there. And the flowers he gave her ? She draws the posy from her bosom—alas, they are withered, and no tears of hers can bring them back to life. Warned by the Count, the much-moved villagers do not dare to disturb her, until the penitent Elvino—for Lisa's treachery has now been revealed—gently replaces the precious ring ; the chorus can no longer refrain from shouting their favourite *Viva Amina*, as the happy heroine wakes to find her lover kneeling at her feet, her mother at her side, and all the world once more a place of perfect bliss !

This last Scene has inspired Bellini with music of such direct and poignant expression as is found nowhere else in the opera. Amina's air, *Ah non credea mirarti*, remains one of the best examples of true pathos to be found in the entire range of Italian opera ; it possesses that peculiar elegiac quality in which Bellini excelled, and it owes nothing to vocal ornament, which is appropriately reserved for the brilliant rondo *Ah non giunge*, which ends the opera in a shower of fireworks.

It is easy to understand the enormous popularity of the Scene with early Victorian audiences. It appealed, in the first place, to the sentiment, the ' sensibility,' of the age, and, secondly, to the growing interest in popular science of all kinds. Somnambulism was just coming up as a subject for popular discussion among frivolous and serious alike ; a proof of this is found in an early edition of this opera, the preface of which has some columns devoted to an exposition of this strange abnormality, illustrated by anecdotes and a whole string of references to learned medical treatises in English and Latin.

La Sonnambula, produced at Milan in 1831, was heard in London the same year, and two years later was given at Drury Lane, in English, with Malibran as Amina. Never has any English version of an Italian opera achieved such a popular success ; a knowledge of it spread throughout the length and breadth of the country, and about the time of the Great Exhibition of 1851 there were few persons with any pretensions to gentility who could not hum the tunes of " Still so gently," " As I view," and " Do not mingle." Since not many people now alive can be acquainted with the quality of the ' lyrics ' concealed behind these titles, it may be of interest, in view of their amazing ineptitude, to give some quotations from them ; they should make us a little less dissatisfied with the English versions of the present day, which, whatever their faults, will certainly not suffer by the comparison.

ELVINO.   Still so gently o'er me stealing,
           Mem'ry will bring back the feeling,
           Spite of all my grief, revealing
               That I dearly love thee still.
           Though some other swain may charm thee,
           Ah, no other e'er can warm me,
           Yet, ne'er fear, I will not harm thee,
               False one, no ! I love thee still.

· · · · ·

THE COUNT. As I view these scenes so charming
           With dear remembrance my heart is warming
           Of days long vanished. Oh, my heart is filled
               with pain,

Finding objects that yet remain
While those days come not again.
Maid, those bright eyes my heart impressing
Fill my breast with thoughts distressing
By recalling an earthly blessing
   Long since dead and pass'd away.
She was like thee, e'er Death oppressing
   Sank her beauties in decay.

    .   .   .   .   .

AMINA. Do not mingle one human feeling
       With the rapture o'er each sense stealing ;
       See these tributes to me revealing
          My Elvino true to love.

There has hardly been a prima donna since 1831 who has not endeavoured to make the part of Amina ' her own.' The original exponent, strangely enough, was Pasta, whose reputation is more usually associated with such tragic rôles as Medea and Norma. Malibran followed her immediately, then Sontag, Persiani, and Grisi; in 1842 came Jenny Lind, and effaced all previous impressions, at least so far as England and America were concerned. It would be tedious to extend the list, but it is interesting to know that on the statue of Bellini in Naples the three singers who have been thought most worthy of association with the part are Pasta, Malibran, and Emma Nevada.

NORMA

Music by BELLINI. *Words by* ROMANI.
Milan, 1831 ; *London*, 1833 ; *New York*, 1841.

WHATEVER we may think of the music of *Norma* there is no denying the strength of the libretto. It is a drama of conflict on the highest plane of tragedy ; against a background of warring Gauls and Romans we have the struggle of tremendous passions, of love opposed to patriotism, of pity conquering hate, of jealousy yielding to maternal instinct.

The action takes place in Gaul during the Roman occupation in the first century B.C. Norma, a priestess of the Druids, and regarded by them as an inspired prophetess, has, unknown to anyone, broken her vow of chastity for the sake of Pollione, the Roman proconsul, to whom she has borne two children ; wearying of her, he has formed a new connexion with Adalgisa, a young virgin attached to the temple.

Act I. *Scene* 1. For the opening Scene we may imagine a reconstruction of Stonehenge as it was 2000 years ago, taking care to supply a huge oak thick with mistletoe, and, suspended near, the shield of Irminsul, God of War, whose brazen clang is the signal that calls the warriors to arms. A procession of priests enters, headed by Oroveso the Arch-Druid ; he is impatient for action ; too long have they borne the insufferable tyranny of the Roman invader ; it is time to beat on the sacred shield and rouse the tribes to fury. But that solemn act only Norma, the high-priestess, can perform ; Oroveso, her father, bids them all return at the rising of the moon,

when Norma shall be there. Pollione, the Roman governor, now enters to tell us, or rather his centurion Flavio,
of his new passion for Adalgisa. Flavio warns him of his
danger should he be caught in the sacred precincts, and
he retires after hurling defiance at the priesthood in the
bold allegro *Mi protegge, mi difende.*

The Druids return singing a solemn chant to the accompaniment of the famous march which still holds its
own among such compositions. When all are assembled,
Norma should enter with superb effect, in flowing white,
the golden sickle in her hand with which to cut
the sacred mistletoe. She is priestess, prophetess, and
their ruler : let them put aside their foolish clamour for
rebellion ; the power of Rome indeed must be broken,
but the time is not yet.

The full moon floods the scene as Norma cuts the
mystic branch, while she sings the great aria, *Casta diva,*
to the chaste Queen of Heaven, and the sequel, *Ah bello
a me ritorno,* in which she laments for Pollione's love
grown cold.

The rite being over, and all departed, Adalgisa takes
the stage to ask pardon of the gods for her guilty passion
from which she cannot free herself. She is soon joined
by Pollione, who in a long duet persuades her against her
conscience to fly with him to Rome.

Scene II. Here in her private dwelling we see Norma,
no longer the awe-inspiring prophetess, but a tender
mother with a bleeding heart. Her children are with
her—hers and Pollione's—but they can comfort her no
longer ; she fears that their father is about to abandon
her and them, and what then will be their fate ? Sadly
she sends them from her presence, and turns to welcome
one who, like herself, is in sore need of consolation. It
is Adalgisa, who, conscience-stricken, has come to seek

counsel of Norma, her dearest friend, of whose relations with Pollione she is of course ignorant ; to her she confesses her fault, and asks to be released from her vow. The priestess, moved to instant sympathy by an experience so like her own, gives her ready absolution, when Pollione appears upon the scene, and the true state of affairs is revealed, Norma's love turns to hate, and Adalgisa is so horrified at Pollione's treachery that she resolves to give up her lover, and remain faithful to the friend who has shown her a mother's tenderness.

Act II opens with Norma's half-hearted attempt to kill her children, in her mad desire for revenge ; her mother-love, however, prevails against the evil impulse, and she commits them to the care of Adalgisa, whom she advises to trust her happiness to Pollione and to follow him to Rome ; for herself, she declares, death is the only refuge.

But Adalgisa's infatuation is over—she has resolved to end her life in the service of the Temple ; Norma's happiness, she feels, may be restored by Pollione's return to his first love, and she herself will go to him and persuade him to his true duty.

The last Scene is a court in the temple, where Norma is waiting for news of Adalgisa's success. The messenger returns, to tell her the worst ; Pollione refuses to give up Adalgisa—nay, should she persist in flying from him, he will drag her from the very precincts of the Temple. On hearing this, Norma is roused to the wildest fury— Pollione, and Rome with him, shall be made to suffer for this insulting threat. Hastening to the tree where hangs the brazen shield of Irminsul she strikes three times thereon, and at that sound the Druids all assemble. War, she tells them, is now the will of the gods—war against the Romans, fierce and determined. At the same moment a tumult is heard without—some Roman has actually dared to pollute the sacred groves with his presence ; it is Pollione, who has fulfilled his threat to Adalgisa. He is brought in and condemned to instant death ; indeed, his intrusion is almost welcome, as it supplies the human victim that must be sacrificed in order to ensure the success of the expedition.

And Norma's is the hand that must strike the blow. But at the last her old affection wakes again within her —she tries to save him ; if he will but give up Adalgisa his life shall be spared. But Pollione refuses life on such terms, and Norma, in despair, resolves to end her suffer-ings by death. The gods, she announces, have chosen another victim for the sacrifice, a virgin priestess of the temple, who has broken her vows, and brought disgrace upon her country and her father ; the punishment is death by fire. Amazed and wrathful, the Druids demand her name—" It is I—Norma ! " comes the terrible reply. Her father, Oroveso, incredulous, joins with the others in imploring her to take back her words. But no— " Norma cannot lie ! " Unfaltering, exalted by her pur-pose of atonement, she ascends the sacrificial pile—and by her side is Pollione, awake at last to the lofty nature of the woman he has wronged, and rejoicing to share in the only expiation which holds for both the hope of a future reunion.

Such is the ' book ' that Felice Romani, the skilful librettist of *La Sonnambula*, prepared for Bellini as a successor to that simple pastoral. That the young com-poser was overweighted by so tragic a subject is not surprising ; we certainly find a considerable advance in breadth of treatment as compared with the earlier opera— there is a spirited March of Druids at the outset, and a rousing chorus, a call to battle, in Act II—but Bellini could not command the note of tragedy, and the music moves too often with a stilted, mechanical swing. On the other hand, in the purely lyrical passages the true Bellini triumphs as before; he is at his very best in Norma's lovely prayer to the rising moon, *Casta diva*, her scene with the slumbering children, *Teneri figli*, and the duet for Norma and Adalgisa, *Mira, o Norma!* Granted that there are tunes in *Norma* that a self-respecting barrel-organ might kick at, nevertheless it contains so much melodic beauty, to say nothing of the dramatic interest, that an occasional revival of the opera will always be welcome not only to opera-goers, but to all save the most narrow-minded of musical *connoisseurs*. The one indispensable condition is a really strong cast; the three chief parts require singers of exceptional gifts, while the heroine must be not only a perfect mistress of *il bel canto*, but also a tragic actress of a high order; it is small wonder, then, that for many years *Norma* has been practically out of the repertory.

The opera started on its career with every advantage. In the previous year Bellini had made an enormous success with *La Sonnambula*, the leading part in which was designed especially for Mme Pasta, one of the greatest actresses of the time, from whom even those of the 'legitimate' stage did not disdain to learn. In the rôle of the Druid priestess Pasta found a part far worthier of her tragic powers and gave a performance that was one of the sensations of the time. But even a perfect Norma is handicapped unless supported by the right Adalgisa, and here, too, Bellini was equally fortunate; in the first production this rôle was assigned to no less an artist than Giulia Grisi, who was soon to succeed to Pasta's laurels in the part of the heroine, and to remain the ideal Norma for close on a quarter of a century. [During Grisi's reign

Mario was the accepted Pollione, and the great Lablache did not despise the small part of Oroveso.] Pauline Viardot-Garcia, Johanna Wagner, Adelaide Kemble, were all notable Normas; Sontag, Jenny Lind, great singers both, were hardly equipped by nature for such heroic flights. The second half of the 19th century produced no distinguished representatives of the part until Mme Lilli Lehmann, quite late in her career, chose to demonstrate that one of the greatest interpreters of Wagnerian heroines could be equally great in 'old-fashioned Italian opera.' The performance of *Norma* at Covent Garden in 1899, with Mme Lehmann in the title-part and Mme Giulia Ravogli as Adalgisa was as near an approach to the standard of the original production as can be hoped for. Each of these ladies was vocally superb, while Mme Lehmann was a rare combination of all that is best in both the German and Italian schools. After a long course of Wagner, she revelled in a part which, while providing full scope for the tragic actress, allowed her a whole evening of that pure Italian singing her devotion to which she had never lost. Of especial value in this rôle was her remarkable faculty of clothing the most elaborate florid passages with a dramatic significance which completely hid their apparent banality; so intensely did she apply herself to the task that she—an artist who hardly knew what fatigue meant—confessed that a single performance of *Norma* tried her more than all three evenings of Brünnhilde in *The Ring*. These are the words of an exceptional artist, but their general application would bring about a much-to-be-desired reform in the operatic performances of to-day; let every aspirant to Wagnerian honours first school herself to sing the part of Norma—she will then find that, vocally, Isolde, Kundry, Brünnhilde, are mere child's play by comparison.

L'ELISIR D'AMORE

Music by Donizetti. *Words by* Romani.
Milan, 1832; *London,* 1836; *New York,* 1883.

WHEN Donizetti was asked whether he believed the story that Rossini took thirteen days to write *The Barber of Seville,* he replied: "Very likely—Rossini is such a lazy fellow!" Truly, at the rate at which Donizetti composed—the last Act of *La Favorita,* which ranks among his best work, was written in a single night—a fortnight may well have seemed a long time to spend on any opera. He must have written habitually at a furious pace; his first opera was produced at the age of twenty, and in the quarter of a century of activity that remained to him he added sixty more to his credit.

But the composer's power of invention was not robust enough for such a strain—we find him often spinning too slight a thread. The writer of the article in Grove remarks that "of Donizetti's operas at least two-thirds are quite unknown in England"; he would be considered a specialist to-day, we imagine, who could name even ten of them. Besides the three or four works which may be said to have a place in the repertory, the names of a few others are remembered by certain melodious numbers which still survive. *O mio Fernando* may be said to have outlived the opera *La Favorita* in which it occurs, as *Don Pasquale* has bequeathed to us the delicious serenade *Com' è gentil,* and *Convien partir* will probably be heard when *La Fille du Régiment* is laid aside. *L'Elisir d'Amore* also has its popular attraction in the lovely tenor romance *Una furtiva lagrima,* but is by no means dependent on it, as the entire opera is essentially attractive. *L'Elisir* was written early in Donizetti's career, when he was strongly influenced by Rossini, and much of the music is delightfully reminiscent of that great master's gayest manner, while Dulcamara, the quack doctor, is one of the great *buffo* figures in Italian opera, worthy to rank with Rossini's Figaro and Mozart's Osmin.

This Dulcamara is the centre of the rather flimsy little plot. Adina, the heroine, a capable young woman who farms her own land, has two suitors, Nemorino, a diffident young farmer, who does but sigh for her, and Belcore the sergeant, who courts her boldly. The latter seems likely to carry all before him, when the arrival of the great Doctor Dulcamara alters the probable course of events; Nemorino obtains from him a love-potion warranted to make any girl his willing slave; under its influence Adina gives her hand to the young farmer, Belcore cheerfully accepts the situation, every girl in the village lays in a bottle of the magic draught, and Dulcamara's reputation is made for ever.

Act I. *Scene* 1. The scene is in the garden belonging to Adina's comfortable homestead; it is high noon and harvest-time, and the reapers are resting in the shade. The lady is reading, and chuckling over her book. Challenged by the others, she tells them that it is an old romance called *Tristan and Iseult*: "Just listen! Tristan is in love with the lady, who will have nothing to do with him; he therefore procures a certain elixir [*l'elisir d'amore*], drinks it, and Iseult at once falls into his arms! Now, isn't that delightful!" Very; all the girls would like to know where such useful draughts can be obtained; so would Nemorino, who has been lurking and listening, not daring to come forward.

[The reader will notice that we have here a curious

variation of the usual tradition of the love-philtre ; as a rule the potion must be mixed with the drink of the one whose love it is desired to gain, whereas in this case it is drunk by the rejected lover and endows him with the power of inspiring love. The reason probably is that this scheme fits in best with the development of our innocent little story.]

Martial music now prepares us for the entrance of the gallant sergeant Belcore and his men. The son of Mars has no use for love-philtres—he believes in simpler methods ; he is of opinion that he can " put the come-ther " upon any woman he chooses, in double-quick time. Just now his object is the very wide-awake Adina. Without hesitation he marches smartly up to her, presents his bouquet, and after a few *roulades* in the true Rossinian manner, lays siege to her heart in a fine bold melody, *Più tempo, oh Dio, non perdere*, in which he urges the lady to waste no more time since, as he points out, she is bound to yield at last. This theme serves as material for the *ensemble* that follows, in which Adina keeps him well in hand—she herself declines to be hurried, but will take time to think it over.

The sergeant having withdrawn his men for refreshment, the timid Nemorino comes out of his retirement and begs a word with her. Now though Adina's heart secretly inclines toward this too modest wooer, she finds his long face and woebegone speeches a little tedious. " If you can't stop sighing," she tells him, " would it not be better to go right away for a time ? Go and visit that sick old uncle of yours—if you don't hurry up he may die before you get there, and you'll find yourself cut off with a shilling ! Then, of course, *you'll* die—of hunger ! " " Better die of hunger than of love ! " is the desperate retort. " Well," she says coldly, " I'm sorry—but *I* can't love you!" "Why?" asks the fatuous young man. It takes Adina several pages of elegant filigree-work to explain her reasons—and even then poor Nemorino is not satisfied.

Scene II. Now the fun begins in earnest. The village square is empty when the curtain rises, but the blare of a trumpet brings the women out of the houses and the men from their labour. The advancing trumpeter is but the herald of a truly imposing spectacle; on the stage there rolls a golden chariot, only less dazzling than the magnificent and spanking personage who stands upright in it with an air of lordly patronage for all the world. This is the great Doctor Dulcamara, most picturesque, most genial of all stage quacks and charlatans.

[The colossal Luigi Lablache, who created the part, seems to have set a standard of perfection which no one since has ever approached; a superb presence, an unctuous humour, a perfect method applied to perhaps the finest bass voice on record, all these combined to make that wonderful artist unique in this as in many other parts.]

The Doctor's hands and pockets are full of little phials and boxes, the virtues of which he extols in the long patter-song *Udite, o rustici*, a piece of Rossinian gaiety, only comparable with that master's *Largo al factotum* or *Miei rampolli feminini*. Have you toothache, heartache, wrinkles? Here is an ointment that will banish them for ever! And here, still greater marvel, is the universal remedy that will cure all diseases, dry a widow's tears, and make an old man young and lusty! As for the price—well, everyone knows that Dulcamara's Grand Specific is worth a guinea a bottle, but to them, his own dear countrymen, the price is half a crown!

When the grateful peasants have departed, well satisfied with their treasures, Nemorino seizes the oppor-

tunity; has the Doctor perchance any of that patent
fluid that Sir Tristan used in order to bring Madame Iseult
to reason—the elixir of love? The Doctor beams with
satisfaction—why, he himself is the distiller and sole
proprietor of that magic potion! [The lively duet
Obbligato! exactly expresses Nemorino's joy at his good
fortune and Dulcamara's opinion of him as the silliest
pigeon he has ever plucked!] The amorous youth puts
down his last coin for a flask of formidable size with which
he is eager to experiment at once. "Certainly!" says
the benevolent Doctor, "drink it now! But remember
it will not take effect till to-morrow, by which time,"
he confides to the audience, "I shall be far enough away!"
After another delightful duet, *Va, mortale fortunato,*
Nemorino is left alone to try what effect the elixir will
have on himself. The first draught delights him, the
second excites him; by the time he has drunk it all he
feels a new man—and no wonder, since, as the Doctor
has informed us in an undertone, the famous elixir is
just a bottle of good red wine!

Adina enters—she can scarcely believe her eyes: this
is never Nemorino, this laughing, singing, rollicking loon!
Their duet, *Esulti pur la barbara,* sung for the most part
'aside,' allows sufficient musical dialogue for Nemorino
to assure the lady that he has taken her advice to heart;
no more sighing for him—he feels quite jolly already!—
and to-morrow—"Well, to-morrow," he says, "you will
see!" "Yes!" retorts Adina, now thoroughly nettled,
"we *will* see!" The opportune entrance of Belcore
determines her course of action. She is all smiles and
complaisance for the newcomer, and, as the sergeant is
out for victory, in less than five minutes he has asked her
to name the day. "Say a week from now!" says Adina,
with her eye on Nemorino, to see how he will take it.

To her discomfiture, and Belcore's indignation, her once bashful adorer does nothing but chuckle to himself, or laugh aloud, to think how the tables will be turned to-morrow, when the elixir has begun to work its magic on Adina.

But alas! how easily things go wrong! A messenger arrives with despatches: marching orders for to-morrow morning—and the wedding indefinitely postponed! Nemorino, well pleased at this new turn of affairs, is still chuckling, when Belcore forces the pace and carries all before him: after all, why should they wait? Why not get married to-day? Adina assents to the proposal with the greater alacrity as she notices the astonishing effect it has on Nemorino. The poor fellow almost collapses; he sees all his hopes vanish in a moment—the elixir he knows will not take effect until to-morrow, and by that time Adina will be another's! He implores her not to act so rashly—to wait until the morning! But the lady is obdurate; Nemorino's assumed indifference has wounded her pride, and she will make him smart for it.

All through this scene we are left in doubt whether Adina may not be using the sergeant merely as a blind, in order to bring the young farmer back to his old allegiance. However, the hour for the wedding is fixed, the neighbours bidden to the feast, and the curtain falls on the distracted Nemorino, jeered at by all and calling wildly on the Doctor to come to his aid.

[The closing quartet and chorus are a worthy climax to an Act the music of which is consistently graceful and exhilarating; in the elaborate middle section, *Adina credimi*, and the delicious final frolic, *Fra lieti contenti*, we see how admirable was Donizetti's talent so long as he confined himself to his proper sphere of comic opera.]

Act II. *Scene* I. The preparations for the wedding have begun already ; there is some jolly feasting at the tables in the big farmhouse kitchen, and Belcore's men are making a jolly noise on their brass instruments. The only personage not there is Nemorino, and it is significant that Adina's first words are an expression of regret at his absence. Dulcamara, of course, is in his element ; he earns our gratitude by introducing a really captivating little duet —a *barcarolle* he calls it—in which he induces his fair hostess to join him ; it is only just out, he says, as he produces the music from his pocket and hands her her part, and we are all the more delighted when we find that Adina, who is certainly one of the most attractive of light-opera heroines, includes among her many gifts the ability to sing at sight.

On the arrival of the Notary all leave the room except Dulcamara, who calmly goes on with his feasting. Nemorino enters in desperate plight : much good the elixir has done him ! What's the use of winning Adina's love to-morrow if she is married to someone else to-day ? Can't the Doctor do something ? Certainly ! Nemorino has only to take another bottle, and the charm will begin to work in half an hour. " That," adds the Doctor for our benefit, " gives me plenty of time to get away ! "

This is good hearing, only Nemorino has no money— well, the Doctor has to go back to his inn, so Nemorino must raise the money and bring it to him there in a quarter of an hour.

Belcore enters most opportunely—Nemorino tells him his need, though not the reason for it. The sergeant, eager to get him out of the way, advises him to enlist for a soldier, and put money in his pocket that way. Nemorino agrees, signs the paper, and the two go off together.

Scene II. We begin with a really humorous little chorus for female voices.

The girls in the square are evidently much excited. Such a piece of news! "Can it be possible?" "'Tis all nonsense, I believe!" "No indeed, 'tis true!" "But what is it?" "Well—not a word to anyone!—but they told me at the shop that—but you're sure you won't let it go any farther? Then I'll whisper it: Nemorino's old uncle is dead, so now he's a millionaire, the richest man for miles around! But—silence—here he comes!"

Nemorino has just finished the second bottle of elixir, and is so absorbed in analysing its effects that he has no eyes for anything else; he suddenly wakes to find himself the centre of attraction for a bevy of village beauties, all bowing and curtsying and eyeing him with unmistakable meaning. And the things he hears them say! "Oh, isn't he a darling!" "So modest and amiable!" "And what a gentlemanly air!"

Nemorino, who has heard nothing of his rise to fortune, is taken aback for a moment—then he remembers: of course, it's all the result of that elixir—bravo Dulcamara! And as he is now beginning to feel all the better for so much good wine, he is quite ready for the good time coming, and lets himself be dragged off to the dance, where he seems likely to have more partners than he can conveniently do with.

Now of this very lively scene—and it must be said that the conduct of the girls, especially of a minx named Giannetta, is rather scandalous—Adina has been a pained and horrified spectator. Nemorino, then, is really indifferent to her—her approaching marriage with Belcore is nothing to him! This discovery—and perhaps the fact that she has never before seen him in so favourable a light —serves to fan to a flame the love that has long smouldered in her heart. Resentment is forgotten—the tables are

turned indeed—she is now a suppliant for love, to whom
Nemorino can dictate his terms.

But still she cannot understand why all the girls in the
village have suddenly gone mad about him! When the
others have danced off the stage, Dulcamara (who knows
all about that uncle) condescends to enlighten her. She
has read of the magic philtre by means of which Sir
Tristan gained the love of the lady Iseult? Well, he,
Dulcamara, is the only living man who has the secret—
he has given the elixir to Nemorino, and this is the result!
All the girls on fire for him! "But," inquires Adina,
"has he made his choice yet?" "I think so," says the
cunning Doctor, "when he came to beg me for the
potion, he certainly mentioned someone for whom he was
dying—and he must have been in deadly earnest, for I
know he enlisted for a soldier just to get the money to
pay me for it!"

Adina is now all remorse and tenderness—the faithful,
noble fellow, how can she have wronged him so! The
Doctor's heart is touched: "Ah, my dear," he says,
"it's a bottle of my elixir would do you a world of good
—so be advised, and take it!"

Adina is now all smiles again—but no elixir for her!
Like Mozart's Zerlina she prefers to rely upon her own
fascinations. Her unpretentious little air *Una tenera
occhiatina* has a winning archness about it that should
appeal to all light sopranos.

> With a tender look I'll charm him,
> With a tear or sigh disarm him.
>
> Never man was yet so mulish
>   That I could not make him yield;
> Nemorino's fate's decided
>   When Adina takes the field!

He would be a bold man who should suggest to the

tenor that his solo, *Una furtiva lagrima*, were better
omitted ; in any case the suggestion should be made with
a wink of the eye, for though the graceful number is a
mere sop to the singer, and dramatically indefensible, it
is generally ' the hit of the evening,' and its popularity
on the concert platform seems inexhaustible.

Adina's course is not yet all plain sailing. To make
sure of Nemorino she takes the very sensible step of
secretly buying him out of the army, but when she waves
the document triumphantly in his face, the wretch pre-
tends not to understand her motive. " To a rejected
suitor like me," he cries, " of what use is liberty ? Better
to die on the field of glory than stay at home and die of
love ! " [He has said something very like this before, we
remember.]

But Adina has her way. When Belcore enters a few
minutes later he finds the pair in each other's arms, and,
rightly concluding that he is no longer wanted there,
marches cheerfully off to fresh conquests.

Dulcamara, we may be sure, improves the occasion :
the blissful lovers owe it all to him, and, mark you, what
his elixir has done for them it can do for the rest of them
—so be in time ! be in time ! be in time ! In a few
minutes his entire stock is sold out, and the magnificent
creature, mounting his golden chariot, departs, as he came,
in a blaze of glory.

So ends this sparkling little opera, which all lovers of
true musical comedy should pray to see revived, not at
one of the big houses, with star performers, but put on
for a run at some little theatre, where it could be played
in the intimate manner that it demands.

LUCREZIA BORGIA

Music by Donizetti.   *Words by* Romani.
Milan, 1834 ; *London,* 1839 ; *New York,* 1847.

*L*UCREZIA BORGIA, produced at Milan in 1834,
was first seen in London, at Her Majesty's Theatre,
in 1839, and at once established itself in popular
favour.   It would seem that the moral vigilance of that
period was somewhat lax in comparison with the standards
of 1854, when *La Traviata* found all the forces of virtue
ranged against her, for it must be admitted that the story of
the earlier opera is open to far more serious objections.
There are few names in history so infamous as that of
Lucrezia Borgia, most shameless member of a shameless
house.   It is true she has not wanted for apologists, but
Victor Hugo, author of the drama from which the opera
is taken, was not of their number ; his play is as unpleasant
as his 'romantic' pen could make it, and although
Romani, the librettist, has toned down many a flagrant
detail of the French original, much of the unpleasantness
still remains.

The opera is described as being in a Prologue and two
Acts, but the three parts are of equal length, and the action
continuous.   The first Scene is laid in Venice, where, in a
moonlit garden, some young gentlemen-at-arms are revelling on the eve of their departure for Ferrara, on a mission
to the Duke, Don Alfonso d'Este, fourth husband of
Lucrezia Borgia.   One of the revellers, Gennaro, falls
asleep, and the rest retire.   A masked female arrives in
a gondola, dismisses her attendant, and, unmasking,
breaks out into lyrical admiration of the slumbering youth ;

in the last line of her long and sickly song she mentions the fact that she is his mother, and proceeds to wake him with a kiss.

The awakened youth takes fire at once at the sight of this lady, as fair as she is kind. " Whom perceive I ? " he cries in rapture, only to be repulsed by a coy " Oh ! leave me, Sir ! "

What follows is best given in the delicious English version of 1850 :

> HE. Nay, nay, my gentle creature,
> I long to learn ev'ry feature !
> To Beauty ne'er I blind me !
> SHE. Gennaro ! can this be possible !
> Your breast for *me* doth warm ?
> Speak candidly !
> HE. Then, by my knighthood, I love thee !
> SHE (*aside*). Too joyous !

But Gennaro is the soul of honour : " I must tell you," he says—

> There is a prior selection
> To whom I owe more affection !

He refers, it seems, to his mother—whom he has never seen—little dreaming that it is she with whom he is speaking ! This ineffably silly scene is interrupted by the return of Gennaro's companions. The lady hastens to replace her mask—" To fly doth behove me ! " she remarks (" struggling to free herself from Gennaro "). But it is too late—she is recognized, and they approach her each in turn with a mocking reverence. " Madam ! " says the first, " my name is Maffio Orsini ! you poisoned my brother ! " " You murdered my uncle," says the second, " and stole his estate ! " " And what did you not do to my nephew ! " cries a third. Then, all together :

> She is wanton—a faithless betrayer !
> An incestuous night-loving slayer !

Nature, owning abortion so hideous,
Stands convulsed at the awful offence !

Meanwhile the indignant would-be lover of the lady is
preparing to do battle for her honour, when Orsini tears
the mask from her face and reveals the dreadful truth :
" Look on her ! " he cries, " 'tis the Borgia ! "

Gennaro " dashes her from him with horror and detestation," the others hurry him from the scene, and
Lucrezia is left alone, in tears and rage, to think out some
dark scheme of vengeance.

The scene is transferred to Ferrara. Gennaro, after
some late festivities, is saying farewell to his friends at the
door of his house which faces the Ducal Palace. Charged
by them, in jest, with cherishing a passion for the lovely,
if infamous, Lucrezia, he proceeds to show his detestation
of the lady in practical fashion. On one of the palace
gates is a heraldic shield bearing the word

BORGIA

in raised letters ; with his sword the young man strikes
off the initial ' B,' leaving the horrid word

ORGIA

for all to jeer at. This ingenious insult is immediately
punished. The Duke has long suspected his wife of being
infatuated with Gennaro, and seizes this opportunity to
have him arrested on the spot.

The next day Lucrezia, informed of the outrage but
ignorant of its author, demands the instant punishment
of the culprit ; and the Duke gladly swears an oath, at
her request, that he shall die before the day is ended.
Gennaro is brought into the presence. Lucrezia, beside
herself with remorse and fear when she sees how she has
been trapped, pleads desperately for his life ; the Duke is
inexorable, but, after Gennaro has been led out to prepare

for death, tells his wife she may choose whether the culprit shall die by the sword or by poison—she decides on the latter. The prisoner is brought back; the Duke informs him that, in response to his wife's entreaties, he has resolved to pardon him, and pleasantly invites him to drink a parting cup before he goes. Two flagons stand ready, the silver and the gold—from the one the Duke and Duchess are served—the other holds the wine of the Borgias, the wine of death. From this the Duchess is made to fill a goblet and present it with her own hands to Gennaro, who unsuspectingly drinks it off. The Duke at once leaves the room with a smile of satisfaction on his face—for one who has drunk the wine of the Borgias is not likely to trouble him much longer. Lucrezia, however, is in possession of a remedy known only to herself; hastily revealing the truth, she makes Gennaro swallow the antidote, and assists him to escape by a secret door in the wall of the audience chamber.

Act II. Anyone who loves to sup on horrors might do worse than look in—already well fortified by a good dinner —on the last Act of *Lucrezia*. Dramatically it is not without merit of a certain kind—the action is swift, the contrasts undeniably effective; sensation can hardly go farther than the closing scene. The music is vigorous and full of garish colour; moreover, it includes the dashing 'brindisi,' *Il segreto per esse felice*, with which everyone is familiar.

Lucrezia has not forgotten her discomfiture of the opening scene; she has waited some time for her revenge, and now an operatic providence has placed her assailants in her power.

Still at Ferrara, we are invited to a midnight banquet (the third in the opera) at the palace of the Princess Negroni, a close friend of the Borgia. Lucrezia's enemies, five in number, are all present, as well as Gennaro, who has accompanied his friend Orsini, a fact of which his infatuated mother is ignorant. A too boisterous incident in the revels has driven the ladies from the room; the men settle down to the serious business of drinking, and a special flagon of ' wine of Syracuse ' is sent up for their better entertainment—it is, of course, the Borgian wine, the wine of death. Under its rousing influence Maffio Orsini—the gallant young captain who, for musical reasons, must be impersonated by a lady with a rich contralto—volunteers the drinking-song to which reference has been made, a reckless effusion in which we are exhorted to care not a hang for the morrow, so long as we're jolly to-night.

The noisy chorus which follows is killed by the tolling of a funeral bell—but the dare-devil Orsini still goes on. As the second verse proceeds the lamps are seen to grow gradually dimmer, until at the end but few are left alight; yet the stage is filled with a strange unfestal glare as the great doors of the banqueting-hall are slowly parted, to reveal a large apartment, hung all with black, and lit by the inverted torches that speak of death.

A procession of monks, black-robed and hooded to the eyes, advances slowly, chanting a mournful Latin psalm, and lines both sides of the hall, while a third rank is drawn across the far end of the inner chamber. The terror-stricken revellers attempt to escape, but find that every door is locked.

Now through the torchlight gloom is seen advancing with tragic stalk a woman's figure, trailing the sombre robes of death, a smile of awful triumph on her face as she salutes her victims: " Yes! look on me! 'Tis I, the Borgia! In Venice, Sirs, you entertained me finely— now in Ferrara I return your kindness! I trust the

Borgia's wine was to your liking!" At a sign from her the monks in the background, the Black Penitents that guard the secret of the inner chamber fall back on either side and disclose—shades of Mrs Radcliffe, Monk Lewis, and Maria Monk!—five coffins raised upon a platform, draped in black and set round with funeral tapers. Lucrezia is watching her wretched victims—already the poison has begun to work. "Gentlemen!" she says, "I see you have drunk deep! you may desire to slumber—see where your beds await you!"

But the Borgia has reckoned amiss. "Madame!" a clear voice cries behind her, "there are but five! Is there no resting-place for me?" She turns to find herself confronted with Gennaro, whose presence at the banquet she has never suspected. With a cry of horror the wretched woman bids the monks hurry her drooping, staggering victims from the room. The folding doors are shut; she is alone with the dying Gennaro.

[At this point the librettist has very wisely shied at the text from which he was working; those who wish to shudder, or laugh, at the impossible horrors of the original are referred to *Lucrèce Borgia*, the drama by Victor Hugo.]

A few drops of the precious antidote still remain; Lucrezia frantically implores Gennaro to swallow it in time, but he refuses to survive his comrades. Weak as he now is, the piteous farewells of his bosom friend Orsini, heard from the inner room, rouse him to fury; he seizes a knife and is about to rid the world of this monstrous woman when Lucrezia, driven to bay at last, reveals a part, at least, of her terrible secret: "Stay!" she cries, "thou darest not slay a Borgia, for thou thyself art one! Gennaro! dear Gennaro! *I am thy mother!*"

With this disclosure the horrors of the past seem all forgotten ; Gennaro finds some strange consolation in dying in the arms of even such a mother, and Lucrezia, allowing herself time for a last *cabaletta*, falls dead upon his body.

Of the music as a whole there is little to be said ; it is largely of the rocking-horse order, and generally undistinguished ; the waltz tunes, marches, *boleros*, and *cabalettas* in which it abounds make excellent pianoforte duets for schoolroom practice. One number, Orsini's drinking-song (*Il segreto per esse felice*), is still an effective contralto solo for the concert platform.

Lucrezia, in short, belongs to " the palmy days of opera," the 'forties and 'fifties of the Victorian era, when the favourite singers of the day carried all before them. And this opera was well served : Mario chose it for his London *début* ; Grisi, Brambilla, Tamburini, Lablache, and, later, the luscious Alboni, all seem to have revelled in the showy melodies and thrilling situations it offers. Titiens was probably the greatest interpreter of the name part, and sang it with superb effect a few days before her death. It was revived for Caruso not so long ago in New York, and there seems no reason why some exceptionally gifted soprano who fancies herself in the part of the lurid heroine should not bring *Lucrezia Borgia* once more into temporary popularity.

LUCIA DI LAMMERMOOR

Music by DONIZETTI.   *Words by* CAMMARANO.
Naples, 1835 ; *London*, 1838 ; *New York*, 1845.

APART from the fact that our Queens of Song seem still to find in the part of Lucia an irresistible opportunity for vocal display, it is difficult to see why this opera retains its place in the repertory. The Waverley Novels, stripped of their atmosphere and their rich Scottish humour, are but dry bones at the best, and *The Bride of Lammermoor* emerges badly from the skeletonizing process. Scott's piteous romance of poor Lucy Ashton and the Master of Ravenswood, as treated by Donizetti's librettist, Cammarano, becomes a chronicle of gloom unrelieved by any lighter touches ; a commonplace plot moves heavily through three Acts to the accompaniment of music that is at once pretentious and undistinguished ; the various persons of the drama hardly admit of characterization, and Donizetti has attempted none, but, for the delight of amateurs of *il bel canto*, there is always the limelit heroine with her boundless prodigality of trills and *roulades*, vainly attempting to conceal the poverty of the melody under a tangle of trumpery ornament.

To the general public *Lucia* means the Mad Scene with its flute obbligato ; the soprano romance, *Regnava nel silenzio*, the tenor solo, *Fra poco a me ricovero*, are to be found in all ' operatic albums,' and the sextet, *Chi me frena*, had an immense reputation until the advent of *Rigoletto*, with its famous quartet, *Un dì se ben rammentomi*, gave the *cognoscenti* something more deserving of their enthusiasm.

That the action is supposed to take place in Scotland just at the close of the seventeenth century need send no one to his Scottish history nor even to Scott's novel; this puppet drama is played in the shadowy region of operatic convention, which has scant relation to place or period.

Act I. There is little doing in the first Act. In the opening Scene we gather that there is an ancient feud between two noble families—that Enrico, who is in difficulties, ascribes all his bad luck to Edgardo, whom he hates accordingly. In order to repair his fallen fortunes Enrico has arranged to give his sister Lucia in marriage to the wealthy Arturo, before consulting her wishes in the matter, and is naturally furious on learning from his retainers that she has already given her heart to the hated Edgardo.

[It may be as well to explain that ' Enrico ' stands for Sir Henry Ashton, ' Edgardo ' for the Master of Ravenswood, ' Arturo ' for Lord Arthur Bucklaw, while ' Lucia ' is Lucy Ashton, the Bride of Lammermoor.]

Scene II shows us the moonlit garden and the fountain where Lucia is waiting for her lover; an elaborate solo on the harp forms an appropriate prelude to Lucia's air, *Regnava nel silenzio,* in which she relates how she had lately seen a spectral form appear beside the fountain which, to mark the occasion, had run with blood—an evil omen, thinks Lucia. And, indeed, ill news is on the way. Edgardo enters, only to tell her that they must part at once—he leaves for France that night; in a long duet they plight their solemn troth, and say farewell. [The sugary waltz-tune, *Verranno a te sull'aura,* must be noticed; it is usual to refer to it as one of the ' gems ' of the opera.]

Act II. We do not get far in this Act before we

discover that Enrico is a black-hearted fellow, as are also Normanno, his henchman, and Raimondo, his chaplain: the three have conspired to wreck the happiness of poor Lucia.

Edgardo has now been for some months in France; he has never failed to write regularly to his affianced bride, but not a single letter has reached her—all have been intercepted by her brother Enrico. Still worse, that gentleman has not hesitated to forge a letter showing that her lover has been faithless to his vows. Thus armed, and with the ready help of Raimondo, he works upon the heart of the unhappy girl until she has abandoned all hope, and then tells her that he himself is on the brink of ruin from which she alone can save him by an immediate marriage with Arturo. Lucia's consent is at last wrung from her. Arturo arrives, the guests assemble (to the music of a choral march, *Per te d'immenso giubilo*, which is first cousin to the first Druids' chorus in *Norma*), the marriage-contract is produced, and Lucia has just signed it when Edgardo makes a dramatic entry, in time to confound the guilty, but too late to save the wretched lovers from their doom.

All are paralysed for the moment—"Edgardo! oh thunderbolt!" is Lucia's strange remark—and the great sextet *Chi mi frena?* begins.

Those who are familiar with the quartet in *Rigoletto* are not likely to be greatly impressed by this composition for six voices, only three of which attain to individual importance. The music throws little light on the situation, but from the words we gather that Lucia's stony despair admits not even the relief of tears, that Edgardo is torn between love and a desire for revenge, while Enrico is a prey to late remorse—Normanno, Raimondo, and Alisa (Lucia's *confidante*) serve merely to fill in the harmonies.

The sextet over, Edgardo's wrath against the treacherous Enrico seems likely to get the better of him, when the chaplain, Raimondo, comes suddenly into the limelight ; after cautioning Edgardo against the wickedness of harbouring revenge—he even quotes Scripture for his purpose—he proceeds to convince him of the hopelessness of his case by drawing his attention to Lucia's signature on the contract of marriage.

Edgardo, in a frenzy, flings his engagement ring at Lucia's feet, and demands his own in return ; he then requests to be butchered immediately, in order that Lucia may have the pleasure of trampling on his bleeding corpse on her way to the altar with Arturo.

The six solo voices are now " supported by the entire strength of the company," and the result is one of Donizetti's most substantial *finales*, conventional and rather colourless, but undeniably effective.

Act III opens with a stormy scene between Edgardo and Enrico ; in a long hammer-and-tongs duet they express a mutual desire for each other's blood, and arrange for the inevitable duel, which the Master of Ravenswood insists shall be fought among the tombs of his ancestors.

A jubilant chorus of retainers is interrupted by Raimondo, who breaks the awful news—Lucia's reason has given way, and she has murdered poor Arturo in their bridal chamber !

The heroine now wanders on to the scene to show us that, whatever the state of her mind may be, she has her voice under perfect control. The meanderings of distraught maidens, on the lyric stage at least, are apt to run on much the same lines both in matter and method, and Lucia, in her Mad Scene, has points of resemblance with sleep-walking Amina, Dinorah with her shadow, and Marguerite in prison.

In the opening andante, *Il dolce suono*, she imagines herself once more in the moonlit garden waiting for Edgardo [the orchestral reference to her earlier solo, *Verranno a te sull'aura*, anticipates Gounod's masterly use of this device in the Prison Scene in *Faust*], but the phantom rises from the fountain, as of old, and puts the dream to flight. Now, like Amina, she is standing with her beloved at the altar (*Ardon l'incensi*) and life henceforth is to be a heaven on earth. [It is at this point that the flute obbligato is introduced with such happy effect.] But the entrance of Enrico recalls the signing of the marriage-contract, and its awful consequences; again, in fancy, Edgardo stands before her, but only to denounce and cast her off for ever, and poor Lucia exhausts herself in a piteous appeal for forgiveness. At last in the aria *Spargi d'amaro pianto* she resigns herself to the approach of death; Enrico will mourn over her ashes, while she, in heaven, will pray for their swift reunion.

It is a pity that the opera cannot end here—but Edgardo, of course, has to be provided for. To the tomb of his ancestors he comes in the last Scene, not, however, to fight the intended duel; before Enrico can arrive he hears of Lucia's death and puts an end to his own existence, impatient to join his beloved in the skies (*Fra poco a me ricovero*).

It is difficult to say much in favour of *Lucia* as an opera, and easy enough to laugh at the Mad Scene, but, after all, ours is not an age that can afford to discourage such vocal exhibitions; there are not many sopranos to-day who can do justice to its extremely difficult passages, and, should the tradition wholly die out, it would be a real calamity for the singer's art. The prima donna who in the great air from *L'Étoile du Nord*, in *Ombra leggiera* from *Dinorah*, or in the Mad Scene from *Lucia* can triumphantly assert her claim to rival the competing flautist, deserves all possible praise, since she reminds us of what we are too apt to forget—that the human voice is æsthetically the most beautiful, and may be made the most perfect, of all instruments.

LA FILLE DU RÉGIMENT

Music by DONIZETTI. *Words by* BAYARD *and* ST GEORGES.
Paris, 1840 ; *New Orleans*, 1843 ; *London*, 1847.

LA FILLE DU RÉGIMENT, better known to us in the Italian, *La Figlia del Reggimento*, was written in 1840, toward the end of the composer's career ; like most of his work it strikes our modern ears as painfully thin, such musical interest as it possesses being confined to the popular numbers *Ciascun lo dice, Convien partir*, and the *Rat-a-plan* Chorus.

The libretto is of little merit, but it had the advantage of introducing a new type to the operatic stage in Marie, the *vivandière*, and a certain piquancy is introduced by placing the heroine in two well-contrasted settings—the freedom of camp life, and the old-fashioned proprieties of the castle. At the same time, it must be confessed that the ' book ' is naïve to the verge of banality ; the fact that it is so emphatically *pour les jeunes filles* has undoubtedly contributed largely to its popularity in England.

The part of Marie was a favourite with a succession of prima donnas in the Victorian era, Jenny Lind being the most illustrious example ; but it is hardly likely in the present century to appeal to any artist of the first rank.

Act I. The scene is a valley in the Austrian Tyrol, which at the time is in the occupation of Napoleon's army. There has evidently been a skirmish in the neighbourhood just before the rise of the curtain, for we find a chorus of ladies on their knees, entreating heaven to protect them against the foe, and a ridiculous Countess in a fainting condition, being supported to a seat by her servant, Ortensio; she is evidently a prey to war's alarms, and hints darkly to Ortensio of terrible experiences in the past. But, the last shot fired, and the danger over for the present, the Countess retires to a cottage, while the frightened peasants gather together and break out into a chorus of "Tra-la-la!" according to the well-known custom of their country.

Sulpizio, a French sergeant, now swaggers in to tell how the Tyrolese took to their heels; and close behind him comes Marie, the pride, the pet, the Daughter of the Regiment. The regiment is her official father, so to speak, but she regards each man in it as her particular papa, more especially the sergeant, who found her, a mere infant, abandoned on the field of battle, and has brought her up in the lap of the army. And in her duet with Sulpizio she knows plainly that she takes after her father—or fathers; she is all for "allonging and marshonging"—"Plan-rat-a-plan!" comes as naturally to her lips as does "Tra-la-la!" to those of the Tyrolean peasant.

Still, there are other things to be thought about; as Sulpizio reminds her, she is getting a big girl now and it is time she got married; she has the whole regiment to choose from, and hardly a man of them but would be glad to exchange his paternity for a tenderer relationship. Pardon!—but she has chosen already, and *not* from the regiment! He is just a young Tyrolese, Tonio by name who recently saved her from falling over a precipice.

A noise without—and on come the soldiers, dragging Tonio with them; he is suspected of spying, and must die the death. Marie's explanations, however, soon alter their attitude; a friend of hers is a friend of theirs; so they must clink glasses together, and, as the rum goes round, the Daughter of the Regiment shall sing them the song they love best to hear, *Ciascun lo dice*, a catchy, spirited tune in praise of "the glorious Twenty-first." The drums are heard beating the roll-call, and the soldiers march off, taking Tonio with them. He manages to give them the slip, however, and in less than no time is back at Marie's side for his share in a love-duet of unsophisticated but not ungraceful humour. The sergeant, indignant at finding him there, puts a stop to all further philandering by the blunt declaration that none but a soldier of the glorious Twenty-first may aspire to the hand of the Daughter of the Regiment. Tonio accepts the decision, but is of opinion that the obstacle is not insurmountable, and retires to see what can be done.

Now re-enters the Countess, still in a highly nervous condition, to beg a military escort to see her safe to her Castle of Birkenfeld ; the name awakens memories in Sulpizio's mind in connexion with the finding of Marie ; a paper found on her at the time, and now produced by the sergeant, establishes the fact of her aristocratic birth, and the Countess claims her as her niece. " I trust," adds the stately dame, " that Marie has been educated as becomes a lady ! " " Oh, perfectly ! " says the sergeant, " her manners are most correct ! " At this instant the voice of the young 'lady' is heard behind the scenes, swearing like the little trooper that she is : " *Parbleu ! Morbleu ! Corbleu !* "—a whole string of horrid oaths ! The shocked Countess, however, makes the best of it, and hurries her reluctant niece away, to instruct her in the responsibilities of her new position.

The soldiers once more crowd the stage. After the popular noise of the famous *Rat-a-plan* Chorus has died away, Tonio reappears, with the French colours in his cap, and succeeds in convincing Marie's assembled ' fathers ' that he is now as eligible a suitor for her hand as any other man—besides, she happens to prefer him, so there's an end of it! The brave fellows take the philosophical view :

> Then she has selected !
> 'Tis most unexpected !
> But yet, if she loves him,
> She *must* be his wife !

But Tonio's dream of happiness is shattered by the return of Marie, in the custody of the Countess ; the Daughter of the Regiment is on her way to the Castle of Birkenfeld, to assume her rightful position in high society ; she must leave her low associations behind her, and try to forget that she was ever the humble comrade of " a brutal and licentious soldiery." Such at least is the Countess's view. But Marie feels differently ; with a breaking heart she prepares to take farewell of her dear companions, in music worthy of the pathetic situation. *Convien partir* is one of those really lovely and significant melodies with which Donizetti occasionally surprises us ; it stands side by side with *O mio Fernando* (*La Favorita*) and *Una furtiva lagrima* (*L'Elisir d'Amore*), and is likely to live long after the opera has ceased to be performed.

The interest is well sustained in the short *finale* that ends the Act. With tears in her voice and on her cheek, Marie takes leave of them one by one—Pietro, Matio, dear old Tomasso—Sulpizio she embraces fondly, to the scandal of her aunt ; as for Tonio, well, they part to meet again. The chorus meanwhile console themselve by consigning the Countess to the care of the Devil fo robbing them of their treasure ; they present arms a Marie passes through their ranks, and as the curtain fall Tonio is seen to tear the French ribbon from his cap an trample it underfoot.

Act II. We find Marie unhappy amid the luxurious surroundings, the old-fashioned etiquette, of the Castle of Birkenfeld. She is being trained in the elegant accomplishments—to dance the minuet, to sing the 'classical' compositions beloved by the Countess; worst of all, she is to be married to the Duke of Crakenthorpe without delay. Her only comfort is that old Sulpizio, the sergeant—for reasons purely operatic, apparently—is still allowed to attend her.

The Countess enters, in a gorgeous toilette, to perfect Marie in a song with which she is to charm the company that evening, a *canzonetta* by the *maestro* Caffariello. While the former Daughter of the Regiment sings, to the Countess's accompaniment, of the loves of Venus and the woes of Philomela, Sulpizio sits gloomily by, exchanging sympathetic asides with Marie on the dullness of such stuff compared with the jolly camp-songs they sang together in happier days. At last, when the Countess requires her niece to " sing like a nightingale " the limits of endurance are reached ; carried away by a flood of old associations, they throw etiquette to the winds, and break out into the rowdy *Rat-a-plan*, " allonging and marshonging," up and down the room to the disgust of the dignified old lady, who goes out in high dudgeon. The sergeant, too, is fetched away to speak with a wounded soldier, who is waiting for him outside—some ruse of Tonio's, he suspects. Left to herself, Marie sings of her constant longing for her old companions of the army ; she has just ended on the theme of her air in Act I (*Convien partir*) when the roll of approaching drums rouses her to a wild enthusiasm, as the boys of the Twenty-first pour on to the stage for a joyful reunion. Tonio, of course, with a wounded arm, is among them, and—the rest having retired for refreshment—he, Marie, and the sergeant join in a really spirited trio, *Stretti insiem tutti tre*, which well deserves attention. This is the last point of interest in the very huddled finale. The Countess confesses to Sulpizio that she is actually Marie's mother, and proceeds to use her maternal influence to hurry on her daughter's wedding with the Duke. However, the regiment, headed by Tonio, returns to enter a vigorous protest against any such coercion, and quite prepared to enforce their ' paternal ' claims by direct action, if necessary. Fortunately the Countess, moved by her daughter's grief and Tonio's obvious devotion, consents to their union; she joins their hands amid general cheers, and a patriotic chorus, *Salvezza alla Francia!* led by Marie, brings down the curtain, and assures us that the Daughter of the Regiment will always remain faithful to her adopted fatherland.

LES HUGUENOTS

Music by MEYERBEER.   *Words by* SCRIBE *and* DESCHAMPS.
Paris, 1836 ; *London*, 1842 ; *New York*, 1850.

THE name of Meyerbeer means little more to the present generation than three popular vocal pieces, *Nobil signor, O mon fils,* and *Ombra leggiera* ; yet each of the operas from which these are taken —*Les Huguenots, Le Prophète,* and *Dinorah* respectively —was a prime favourite with the public up to the end of the last century—the first-named was given as late as 1912 at Covent Garden, and at the Metropolitan Opera House, New York, in 1918.   Should there come a Meyerbeer revival, the choice would probably fall on this opera.

Yet it is doubtful if *Les Huguenots* would ever regain its former popularity in England.   It belongs to an age of grandiosity quite alien to our own ; it makes no strong emotional appeal ; as a spectacle it has been superseded by *Aïda* ; and, musically, it certainly does not contain the seed of immortality.   On the other hand, there is no denying its strong superficial attractions ; those who demand the pomp of Courts, marching soldiers, brawling mobs, duels, bells, and cannonades will find here all they want.   The piece is like some crowded historical canvas, showily painted.   Showy, too, is the music—showy and vastly clever, but having too often that ring of insincerity with which so much of Meyerbeer's work is chargeable. The best plea, perhaps, that can be urged for its retention in the repertory is that it furnishes an almost unique opportunity for vocal display ; for its adequate performance it demands no less than six singers of the first rank, thoroughly schooled in all the brilliance and elegance of style which seems essential to this opera. This, it need hardly be remarked, is at the same time a formidable obstacle to its revival. At the Metropolitan Opera House, New York, in the winter of 1894, *Les Huguenots* was given with Melba, Nordica, Scalchi, Maurel, Plançon, and the two De Reszkes. An impresario who can get together a cast like that may put on *Les Huguenots* any time he likes with a fair certainty of being able to run it for just so long as his singers hold out.

The first thing that strikes us about this opera is that there is altogether too much of it—that the five Acts are crowded with too much noise, too much *bravura*, too much plotting, too many improbable incidents, with the actual Massacre of St Bartholomew's Day as an overwhelming *finale*. At first we are inclined to grumble at a plot which seems to require almost as much preparatory study as *The Ring* itself; but, soon or late, we come to see that the whole thing resolves itself into the tortuous love-story of Raoul and Valentine, shown up against a highly coloured historical background.

Raoul de Nangis is a Huguenot gentleman, Valentine the daughter of a Catholic noble, the Count St Bris. The lady is betrothed to the Duke de Nevers, a Catholic like herself; but Marguerite de Valois, who, though a Catholic, is espoused to the Protestant Henry of Navarre, is anxious to reconcile the two political-religious parties, and so determines to break Valentine's engagement with Nevers, and marry her to Raoul instead. This is the situation when the play begins. The Scene is in Touraine, the year 1572, and, for the benefit of readers with a theological bias, it may be well to state that all the characters are Catholic, with the exception of the Huguenot Raoul de Nangis, and Marcel, his grim old Puritan retainer.

Act I. The short Prelude, an ingenious setting of the Lutheran chorale *Ein' feste Burg*, serves rather to emphasize the title of the opera than as a key to its contents. With the rise of the curtain, it is true, there is just a little talk of both religion and politics—the great names of Medici, Coligny, and Calvin are mentioned—but we soon pass to lighter topics. The Count de Nevers is entertaining his brothers-in-arms at a banquet, to which they cannot sit down before the arrival of an expected stranger, Raoul de Nangis, whom, although a Huguenot, he is desirous of treating with special courtesy; there is a movement in the Catholic party toward an agreement with the Protestants, and Raoul is necessary for their purpose. The young Huguenot on his entry proves to be as comely a figure as any in the room, and breathes quite freely in the atmosphere of gallantry that prevails. To pass the time it is suggested that each hot young lover shall reveal the secret of his heart. As for Nevers, he confesses that his is already plighted in earnest—no more amorous adventures for him! Raoul too, it appears, is very much in love, but with little more than a fleeting vision, a " phantom of delight "; in the romance *Plus blanche que la blanche hermine*, he tells us how he rescued, lately, a lady fair from insult, how she raised her veil, gave him one smile and left him, and how henceforth he is her slave for evermore. While a merry toast is being drunk in Raoul's honour, a booming bass breaks in upon their chorus—it is his old servant Marcel, a fanatical Huguenot who, shocked to see his master thus consorting with the ungodly, strikes up the Lutheran chant of the Prelude (*Ein' feste Burg*) as a protection against the Powers of Evil. The amused company hear him out to the end and even clamour for more.

The grim old Puritan relaxes so far as to give them a longer
and far livelier performance; this is the famous *Piff! Paff!*
a fine rollicking ditty in spite of its ferocious sentiments,
" Down with the Pope, and a plague on all women ! "

This outburst against femininity is, very fittingly, the
cue that brings the first woman on the scene. A veiled
lady passes across the back of the stage, attended by a
servant who presently summons Nevers to wait on his
mistress.   Here is an adventure indeed to the taste of
the jolly company ! After their host has left the room
their curiosity rises to a pitch where manners are forgotten
—they crowd eagerly to the window, and there, in the
garden, is the loveliest of ladies in earnest conversation
with the young Count. They are so enthusiastic about
her beauty that even Raoul is tempted to take a look.
The next moment he regrets his action, for there, in
close communication with Nevers, is the fair one of whom
he has already told us. The others, whom of course he
takes into his confidence, must have their laugh at him in
a gay little chorus, but this time they, as well as Raoul,
have read the situation wrongly. The audience, however,
are not left longer in the dark. Nevers is seen in the
corridor to take a most respectful farewell of the lady ;
then, managing to evade his guests, he comes to the footlights and lets us into the secret. The lady is or was his
fiancée, and a maid of honour to Marguerite de Valois,
Queen of Navarre ; at her royal mistress's command she
has come to ask Nevers to release her from her engagement, for reasons of state. " To this," says Nevers, " I
am bound, as a gentleman, to consent ; at the same time,
I must say, I am infernally annoyed " or, in the politer
language of the English version :

> As a courteous knight I my promise engage,
> But I secretly burn with direst rage.

[Here we have an excellent example of the difficulties presented by the ordinary opera libretto ; this explanation by Nevers is absolutely necessary to the understanding of the plot, yet, conveyed as it is in a single page of dry recitative, it is almost sure to pass unnoticed by the audience.]

Nevers now turns again to his guests, who have scarcely time to rally him over his supposed new conquest when they are interrupted by a new arrival. This is a page, a glittering, impressive, and, as we shall soon find, far too florid page. His name is Urbain. [Urbain started his career as a high soprano, but when, in 1844, the luscious - voiced Alboni ("Venus-contralto," as Walt Whitman calls her) took a fancy to the music, Meyerbeer rearranged it to suit her voice, since when most of the great contraltos have revelled in the part.]

To Urbain is assigned the best-known number in the opera, generally referred to as *Nobil signor*, which are the first words of the Italian version of the recitative. The air, made so pretentious by its trills, *roulades*, and *cadenzas*, has but the slightest dramatic significance ; it merely tells us that the page is the bearer of a letter from a great lady to one of the present company. Nevers naturally concludes that he is the man ; but no, the letter is for le Sieur Raoul de Nangis, who reads it aloud for our benefit. The lady's request is a strange one : Raoul, after allowing himself to be blindfolded, is to be conducted by Urbain into her presence ; as to whom she is, and what her object may be, not a word is said. The young man's amazement on reading the letter changes to utter bewilderment at finding himself the centre of extravagant interest—the others crowd around him with most obsequious congratulations on his good fortune ; love and luxury, power and glory, all these, they hint, are henceforth his for the taking. The only discordant voice is that of old Marcel, who scents the world, the flesh, and the Devil in such irregular doings, and bawls out a few staves of a *Te Deum* to keep the enemy at bay. The explanation of the company's change of attitude toward Raoul is simple enough; Nevers and the others have seen the seal and signature of the letter, and have recognized them for those of the greatest lady in the land.

The young Huguenot is led submissively away by the giddy page. This is the second time since the rise of the curtain that he has found himself involved in mystery; first came the affair of the veiled lady in the garden, and now we have this strange summons from the fair unknown, who is evidently accustomed to be obeyed. The audience are left almost equally in the dark as to the real significance of the two incidents; however, we have only to wait for the explanation till the next Act, when we shall find them to be intimately connected.

Act II. This is often played as the second Scene of Act I, but even by itself it is rather a formidable affair when given in its entirety. It deals with Raoul's interview with the sender of the letter—who is no less a person than Marguerite de Valois, Queen of Navarre—his introduction to Valentine, the bride she has selected for him, his violent rejection of the alliance, and the consequent quarrel between him and the lady's father, the proud St Bris. The dramatic content, it will be seen, is not large in itself, but the Act is considerably inflated by show pieces for the solo voices and other music of a purely decorative nature.

We begin with a long and brilliant *scena* for Marguerite de Valois. The scene is in the garden of her castle of Chenonceaux; seated in her pavilion by the riverside, revelling in the beauty of a perfect day in her own fair land of Touraine, she sings the praises of nature and the joys of life and love, *O beau pays de la Touraine !* It is plain that the gloomy band of Puritans will find no favour at her Court. Echoing her lively mood, her ladies furnish a graceful harmonic background for the vocal fireworks of their mistress, who ends with an air of a more vigorous character, *A ce mot tout s'anime.* Urbain the page is, of course, in attendance. In this Scene he finds ample opportunity to show himself a true descendant of his more famous predecessor Cherubino ; he is in love with every one of the maids of honour, and with his royal mistress most of all.

And here comes another fair one with whom he falls in love at first sight. This is the veiled lady whom we saw in Nevers' garden, sent thither, we remember, by the royal command. Her name, we learn, is Valentine, daughter of the Count de St Bris. She has but a short interview with the Queen, who tells her of the project she has formed for marrying her to Raoul. Valentine offers no objection, and retires to prepare herself for her prospective bridegroom, to whom we may assume her to be, in elegant Victorian language, ' not indifferent.'

Here follows what is generally known as the Bathing Chorus. The ladies of the Court retire to a shady grove close to the river bank and entertain us pleasantly with song and dance ; the amount of actual bathing permitted depends, of course, upon the taste and discretion of the management. In any case, the Queen does well in banishing from such a scene the amorous page who is caught lurking in the bushes ; the next moment, however, he is here again to announce the arrival of a young nobleman ; the ladies need not fear him—his eyes are safely bandaged ! This, of course, is Raoul, for whose admittance the Queen at once gives orders. Meanwhile the irrepressible Urbain

takes the stage with a lively solo (written in for Alboni),
"No, no, no, no!" in which he relates the sensation caused
among the villagers by the sight of a cavalier with bandaged eyes being led through the streets to the castle by
the Queen's own page—how the boys made fun of him,
while the girls pelted him with flowers! Urbain paints
so vivid a picture that the ladies are all curiosity to see
this mysterious personage. On his entry they move on
tiptoe round the blindfolded man, peering into his face
and singing, or whispering, a really dainty and effective
little duet, *Le voilà!* ; they can scarcely tear themselves
away even when the Queen arrives and orders all to leave
the room.

Raoul and Marguerite de Valois are now alone. The
long duet *Beauté divine! Enchanteresse!* is little more
than an elaborate and graceful vocal exercise for two
gifted singers ; the musical texture, a thing of shreds
and patches, is scarcely adequate even for the expression
of the artificial sentiment. Raoul is dazzled by the gracious beauty of his royal mistress, who is by no means
indifferent to the charm of his youthful ardour. Words
and music alike are mere tinsel, and not too well put
together. After the Queen has explained her reasons for
summoning Raoul to her presence and prepared him for
the meeting with Valentine, on whom he is supposed
never to have set eyes before, we pass to matter more
worthy of Meyerbeer's peculiar talent.

To the strains of what is described as a minuet, though
sadly lacking in the grace which we usually associate with
that measure, her Majesty's subjects assemble to do her
homage ; Catholics and Protestants in about equal
numbers, they give occasion for one of those crowded
scenes which the composer so loved to handle. After
the Queen has introduced Raoul to the company she

requires that all shall in her presence swear an oath to keep
the peace and lay the foundation of an enduring friendship. With lamb-like submission, though with voices of
thunder, the Huguenots and their inveterate foes, the
Catholics, with hands upraised to heaven, proceed to take
the solemn oath demanded of them : " By the faith of
our fathers, by the honour of our swords, by our fealty to
our King, by the God of all truth, we swear to keep the
bond of everlasting peace and friendship ! "

Amidst the tremendous volume of sound one dissen-
tient voice has no effect ; we must search the printed
page to find how carefully that stout old Protestant,
Marcel, while keeping time with the rest, contrives to
alter the words so as to satisfy his conscience—courtiers
may swear their souls away, but Marcel is not one of
them : " Neither friendship nor peace will I swear," he
sings, " and may God turn my master from the error of
his ways ! "

All this hard choral swearing is perhaps more noisy than
convincing, and we are grateful for the relief of even a
short unaccompanied passage quietly sung ; but, once
started on his sonorous career, Meyerbeer was always ready
to go from strength to strength—the *ensemble* with which
the Act concludes almost wipes out the impression of the
one from which we are just recovering. Truth to tell,
there is good reason here for sound and fury. The business of the oath concluded, Marguerite proceeds to bring
Raoul face to face, for the first time as she supposes, with
his future bride. The Queen's hopes are centred in this
union, and she has no misgivings as to the issue of their
meeting ; like the "*jeune et brave Dunois*" of a later
Queen's imagining, Raoul is " bravest of the brave," while
Valentine is " fairest of the fair "—surely they were made
for one another ! Valentine enters on the arm of her

father, the haughty St Bris. Raoul starts back in horror. In the lovely vision before him he recognizes one whom he has already seen on two occasions—she is the maiden in distress whom he had succoured and who had become for a time the idol of his dreams, but, alas, she is also the veiled madame whose compromising visit to Nevers had meant for Raoul such a rude awakening. He turns away with a sneer : " What ! ally myself with her ! Never ! "

No wonder if " most things twinkled after that ! " In the general uproar that follows we distinguish the indignant amazement of the Queen, the despair of Valentine, the furious wrath of St Bris and Nevers, and the bewilderment of the chorus, who sing throughout in a sustained *fortissimo*. The outraged father is for taking instant vengeance on Raoul for this gross insult, and it needs all the Queen's authority to make them postpone the inevitable conflict. A welcome touch of character is added by old Marcel, who throughout the tumult consoles himself by calling good Dr Luther to his aid, and in the pauses of the chorus is allowed to bawl out snatches of *Ein' feste Burg* without attracting the least attention.

Act III. The scene is the *Pré-aux-clercs* in the late 16th century—a good opportunity for a presentment of old Paris with the glamour of the Middle Ages still hanging about her. But let no one look for the atmosphere of Hugo's romances—we must try, too, to forget the wonderful pictures of mediæval life in Wagner's *Mastersingers*. Meyerbeer has no such magician's wand. The result of his collaboration with Scribe in this opera has been compared to Shakespearean drama, and to the novels of Sir Walter Scott ; it reminds us rather of the puppet-plays for which, as children, we used to cut out the coloured figures and mount them on cardboard.

However, we have here a brave array of puppets, a rich background, plenty of action, and more than enough of noise. The essentials for the stage setting are as large an open space as possible, a church on one side, and a tavern on the other.

It must be understood that, as a set-off to Raoul's contemptuous rejection of Valentine, it has been decided to marry her at once to Nevers, her former *fiancé*; it is already the evening of the day which has been chosen for the ceremony.

First to fill the stage are a crowd of citizens, who inform us that this is a day for feasting, a fact confirmed by the noisy groups of Huguenot soldiers seated round the tavern—roaring fellows, who drink to the health of Coligny, and down with the Catholics! [Another famous "*Rat-a-plan* Chorus," in which the singers clap their hands in time to their vocal imitation of the drum.] In contrast to this boisterous outburst comes a procession of Catholic ladies chanting an *Ave Maria* on their way to the church, where Valentine and her father are passing the time previous to the nuptial ceremony which is to take place, apparently, about midnight. The Protestants do their best to drown the gentler voices with their *rat-a-plan*, to the great indignation of the populace, who are only prevented from falling on them by the opportune arrival of a troop of gipsies, introduced solely for the purpose of the ballet which follows.

When the stage is clear again, St Bris, with an attendant, appears from the church and is met by Marcel, who brings a letter from his master, Raoul, challenging St Bris to mortal combat, at short notice, and in that very place. Having signified his acceptance, St Bris consults with his friend how best to secure the death of Raoul, by fair means or foul; it is agreed that should fortune favour the young Huguenot in the duel there shall be those lurking near who will quickly despatch him.

The curfew now rings out and sends all Paris hurrying home to bed. The stage is empty and nearly dark.

Out of the darkness emerge two figures—Valentine, who comes from the church in deep distress, and Marcel, determined to be within his master's call in the hour of peril. In the interminable duet that follows, *Dans la nuit où seul je veille* (which might well be passed over in silence so far as its musical interest is concerned), Valentine tells Marcel of the trap that is being laid for Raoul, the details of which she has overheard ; she also confesses that her love is all given to the young Huguenot, for whom she is prepared to die should need arise. She re-enters the church, and Marcel lurks in the shadow, as the combatants Raoul and St Bris arrive on the scene, each with his brace of seconds. With Marcel in the background, all six of them advance to the footlights and join in the admired septet *En mon bon droit j'ai confiance*, in which they swear by all that is holy to conduct the affair in strict accordance with the code of honour, " Each for himself, and God for all ! " It is plain, however, that certain of these gentlemen do protest too much, for Marcel presently detects no less than three armed men stealthily approaching, prepared to lend most dishonourable assistance to the cause of St Bris. The faithful old servant starts up in their path, and things begin to look ominous both for him and his master, when from within the tavern is heard the rousing *Rat-a-plan !* of the Huguenot soldiers, to which Marcel replies with a stentorian version of his favourite Lutheran chorale. In quick response, his comrades pour out of the tavern, followed by a band of Catholic students, also warmed with drink. Women of both parties spring up from somewhere to join in the fray,

and a most lively struggle is in progress when the arrival
of the Queen brings all to their senses.

The remainder of the Act is kaleidoscopic. St Bris and
Marcel both lay their different accounts of the quarrel
before the Queen, each accusing the other side of treachery,
when the old Huguenot produces his chief witness in the
person of Valentine, who again comes forward from the
church. Valentine it was who overheard the plot and
revealed it to Marcel! But why? In whose interest?
Amid the general astonishment the Queen, with an amazing lack of discretion, proceeds to tell Raoul the truth—
or at least a part of it; Valentine's visit to Nevers, she
hints, originated in her own wish to break off an engagement which she detested—Raoul has always been the
choice of her heart. This disclosure, however flattering
to Raoul, comes rather late to afford him much consolation. It is followed immediately by the arrival of the
lucky man, Nevers; he comes in a gorgeously illuminated
state barge to bear Valentine away to the scene of their
midnight nuptials. Here, of course, is all the material
for a colossal *finale*. In addition to the usual orchestra
there is a band of music on board, both of which support,
or possibly drown, the huge body of singers in one of the
most blatant of choruses, as the bridal procession is
formed and passes on to the barge. The tumult of the
mob is by no means ended, and Huguenots and Catholics
are still hard at it till the very fall of the curtain, breathing
out threatenings and slaughter one against the other, in
sad contrast to the peace and friendship they had sworn
at the beginning of the Act.

Act IV. This is the best-esteemed Act in the opera,
largely on account of the impressive Scene known as
" The Blessing of the Poniards," and was often chosen to
form part of those mixed programmes which we associate

with state and gala performances. We are in Nevers' castle, to which he has brought home his not too willing bride. Poor Valentine opens with a *romance* (for which a long recitative is sometimes substituted) concerned with her love for Raoul and her struggle to drive his image from her heart. Raoul, made reckless by the Queen's revelation of the truth, promptly appears on the scene, merely, as he says, to see her once again and then to die. His wish seems likely to be fulfilled without delay, as the voice of St Bris is heard without. Valentine has just time to hide her lover behind the curtain when her father, Nevers, and a number of their adherents enter the room. St Bris would have his daughter retire, but Nevers obtains permission for her to stay—perhaps with a view to the effective assistance she is able to lend in the coming *ensemble*.

Neither here nor throughout the Scene does the music suggest the horror of the purpose for which they have met together—nothing less than to plot the extermination of all the Huguenots in Paris that very night, the Eve of St Bartholomew. One voice alone is raised in protest— Nevers will never consent to stain his ancestral sword by such ignoble butchery! He is promptly arrested and led away. St Bris is left to work up the feelings of the others : the evils that affect the realm, the dangers that threaten the Royal House, the plots and conspiracies that are everywhere afoot, all are the work of that accursed band of heretics, the Huguenots! It is time to make an end, to wipe them from the face of the earth! Are all agreed ? They are agreed ; it is the King's command—it is the will of Heaven !

St Bris then proceeds to allot to each man his place and share in the coming massacre. Coligny, the leader of the Huguenots, must be the first to fall; afterward, all must assemble at the Tour de Nesle ; the signal will be the tolling of the great bell of St Germain.

For such a holy enterprise one thing, of course, is needed—the sanction of Holy Church. All swords are drawn and solemnly blest by three monks who, led vocally by St Bris, proceed to work the others up to a state of frenzy by their bloodthirsty exhortations :

> Holy and sacred swords, receive Heaven's
>   blessing !
> Eternal wreaths of glory
>   Shall deck the warrior's brow
> Who now, great Heaven, before thee
>   Shall make the impious bow !
> No pity for them show !
>   Let none escape your vengeance !
> Our swords shall lay them low !
> 'Tis Heaven wills it so !

[So much for the black villainy of the Monastic Orders ! As a companion picture old opera-goers may recall the renegade nuns whose restless phantoms figure in the churchyard ballet in *Robert le Diable*.]

After St Bris has distributed the white badges marked with a cross by which his party may be recognized, the entire chorus line up to the footlights, brandish their swords, and give vent to their feelings in a ' barbaric *yawp* ' to which we feel a war-dance would be the appropriate accompaniment : " Strike them down and show no quarter ! Let not one of them escape ! "

> So shall we gain the grace of Heaven
> And all our sins shall be forgiven !

The monks, in giving a final blessing, implore them to go softly ; they even exhort each other to silence with the words :

> Whisper low ! Not a word,
> Not a breath should be heard !

But all in vain—the holy zeal within them burns too fiercely for restraint; once more do they return to the footlights and rend the air with a mighty shout of " Heaven's will be done ! "

Such is the famous Scene which so impressed our forefathers ; it belongs frankly to the ' palmy days ' of Italian opera, when the immense chandelier with its blaze of cut-glass lustres that hung from the roof of Covent Garden Theatre seemed like the presiding spirit of the place. The situation is effective, if absurd, and, with adequate performers, must always make a sensation through mere violence and volume of sound, but, musically, it would be difficult to find its defender at the present day ; we feel that here, at least, Meyerbeer deserves the hardest things that have been said of him.

Happily the Act does not end here, and the duet that follows between Raoul and Valentine is the one number in the opera which musicians have agreed to praise, *Oh ciel, où courez-vous ?* It is of great length and of supreme dramatic importance, as it is not only the *finale* of an Act, but constitutes the end of the opera as usually played. As soon as the stage is clear Raoul comes from his hiding-place and rushes to the door, but is stopped by Valentine, who uses every persuasion to prevent his going. His situation is a terrible one—he burns to fly to his comrades and warn them of the coming disaster—even now it may be too late—and here is Valentine, his one and only love, imploring him to stay. The conflict between love and duty could hardly be more poignantly presented. Duty holds her own, and Raoul makes another attempt to go, when Valentine throws herself in front of the door : " Nay, nay ! not to thy death ! Or, if thou diest, I will die with thee ! For know, Raoul, I love thee ! " To Raoul at last has come, if only for a brief moment, the realization of his dream of love, and he abandons himself to it wholly.

[The long section *Tu l'as dit, oui, tu m'aimes!* contains perhaps the best melody Meyerbeer ever wrote, of a kind which finds an echo in Gounod and Saint-Saëns.]

Valentine's distress is intense—she is conscious of the guilty nature of her love, and is torn by anxiety for her beloved's safety; Raoul is lost in an ecstasy, and for the time has no other thought but her. The awakening comes with the ominous booming of the slaughter. Already the flames light up the Scene; Raoul sees in imagination the Seine run red with blood, the dead bodies of his comrades on every side. There is but one place for him, beside his own people, to fight and die with them. Valentine has fainted; commending her to God's protection, he leaps from the balcony into the raging fury of the streets.

In order to bring the opera within reasonable limits it is customary to end it with this dramatic climax, in which case a vigorous fusillade following on our hero's disappearance gives us to understand that he has fallen in the cause of duty; lovers of sensation, however, will find it well worth their while to make themselves acquainted with the still more exciting finish provided in the next Act.

Act V. In certain respects this short Act is the best of the five. The necessity for cramming such an amount of incident into so small a space seems to have had a salutary effect upon the composer; there is no time for prolixity, there is no need for mere musical noise amid the rattle of musketry and the cries of the wounded; even the melody, always Meyerbeer's weakest point, seems to flow more easily under the increased pressure of events.

There are two Scenes: the first at the Tour de Nesle, where the Huguenots are celebrating the festivities in honour of the royal marriage. The music of a minuet is interrupted by that booming bell, the meaning of which is already known. They pause for a moment in wonder, but resume their dancing to a livelier measure. Suddenly Raoul makes a wild entry, an awful figure, his clothes all stained with blood. He tells them the dreadful news ; he has seen Coligny slain, his house destroyed ; a general slaughter is in progress, that spares neither man, woman, nor child. His heroic call to vengeance and the frenzied response are the more effective from not being unduly prolonged.

The scene changes to the cloisters of a church to which many of the Huguenots have fled for shelter. The cold-blooded massacre is in full swing, the tumult comes ever nearer and nearer. Raoul now appears, with Marcel ; the two are about to rush into the thick of the *mêlée* when Valentine appears, and struggles desperately to keep her lover at her side. She knows of a certain method by which he may be saved—if only he will let her bind this white scarf round his arm, as a sign that he is a good Catholic ! But no—never will Raoul abjure his faith ! Besides, why should he wish to live ? Valentine, wedded to Nevers, can never be his. But here Marcel intervenes with the welcome information that Valentine no longer has a husband—Nevers has just died a hero's death in a successful effort to save the old Huguenot's life ! The lady promptly grasps the situation ; she is now free—she will become a Protestant and marry Raoul, if only to die in his arms. If anything could surprise us now, it might be the fact that Marcel is called upon to play the part of priest and to pronounce a marriage blessing, to which a fictitious dignity is lent by the chanting of the Lutheran hymn by the wretched fugitives in the church. The assassins have by this time broken in, and are at their brutal work ; snatches of the hymn are still heard amid the gunfire and the shrieks of the dying, until the silence tells us that the grim work is completed. Here Marcel, wrought to the height of religious ecstasy, has a vision in which he sees the souls of the victims ascending straightway to their reward in heaven ; Valentine and Raoul join him in what is perhaps the most melodious number in the opera. Raoul next receives a mortal wound, and is being helped away by Marcel and Valentine when they are met by a small band of the enemy and the challenge " Who goes there ? " " Huguenots ! " gasps the dying man, while Marcel repeats the word in a shout of defiance. Then comes the order : " In the King's name—fire ! " " Great Heavens ! " exclaims Valentine, " it is my father's voice ! " But it is too late—the shots ring out— and St Bris finds that he has added to his list of victims Raoul, Marcel, and his own daughter, Valentine.

" Room for the Queen ! "—it is Urbain's voice we hear —and the *tableau* is completed by the arrival of Marguerite de Valois, Queen of Navarre, returning from the ballroom to her palace. She recognizes the dying Valentine, and, overcome with horror, raises her hand as a signal to stop the carnage, as the curtain falls.

RIGOLETTO

Music by VERDI.   *Words by* PIAVE, *from* VICTOR HUGO'S
"*Le Roi s'amuse.*"
Venice, 1851 ; *London,* 1853 ; *New York,* 1857.

MANY causes contribute to make *Rigoletto* one of the most memorable of operas ; it has a plot unsurpassed for thrilling interest : musically it is Verdi's greatest achievement before *Aïda* ; its leading part is assigned to a baritone, and contains some of the finest dramatic music ever written for that voice ; finally, it has the distinction of having been prohibited in its original form owing to the alleged anti-monarchial tendencies of its story.

Victor Hugo's drama, *Le Roi s'amuse*, from which Piave's libretto was taken, was produced in Paris in 1832 : the story of its immediate withdrawal belongs, like the first night of *Hernani*, to the political and literary history of France during the Romantic Movement. Though it was not till 1851 that Verdi's opera was offered for production at the Fenice Theatre, Venice, similar objections were raised ; permission was refused to the performance of the original version, but by changing the scene from France to Italy the difficulty was overcome. Hugo's French king was transformed into a Duke of Mantua, and Triboulet the jester became Rigoletto. *La Maledizione* (The Curse) was the title under which it was first performed. Following Hugo's conception, Verdi has put all his strength and sympathy into the tragic figure of the hunchback ; but two other parts (Gilda and the Duke) are so well provided for that a favourite prima donna or the tenor of the hour will sometimes contrive to have the production so faked that their own vocal displays become the centre of attraction, greatly to the disturbance of the artistic balance. Moreover, the rôle of Rigoletto demands such a combination of dramatic and vocal endowments that worthy revivals of this fine opera are unfortunately rare.

The story is woven around a strong and fiercely passionate nature warped by physical deformity and the degrading influence of his surroundings. Poor Rigoletto, the despised hunchback with something of a lion's nature, is the paid ape of the profligate Duke of Mantua ; grotesque with cap, bells, and bauble, he affords fine sport for the idle courtiers, on whom he often revenges himself by lashing them with his stinging wit. The Duke, who lives only for the seduction of women, finds him invaluable for his own evil purposes ; embittered by misfortune, fouled by association, Rigoletto has become the willing tool of his master, and even finds pleasure in the ruin and anguish he helps to spread. His insolent indifference to the sufferings of others calls down on him a father's righteous curse, the fulfilment of which is the theme of the opera.

For there is another side of Rigoletto's nature which is unsuspected by the heartless nobles of the Court. In his youth, poor, wretched, misshapen as he was, a woman's faithful love had raised him to the height of happiness, only to be plunged into deeper misery than before by her early death. But consolation still remained in the little daughter his dying wife had left him, and to whom all the devotion of his passionate nature was transferred. After accepting his position at the ducal Court, in his anxiety to keep the young girl far from that ribald company, yet always within his reach, he had placed her in the care of a seemingly faithful servant, with orders never to let her stir abroad unless attended, and always to keep her from the public eye ; even his own visits to her were made in strictest secrecy.

When the drama opens, Gilda is in the first bloom of lovely girlhood—but the plot for her ruin is already on foot. The Duke has often noticed her on her way to Mass, and his looks of open admiration have awakened love in her innocent breast. His courtiers contrive to carry her off and place her in the Duke's power. Rigoletto, enraged and broken-hearted, succeeds in recovering his daughter, and, after learning the truth from her lips, resolves to take a swift revenge. He hires an assassin to lure the Duke to a house of ill repute on the outskirts of the city ; at midnight, after the deed is done, he will visit the murderer, pay him his reward, and himself dispose of the victim's body. Gilda has confessed that she still loves the Duke ; in order to break her infatuation, her father takes her with him to the place before the time appointed, that she may be convinced of the baseness of the Duke's true character. Outside the dwelling he leaves her for a time. In the utter darkness of the scene Gilda, still faithful to the Duke, contrives to receive the assassin's blow, and to die the death that was designed for her lover. Rigoletto soon returns, and is carrying off the sack that contains, as he supposes, the body of his enemy, when the groans of a dying woman reveal the awful truth—it is his own daughter, Gilda, slain by the assassin whom he himself had hired.

Act I. There is no overture. After the orchestra has sounded some thirty bars of solemn warning, the curtain rises on the frivolities of the wanton Court of Mantua. The small orchestra on the stage, the succession of gay dance tunes, can scarcely fail to recall the similar scene

in *Don Giovanni*; the delicate minuet in particular is
not unworthy of its great original.

There is much intrigue in the first few pages. The
Duke has no secrets from his courtiers; after referring to
his latest conquest, the young girl he has met so often
on her way to Mass (none other than Gilda, the jester's
daughter), he draws their attention to the beauty of the
Countess Ceprano, and proceeds to make love to her
under her husband's very eyes. [His air *Quest' o quella*
is a delightful insistence on the virtues of infidelity.]

Rigoletto now comes forward, to insult the Count in
his most offensive manner; even the Duke has to tell
him that he goes too far, and Ceprano engages the courtiers to join him in a scheme to avenge themselves on the
common enemy—a scheme suggested by the recent discovery that the hunchback himself pays secret visits to
one whom they suppose to be his mistress.

But Rigoletto is soon to arouse an even more terrible
spirit of vengeance. Struggling with the retainers, a man,
grey-haired but vigorous, forces his way into the hall. " I
say the Duke *shall* hear me ! " he thunders out. It is the
aged Count Monterone, whose daughter the Duke has
recently dishonoured. His indignant denunciations are
cut short by the hunchback, who swaggers to the front :
" Let *me* answer him ! " With every insult that tone
and gesture can convey, he mocks the broken-hearted
father to his face : " What folly is this ! " he sneers—
" your daughter's honour gone ? Well, why make so
great an outcry over such a trifle ? "

With these words Rigoletto invites his own destruction
—Heaven itself will not suffer an outrage such as this.
The aged Monterone becomes an instrument of fate :
awful in his fury he calls down Heaven's wrath upon them
both—living or dead he will not cease until his vengeance

be accomplished. " Shame on you, tyrant," he cries to the Duke, " who can set your mongrel on a dying lion ! And for you "— turning to the cowering hunchback— " vilest of creatures, who can make sport of a father's anguish—for you, what punishment can suffice ?   God's curse go with you for evermore ! "

As Monterone is led away to execution, Rigoletto lies writhing on the ground, a father, justly stricken by a father's curse.

Scene II.   The short Scene that follows, with its admirable terseness of expression, is a triumph for both librettist and composer.

Rigoletto, his tell-tale form concealed as well as may be in a heavy cloak, is making his way cautiously, after nightfall, to the house where his daughter is kept secluded.   He is gloomy with a sense of coming disaster : " That old man laid his curse on me ! " he mutters—and its power is even now at work.

The orchestra begins an oddly sinister theme which persists throughout the dialogue.   A stealthy footstep and a few low words; it is Sparafucile who accosts him, an assassin who may be hired to rid any man of his enemy. " You too," he says to Rigoletto, " may need my aid, for you have a mistress " (pointing to Gilda's house) " and— a rival ! "

Rigoletto's fears increase ;   he inquires further of the man and his methods.   He lives outside the city walls with his sister Maddalena ;   it is her part to lure the victims to their dwelling—Sparafucile's dagger is swift and sure.   Though the hunchback has no need of him at present, he will do well to remember.

With the ending of this short dialogue the preparations for the drama are complete.   The Duke, we know, is hot in pursuit of Gilda, not guessing her to be the hunchback's daughter ; Count Ceprano, whom Rigoletto has made his enemy, will, in his desire for revenge, unconsciously assist the Duke to gain his ends ; by his heartless insolence toward Monterone, Gilda's father has incurred an outraged father's curse ; and in Sparafucile we see the agent who is to bring that curse to its terrible fulfilment.

We have by this time seen the worst of Rigoletto ; for the rest of the opera he is a pathetic figure to whom we can hardly refuse our sympathy.

His fine soliloquy, *Pari siamo*, a dramatic outburst of convincing sincerity, goes far beyond anything that has yet been done in Italian Opera. It is the lament of the melancholy buffoon who is paid to make laughter for others while his own heart is aching—an idea that has been handled since by more than one composer, though never so finely. In this case there is a tragic fierceness in the music, perfectly in keeping with Rigoletto's character ; he despises himself and his surroundings, he curses the corrupt tyrants whom he has to serve—if he is vile, it is they who have made him so. And all the while he is haunted by an awful memory—

That old man laid his curse on me!

Forcing all gloomy thoughts aside he unlocks the door that opens on the courtyard of his daughter's dwelling, and Gilda flutters gaily down the stairway to be folded to her father's breast. Now indeed is Rigoletto a changed man, all gentleness and love ; there are few pages in opera more gracious than this duet between father and daughter. Gilda asks him to speak of her mother. In a solo of poignant pathos, *Deh! non parlar al misero*, he laments his angel and her early death, and thanks God for the daughter left to fill her place in his heart.

But his fears again awake—suppose someone should

discover his secret, and rob him of his only treasure—is Gilda careful of her father's command never to go beyond the garden walls ? Does she never go into the town ? "Only to Mass!" Hardly satisfied, he summons Giovanna, the servant, and recommends the strictest watchfulness in the lovely air *Ah veglia, o donna, questo fiore.* Alarmed by the sound of footsteps, he leaves his daughter for a moment, and the Duke slips in unnoticed by the garden door. After Rigoletto's departure he discovers himself to Gilda, who has known him hitherto only by sight ; he is a poor student, he tells her, Gualtier Maldé by name, and has long been her worshipper. The young girl listens entranced, for she too has long been in love with his handsome face. In the midst of their impassioned duet, *È il sol dell'anima,* Giovanna warns them that someone is coming. The Duke tears himself away, leaving Gilda to a delicious meditation on her lover's name : Gualtier Maldé! was ever melody so sweet ! The song *Caro nome* well deserves its universal popularity ; it is a true and fresh expression of a young girl's first experience of the mystery of love, and the florid graces with which it is overlaid, so far from being superfluous, form an essential part of its charm. [It should be mentioned that the concluding shake on the E above the stave is not due to Verdi ; it is a foolish tradition, like the high C in Manrico's song in *Il Trovatore,* and might very well be discontinued.]

The short remainder of this Act contains an amount of rapid action that is not easy for the audience to follow. Gilda has retired ; the night is dark, but by the aid of guarded lanterns is seen a group of men, cloaked and masked, outside the wall of Gilda's house, next to which is the Ceprano palace—it is Ceprano himself, with other courtiers, coming to carry out their threat of vengeance on the savage jester by abducting his supposed mistress. Rigoletto himself, for some unexplained reason, comes on the scene, suspicious and alarmed ; Ceprano hides ; the others hasten to explain that they have come to carry off the Countess for the Duke's pleasure, in accordance with the hunchback's own suggestion. He falls into the snare, and offers to assist them. Provided with a mask, secured by a handkerchief so that he is prevented from using his eyes, he is set to hold the ladder by which the others scale the wall. Placed as he is, he can hardly hear a woman's stifled call for help, or the stealthy steps of the conspirators as they escape with their victim through the courtyard. Alarmed at last by the silence, Rigoletto tears the bandage from his eyes and hurries to the door of Gilda's dwelling—it is open, and there on the pavement is a scarf that only Gilda can have dropped. The awful truth is plain ; it is Gilda, his own daughter, who is now in the hands of the shameless courtiers, and he, her own father, has assisted in her abduction. He enters the house, rushes wildly, vainly, from room to room, and staggers out again, only to fall to the ground with the terrible cry :

A father's curse is on my head !

Act II. The opera would certainly gain in dignity and consistency by the omission of the first number of this Act ; the Duke's solo, *Parmi veder le lagrime*, is an unworthy concession to the exacting vanity of tenors. Having revisited Gilda's house and found it empty, his Grace concludes that she has been stolen from him by some rival gallant ; he proceeds to lament her loss and to shed the tear of sensibility, but his avowals that Gilda is the guiding star of his existence, for whose sake he intends to turn over a new leaf, do not convince us—they are merely a blot on the picture of an otherwise consistent blackguard. Verdi has certainly made good use of the opportunity for an air of sentiment, but the chorus, in which his courtiers enlighten him as to the actual situation, is in his worst 'conspirator' manner. However, brave amends are made in what follows. It would be difficult to overestimate the mastery with which the great composer has managed to convey the complex emotions of the next scene, especially when we consider how inadequate for such expression were the cramping formulas in which he worked.

Rigoletto, ignorant of the sequel to last night's villainy, swaggers in among the courtiers, desperately trying to keep up his usual manner of careless insolence, while his heart is racked with fear and anguish. The courtiers observe his feverish anxiety, and play upon it ; for a time he can get nothing from them ; when at last some chance words assure him beyond all doubt that Gilda is actually in the power of the Duke, his control gives way. Telling them that it is his daughter, not his mistress, whom he is seeking, he struggles madly to get through the doors that lead to the Duke's apartments ; but all his efforts are in vain, and he exhausts himself in a furious outburst against the whole race of courtiers and their infamous lives. Finally his rugged spirit breaks down altogether—with trembling voice and humble gestures he goes from one to the other imploring their pity, their pardon for his insults of the past—if only they will let him pass, to save his daughter while there may yet be time !

At this crisis Gilda herself enters the hall, to hide her shame in Rigoletto's sheltering arms. The courtiers retire ; the frightened girl pours out her pitiful tale, and receives her father's pardon and his blessing. [Gilda's opening solo, *Tutte le feste al tempio*, and Rigoletto's

pathetic outburst, *Piangi, piangi, fanciulla,* are noticeable episodes in this long and finely sustained duet.]

A dramatic interruption is here made by Monterone,
who is being led to execution ; pausing to hurl one last
curse on the Duke, who is still apparently untouched by
his former imprecations, he is suddenly confronted by
Rigoletto, who, too late repentant of his own misdeeds,
bids Monterone have no misgivings as to the Duke's
future—he, Rigoletto, will see that justice is done. The
scene ends with another duet for father and daughter, he
breathing vengeance against the Duke, she, still tender to
her first lover, imploring Rigoletto to have mercy on him.

Act III. The last Act of *Rigoletto*, like that of *Il
Trovatore*, is one of the outstanding triumphs of Verdi's
genius ; masterly throughout, it contains one of the most
famous solos, and unquestionably the finest quartet, to be
found in the whole range of Italian Opera. Indeed,
although he treats the vocal part as always of first importance and never stints the flow of suave or brilliant
melody, Verdi has here made such progress in avoiding
set forms and in employing the orchestra as a means of
dramatic and picturesque expression that we feel we are
no longer dealing with ' Italian Opera ' in the olden
sense ; although *Rigoletto* precedes *Aïda* by twenty years,
it may fairly be considered as the composer's first excur-
sion into the domain of modern music-drama.

The action takes place in the riverside cottage outside
the town, where Sparafucile, the assassin, lives with his
sister Maddalena. The scene is so set as to allow us a
view of the interior as well as of what goes on outside.

Under cover of the dark and heavy summer night
Rigoletto has brought his daughter here to convince her
of her lover's infamy ; they stand concealed outside the
door of the house, where they can see through the window.

"And you still love this man?" the father asks. "Ah, yes!"

"Oh piteous folly of a woman's heart! And if I prove him false to you—would you still love him?"

Gilda is not to be moved: "Nay, but he loves me dearly!"

Rigoletto leads her near the window; there is the Duke in rough soldier's dress; while Maddalena and her brother prepare for his entertainment, he sings the famous air, of which, in its place, one can never tire, *La donna è mobile.*

> Women are all the same—
> Never believe them!
> Love them and leave them—
> That's how to play the game!

Now comes the great quartet, *Un dì se ben rammentomi.* Inside is the amorous Duke with Maddalena on his knee—outside, poor Gilda and her indignant father.

We begin with the libertine's practised gallantries and the coquettish repulses of Maddalena, who is well able to keep him at a distance so long as it suits her. Then comes the Duke's solo, *Bella figlia dell'amore,* of an entrancing elegance, which well bears repetition in the closely woven quartet that now follows, in which each voice is of about equal importance to the dramatic effect. Above the seductive melody for the tenor soar the piercing soprano notes which tell of Gilda's anguish; mingled with these are Maddalena's boisterous gaiety, and Rigoletto's stern demand for vengeance.

After the quartet the drama runs swiftly to its awful end. The recitative which follows must be carefully noted. Rigoletto bids his daughter set out at once, alone for Verona, in the man's dress he has provided for her he will join her later. He then hands to Sparafucile ha of the price agreed upon—the remainder to be paid when he returns at midnight, to find the murder done. The assassin's custom is to sew the victim's body in a sack, and throw it in the river close at hand—but this last ceremony Rigoletto reserves for his own satisfaction. "Tell me his name!" says the assassin. "His name is Villainy, and mine—Revenge!" is Rigoletto's answer as he departs.

A storm is gathering—the most effective storm in Italian Opera until this amazing composer surpassed it thirty-six years later in his *Otello*. The Duke resolves to stay the night, and is shown to an upper chamber, where he is heard singing snatches of his wanton ballad as he lies down to rest :

> Women are all the same !
> .   .   .
> Love them and leave them !

It is plain that the gathering storm is close at hand—in this last grim scene the elements assume almost the importance of *dramatis personæ* ; in the moaning wind at least there is an actual human cry, as the effect is produced by an invisible chorus, whose voices, through closed lips, rise and fall in chromatic thirds ; the part of the lightning (as vivid in the orchestra as on the stage) is to show us poor Gilda, who has crept back in her male attire, cowering against the wall, lashed by the rain which seems furiously to demand admission to the evil house. Through chinks in the boarding Gilda can see and hear all that goes on inside.

Sparafucile is handling a large sack, which he bids Maddalena repair for the safe conveyance of its lifeless burden ; but the caresses of the handsome Duke have awakened some feeling of tenderness in the woman's heart, and she beseeches her brother to spare his life. Sparafucile is greedy for the ten ducats that Rigoletto has still to pay him, and which he will not get if the Duke escape. "Then," says Maddalena, "kill the hunchback!" But the assassin's code of honour will not allow him to murder one of his own clients. However, as Maddalena becomes more urgent, he makes a slight concession : supposing, before the hour of midnight, some traveller, seeking shelter from the storm, should knock at their door, his murdered body shall fill the sack instead of the Duke's.

Gilda, who has followed their talk with growing terror, has now taken her resolve. What hope is there, on such a night as this, of any wanderer near that lonely spot ? She herself will be the victim. She thanks God that, although her lover has betrayed her, she is allowed to give her life for his. She knocks at the door. All light is extinguished in the cottage—the practised hand of Sparafucile needs no such guide—and the victim's stifled cries are scarcely heard amid the crashes of the thunder. The tempest is now in all its fury ; it rages for some considerable time in the orchestra before Rigoletto returns, impatient to enjoy the full flavour of his vengeance.

Sparafucile is at the door to receive the price of blood ; at his feet lies Rigoletto's share of the awful compact. With hideous joy he proceeds to drag the body toward the river bank—he must even stop on the way to gloat over his murdered enemy. "Here then," he cries, "here lies my master, the betrayer of my daughter, the all-powerful tyrant, dead at my feet—and I, his poor despised buffoon, shall pitch him like any dead dog into the river, a sack for his only covering."

The storm is passing over ; the wind has dropped, but the lightning still flashes from time to time. A well-known voice cuts short the hunchback's triumph :

> Women are all the same—
> Never believe them !

Rigoletto turns his head, to see the Duke step out, alert and strong, from his bedroom window on to the city wall, and walk homeward, singing !

Frantically he tears the sack's mouth apart—Gilda is not quite dead—there is still time to ask her father's forgiveness, " For," she whispers, " I loved him too well —and for him I chose to die. Father ! your pity, your pardon, for him as for me ! "

But it is Rigoletto who has most need of pardon—who but he had mocked at Monterone's anguish ? He recalls the outraged father's curse, and can but recognize the justice of its fulfilment.

IL TROVATORE

Music by VERDI. *Words by* CAMMARANO.
Rome, 1853 ; *London*, 1855 ; *New York*, 1855.

IT is merely a parrot-cry that insists on the unique
absurdity of the plot of *Il Trovatore* ; compared with
that of many another opera—say *Robert le Diable* or
Dinorah—the libretto is a masterpiece of sane lucidity and
dramatic inevitableness. It is true that you cannot expect
to understand *Trovatore* on the first visit without a little
previous study of the 'book,' but that is no uncommon
case—what about *Figaro* ? How about *The Ring* ? No ;
as sheer melodrama the plot of " The Troubadour, or
the Gipsy's Vengeance," is good and strong—we must
admit that " the statements is interesting but tough,"
as Huckleberry Finn remarked of a very different work.
The chief difficulty in keeping hold of the thread of the
drama in performance lies in the fact that so much that
is necessary for us to follow is packed into a couple of
narratives (one by quite a subordinate character), and
these are poured out in a flow of such fascinating melody
that our attention is distracted from their logical contents.

Yet the story of *Il Trovatore* must be mastered if we
would properly enjoy the music, which is far more closely
wedded to the dramatic development than is generally
supposed. Of course, when we find the soprano labelled
Leonora, the tenor Manrico, the old seneschal Ferrando,
and the *confidante* Inez, we prepare at once for a drama
of incident rather than of character ; nevertheless, the
play contains one of the strongest personalities in the
whole of opera—the aged gipsy Azucena, a true figure of

tragedy and one of Verdi's greatest triumphs in musical characterization.

Many years before the opening of the drama, Azucena had seen her mother burnt at the stake on a charge of having by witchcraft caused the illness of one of the Count di Luna's infant sons. The girl, herself a mother, had, in her frenzy of grief and hate, stolen the sickly child and flung it on to the still flaming pyre in which her mother had just perished ; such, at least, was her intention, but, actually, it was her own child whom, in the blindness of her rage, she had snatched from the cradle where the two infants slept side by side, and had sent to such an awful death. So far her efforts of revenge have recoiled upon herself ; but the stolen child remains in her hands —she flies with him to the mountains of Biscaglia, her old home, where she brings him up as her son, to be used as the instrument of her vengeance in the future.

When the play opens, the old Count di Luna has long been dead, and his son, succeeding, imagines himself the last of his race. Meanwhile Fate and Azucena have so contrived that Manrico, the Count's unsuspected brother, has become his bitter opponent in feudal warfare and his rival in love. At the Court of the Princess of Aragon, to which the Count is attached, dwells the lovely Leonora, whom he designs to marry ; she, however, has been captivated by the gallant figure of Manrico, the troubadour, famous alike for song and knightly prowess, at whose triumph in the tournament she has herself assisted. As Manrico is in the service of the Prince of Biscaglia, the enemy of the Count, the two brothers are in perpetual conflict and from a double motive. Manrico at last succeeds in carrying Leonora off to his own castle, where he is just about to " to lead her to the altar " when the news arrives that Azucena, his supposed mother, has fallen into the Count's hands, and has been condemned to the flames. He rushes off to her rescue, only to be captured by the Count's men and thrown into prison.

Leonora returns to the Count and offers to yield to his wishes if he will set Manrico free ; but in order to escape from her promise she takes poison and dies in the arms of her true love. The Count, baffled and furious, orders Manrico to instant death by fire. As the flames of the pyre in the castle leap high around the victim and throw their glare on the dungeon walls, the Count drags Azucena to the iron grating of the cell : " See ! " he cries, " that is thy son ! " " Nay ! " comes the awful answer, " *that is thy brother !* " The gipsy's revenge is accomplished—she falls dead at the Count di Luna's feet.

Act I. Terraces and gardens of the castle of Aliaferia, where Leonora and the Count di Luna both reside, in attendance on the Court of Aragon. A moonlit night, with flying clouds. Soldiers are on guard, to prevent the expected intrusion of the Troubadour, whose nocturnal serenades of late have made the Count uneasy. Ferrando, an old retainer, tells once again the old story of the mysterious fate of the Count's infant brother, the gipsy-mother's fiery death, and the escape of the daughter. Even now some malevolent influence lingers round the place ; the spirit of the old witch has been seen by many in the form of a gigantic owl, fluttering round the battlements, and shrieking horribly at dead of night. The midnight bell now sounds, and Ferrando and his listeners retire.

[In this short but significant scene Verdi begins at once to batter our ears with his too persistent dance rhythms ; Ferrando's long narration, *Abbietta zingara*, is in mazurka form, while the reference to the spectral owl, *Sull'orlo dei tetti*, in which the chorus join, has the effect of a tarantella, though written in three-four time ; nevertheless, these materials, if properly handled on the stage as well as in the orchestra, produce an undeniable, if crude, effect of mystery and terror.]

Now Leonora, in white satin, and attended by Inez, her *confidante*, floats down the marble steps into the moonlit garden, and soon transports us to a region

Where moonlight and music and feeling are one.

She expects her Troubadour, Manrico ; meanwhile Inez must have the story of their first meeting at the tourney, and of his serenades beneath her window. [Her solo, *Tacea la notte placida*, is the first of the many exquisite melodies in this opera which exalt so beautifully the spirit of the early days of the romantic movement, as expressed in Byron, Mrs Radcliffe, and certain of the tales of Edgar Allan Poe.] Inez warns her against cherishing " so perilous a flame," to which the soprano replies in the inevitable *cabaletta* which had to follow the *andante*, according to the operatic formula of the time.

They retire to Leonora's apartments, beneath the windows of which the enamoured Count di Luna now appears. He cannot sleep for love of Leonora, whose heart he hopes this very hour to move to pity. Barely has he time for his short recitative when a distant harp is heard, preluding to a thrilling melody, such as only a troubadour could sing, *Deserto sulla terra*. Leonora too has heard it, and comes rushing on to the scene just as Manrico enters. Confused by the uncertain light, she throws herself most unfortunately into the arms of the Count, to Manrico's natural indignation. [This seems a quite unnecessary complication, which merely serves to perplex the spectator.] A few bars, however, suffice to put the matter right, and the two lovers enjoy a whole page of mutual rapture before the Count finds voice to interrupt them. In a tempestuous *allegro assai mosso, agitatissimo* (*Di geloso amor sprezzato*), he pours out his furious jealousy, and demands Manrico's blood; the Troubadour's haughty defiance and the shrill pleadings of Leonora make up a perfect whirlwind of a trio which lasts to the end of the Act, leaving, if not the singers exhausted, the audience breathless with excitement. Leonora falls senseless to the ground, while tenor and baritone prepare for what promises to be a mortal combat.

Such is the first Act, effective, swift, and simple. We have already had a feast of melody, in three of the composer's most characteristic manners: the true romantic beauty of Leonora's opening solo and Manrico's song behind the scenes; the rather incongruous dance tunes of Ferrando's legend; and the amazing, almost brutal, energy of the Count's jealous outburst in the concluding trio. Yet each of these models will be improved upon as the opera proceeds.

Act II. *Scene* 1. We are now to make the acquaintance of the one great personage of the play, the gipsy Azucena. The scene is a gipsy encampment; the men are busy at the forge, the maidens dancing to their tinkling tambourines; all is life and gaiety, musically crude and highly coloured. The famous Anvil Chorus, to which the men beat time with their blacksmiths' hammers, runs its noisy course. The song, the dancing, cease, to be succeeded by music of a very different order.

Azucena has been cowering over a fire of logs, seeing, hearing, nothing of what goes on around her. Sunk in her brooding sorrow, bowed and withered not so much by age as by the awful experience of her girlhood, she lives for one thing only—revenge. It is true she has a mother's love for Manrico, whom she has reared from infancy to manhood, but even him she would sacrifice on the altar of her vengeance. Now she rises, a dark, menacing figure, under the influence of some terrible emotion ; without prelude or preparation she begins her air *Stride la vampa*—' Azucena's Fire-song ' would be its best description. Softly at first, as if her reverie by the camp-fire had not yet been broken, she paints the scene of her mother's awful fate : she sees her in rags, barefoot, bareheaded, her grey hair fallen about her shoulders, dragged to the stake amid the jeers and howls of the piti-less mob. The first part of the song is given with a tense and ominous quiet, but as the fire is kindled at the stake and the flames leap high around the victim, so does the voice gather strength and rise to a cry of agony. By the end of the second verse Azucena is exhausted, and has just sufficient strength for the *Mi vendica !* which was her mother's last utterance, and is her own life's one object.

The gipsies are now on the move, but Azucena remains, to explain to Manrico the meaning of her appeal for vengeance. In what is musically one of the finest numbers of the opera she describes how her mother in her death-agony bequeathed to her daughter the awful duty of revenge. She then goes on to reveal her own dreadful secret—how having stolen the old Count di Luna's son, intending to throw him into the flames, she finds that in her blind fury she has sacrificed her own child instead.

Here, it must be noted, we have the weakest link in the dramatic chain. Manrico draws the only possible conclusion from Azucena's narrative—that, as she never had more than one child, he cannot be her son. Her only reply to his challenge is that, in her excitement, she has told her tale amiss ! Yes, he is her son ! Has she not been to him the tenderest of mothers ? So it is he who must take up her cause and the task of vengeance imposed upon her. " *Mi vendica ! Mi vendica !* " she reiterates.

The Count must be made to suffer for his father's crime. She urges Manrico to a keener sense of this duty—did he not lately, when the Count was in his power, refrain from his advantage ? What moved him to act thus ?

Manrico's reply is one of the curiosities of the opera— a point which probably very few have noticed. His air, *Mal reggendo*, is a striking melody, yet of the vaguest significance, and the general attitude is to accept it, without further question, as one of those haunting tunes with which Verdi, at this period, could scarcely help plastering his score. The words, however, are full of quite unexpected interest; they relate how Manrico, when the Count lay prostrate at his feet, and his sword was poised for the fatal blow, was turned from his purpose by a voice from heaven saying to him, " Forbear to strike ! " This subtle touch of psychology, suggesting a secret affinity between the two brothers, is rather surprising in an opera of the period and calibre of *Il Trovatore*.

Just as Azucena is spurring him on to greater ruthlessness in the future, a messenger arrives with the tidings that his presence is needed in two places—the Prince of Biscaglia has appointed him to the defence of a certain fortress, and Leonora, deceived by a false report of his death, is on the eve of entering a convent, there to take the veil. No need now to urge the Troubadour to action —he is on fire to be gone. But Azucena becomes all tenderness and apprehension ; she cannot bear to let him go—and it is only after a lengthy duet that he succeeds in tearing himself away.

[Azucena's music all through this Scene is worthy of the closest attention ; it shows an advance in the direction of ' music-drama ' beyond anything yet achieved in Italian opera. The air *Stride la vampa*, which may be regarded as the central point of interest in the opera, is treated in a strikingly original manner ; without any recitative to introduce it—the usual " Where am I ? " " O day of horror ! " or " Well, I will tell you "—it cuts straight into the scene of noisy gaiety with compelling effect ; the melody is given to the orchestra later on, quite in the Wagnerian manner, and is introduced with still greater point into the Prison Scene at the end.

But far finer music is to be found in the scena that follows, *Condotta er' ella in ceppi*, in which Azucena reconstructs the tragedy of her mother's death, and her own fatal mistake ; here the vocal phrases, broad and melodious as they are, serve admirably to conduct the narrative, while the independent figures in the orchestra suggest most vividly the tragic idea of the aged gipsy, dragging herself wearily through life under a burden too great for her to bear ; the long, low notes of the concluding bars, *Sul capo mio le chiome sento drizzarsi ancor*, sung in the contralto's deepest tones, leave an impression of hopeless misery not easily forgotten.]

Scene II. Moonlight in the convent grounds. The Count, who has heard of Leonora's intention of retiring from the world, is determined to prevent her ; he has come, with his retainers, just in time. He sings of his passion in the famous *Il balen del suo sorriso*, which, under the title of ' The Tempest of the Heart,' was the delight, or torment, of generations of Victorians. The convent bell is heard, and a chanted chorale ; the Count's men stealthily prepare for action. From the chapel come the nuns in procession to receive Leonora, who arrives, attended by Inez ; just as the convent gates are about to close on her for ever, the Count steps forward to claim her—and at the same moment Manrico and his men arrive, with a similar purpose. Leonora flies to the arms

of her lover, whom she had supposed to be dead.   Her
song of ecstasy, *Deggio e posso crederlo*, permits the most
interesting material for the *finale*, in which the chorus of
soldiers, retainers, and religious lend but feeble support ;
it is made plain, however, that Manrico's party is the
stronger, and Leonora passes without a struggle into his
possession.   The heroine is allowed to end the Scene,
sola, with a four-bar repetition of the loveliest phrases of
her song of ecstasy.

  Act III.   *Scene* 1.   An armed camp near the fortress
of Castellor in the Biscaglia territory.   The Count is be-
sieging the castle, to which Manrico has brought Leonora.
The Soldiers' Chorus with which the Scene opens is, of
all such compositions, perhaps the most blatant and banal
—though ample amends will soon be made.   The Count
enters, deploring his loss, and threatening swift revenge
on his rival ; on the morrow Castellor shall fall, and Leonora shall be his.   A tumult in the orchestra heralds the
noisy entrance of a band of soldiers, dragging in the unhappy Azucena, on whom they have just laid hands.   To
the Count and old Ferrando a gipsy is always an object
of suspicion—the family legend is never forgotten.

  Azucena, on being questioned, admits she is from
Biscaglia, a hostile territory ; on closer scrutiny Ferrando
discovers, or decides, that she is the very gipsy who stole
the Count's infant brother.   The Count, of course, accepts
his word, and when Azucena in her despair cries out :
" Manrico, my son ! why art thou not here to help
me ! " the discovery that the mother of his rival is in his
hands rouses him to greater fury.   Azucena must die the
fiery death !   The old woman makes a brave struggle for
freedom, but is bound fast and dragged away, calling
down the curse of heaven on the Count and her tor-
mentors.

[In this short but very dramatic Scene, Azucena's music again creates the right atmosphere, that of the weary, desolate woman driven on to her doom. In spite of its set, monotonous rhythm, the solo *Giorni poveri vivea* has a sombre sense of tragedy, as have also the rest of her broken phrases, while the frenzied vigour of her curse, *Deh ! rallentate barbari !* seems almost to break its formal fetters, and works up the *finale* to a perfectly appropriate climax.]

Scene 11. This Scene, which passes inside the fortress of Castellor, consists virtually of but two solos, one of which is among the loveliest, the other the most sensational, in the entire opera. The lovers are about to be joined in marriage, but even now Leonora cannot quite shake off her fears of the dangers that surround them. Manrico bids his bride put all her trust in love : whether on earth or in heaven, no power can separate them—they are eternally united. [This is the meaning of the suave and finely developed air, *Ah sì, ben mio,* which for sheer melodic beauty Verdi himself has rarely surpassed.] This is followed by the sound of the organ, and a most effective passage for the two voices, which is too often omitted. They are on their way to the chapel when a breathless messenger breaks in on them with the dreadful tidings that Azucena has been captured by the Count di Luna's men, and is in instant danger of being burnt at the stake. There is not a moment to be lost—Manrico takes leave of his weeping bride, and expresses his passionate desire for his foster-mother's release in the famous *Di quella pira,* which calls for robuster vocal chords and a more heroic style of delivery than any other tenor solo in the whole of Italian Opera. For the wholly unnecessary parade of the high C, which is now universally expected at the end of the second verse, the vanity of tenors, and not Verdi, is responsible; he finishes the Scene with the aid of a male chorus, an arrangement in every way more satisfactory.

Act IV. Even if *Il Trovatore* should disappear from the repertory, it seems probable that the last Act would still survive; it is a compact masterpiece, in which lyric beauty and dramatic significance are closely blended, and seventy years of continuous popularity have failed to dispel, or even to diminish, its glamour of romance.

Scene 1. Outside the castle of Aliaferia. Manrico, in his attempt to rescue Azucena, has himself been taken prisoner; he and his foster-mother lie in the same dungeon awaiting execution.

Leonora, accompanied by one of Manrico's men from Castellor, is here; she has come inspired by one fixed purpose, to save the Troubadour's life even at the cost of her own. To the Count she will give her promise, if necessary, but herself, never! " Here," she says, raising the hand on which is a ring which conceals a deadly poison, " here is my sure protection! "

Turning toward the tower in which she knows Manrico to be confined, she pours forth her soul in a gush of warm and tender melody. *D'amor sull'ali rosee* far surpasses even her first air, *Tacea la notte*, as an example of romantic beauty. Hardly is it finished when the choir in the chapel are heard chanting the *Miserere*, the penitential psalm which implores mercy for the parting soul. " Have mercy, O Lord, on the souls of them that are so soon to leave this world! Let them not fall into the pit of darkness! "

[It is this simple chorus which has given this Scene the popular name of ' The Miserere,' now often misapplied to the great tenor solo which is to follow.]

All Leonora's terrors are aroused by these funereal

sounds; in the poignant, broken phrases which follow we may hear her sobs, and count the very beatings of her heart.

Now from the tower floats down Manrico's pathetic farewell to life and Leonora, *Ah, chè la morte*—short, simple, and of flawless outline, it is probably the nearest approach to an ' immortal ' melody that is to be found in Italian Opera. Of rare intrinsic beauty, its effect on the stage is prepared and heightened by every circumstance. With the initial advantage of being sung by an invisible tenor, its broad phrases in the major key, breaking in upon the heartrending sobs of the heroine, come as a complete surprise, and seem to lend a touch of resignation, if not of hope, even to her despair, while it gains enormously by mingling with Leonora's fervent responses, and the sombre strains of the religious choir. But even removed from its setting, and divested of all these advantages, sung in the concert-room or played on a barrel-organ, the melody of *Ah, chè la morte* never fails to cast its spell upon those who hear it—it seems to be made of the same imperishable stuff as Gluck's *Che farò senza Euridice* and Handel's *Largo in G.*

The Count enters, and in the long and exciting duet which follows Leonora has a hard struggle for the life of the Troubadour. Her first plea—" Slay me—but set him free ! "—serves only to increase the fury of her rejected suitor, but he yields at last on her offering herself as the reward of his clemency ; on condition that she marries the Count, she is to be allowed even to visit Manrico in his cell and be the bearer of his pardon. Leonora breaks into an ecstasy of rejoicing at this, and in the midst of her *roulades* finds opportunity to drain, unnoticed, the poison from the fatal ring.

Scene 11. A dungeon in the tower of the castle. Azucena is lying on her wretched bed, but cannot sleep. Manrico tries to comfort her, but in vain—the gipsy already feels the hand of death upon her, and her only hope is that she may die before they come to drag her away to execution. Always before her eyes is the horror of the blazing pyre, and her mother's agony repeated. [The fire-*motif* is here introduced in the orchestra with admirable effect.] She works herself up to a frenzy of terror, and sinks once more exhausted on the bed. Manrico takes his lute and soothes her to a calmer mood ; between waking and sleeping she sees again in vision the hills of her native land, to which they both will surely soon return ; and so she sinks to slumber. [The music of this scene—*Sì, la stanchezza* and *Ai nostri monti*—in its touching pathos, gained by the simplest of means, is more than worthy to stand side by side with the *Miserere* music, only it can hardly bear separation from its dramatic surroundings.]

Leonora enters, and the end follows swiftly. After the first rapture of meeting, her good tidings only awaken Manrico's suspicions ; on what terms has she purchased his freedom ? Guessing at only half the truth, he casts her from him, with reproaches for her infidelity. But the poison has nearly finished its work, and Leonora sinks into the arms of her repentant lover. The Count enters, discovers how he has been tricked, and orders Manrico to instant execution. Azucena awakes to find Leonora dead and Manrico gone. She grasps the truth—the moment for revelation has come, but it is too late. The Count drags Azucena to the grating of the cell to see Manrico already in his death-agony : " See ! yonder is thy son ! " " Nay ! thy own brother ! " is the terrible answer. With the cry " Mother ! thou art avenged ! " she sinks lifeless to the ground ; the Count is left alone, to bear the burden of the gipsy's curse.

LA TRAVIATA

Music by VERDI. *Words by* PIAVE.
Venice, 1853 ; *London*, 1856 ; *New York*, 1856.

ALTHOUGH *La Traviata* is perhaps the most faded of all Verdi's surviving operas, containing few numbers of outstanding beauty, and several that show the composer at his worst, nevertheless its production must rank among the most important events in the history of the lyric drama. It marks a definite advance in Verdi's musical development, and introduces an entirely new *genre* of subjects capable of operatic treatment.

Its vigorous survival—and it is doubtful if even *Il Trovatore* enjoys so great a popularity at the present time —is due to two causes, one being the irresistible attraction it has always had for the prima donna, the other the genuine human interest of the story. Yet this story was in the beginning a fruitful source of trouble. The libretto is based on the French play *La Dame aux Camélias*, by the younger Dumas, written in 1849, but not produced till 1852 owing to the objections raised by the licensing authorities of Paris. In this country the Lord Chamberlain absolutely refused to sanction any English version of the play, and when in 1856 *La Traviata* managed somehow to evade his vigilance and make a triumphant appearance at Her Majesty's Theatre it raised a storm of protest. Clergymen thundered at it from the pulpit, the *Times* denounced its " foul and hideous horrors," but the public found it neither foul nor horrifying, and with the enchanting Piccolomini as the heroine it drew crowded houses at each performance.   So widespread was the interest excited that even those pious persons who were loudest in their condemnation managed to satisfy their curiosity and their conscience by attending the concert performances of the work given at Exeter Hall, the stronghold of Puritanical principles.   The situation is well summed up in Albert Smith's satirical comment:

> The chance won't come again to us, the world's regenerators,
> To hear improper music, and not in the vile theayters;
> The *Times* condemned its playhouse form, but—bless our happy
>   land!—
> What's sin in the Haymarket is religion in the Strand!

An actual acquaintance with the opera soon convinced all sensible people that such prejudices were unjustifiable; *La Traviata* might be called silly or sentimental, hectic or in bad taste, but immoral it certainly was not.

Nevertheless Verdi's new opera was a daring experiment: not only does it mark the first intrusion of psychological problems into the lyric drama; it is also the first to deal with contemporary society in modern dress.   This innovation was so little to the taste of an Italian audience on its first production (Venice, 1853) that the opera was a complete failure; but on its revival in the following year it was put back into the Louis-Quatorze period, and at once started on its successful career.   This concession to convention, however, was soon dropped, and the opera is generally played, in accordance with Verdi's original intention, with the setting which Dumas' realistic drama demands.   This is undoubtedly the proper treatment, for the atmosphere of *La Traviata* is unmistakably that of Paris in 1850.   Another plan for which there is much to be said is to dress the piece according to the fashion actually in vogue at the time of the particular revival; whichever method is adopted, the opera retains its almost unique privilege of enabling the prima donna to wear all the diamonds her heart can desire without any risk of overdressing the part.

La Traviata, indeed, calls aloud for diamonds, emeralds, rubies—any jewellery you like, with the possible exception of pearls—dealing as it does with all the glitter of the fashionable *demi-monde* at a period when Paris might with truth be called ' the gay city.' The subject, considered so daring in its day, but seeming so hackneyed in our eyes by reason of its wearisome iteration on the stage, is the reformation of a courtesan through the influence of a genuine passion, and her sacrifice of wealth, happiness, her newly acquired self-respect, everything, to the fancied interests of the man she loves. The story, so admirably handled by the younger Dumas, has been condensed by Piave, the librettist, into a well-knit play in which the pathetic figure of the consumptive heroine makes a strong emotional appeal.

Act I opens with a supper-party in the *salons* of the beautiful and notorious Violetta Valéry. The conduct of this scene, with the constant *va-et-vient* of the guests, the short phrases of vocal conversation, and the continuous brilliancy of the orchestral background, reminds us of the opening scene in *Rigoletto*. There, it will be remembered, the Duke, the *primo tenore*, emerges from the crowd to sing his first solo; here a still greater sacrifice of operatic convention is made, as the prima donna has no *aria d'entrata*, but is ' discovered ' among her guests, and joins at once in the general conversation.

Violetta is the leader of the revels; an admirable hostess, she is constantly contriving some new pleasure, some fresh excitement, for the company. But from the very outset it is obvious that her intimate friends—Flora Bervoix and Gaston de Letorières—are anxious that she should not overtax her strength, for, as we learn, she has only just recovered from a severe illness, and her cough still troubles her. Gaston, in introducing his young friend Alfredo Germont as a new admirer, mentions that the latter has called every day of her illness to make inquiries. Violetta is evidently touched by this, though she treats it lightly, and laughingly holds such conduct up as a model to the Baron Douphol, who, though an old acquaintance, had paid her no such attentions.

Alfredo, in fact, has worshipped " *la belle Valéry* " for many months in secret, though they had never met before ; his youth and ardour could hardly fail to move the poor *demi-mondaine*, who from time to time had allowed herself to dream of some such faithful lover. She calls for more champagne, fills his glass with her own hands, and demands in return a song in praise of the good wine. Alfredo then sings the song generally known as the ' brindisi,' *Libiamo ne' lieti calici*. Violetta adds a second verse, and the two voices in unison are supported by all the rest in a brilliant *ensemble*.

The strains of a waltz are now heard from an adjoining room, and Violetta will have all join in the dance. She herself is preparing to lead the way when a sudden faintness stops her. She insists, however, that her guests shall not lose their pleasure, which she hopes to share with them in a little while.

Left to herself, the poor girl begins to suspect the true nature of her complaint. Dragging herself to the mirror, she gazes, horrified, at what she sees there. The deathly pallor, the hectic spot, the wasted muscles of the throat, all warn her that the hand of consumption is laid upon her. However, the actual faintness has passed, and she turns back to the room—to find Alfredo at her side. Touched by her obvious frailty, he urges his chivalrous passion, his desire to protect her, to remove her from the perilous conditions of her present existence. Violetta, half incredulous, laughs at what she assumes to be a sudden fancy—how long, pray, has he loved her ? From the moment when first he saw her—'twas then that the true meaning of love was first revealed to him.

This dialogue has been carried on to the accompaniment of the gay waltz music in the adjoining room ; now the music stops as Alfredo begins his solo, *Un dì felice*, the second section of which should be specially noted :

> *Ah quell' amor ch'è il palpito*
> *Dell' universo intero,*
> *Misterioso altero,*
> *Croce e delizia al cor !*

> Ah Love, mysterious ecstasy
> By every heart confessed !
> Thou strange, delicious mingling
> Of rapture and unrest !

These words are set to a haunting melody which Violetta uses, with even finer effect, in her great *scena* which ends the Act. Violetta still keeps him at a distance ; against his impassioned love-song she throws off some playful passages of brilliant *coloratura*—she warns him that he would do wisely to forget her.

The intrusion of Gaston for a moment seems to draw them more closely together ; on his departure Violetta, in softened mood, gives Alfredo a flower, which he has permission to bring back to her as soon as it is withered. "To-morrow then ! " cries the enraptured lover, and departs full of joyful anticipation.

The guests now troop in to take a noisy farewell. It is plain that Violetta's absence has not damped their gaiety, but the red light of dawn is already paling the candles, and warns them that day is the time for slumber.

Violetta, left alone, begins her great scena, *Ah fors' è lui*, in which she debates the choice, which seems at last to offer, between her present way of life and one that promises a happiness that she has never known.

The situation is finely conceived. The light of day begins to stream in through the half-curtained windows, shaming the guttering tapers, the gilded mirrors, the tumbled luxury of the apartments. Of all her flattering friends not one has stayed behind ; she is alone—but her new lover has just left her with the promise of a speedy return, and new hope has sprung up in her heart. Old memories now awaken—how, in her innocent girlhood, she had dreamed sometimes of a perfect union with the ideal lover who should offer her a life's devotion—was this her lover come at last ?

Softly, timidly almost, she begins her song, as if afraid to drive the lovely dream away ; but her voice gathers strength and passion as she glides into the melody she has heard so lately from Alfredo's lips—she repeats his very words :

> Ah Love, mysterious ecstasy
> By every heart confessed !
> Thou strange, delicious mingling
> Of rapture and unrest !

By the time Violetta has finished her second stanza we have to acknowledge that *Ah fors' è lui* is one of Verdi's most successful creations—the melody has a quite peculiar charm of its own, exactly appropriate to the character and situation to which it is assigned. We can only wonder, regretfully, remembering *Aïda*, what the composer might have made of it in the later stages of his development.

But she awakes from her dream : she, the practised courtesan, hardened in all the sordid shifts of her world.

fighting her friendless way through " the crowded desert that men call Paris "—what has she to do with dreams of a better life and of an honest man's fidelity ? 'Tis folly ! Abandoning herself to a reckless despair, she breaks out into an elaborate air of forced gaiety, *Sempre libera degg' io*—a composition far exceeding the ' brindisi ' in brilliance. Her only way is to plunge yet deeper into the pleasure of the hour, and drown all tender memories, all foolish aspirations, in a constant whirl of ever fresh excitements—true love is not for her.

Only the voice of Alfredo outside her window, still singing of that mysterious power that moves the universe, allows us to hope that Violetta may yet attain to her heart's desire.

Act II. *Scene* I. Violetta's country house, where she and Alfredo have been established for some months. It is within an easy carriage-drive of Paris, but the gay city rarely sees them now ; they have passed from the first flush of passion into that serener stage where the mere sharing of a common life is sufficient for their perfect happiness. Violetta has found her dreams come true ; it is to Alfredo she owes her redemption, her second birth, and richly has she repaid him. In his air, *Di miei bollenti spiriti*, he sings of how her tender, gracious influence has calmed the turbulence of his youthful passions and brought him into the tranquil haven of love. Alas, both are living in a false security ; they

> Have not raised the veil to see
> If still their heaven be lit above.

The entrance of Violetta's companion, Annina, is accompanied by an ominous restlessness in the orchestra ; she has just returned from Paris, and her explanations, in answer to Alfredo's questioning, are sufficient to rouse him from his dream of peace. The visit to the city was made at Violetta's request, with the object of raising money, by the sale of her property, to meet her current expenses. In the absorption of his present happiness Alfredo has failed to realize that the upkeep of their establishment has been borne by Violetta alone. Hitherto she had depended on the lavish generosity of her many admirers ; now that these supplies have long been cut off she is at her wits' end to find the necessary funds ; unwilling to apply to Alfredo, she had commissioned Annina, under a pledge of secrecy, to arrange for the sale of horses, carriages, valuables of all sorts, in order to replenish her purse. Alfredo is now fully awake to his dishonourable position ; filled with shame and remorse, he determines to hurry off to Paris, unknown to Violetta, in order to raise the necessary money and stop the sale of her property.

Violetta now enters the room ; she is no longer the painted, bediamonded *demi-mondaine* of the first Act, but a gracious, gentle figure, glowing with quiet happiness, and with at least the appearance of radiant health. Her first inquiry is for Alfredo ; on learning that he has left the house she turns to her correspondence. There she finds a note from Flora Bervoix, her old acquaintance, inviting her to some festivity at her house that evening. She shakes her head with a quiet smile—such gaieties are no longer to her liking, and never again will she enter such society.

But destiny is implacable ; moreover, there is much to be done in one short Scene, and the librettist is in a hurry. Violetta has just given the servant permission to admit, as she supposes, the man of business whom she is expecting when, on raising her head, she finds herself confronted with Alfredo's father, whom she now sees for the first time.

The elder Germont (an operatic *père noble* of the most tedious kind) has come prepared to curse, to threaten, to insist on an instant separation of the lovers, but Violetta's air and manner convince him of his mistake ; this is not the woman he had expected to find. Still, his errand must be accomplished. Divining the nobler strain in her nature, he makes a subtle appeal to her generosity. He has a daughter—*Pura siccome un angelo*—a young girl just on the threshold of happiness ; she is betrothed to the man she loves, but social conventions make it impossible for them to marry so long as the scandal of Alfredo's connexion with Violetta continues. Can she endure to blight this young girl's life ? Will she not sacrifice herself for the sake of Alfredo's sister—nay, for Alfredo's sake, whose future prospects are gravely injured by this present *liaison* ? Let her consider her own future also ; to-day she is beautiful, she is young —though Alfredo is younger still ; when her charms begin to wither, what other hold is she likely to have upon him ? Would it not be better to part from him now, and leave a fragrant memory behind her ? Violetta has listened in terrible distress to the elder Germont's arguments, struggling with all her might against their convincing logic. As he proceeds, his respect, his pity, increase ; he feels toward her some of the compassion which he claims for his own daughter, and it is to the tender earnestness of his pleading that she yields at last. " Tell your daughter," she says, " that to ensure her happiness another woman has sacrificed her last hope on earth. I will leave Alfredo this very day, and, in order that he may not follow me, he shall be made to believe that I am faithless to him, though God is my witness my love is his and his alone for evermore.   I feel I have not long to live. When I am dead promise that you will tell him the true story of my sacrifice." Full of gratitude the father takes his leave, after pressing to his heart the woman whom he would gladly have welcomed as his daughter had Fate allowed.

"Heaven give me strength to endure to the end!" is Violetta's cry when left alone.   Alas, she does not yet know the fearful nature of the trial that awaits her.   Her intention was to leave the house before Alfredo's return, and so escape the intolerable torture of a last farewell. She writes a note to Flora, accepting her invitation, and is planning the letter to her lover when Alfredo enters the room.   He questions her as to what she is doing, but hardly waits for an answer, and even fails to notice her agitation ; he has troubles of his own.   His father has written him a stern letter to demand an interview, and he expects him at any moment.   Ignorant of the scene which has just taken place, he sets his hope on the influence that Violetta's charm is sure to have over the elder Germont.   "Ah!" he says, looking fondly at his beloved, "how he will love you when he sees you!"

This is almost more than Violetta can bear.   His father must not find her there—she must retire, she says, for a time ; on her return she will throw herself at his father's feet—he will forgive them—they will live henceforth happy for ever in their perfect love.   Happy for ever! As she says these words the tears are streaming down her cheeks.   She clings to Alfredo, repeating, with a feverish insistence, the question, "You do love me, Alfredo ? You truly, truly love me ? "   Ah, how truly, how dearly ! But why does she weep ?   " 'Twas only a passing cloud ! Now I am calm again—see !   I can smile at you, Alfredo !

In a little while I will return to find you here—here,
among the flowers! We will make our peace with your
father, and no one, nothing, shall ever come between us!"
Acting her part out bravely to the end, the broken-hearted
girl takes, as she supposes, her last farewell.

[The closing passage of this Scene is perhaps the most
affecting in the opera; the dramatic situation finds its
direct and natural expression in the simplicity of the words
and the poignant melody to which they are allied:

> *Amami, Alfredo, quanto io t'amo!*
> *Addio!*
>
> Love me, beloved, as I love thee, for ever!
> And now, farewell!

Words and music may seem bald on paper, but no one
who has heard them rightly sung can ever forget the cry
of the heart which they convey.]

Alfredo has had but a little while to ponder happily
on the depth of Violetta's devotion when Fate knocks at
the door—a messenger with a note entrusted to him by
a lady in a carriage, on the road to Paris. It is in Violetta's
handwriting; he opens it—and in a moment his world
had fallen in ruins around him. She has gone—she, who
seemed to live only in his love, has left him, to return to
her old associates, her old way of living—her love for him
was merely a passing fancy. The blow is too heavy.
Alfredo staggers and falls—into his father's arms, who has
entered unobserved. Tenderly condoling with his son,
the elder Germont uses every argument to induce him to
return home with him—home to the fair land of Provence,
where skies are brighter and hearts more true. His
father's love, the family honour, the warm welcome that
awaits him—to all these considerations the younger man
is deaf; his grief has already turned to raging jealousy;
he suspects the Baron Douphol of being the cause of

Violetta's desertion. Vengeance is now his only thought. Finding Flora's invitation for that evening on Violetta's writing-table, he concludes at once that she will go there to meet his rival. He hurries off to Paris to prepare for his revenge, and the distracted father follows him.

[It is obvious that the librettist has attempted too much in this short Scene; the action is so hurried that it misses its proper effect; *e.g.*, the interval between Violetta's adieu to Alfredo and his receipt of the letter which transforms the tenderest of lovers into a jealous madman is far too short—we are not convinced. Verdi must have found his task one of great difficulty; he seems divided between his own desire to write music that shall preserve the dramatic continuity and the necessity of providing his singers, and the public, with the conventional arias which he knew they would expect of him. These, unfortunately, are among the worst specimens of their kind; Alfredo's two solos may be passed over in silence, but the air for the 'heavy father'—*Di Provenza il mar, il sol*—really provokes comment as being the most exasperating jingle that ever masqueraded as a pathetic melody. On the other hand, Violetta's music makes fair amends; her part preserves as much dramatic consistency as is possible in the circumstances; no florid passages are admitted, her two short-set melodies, *Non sapete* and *Dite alla giovine*, are not inappropriate to their sentiments, while her farewell is, as we have said, a masterpiece of expression.]

Scene II. This being the second drawing-room Scene in the play—for Flora Bervoix has thrown open her *salon* to the gay world of Paris—Verdi has taken care to avoid any monotonous repetition of the musical atmosphere of Act I. Consequently we find Flora entertaining her guests with a masquerade—first come the Zingari (with a little byplay of fortune-telling), then a chorus of Spanish matadors. There is no ball-room dancing, the gaming-tables being the chief object of interest on the stage. Alfredo is the first to arrive, then Violetta escorted by the Baron Douphol ; the latter, enraged at the sight of his rival, roughly warns Violetta against holding any intercourse with him, and the poor girl bitterly repents of her imprudence. (Her pathetic phrase *Ah, perchè venni incauta ?* although a stage 'aside,' is heard more than once above the other voices as the action proceeds.)

Alfredo seats himself at a gaming-table—his amazing run of luck draws the attention of the whole assembly. The Baron challenges him to play, Alfredo's luck still holds, and it is plain that the passions of both are rising high, when the announcement of supper separates them for a time, but not before Alfredo has promised to give Douphol full satisfaction on some future occasion, by which all understand that a duel is intended. Dreading the consequences to Alfredo, Violetta contrives to keep him with her when the other guests have gone to supper. She implores him to leave the house at once and so avoid further trouble ; he will agree on one condition only—that she will accompany him. With a breaking heart, but strong in her resolution, she refuses—she has given her promise to another, who has a better right. " To whom ? " he asks. " To the Baron Douphol." " Then," he persists, " you love him ? " " Yes," replies Violetta, *splendide mendax*, a heroine indeed at this moment, " I love him ! "

Beside himself with fury, Alfredo calls the astonished guests from the supper-room. He tells them the story of his long association with Violetta, of how he was led into allowing her to bear all the expenses of their establishment, of her subsequent desertion, of which they are all aware, and announces his intention of at once discharging the humiliating obligation. "And here," he cries, "I call you all to witness that I have made reparation in full!" With these words he flings the heavy purse containing the whole of his evening's winnings at Violetta's feet.

A general chorus of execration is heard—not one in the assembly but is shocked and disgusted at this wanton outrage. Loudest in his indignation is the elder Germont, who denounces his son's conduct as unworthy of his house; Alfredo, his fury dead within him, is stricken with shame and remorse; and above all the storm of the elaborate *ensemble* is heard the cry of Violetta, heartbroken at Alfredo's cruelty; yet even that cannot shake her faithful devotion—she is his, and his only, till death and beyond the grave.

[This Scene suffers, like the preceding, from the attempt to crowd too much into a short period. We become aware, too, of something amiss in the psychology. It is difficult to account for the unanimous outburst of sympathy with Violetta and of strong indignation against Alfredo for denouncing his late mistress; only in the elder Germont, who knows the truth of the affair, is such indignation explicable; to the others Violetta's sudden desertion of her devoted lover, apparently from mere caprice, must seem altogether blameworthy, while the behaviour of Alfredo, who believes himself to have been basely deceived, is natural and excusable. Admirers of Verdi may find their comfort in the elaborate and effective *finale* which he has managed to construct out of so unsatisfactory a situation.]

Act III. The tranquil beauty of the orchestral prelude—of a refinement quite remarkable for this stage of Verdi's development—prepares us for the quiet close of poor Violetta's stormy day. She has been for some time prisoner in her modest Paris apartment—far gone in consumption, she is but a shadow of her former self, and death is nearer than she imagines.

In all respects she is a changed woman; she has made her peace with God, and awaits the end with resignation, grateful for the careful ministrations of her faithful Annina and the good doctor Grenvil. When the scene opens, her room is still curtained for the night, but at her request Annina lets in the daylight. The streets are ringing with songs and mirthful cries; it is the Carnival, as Annina reminds her. Violetta's instant thought is for the many poor who will go hungry in the midst of so much feasting; she bids Annina take half the contents of her purse for distribution among them. The doctor enters, and tries to cheer her with promises of a speedy convalescence—but to Annina he whispers that her mistress has but a few hours to live. Left to herself, Violetta looks over the morning's correspondence.

The love-motive, *Ah, quell'amor*, is heard in the orchestra as she opens a letter from the elder Germont: "The duel was fought, the Baron wounded, but not seriously—Alfredo was obliged to leave the country. I have since written to him, telling him the full story of the noble sacrifice you made for his sake. Bravely have you kept your promise to me! Alfredo is hastening back to plead for your forgiveness—and I shall come with him. Only get well, and enjoy the happiness you so richly deserve."

Sweet comfort indeed—but it comes too late. Violetta drags herself to her mirror—one look is enough: she sees the shadow of approaching death. At the thought of her lover's return the longing for life awakes once more within her—but she knows it cannot be; farewell now to those false visions of recovery, farewell to all earthly hope;

Alfredo will not come in time; she must die the lonely death allotted to those of her class—no cross, no springing flowers, will mark her grave. May God have mercy on the soul of the poor 'Traviata,' and give her rest at last!

[This solo, *Addio del passato*, ranks with Violetta's *Amami, Alfredo*, in Act I, as an admirable example of true melodic expression—it has the ring of absolute sincerity. Even the fetters of the metrical form are less rigid than usual, and may easily be loosened by a skilful artist; sung throughout in a sustained *mezza voce* it makes an appeal of infinite pathos—it is the very dirge of perished hope.]

After the relief of a gay chorus from the revellers in the street Annina enters in great excitement—is her mistress well enough to hear some good news? Ah, Violetta needs no further hint—the door opens, and she is once more in the heaven of her beloved's arms.

The remainder of the Act is practically a duet between the two. In the first flush of joy Violetta seems to drink new life with every breath—even Alfredo is for a while deceived. They make plans for the future; they will leave Paris at once and live again the quiet country life in which they found such happiness.

[The duet *Parigi, o cara*, is one of the most popular numbers in the opera; it has, however, worn badly, and is singularly unfortunate in inviting comparison with the lovely *Ai nostri monti* in *Il Trovatore*, of which it might almost pass for a parody.]

Violetta is eager to take advantage of her recovered energies; she will go out—they will go together to church to thank God for their reunion—but the effort is too much for her; she falls back, exhausted, and the doctor is sent for. Again she gathers some feverish strength, enough for the passionate protest against her cruel fate: *O Dio morir si giovane !*—to die so young, and when happiness seemed once more within her grasp !

However, when the doctor comes he finds her calm and resigned, and the arrival of the elder Germont adds much to her contentment—in Alfredo's arms, and with his father reconciled to their union, she can smile in the face of Death.

Her last act is to give Alfredo a miniature of herself, radiant with youth and health ; he in turn is to give it, with her blessing, to the imaginary bride, more virtuous, but not more loving, to whom she commends his future.

Once more the throbbing violins whisper the love-motive *Ah, quell'amor*—so softly it hardly seems of earthly origin ; as if in answer to the call, Violetta rises to her full height ; with outstretched arms she utters a last cry, not of agony, but of joy and triumph, as her soul escapes from the prison of this mortal life.

Indeed, Violetta has made a good end, and no one will feel inclined to think harshly of the poor 'Traviata' ; when contrasted with many of the 'heroines,' erotic, neurotic, exotic, that have been exploited on the operatic stage in recent years, she stands out as a shining example of faithful devotion and heroic self-sacrifice.

UN BALLO IN MASCHERA

Music by VERDI. *Words by* SOMMA, *adapted from* SCRIBE'S
"*Gustave III.*"
Rome, 1859; *London*, 1861; *New York*, 1861.

A LONG chapter might profitably be written on
the libretto of this opera, coupled with reflections
on the curiously elastic and elusive nature of
librettos in general. Many a musically fine opera has
failed, or fallen into neglect, owing to the insipid or in-
coherent quality of the text ; some, making preliminary
shipwreck, have been successfully refloated after a drastic
revision of the 'book,' while certain old-established
favourites, though still surviving, find the burden of a
bad libretto ever a greater handicap as the years go on.

Among the last we may include Verdi's *Un Ballo in
Maschera*. Although unusually well served by his librettists on the whole, our composer was peculiarly unfortunate in one respect. The subjects chosen by him were
constantly bringing him into conflict with the political
authorities, so that opera after opera was in danger of
being 'choused' on the very eve of production. In
every case Verdi contrived to win the day, but only by
the sacrifice of certain situations in the drama, or by
changing the scene, the period, and the names of the
characters. In the cases of *I Lombardi* (1843), *Ernani*
(1844), *Rigoletto* (1851), *I Vespri Siciliani* (1855), not one
of these but had a tough struggle with the political
authorities, while the titles of the two last operas had to
be changed before the Austrian police would permit their
production in Italy.

But the climax was reached with the work which we are now considering. Its original title was *Gustavo III*, as it dealt with the historic incident of the King of Sweden's assassination at a masked ball in 1792. The opera was actually in rehearsal for production at Naples, in 1853, when the news of the attempted assassination of Napoleon III by Orsini decided the authorities to forbid the stage presentation of a similar incident. Verdi was told that he must either adapt his music to an entirely different libretto or withdraw it altogether. As he flatly refused to make such an alteration, the opera was withdrawn, to the intense indignation of the people. Verdi was immensely popular by this time, and the young Italy of the day nearly caused a riot by their processions through the streets of Naples ; the name of ' Verdi ' inscribed on their banners was well understood to represent the initial letters of Vittorio Emanuele, Re D'Italia, on whom they built their hopes of a free and united Italy.

When *Un Ballo in Maschera* was produced the following year, not at Naples but at Rome, Verdi had seen his way to altering, not the plot, but the period and place of his drama. The scene was now laid in Boston, Massachusetts, at the end of the 17th century, and the victim of assassination was the English nobleman who acted as Governor of that town. Oddly enough, this arrangement appears to have satisfied all political requirements, and the opera won an immediate success, which was repeated two years later in Paris, in London, and in New York. In the French version, *Le bal masqué*, the scene is changed from Boston to Naples, where the rather lurid happenings certainly seem more at home. However, we shall base our description on the Italian version, which is the one usually given.

Here is the outline of the story. Richard (Riccardo), Count of Warwick and Governor of Boston, is in love with Adelia, the wife of Renato, a Creole, his secretary and devoted friend ; she returns his love in secret, but tries to check her inclination, as she is a true wife in intention. Circumstances, however, force them to an avowal of their mutual passion, and Renato discovers what he believes to be their guilty secret ; at a masked ball given at the Governor's house he plunges his dagger into the heart of Riccardo, who lives just long enough to proclaim Adelia's innocence, and to pardon his assassin.

This simple plot is set forth in picturesque and melodramatic fashion ; the result of its association with Puritan Boston in its early days may be imagined. The height of wild incongruity is reached when the English Governor, on the occasion of his visit to a negro sorceress named Ulrica, is made to express his feeling in a Venetian barcarole.

Happily the day of the purely fatuous type of libretto was nearly over. The year of *Un Ballo* saw the production of a far crazier specimen in Meyerbeer's *Dinorah*, but it also gave us the excellent ' book ' of Gounod's *Faust*, the work of MM. Barbier and Carré,[1] since when there has been no lapse into sheer inanity. It is somewhat astonishing, however, to reflect that in 1859 *Lohengrin* had been nine, and *Tannhäuser* fourteen, years before the public.

Act I. And so the curtain rises on a scene that hardly prepares us for the highly coloured events that are to follow. We are in Puritan Boston, say, in the year seventeen hundred. The good townsfolk are assembled in the audience chamber of Government House awaiting

[1] It is only fair to add that these busy collaborators were also responsible for the absurdities of *Dinorah*.

the appearance of their popular Governor, Riccardo, Count of Warwick. The suavity of their opening chorus is mingled with the ominous mutterings of two gentlemen of colour—Sam and Tom by name—on whom it would be well for us to keep an eye, so plainly does their music suggest the whisperings and tiptoeings which mark the stage conspirator.

On the entrance of Riccardo the Governor, we learn that a masked ball is arranged for the next day ; a list of the invitations is submitted by Oscar (Edgar, in some versions), a particularly sprightly page, whose graceful share in the opera is among the chief causes of its success. The first name to meet Riccardo's eye is that of Adelia, the wife of his friend Renato, and he at once breaks into a rapturous avowal of his love for the lady in the aria *La rivedrò nell'estasi.*

The chorus having retired, Renato enters, full of affectionate anxiety for his friend and chief, whose life, he tells him, is threatened by a conspiracy in his own household. In spite of Renato's earnest exhortation, *Alla vita che t'arride,* Riccardo laughs all such fears away, and turns to receive the Lord High Judge who comes to demand the banishment of Ulrica, the black witch and prophetess, whose activities he regards as a danger to the city of Boston. Here Oscar the (soprano) page gets his (or her) first opportunity, as he pleads Ulrica's cause in a sparkling cavatina, *Volta la terrea,* which has the double effect of delighting the audience and of influencing the Governor in Ulrica's favour. He is determined to look into the matter himself, and as the chorus have by this time meandered back to the stage, he invites them all to meet him at the witch's hovel that afternoon. They express their pleasure at the prospect in a lively chorus, in which the sinister voices of Tom and Sam are hardly noticed, though it is plain that they are busy as ever with their black designs.

Scene II.   Though it is difficult to take the libretto of *Un Ballo* seriously, it is possible to say a good word for the picturesqueness of the *scenario* and the varied interest of the action.   After the rather hasty exposition of the opening Scene, which owes its attraction largely to three frankly popular tunes, so characteristic of the composer at this period, we pass to the highly fantastic atmosphere of the black witch's dwelling.   The rich and sombre colouring of the short orchestral introduction prepares us for the apparition of Ulrica, a figure of dread, intent on the magic brew that is simmering in her cauldron.   There are few finer opportunities for a real mezzo-contralto— with an easy command, be it noted, of more than two octaves—than the opening Invocation, *Ré del abisso*, *affrettati*.   A chorus of women has but little to sing, and Riccardo only a couple of bars as he passes, disguised, across the stage into hiding.

The prophetess is now prepared for the exercise of her powers.   Her first client is Silvano, a sailor, in the service of the Governor.   Ulrica dismisses him curtly with promises of speedy good fortune, which Riccardo, who has heard all, hastens to fulfil by placing, unobserved, a purse of money and the warrant for a commission in the man's pocket !

Adelia now enters, to seek, not prophecy, but counsel and help in her affliction.   She, Renato's true-hearted wife, is the victim of an unlawful love for Riccardo, the Governor and her husband's friend—she can have no peace unless Ulrica will find a way to rid her of this obsession.   The sorceress has her remedy pat; in the short solo *Della città all'occaso* she gives Adelia her instructions.   On the confines of the town, under the gibbet where the bones of malefactors dangle to the wind, there grows a plant the leaves of which can bring oblivion ; this plant Adelia herself must gather, at midnight, and alone. The listening Riccardo thus learns for the first time that his passion is returned, and determines to meet his beloved at midnight in the appointed place. Adelia having left by a secret door, the Governor's friends arrive on the scene, together with the sinister couple, Tom and Sam, and, of course, the sprightly page whose high soprano is given every opportunity in the *ensembles* that follow.

All are anxious to put the prophetess' pretensions to the test. The disguised Riccardo in light-hearted mood leads off with an almost rollicking number, in the form of a barcarole, *Di' tu se fedele*. But the sibyl assumes her sternest aspect ; taking Riccardo's hand, she foretells his awful fate—he is to die, and soon. " In battle, doubtless ? " asks the scoffer. " Nay ! " she answers, " by the hand of a friend ! " Still unconvinced, Riccardo begins a lively quintet, *È scherzo ed è follia*, which must rank among the very best of Verdi's concerted pieces.

But cannot the witch, he asks, describe this destined minister of fate ? " Know then," she says, " 'twill be the man whose hand you next shall take in yours ! " More than ever convinced of the imposture, Riccardo laughingly offers his hand to any or all of the familiar company who surround him, but none will dare to take it. At this moment Renato enters the room and seizes the Governor's hand in the warm grasp of friendship. The tension is relaxed, Riccardo's identity is revealed, and Ulrica's gloomy prophecies are all forgotten. The Act is brought to an effective close by the device of bringing Silvano back, with a troop of friends, bent on finding the Governor and thanking him for his generous favours. We are thus provided with a largely augmented chorus to join in the hymn of praise, *O figlio d'Inghilterra*, which seems to augur nothing but a happy future for their well-beloved ruler.   Only Tom and Sam know better.

Act II.   Although *Un Ballo* was written five years after *La Traviata*, on which it is in some respects a great advance, the later opera contains some clear echoes of the earlier.   The prelude and opening scene before us irresistibly recall the last Act of *La Traviata*, with its tender melancholy and its attempts to reach a certain atmosphere of spirituality.

Adelia, alone at the foot of the gibbet at the ghostly hour, is hardly equal to the strain of her varying emotions. She is loth now to accept the gift of oblivion that she had craved—the beloved's image once torn from her heart, what has she left to live for ?   As she still hesitates, the bell tolls for midnight ; she yields to the terror of the place and the hour ; she peoples the darkness with the phantoms of her brain ; she sinks on her knees in a fervent prayer for Heaven's protection—she rises and finds herself confronted, not by a phantom, but by Riccardo, the beloved.   Too late now to pluck the herb of oblivion !

The long love-duet which follows contains much that is stereotyped and banal, but is worked up to a vigorous climax, and the arrival of Renato gives occasion for a trio of the highest interest.   From this point it is almost impossible on a first hearing to grasp the details of motive and action, yet these require careful attention.   Renato has come in hot haste to tell the Governor that the rebels of whom he has warned him are even now in pursuit and will assuredly take him if he lingers.   He, Renato, has overheard their conversation in passing—they know where Riccardo is, and will be here immediately.   Renato, of course, has no suspicion of the identity of Adelia, who is heavily veiled.   In the most admirable section of the trio, both she and her husband urge Riccardo to instant flight. He is at first unwilling to leave Adelia, but at last consents, on the perilous condition that Renato shall promise to escort the lady back to safety without speaking to her or attempting in any way to discover her identity. This the guileless Renato swears to do, and Riccardo hurries away.

The conspirators rush boisterously on to the scene, headed by Tom and Sam. In their disappointment at finding the Governor flown they are inclined to insult the lady, and are about to do violence to Renato when Adelia interposes and, in so doing, lets fall her veil and discovers her identity. This is the tensest moment of the drama, and Verdi has handled it in most original fashion. Adelia's despair and Renato's broken heart find, of course, some immediate musical relief, but their full expression must wait till the next Act for their proper development. Meanwhile the tragedy is overlaid with comedy by Sam, Tom, and their followers, who are delighted with what they regard as a piquant situation. Adelia's cries of distress and the broken phrases of Renato are accompanied by a laughing chorus from the rough band of rebels. This is interrupted for a time by a short dialogue in which Renato hints at his intention of joining their conspiracy, but is again renewed after he has left the stage with Adelia.

They give free vent to their ribald humour :

> To spread the scandal we shall not fail !
> How tongues will wag when they hear the tale !

and the scene ends with the chuckles and guffaws of Tom, Sam, and their companions—surely the merriest band of conspirators to be found in all Italian Opera.

Act III. We now come to the great scene between Renato and Adelia, which contains the most famous number in the opera. *Un Ballo* is noted throughout for its *ensembles* rather than its solos, which are too often of the showy, conventional pattern, but the present situation has inspired Verdi with music of a very different order. Renato, in the fury which has succeeded to the first numbness of grief, is resolved that death, and by his hand, is the only punishment for the wife whom he believes faithless. Adelia's indignant protestations of innocence are all in vain, but one last request he can hardly refuse her—that she may take farewell of her little child. [This touching solo, *Morrò, ma prima in grazia*, with its lovely cello obbligato reminds us inevitably of the softened Violetta in the last Act of *La Traviata*.]

Renato's reply to Adelia's petition is the noble *scena* well known to every concert-goer as *Eri tu*. It may be well to give a fairly close translation of the Italian text in order to show the material on which Verdi had to work.

"Rise, then!" says Renato to the kneeling woman; "I will allow thee to see thy child once more. To yonder chamber go—and there in darkness and in silence hide thy blushes and my shame." With her departure his mood changes. "Nay, not on her, not on a poor weak woman, must my revenge be taken!" Here he strides up to a portrait of Riccardo that hangs on the wall. "'Tis thy blood—*thy* blood, thou traitor, that must wipe out this insult! For 'tis thou who didst sully the whiteness of this innocent soul," etc., etc. Poor stuff, indeed, to inspire a composer; yet Verdi has contrived to use it for the basis of a little masterpiece of lyric beauty and dramatic sincerity; love, hate, and a broken heart, all are here expressed with a truth that is marvellous when we consider the poverty of the text as well as the cramping musical formulas by which the composer was still bound.

The tension is relieved by the arrival of our comic

conspirators. Although they come in answer to a summons from Renato, they can scarcely believe his assurance that he desires to join them in their plot to assassinate the Governor ; but, once convinced, it only remains to decide who is to have the honour of striking the fatal blow. [It is rather sad, after the excellent quality of the previous scene, to be confronted with the blatant trio *Dunque l'onta di tutti sol una*, a piece of cheap conspirator-music which Verdi might have written twenty years before with an easier conscience.] They agree to refer the matter to chance, and the lots are already prepared, when Adelia reappears, and Renato resolves that her hand shall draw the fatal number from the urn ; to his great delight he finds himself the chosen man.

The page, who may always be relied upon to lighten a too strenuous situation, now enters with invitations from the Governor to the masked ball on the following evening, and the scene ends with one of those well-written and significant *ensembles* that are the peculiar glory of this opera.

The materials for the last scene—the masked ball and the assassination—naturally do not admit of much expansion, but the librettist has shown no small ingenuity in providing some variety of incident. First of all we get what we may call a whitewashing solo for Riccardo. The device is not new ; admirers of *Rigoletto* will recall a similar number at the beginning of the second Act of that opera. The rascally Duke, after plotting the abduction of Gilda and discovering that someone has been before him, is provided with a pathetic soliloquy in which he professes himself heartbroken at the loss of her for whose sake, he assures us, he was prepared to turn over a new leaf and live cleanly ever after. Certainly no one ever believed in the Duke's repentance, nor are we prepared to accept our Riccardo as an entirely virtuous person. However, as sympathy has to be worked up for a *primo tenore* who is about to perish, we find him in a virtuous mood. The orchestra is playing the melody of his aria in the first Act, *La rivedrò nell'estasi*, while he makes up his mind not only to see Adelia no more, but also to ship her and her husband off to England, and thus remove temptation from his path. Having signed, after some hesitation, the document that secures Renato an honourable appointment in that far-off island, he takes, in imagination, his last farewell of his beloved—*Ma se m'è forza perderti*. As he prepares to join the dancers, Oscar meets him with an anonymous letter (from Adelia, of course) which warns him that an attempt will be made that very evening on his life. But the Governor will run all risks save that of being thought a coward ; assuming mask and domino, he mingles with the general throng.

Renato now enters with his fellow-conspirators, Sam and Tom, all three in similar disguise. They are afraid at first that the Governor will not be present ; Oscar, however, assures them that his master is in the rooms, though he refuses to give them any clue to his identity. His roguish little song, *Saper vorreste*, sounds the last note of personal gaiety possible in the face of the tragedy so near at hand. The inevitable love-duet between Adelia and Riccardo is woven into the measures of a graceful mazurka, but the emotion of the lovers is well brought out in the vocal parts. Adelia implores him to fly while there is yet time—the enemy may strike at any moment. Riccardo is obstinate as he is fearless ; he feels he cannot tear himself away ; but he nerves himself to tell her of his resolve, and how he has arranged for her return to England. " And now," he sings, " the hour has come for me to leave you—take, then, my last farewell ! "

A madman rushes in between them : "And thou, too, take this last farewell from me !" thunders Renato, as he stabs Riccardo to the heart. His victim, of course, lives long enough to forgive his assassin, to vouch for Adelia's unspotted innocence, and, as a proof of his own noble intentions, to hand over to her the papers that will secure her husband's position in England. With tender farewells for all, not omitting his "beloved America," Riccardo, Count of Warwick and Governor of Boston, breathes his last amid the sobs of a grief-stricken people and in something rather like the odour of sanctity.

AÏDA

Music by VERDI.   *Words by* DU LOCLE *and* GHISLANZONI.
Cairo, 1871 ; *New York*, 1873 ; *London*, 1876.

THIS is perhaps the one work which can bear without reproach the much-abused name of Grand Opera. Grand, not grandiose, in conception, massive yet simple in structure, dealing with heroic times and primitive passions, it calls for great splendour of setting, great singing, and, in two at least of the parts, for great acting. Musically it offers a superb feast of pure melody such as none but Verdi could have provided, offering a flexible medium for dramatic expression, and orchestrated with a resourceful variety of colour which the composer's previous works had but faintly foreshadowed.

Nor in praising Verdi's masterpiece should the names of the librettists be left unhonoured ; Camille du Locle and Antonio Ghislanzoni, collaborating, managed to produce in *Aïda* one of the finest 'books' ever written for an operatic composer.[1]

The story of true love thwarted by destiny, betrayed by jealousy, yet triumphant in death, has for its setting the Court of the Pharaohs at a time when Egypt was at constant strife with the neighbouring land of Ethiopia. The reigning Pharaoh has a daughter, Amneris, who numbers among her favourite waiting-women a beautiful young Ethiopian, Aïda, brought from her native land among the spoils of recent warfare. Although her slave,

---

[1] My thanks are due to Messrs G. Ricordi and Co. for permitting me to use their text of the opera.

Aïda is actually the equal of her mistress, for, unknown to all, she is the daughter of Amonasro, the reigning sovereign of Ethiopia. She is also her rival in love—the proud Amneris has long been on fire for Radames, the valiant Captain of the Egyptian Guards, but his heart is given to Aïda, who returns his love in secret. Amneris, tortured by jealous suspicion, bides her time. A fresh invasion of Egypt by the Ethiopians is a failure ; King Amonasro is captured and brought with other prisoners to the Court of Pharaoh, where his identity is no more suspected than that of his daughter. Discovering Aïda's passion for Radames, now Chief of the Egyptian forces, he compels her to obtain from her lover a military secret of vital importance. Radames is overheard as he speaks the fatal words ; though perfectly innocent in intention, he is convicted of treason and condemned to an awful death— to be entombed alive in the vaults beneath the Temple of Isis. But he does not die alone ; Aïda contrives to gain an entrance to his dungeon, and the faithful lovers pass together through death to life, locked in each other's arms.

He who comes late to a performance of *Aïda* commits a grievous sin against himself and his neighbours. There must be perfect silence in the house if the first notes of the Prelude are to be heard, a heavenly love-song given out by the violins alone, *pianissimo*, and at a poignant height. After a short contrapuntal development of this theme, the heavy tread of destiny is heard in the bass, the march of the inexorable priests of Isis, to whom the lovers' piteous death is due. But again the song of love soars up, strong and triumphant, until the last notes seem to reach the stars and die away. Not even the most *blasé* of opera-goers, provided he still loves what is best in music, will willingly miss the Prelude to *Aïda*.

Act I. *Scene* 1. In the vast columned halls of the royal palace of the Pharaohs, Ramphis the Chief Priest and Radames, the young and valiant soldier, are in converse; the solemn swing of the orchestral phrases prepares us for heroic scenes and actions. The Ethiopians once more have laid waste the Valley of the Nile—the need is urgent; the Egyptian forces are already in arms, and the oracle of Isis has declared the name of the Captain who is to lead them to victory. " I go," says Ramphis, " to tell the King," whilst his significant look assures Radames that he is the favoured man.

The young soldier is left alone to rejoice at his good fortune, and his thoughts at once fly to Aïda—what bliss to fight for her, to return victorious, to lay his crown of laurels at her feet ! No longer shall she suffer the indignity of slavery, the woes of exile ; to her own country he will restore her, the greener, fairer land of Ethiopia, where they will reign together. [*Celeste Aïda* is perhaps the most conventional number in the opera, and certainly the most popular.]

The entrance of Amneris is heralded by a broad, insinuating melody in the orchestra, expressive of her passion for Radames. The proud Princess of the Royal House of Egypt notices at once the blaze of happiness in his face, and demands the reason ; he tells her of his ambition and his dream of coming glory—his talk is all of war, but hers, alas ! of love. " And have you no sweeter visions of your future ? " she asks—" no tenderer hopes ? " Radames has nothing to reply, but the confusion of his manner wakens her suspicions, which are confirmed at the agitated entrance of Aïda by the glances which she intercepts between them.

[Amneris' jealousy is depicted in the restless melody which now forms the orchestral background for the voices—Aïda is brought on to the accompaniment of the love-theme already heard in the Prelude.]

With all a woman's cunning Amneris gives her slave an affectionate welcome ; calling her ' sister ' and ' dearest,' she implores her to confide to her the reason for her obvious emotion. Aïda pleads her fear for the safety of her fatherland in the coming struggle, of which she has just heard the rumour, but the suspicions of the Princess grow apace ; the jealousy *motif* continues to the end of the trio, while above the broken phrases of the tenor and mezzo Aïda's voice rings out in a really magnificent melody, in which she avows (though only for herself) her fervent love for Radames.

Now begins the first of the many fine *ensembles* to be found in this work. The King enters with his guards, priests, and courtiers, and in full council announces the outbreak of war ; the news is at once confirmed by a messenger who brings tidings that the Ethiopians, led by their King Amonasro—Aïda shudders to hear her father's name—are even now marching upon Thebes. " Vengeance ! Vengeance ! " shout the infuriated Egyptians. The King assures them that all is prepared for battle, and that the Captain chosen to lead the army is Radames. King and priests now begin the impressive march-tune, *Su ! del Nilo al sacro lido*, on which is built a magnificent chorus of patriotic ardour ; Amneris hands to Radames the flag which is to lead him on to victory, and all voices are raised to acclaim him with the cry, " *Ritorna vincitor !* "

The excited multitude, the King, the priests, depart— only Aïda is left on the stage. She, too, has joined in the universal shout : " Go win the victor's crown ! " Victor —over whom ? Over her brother, her father, her own people ! With a revulsion of feeling she calls on the gods to blot out so impious a prayer—for her own country, rather, would she invoke a victory. Yet—that must mean danger, perhaps death, to Radames, the man she loves! Torn with these conflicting emotions the poor girl breaks down, and, bowed to the earth, pours out her soul in prayer (*Numi, pietà !*) :

> Look down, ye gods, on my despair !
> Turn where I will, no help is nigh !
> Almighty Love, hear thou my prayer !
> Come, end my anguish !   Now let me die !

[This number, *Ritorna vincitor !* is a favourite piece for the concert platform, where, unlike most operatic extracts, it can be made almost as effective as on the stage.]

Scene II.   A strangely beautiful Scene is this, in which Radames visits the Temple of Ptah, the God of War, to obtain his blessing in the coming expedition.   A vast hall, with a double row of columns vanishing in the darkness, is lit mysteriously from above, and filled with clouds of incense from a score of golden tripods.   In the centre of the stage is an altar, and ranged between the columns are the priestesses of the temple, who sing a hymn of unearthly beauty, *Possente Ptah !* in which they accompany themselves on the harp.   Ramphis and the priests interpose a few bars of solemn harmony, and the women's voices continue their solemn incantation, which seems to hint the mysteries of a remote antiquity.   This, too, may be said of the sacred dance that follows.

Before it is ended Radames enters, divested of his armour, and kneels before the altar.   A veil of silver tissue is placed upon his head, and Ramphis, as Chief Priest, lays in his hands the sacred sword which shall surely rout the enemies of Egypt.   He then begins a broad and solemn melody, *Nume, custode e vindice,* which

Radames repeats, the chorus of priests joining in, while the full orchestra lends strenuous and brilliant support. The weird strains from the women's voices are heard again, in ever-quickening *tempo*, and a universal shout of " Almighty Ptah ! " brings to an end one of the most picturesque and impressive *finales* in Italian Opera. If it has a fault, it is the rare one of being possibly too short.

Act II. *Scene* 1. The whole of this long Act, which celebrates the triumphant return of Radames with his victorious army, might be described more particularly as "The Triumph of Amneris"; indeed, throughout the work the moments are not few when the spectator is inclined to ask whether the opera should not be named after the haughty Princess rather than her unhappy slave.

The short Scene with which the Act opens discovers Amneris among her tiring-women, busy with her toilette for the approaching festival ; her slaves know well how to soothe and flatter her as they wave their feather fans and sing of the triumphs of Radames and the reward of love which awaits him. [*Chi mai fra gl'inni e i plausi* is a graceful yet vigorous choral duet for female voices to harp accompaniment.]

Amneris, lost in tender dreams of the future, breaks in with a long-drawn, voluptuous phrase, *Ah vieni, amor mio !* and admirable relief is provided by a grotesque dance of what are described as " young Moorish slaves," usually represented as so many tiny Petes and Topsies from " way down upon the Old Plantation."

Played softly by the 'cellos, the love-theme of the Prelude heralds the approach of Aïda, from whom Amneris is resolved to wring a confession of her secret. With unctuous affection she sympathizes with her grief at the slaughter of her countrymen : " But time, dear friend, will heal your sorrows—aye ! and a greater power than time—the God of Love ! "

Moved beyond endurance, Aïda breaks out into the ecstatic love-song *Amore, amore !*

> O Love almighty, I bow before thee !
>   Giver of rapture, hope, and holy fear !
> In pain and anguish I still adore thee !
>   Heaven lies around me when thou art near !

The melody, of which but a part is given in the Prelude, here finds its full development in a glorious outpouring of romantic passion.

A theme of insolent triumph is now heard in the orchestra : Amneris advances to the field on which her rival is soon to lie prostrate. "My sweet Aïda," she begins, "tell me thy secret trouble ! Among the many heroes who fought for thy dear country, was there not one to whom thy heart was given ? But take courage ! A kindly fate perchance has spared him—not all, thou knowest, have perished. We too, alas ! have heavy losses to mourn—our Captain Radames, I hear, is dead."

A piercing cry of anguish is Aïda's answer.

Amneris turns to fury : "And thou dost weep for him ! Then—then—thou lovest him ? I will know the truth ! "

Seizing the unhappy girl by the arm, she brings her face to face : "Look at me, now, and listen ! I told thee falsely ! Radames still lives ! "

Aïda falls on her knees with arms upraised to heaven : "Ye gracious gods, I thank you ! "

"Then it is true ! Thou lovest him ! But hear me —I love him too ! I am thy rival ! *I, daughter of all the Pharaohs !* "

These words are uttered with a superb gesture of *hauteur*. Aïda replies with no less dignity of voice and manner : " My rival, sayest thou ! A Princess, truly— and I no less than thou——" She checks herself in time, for she must not reveal the secret of her birth. Falling at her rival's feet she pleads for pity in a song, *Pietà ti prenda del mio dolor*, which, if rightly given, can move the theatre to tears.

" 'Tis true—I love him with measureless love ! But thou—have mercy ! Powerful and fortunate, pity my misery ! Leave me my love—it is all I have ! "

But Amneris is inexorable : she is the sovereign, Aïda the slave, whose fate is in the hands of her mistress. From outside is heard the noise of the approaching pageant, and the chorus of Act I, *Su ! del Nilo al sacro lido !*

The Princess rises, awful in her exultation : " Listen ! 'tis the song of victory ! Now is the hour of my triumph ! Follow me, and I will teach thee who thou art—no rival, but the meanest of my slaves ! Radames is mine, and mine alone ! "

Amneris sweeps from the stage, and the wretched Aïda is left, crushed and despairing, to cry to heaven for help : " Look down, ye gods, on my despair ! Pity my agony ! Now let me die ! "

Scene II. A vast open space among the palms and temple of the city of Thebes ; the people are gathering for the great pageant which is to honour the return of the victorious armies. On one side of the stage is a high daïs with a canopied throne, and a second seat of hardly less magnificence.

The royal procession enters : first the King, the officers of state, the captives, the priests, all the pomp and power of Egypt. Next comes Amneris, attended by Aïda and others of her slaves : a majestic figure, she takes her seat at the King's left hand.

The chorus, *Gloria all' Egitto*, begins with a great rhythmic shout of exultation over the mighty deeds of Egypt and Egypt's King. After a gentler passage for the women alone, the music takes on an entirely different colour as the solid phalanx of white-robed priests lift up their voice in the significant phrases to which attention has already been drawn in the Prelude. There is something almost brutal about this massive theme, which is used throughout the opera, always with startling effect. " Glory give to the gods on high ! 'Tis they who rule our destinies ! "—such is the burden of their song ; yet in it we seem to detect a sinister note which would suggest that it is the will of the priests rather than of the gods that must be done.

Excitement rises higher as an advance-guard of the Egyptian troops appears upon the scene, magnificent creatures with long silver trumpets on which they perform most manfully (though not always in tune with the orchestra) what is perhaps the most sonorous march ever written for a stage pageant. But Verdi has seen to it that there are no *longueurs* in *Aïda*. The soldiers soon cease to blare, and take up their ordered station to allow of the entrance of the dancing-women.

The ballet is a welcome diversion, gay and graceful, and delicately varied. But the height of the pageant is reached when the main body of the victorious troops enters, bearing aloft the statues of the gods with their different emblems, the bull, the sacred cat, the boat of Ra. The climax of sound is now reached as people, soldiers, priests, all unite in a repetition of the choral material from the beginning of the Act, but now much more elaborately orchestrated.

At last Radames himself appears, borne in a canopied litter on the shoulders of his officers. The King himself comes down from his throne to embrace and thank the saviour of his country ; for him, too, a crown is waiting, the wreath of laurels which no hand but that of the King's daughter is worthy to place upon his brow. [What thoughts are in Amneris' heart the orchestra shows us—the insinuating melody associated with her passion for Radames is played almost in its entirety.] Yet the wreath is but the symbol of glory—what more substantial reward does Radames desire ? Let him ask what he will, and, by all the gods, it shall be his ! [Amneris' heart beats faster ; but the victor's thoughts are not of her.] His answer is unexpected : " First, O King, let the prisoners of war be brought before thee ! " The order given, the sorrowful crowd of captives enters, closely guarded—last of all Amonasro, King of Ethiopia, but showing no sign of his royal rank. [It is interesting to note here the sinister effect produced by the intervention of the priests, who, as their prisoners enter, repeat their inexorable chant *pianissimo*, as if to protest against any undue show of mercy to a fallen but still dangerous foe.] Aïda springs forward into her father's arms ; he has just time to whisper a caution in her ear when the King of Egypt bids him advance.

" Who art thou ? "

" Aïda's father—one who fought for his country ! We were beaten—our King was slain—vainly I sought for death." Then, with a gesture toward the prisoners, " Yet, O King, do thou show mercy ! Not for myself, but for these I plead ! Spare thy slaves here kneeling before thee ! So, in thine own hour of peril, may fate be merciful to thee ! "

[Amonasro's solo, *Ma tu Rè, tu signore possente*, so splendidly worked into the *ensemble* that follows, is one of the unforgettable things in the opera ; like Aïda's prayer, *Pietà ti prenda*, in the preceding Scene, it expresses the dramatic emotion just as far as is possible with a perfectly symmetrical melody in which formal beauty is obviously the first object. It is not merely the humble petition of a suppliant ; a closer observation will detect a hint of self-assertion, of veiled defiance even, in the music as in the words.]

Now begins an *ensemble* of colossal structure and elaborate design : while the prisoners and the Egyptian people join together in the prayer for mercy, the priests, led by Ramphis, are sternly opposed to any such measure. There is something awful in the passage, *Struggi, o Rè, queste ciurme feroci,* in which they urge the King to devote the prisoners to death :

> Turn thy face from this treacherous nation !
> Be thou deaf to their pitiful tale !
> For the gods have decreed their destruction,
> And the will of the gods must prevail !

[Above the immense mass of choral sound no less than six solo voices strive to make themselves heard ; Aïda, Amonasro, Ramphis, the King, are all interested in the petition for pardon, while Radames gives expression to his tender care for Aïda, and Amneris is muttering threats of vengeance.]

Radames now approaches the King to claim his promised reward : it is that all the Ethiopian captives should be set at liberty. The priests at once make violent opposition ; Ramphis takes upon himself to point out to the King the danger of letting such implacable enemies escape. But Radames is firm : " There is no danger ! Now that Amonasro their King is dead, further resistance on their part would be futile." His pleading wins the day : the prisoners shall be sent back to their own country, all with the exception of Amonasro, who, with Aïda, is to be kept as hostage.

But now the grateful King announces to his heroic General the magnificent reward he has reserved for him : " My daughter Amneris I give thee in marriage : when I am dead, thou shalt be King of Egypt."

This is the hour of Amneris' triumph : " Now," she cries, " Radames is mine indeed ! Let the presuming slave try to take him from me if she dare ! "

The Scene ends with another closely woven *ensemble,* in which the patriotic *Gloria all' Egitto* and the gloomy voices of the priests are well contrasted with the triumphant blare from the long trumpets of the soldiers on the stage. Amneris, too, has her song of triumph ; Aïda and Radames are both in dejection ; and Amonasro, noting the signs of their mutual love, already meditates a plan for the recovery of his fallen fortunes.

Thus ends an Act which for sheer magnificence can hardly be paralleled in opera. Pageant follows on pageant, effect upon effect, each contributing its due share to the perfection of the musical structure ; nothing is introduced as mere ornament, each new spectacular element is part of an organic whole, and never was a lovelier ballet so fully justified. With grateful memories of *Il Trovatore* and *Rigoletto,* those " fair and flagrant things," we can only rub our eyes with amazement at the extraordinary advance the composer has made toward perfection in the way of dramatic expression. At the same time, we are thankful to find the essential Verdi still unchanged : there is still the old, generous flow of enchanting melody, only with the additional perfection that the formal beauty of the melodic curve is now enhanced by an entirely fresh wealth of orchestral colour.

Act III. If the previous Act was dramatically a

triumph for Amneris, the present one belongs emphatically to the heroine, Aïda. It is richer in lovely melody than any other part of the work, while the tense interest of the drama never flags.

The scene is one of romantic beauty—we see the banks of the Nile in full moonlight, groves of palms to right and left, on one side the Temple of Isis almost hidden by the trees, though a bright light streams from the columned portico.

From within there comes the softest flutter of stringed instruments at their highest pitch, to be followed by an unearthly sound of chanting voices. No passage in the opera is more striking than this short invocation, so plainly does the music speak of times and a people unimaginably remote.

A boat now approaches, bearing Amneris and Ramphis the High Priest : the Princess is come to spend the night in prayer that the goddess may bless her union with Radames : as they enter the temple, the mystic chant rises to a wild *fortissimo*, then dies away as the doors are shut. But the moon is bright, and the murmur of the Nile is clearly heard in the orchestra, while above it soars the heavenly theme which symbolizes Aïda's faithful love, as a veiled figure enters with cautious step.

Aïda is despondent of the future. Radames will meet her here to-night—but for what purpose ? " Oh, should he come only to take a last farewell "—she turns to the deep waters of the Nile—" then take me to thy bosom, thou dark and dreadful river ! So shall I find peace at last—peace and oblivion."

Another longing, too, is heavy upon her—the longing for home and country. " Land of my fathers, ne'er shall I see thee more ! " Her solo, *O cieli azzuri*, is one of the most exquisite things in the world of opera.

Students of Verdi will find the old-remembered idiom here, as strongly marked as ever—but with a difference! The way in which he contrives by the distribution of the text to avoid monotony of rhythm, to give a new turn to a too familiar phrase, to enrich the sensuous charm of the melody by the delicate orchestral colouring—in all this we recognize the second spring of the composer's powerful inspiration.

The song ends in a mood of resignation, a soft reverie, which is broken by the impetuous entrance of Amonasro, the royal captive. He can read his daughter's heart, her love for Radames, her longing for her country; it is easy to work on her feelings. She, a Princess, to remain in the power of Amneris, her rival, and the bitter enemy of Ethiopia! Never! Her father is there to take her home! "*Rivedrai le foreste imbalsamate,*" he sings:

> Once again shalt thou see our leafy forests,
> Our fragrant valleys, our temples all of gold.

Radames too shall join her there to share her perfect bliss. The Egyptians—has she forgotten how they laid waste her own dear country?

> Burnt in fury our houses undefended—
> Old men, maidens, and children all were slain!

But the day of vengeance is at hand; even now the Egyptians are launching a new campaign; but this time his people are prepared, and will defeat them. One thing it is necessary for him to know—what route the enemy will choose for their march—and that Aïda must tell him. "But how?" she asks. "Radames!" is the answer. "He will meet you here! Does he not love you—and is he not the leader of the Egyptian army?"

Aïda recoils in horror: never will she tempt her lover to commit such treachery!

At once her father's wrath descends upon her in all its fury : she is no child of his : 'tis she who is a traitor to her country !   He calls up to her imagination all the agony of war, the streams of blood, the groans of the dying—and worse than that :

> Horror !   I see the dead arise,
>   Hate in their eyeballs glowing,
> Pointing at thee with jeers and cries :
>   " She hath betrayed us all ! "

Aïda clings in terror to her father's arm, only to be thrown off in savage anger.   " See ! " he cries, " whose form is this that rises from the shadows ?   It is thy mother, with curses on her lips : ' No child of mine art thou ; nay, but the abject slave of the Egyptians ! ' " Aïda is conquered—she grovels at her father's feet—she will do all he wishes.

" But oh, my country ! " she cries in agony.   " What must I suffer for love of thee ! "

Amonasro hides among the palms as the orchestra gives warning of the hero's approach in a striking, oft-repeated phrase ; it is the jubilant cry of one sure of his triumph, in love as well as in battle.   There is nothing now to bar him from Aïda ; already high in the King's favour, he is to lead another army against the Ethiopians ; he will return again victorious, and neither priests nor Princess will dare to oppose their union.   Aïda feigns coldness and suspicion: let him go to Amneris, to whom he rightly belongs !   In any case she, Aïda, can never be his : the King would not consent, and the fury of the powerful Amneris would overwhelm them both.   Yet there is a way—one only—to fly the country !

Radames at first recoils, but Aïda has powerful means of persuasion : her beauty, his love for her, the pro- spect of a life of perfect freedom in her own fair land.

Her air, *Là tra foreste vergini,* is enough to seduce the sternest from his duty :

> There is the forest's fragrant heart
> Laden with sweets uncloying,
> A perfect love enjoying,
> The world we'll soon forget !

She has won the day ; under the influence of her spell Radames is wild to be gone. His impassioned outburst, *Sì ! Fuggiam da queste mure !* is repeated by Aïda, and the two join in the theme of love triumphant with which Radames made his entry. They are hurrying off the stage when Aïda stops : " But tell me," she says, " what route are we to take ? The passes will all be closed by the Egyptian forces."

" Nay, *one* will be open," is the reply ; " the one chosen for our march on Ethiopia."

" And which is that ? "

" The pass of Napata."

" The pass of Napata ! "—a harsh, exultant voice repeats the words—it is Amonasro, who comes from his hiding-place among the palms. " Behold ! " he cries, " Aida's father—and the King of Ethiopia ! "

The horror and despair of Radames are terrible to witness—his thrice-repeated cry, " *Io son disonorato !* " is unforgettable. Amonasro strives to reassure him : " Nay, there is no dishonour ! 'tis Fate that willed it so ! Come ! and in my country shalt thou have both honour and power ! There thou shalt reign, with Aïda for thy queen ! "

But Fate works swiftly for the ending of all such dreams. " Traitor ! "—the cry comes from the lips of a furious woman : it is Amneris, who has overheard them and now comes forward. Amonasro rushes at her with drawn dagger, but Radames puts himself between them.

Amonasro has just time to drag Aïda away when Ramphis and his guards advance. Radames strides proudly toward him : " Priest ! I am thy willing prisoner ! "

Act IV. *Scene* I. A lofty anteroom, dimly lighted ; on one side the heavy portals of a prison, on the other the mouth of a broad stairway leading down into darkness. The orchestra preludes with the restless *motif* associated with Amneris' watchful jealousy ; she is leaning against the prison doors, listening for any sound from within. She has good cause for gloomy reflection—her rival has escaped ; the man she loves is in prison, expecting a traitor's death. No traitor he !—whatever he may have done, she loves him still—is it too late to save him ? She bids the guards bring Radames before her. Earnestly she pleads with him to save himself, and her peace of mind ; if he will but confess his fault and appeal for mercy, she herself will kneel before the throne and obtain his pardon.

" Nay ! " is his answer, " I am conscious of no crime ; nor do I care to live, now that she I love is dead."

The Princess assures him that Aïda still lives—" but," she urges, " if I save thy life, promise me never to see her more ! "

Radames chooses death rather than such real dishonour ; he is led back again to his cell, and Amneris is left to all the tortures of her jealousy and hate. But her mood soon changes. Very softly in the lowest tones of the orchestra is heard the priests' *motif*, now like an awful march that speaks of doom and death ; Amneris sees too clearly all that is to come. The white-robed priests file slowly across the stage and disappear into the vaults below. Despair seizes upon her—she hides her face in her hands : " Ah ! let me not see that sight of terror—those dreadful ministers of death, who feel no pity. And it is I who have placed my beloved in their power—I, who might have saved him!" She sinks back in horror and remorse as Radames is brought once more from prison and led down to the subterranean hall of judgment.

Nothing could well be more impressive than the scene that follows. The stage is empty, save for the solitary figure of Amneris, half frantic with terror and remorse: clear and awful from below rises the chanting of the priests at their work of doom. The trumpet sounds; then the voice of Ramphis, the accuser: "Radames! thou hast betrayed thy country's secrets to the enemy. Answer the charge!" The last words are repeated by the rest of the priests in chorus; deep silence follows: Radames disdains to reply.

"Traitor! Traitor!" they thunder all together, while Amneris makes her frenzied appeal to heaven to save him. Thrice is the trumpet blown, thrice comes the accusing cry, and the silence that truly may be felt— but no word from Radames, no answer from the gods to Amneris' appeal. From the judgment hall below we hear the sentence delivered by the bass chorus: "Radames! thou art a traitor, and hast incurred the wrath of Osiris; hear then thy doom! In the vault beneath the altar of this temple thou must remain a prisoner till death shall set thee free!"

The fateful march is heard once more as the priests come from the crypt and cross the stage: Radames is not among them. Amneris makes her last frantic appeal: "Hear me, ye tyrants! Monsters of cruelty! Pause, ere ye murder an innocent man!" Then, turning to Ramphis: "Priest of Isis! I love this man! If by your act he dies, Heaven's curse be on you for evermore!"

For a moment they pause, implacable, to repeat their thunderous denunciation of the traitor, then go off, unmoved by the wild imprecations which Amneris hurls after them. " Race of devils ! May the wrath of Heaven fall upon you ! Be accursed for evermore ! "

Scene II. Verdi's device of showing us two independent groups of actors in one scene, which we find in *Rigoletto*, is here employed with even greater effect. We have two stages, an upper and a lower. Above is the interior of the Temple of Isis, ablaze with lights and wreathed in clouds of incense from many braziers ; here are the white-robed priests, and the priestesses who move in the sacred dance—two of the priests are seen lowering a mighty slab of stone into its place in the centre of the stage—it is the ceremonial sealing of the tomb of Radames.

Below the vaulted roof, the pillars of the crypt are dimly seen ; and Radames, resigned to his fate, knowing that Aïda is in safety—may she live on, and cease to sorrow for him ! But even as he speaks he finds he is not alone : Aïda, learning of his awful doom, has found her way to his side ! In the first rapture of this unlooked-for reunion the past, the present, are forgotten.

> At last united, all our troubles over,
> Ah, my beloved, let us die together !

So sings Aïda ; but Radames is struck with horror to think that she too is now involved in his terrible doom. In a passage of true pathos, *Morir, si pura e bella !* he protests against such an end for one so young, so formed for love. As the mystic hymn is heard from the shrine above, he makes one last attempt to dislodge the fatal stone that seals their prison—but in vain. Aïda is already rapt above the earth in an ecstatic vision :

> Lo ! where some angel hither flies
> From yonder azure dome !
> Ah yes, 'tis death in friendly guise
> Who comes to lead us home

On the upper stage a figure, veiled in robes of mourning, advances to the centre of the stage, and bends low over the stone of death; it is Amneris, "daughter of all the Pharaohs." Broken-hearted, bowed to the dust, she can still pray: "O Isis, grant peace to the soul of my beloved: peace in thy heaven for evermore!"

Below, the faithful lovers, blessed in their death, are clasped in one another's arms. Amneris' prayer is answered.

OTELLO

Music by VERDI. *Words by* BOITO, *from* SHAKESPEARE.
Milan, 1887 ; *New York,* 1888 ; *London,* 1889.

WHEN *Otello* was first produced it was rapturously hailed by most of the critics as the
composer's masterpiece, a verdict which would
be stoutly challenged to-day. But in the late nineties
the world of music was perhaps a little Wagner-mad :
none but ' the Master's ' methods were acceptable, and
these were gulped down without discrimination ; consequently it was considered a sign of grace that in this
new score by the great Italian there was a comparative
dearth of melody and very few separate numbers, while
the musical interest was often to be found in the orchestra
rather than on the stage. Certainly Verdi seems to have
laid aside his Italian singing-robes for the time ; you may
call *Otello* music-drama if you like, a successful experiment
along the lines laid down by Richard Wagner. Indeed,
this opera and its still finer successor *Falstaff* show a
development in method and technique which is nothing
less than astounding in a composer already past his
seventieth year ; both works call forth our affectionate
admiration, the latter gives us unqualified delight, yet
it is open to question whether either is such a genuine
expression of Verdi's peculiar genius as we find in the last
Act of *Il Trovatore*, the close of *Rigoletto*, and Scene after
Scene of *Aida*.

Dramatically, *Otello* is apt to be dull, as any desiccated
version of Shakespearean psychological tragedy is bound
to be. The libretto is graced, but not saved, by the

literary talent of the composer's lifelong friend, Arrigo
Boito ; it is worth noting that two of the most striking passages, Iago's *Credo* and Desdemona's *Ave Maria*
are interpolations by the librettist. The version of the
Willow Song is taken from a very old Italian popular
air, most beautifully treated.[1]

A century ago another *Otello*, by Rossini, was very
popular, and became a showpiece for such artists as
Pasta and Malibran ; this work has long disappeared,
though the Willow Song, *Assisa al piè d'un salice*, was
heard frequently in the concert-room till the end of the
last century. Verdi's Desdemona has been a favourite
rôle with great vocalists—Albani, Eames, Melba ; but the
success of the opera depends upon the exponents of
Othello and Iago. We are not likely soon to see the equals
of the artists who created these parts, Tamagno, the
brazen-throated, and the admirable Victor Maurel—the
latter's Iago is still remembered as one of the most superb
performances of the operatic stage.

Act I. A seaport in Cyprus ; the Governor's castle
near the shore. Without prelude the curtain rises on a
stormy sea ; a ship is seen in peril, but as the wind falls
she comes safe to anchor, and Othello, Governor of Cyprus,
steps on land. He tells the assembled people of the success of his expedition against the Turks, and passes to his
castle, after giving orders for all to celebrate his return
with music and feasting.

Iago now comes forward : in his heart the storms of
envy and malice are never still. He confides to Roderigo
how he hates Othello and despises Cassio, who has been
made Captain over his head. To Cassio he now turns
his attention ; he plies him with wine, and by the aid of

---

[1] My thanks are due to Messrs G. Ricordi and Co. for permitting me to
use their text of the opera.

a drinking-song, *Inaffia l'ugola*, succeeds in making him drunk and embroiling him first with Roderigo and then with Montano, the ex-Governor. Finally he contrives to stir up a general tumult, which brings the indignant Othello on the scene. Desdemona presently follows; the thought that her rest has been disturbed by the uproar rouses her lord to fury; all the blame is laid upon Cassio, who is deprived of his captaincy. Iago, the evil spirit of the play, has scored his first triumph.

The Act ends with a love-duet of sustained lyric beauty. There are echoes here of the Shakespearean text—for instance, of the well-known lines:

> She loved me for the dangers I had passed,
> And I loved her that she did pity them;

but the words are mostly of Boito's invention. Special notice should be taken of the musical phrases accompanying the words *Un bacio! un altro bacio!*—we shall meet this *motif* again in a very different situation. For conclusion the voices mingle in a passage of exquisite tenderness: the Pleiades have set, the crescent moon is rising, the hour is late—but not too late for love, whispers Othello, as he draws Desdemona slowly up the castle steps.

As giving us the only glimpse of happy love to be found in the opera, we feel that this duet might well be longer.

Act II. In this scene the villainous Iago must be regarded, like Milton's Satan in *Paradise Lost*, as the real 'hero' of the piece. In a room with balconies opening on to the great garden of the castle we find him with Cassio, hypocritically condoling with his downfall, yet bidding him be of good cheer—his fortunes may be mended! Does not the fair Desdemona sway her lord

Othello to her slightest wish ? Let Cassio but gain her ear and induce her to plead for him, Othello will soon recall him to favour. The plot is laid with diabolical cunning, and the much-praised soliloquy for Iago, *Credo in un Dio crudel,* in which Verdi certainly manages to suggest the ravings of a lost soul, is finely heralded by a great blast of trumpets such as might attend the clanging of the gates of hell. Man—so runs the sound and fury of the words—is the child of the Monster of cruelty who rules the world ; in His own image He has created him. " I am vile," says Iago, " because I am a man—I feel the primal slime within my veins. He whom you call a just and honest man is but a lying hypocrite. Man is the plaything of malignant fate from the hour of his birth to the last day of his life ; then comes death—and nothingness. Only a fool believes in heaven. That is my creed ! "

This outburst over, he turns to spy on Cassio and Desdemona talking together in the garden ; his poor dupe is bent on ingratiating himself with the lady, who is all gracious sympathy with his misfortune.

The approach of Othello from the castle hall gives Iago his opportunity ; taking up his position behind a pillar he gazes fixedly and with a frown on the pair as Cassio is taking his leave. Just as Othello comes within hearing the villain shoots his first poisoned arrow in the words, *Ciò m'accora !* It is enough—Othello's peace is gone. To his demand for an explanation Iago replies with a feigned reluctance that serves to inflame suspicion : " My lord, before you were married, was Cassio acquainted with your lady ? . . . Beware of jealousy, my lord. It is the green-eyed monster ! Only—keep watch ! "

This conversation is interrupted by a most welcome interval of pure beauty. Desdemona is seen advancing from the depths of the garden, surrounded by the fisher-folk with gifts of flowers and shells, while children strew lilies in her way ; they accompany their delicious chorus with mandoline, cornemuse, and little hand-harps. As Desdemona joins in the closing cadences, even Othello is charmed for the time from his jealous brooding, but her very innocence plays into the enemy's hands. The crowd dispersed, she at once approaches her lord on Cassio's behalf, urging her request with such insistence that Othello can hardly control the growing fever of jealousy ; Desdemona, supposing him to be unwell, offers her handkerchief, which he throws angrily to the ground, from which it is recovered by Emilia, in attendance on her mistress.

Now follows a quartet in which Iago manages to snatch from his wife Emilia the handkerchief on which so much depends, while Desdemona pleads tenderly for pardon if haply she has offended her lord. But the poison is work-ing fiercely in Othello's brain—he dismisses her harshly, and the rest of the Act is filled by a long duet between the Moor and his evil genius.

Othello is provided with a solo, *Ora e per sempre addio* —a piece of pure old-fashioned Italian opera—before his fury breaks loose. In his frenzy he seizes Iago by the throat and flings him savagely to the ground—it is he who has awakened his master's suspicions, now let him furnish proof ! Iago answers with a version of the well-known passage " I lay with Cassio yesternight," etc., and he describes the stolen handkerchief which he declares he has seen in Cassio's possession. Othello needs no further evidence ; Desdemona is guilty beyond question in his eyes—blind eyes indeed that cannot see the arch-villain at his side.

It would be difficult to devise the right operatic ending for this scene ; as it is we have to be content with an undeniably stagey duet, in which Iago and his victim join in a solemn vow that they will never rest till vengeance has been accomplished.

Act III. After a short Prelude, in which the ' green-eyed monster ' motive of the previous Act is repeated, the curtain rises on Othello and Iago in the hall of the castle. Iago, who by this time has his master under complete control, bids him remain while he fetches Cassio; then, in hiding, let him note the young soldier's behaviour, and he shall see that which will change suspicion to full certainty. Desdemona is seen approaching and Iago departs, pausing to hiss the words "The handkerchief!" into Othello's ear.

As the young girl advances, radiant with beauty, innocence, and wifely devotion, even Othello can hardly believe her capable of wrong. Alas, her innocence again destroys her; she comes, she says, to plead once more for Cassio—such great friends as they have been, will not her lord pardon and recall him? Othello is again in the raging furnace of jealousy. He asks her for a handkerchief—no, not that one—the one he gave her! Has she lost it—or given it away? Then woe betide her, for there is a curse attached to it! Even now the poor child fails to understand. "Ah!" she says, "you do but tease me, to keep me from plaguing you with my suit for Cassio!"

Othello loses his control: "The handkerchief! The handkerchief!" he thunders, and charges her to her face with guilt beyond the scope of her imagining. Her protestations, her tears, her prayers, are of no avail—the scene ends most cruelly. Taking her by the hand, he escorts her to the door with a frightful mockery of the courtesy he has shown on her entrance : " Give me once more that lily hand!"—here he breaks off : " But, nay— I ask your pardon!"—then shouting with the voice of a madman, " I did mistake you for that vile strumpet whom poor Othello took to wife!" he thrusts her violently from the scene.

His heartbroken lament for his lost love, *Dio! mi potevi scagliar*, is interrupted by Iago, who bids him hide behind the pillars, for Cassio is coming.

Then follows the scene of Iago's jugglery with the handkerchief. The feather-headed Cassio is led on to jest and laugh over his amorous adventures, while Othello, who can see all, is yet not near enough to catch more than a word here and there, which his jealousy is quick to misinterpret. Yielding more and more to Iago's flattery, Cassio tells him a piquant little secret—how he has lately found in his bedroom a lady's handkerchief—dropped there by an unknown hand. "An unknown hand!" repeats Iago in derision, and loud enough for Othello to hear, " Show me the handkerchief!" Cassio produces it, Iago takes it from him and manages so to display it that Othello can identify it beyond all doubt as the one he had given Desdemona.

[The music of this scene, and especially of the trio, is masterly in its subtle differentiation of the various emotions—Cassio's levity, Iago's delight in the success of his devilish cunning, Othello's furious despair. Notable also is the melodious grace of Iago's bantering song about the handkerchief, *Questa è una ragna*.]

After Cassio's departure, Othello has but one thought —that Desdemona must die ; by suffocation, Iago advises, that very night as she lies sleeping ; he himself will see to the slaying of Cassio.

A long fanfare of trumpets announces the arrival of an embassy from Venice ; Desdemona is summoned to help in the formal reception of the visitors, and even here some unhappy turn in the conversation leads her once

more to speak kindly of her hope for Cassio's pardon—
her old friend Cassio! Othello can endure no further;
he commands her to be silent in so terrible a voice as to
shock the whole assembly.

But still further blows await him; he reads the letter
from the Doge of Venice only to find that he is recalled
to the capital, and that Cassio succeeds him as Governor
of Cyprus. Desdemona weeps for pity to see her lord's
distress, and he, supposing her to grieve for the approaching separation from Cassio, throws her brutally to the
ground: "Lie there! Lie there, and weep!"

A long and most elaborate *finale* delays the dreadful
end. Desdemona makes a heart-broken appeal for pity,
and the rest join in a chorus of sympathy, when the Moor,
who is no longer sane, for whom the very air is filled
with blood, breaks in with an awful cry, "Flee, flee from
Othello!" which sends them hurrying from the hall.
Left alone with Iago, he raves more and more wildly,
and falls at last unconscious to the ground.

From the street come the shouts of the people: "Long
live Othello! Long live the Lion of Venice!" Iago
dares to place his foot upon his master's neck and, pointing
with scornful finger, cries out in fiendish exultation:
"See where your lion lies!"

Act IV. The shortest and most perfect. The scene
is Desdemona's bedroom; words and action follow
Shakespeare with fair fidelity; the short Prelude is a
mirror of the poor girl's sad and wistful thoughts.

While Emilia assists her to disrobe, Desdemona sings
the lovely Willow Song, an old, old strain that tells of
one who died because she loved too well. On her, too,
is the shadow of death; Verdi shows us this with a touch
of true dramatic genius. Her mistress has dismissed
Emilia with a "Good night," sung quietly, on a low

note ; as the woman turns to leave her Desdemona realizes her own utter loneliness, her need of sympathy in the face of peril; with a poignant cry in the highest range of the voice she calls Emilia back, and clings to her as she takes what she feels will be her last farewell.   Then, kneeling before an image of the Blessed Virgin, she says her Ave Maria, sings a quiet prayer, and lays her down to sleep.

The musical interest now passes to the orchestra, as the drama runs its familiar course swiftly to the end. Othello enters, puts out the light, and, parting the curtains of the bed, gazes long on the sleeping Desdemona ; we hear the theme from the love-duet of Act I (*Un bacio : ancora un bacio !*) as he kisses her once, twice, thrice.

The brutal deed is hardly done when Emilia clamours at the door for admission ; Desdemona is still able to reply to her question " Who has done this ? " with " No one—myself !   Commend me to my lord ! "

Iago's villainy and Desdemona's perfect innocence are proved by Emilia and Cassio.   Othello is frustrated in his first attempt at suicide, but he has another weapon at hand, and the orchestra for the last time plays with the tender love-*motif* as he falls dead beside the body of his innocent victim.

> I kissed thee e'er I killed thee—No way but this,
> Killing myself, to die upon a kiss.

FAUST

Music by GOUNOD. *Words by* BARBIER *and* CARRÉ.
Paris, 1859 ; *London,* 1863 ; *New York,* 1863.

THE subject-matter of Gounod's *Faust* makes probably a more universal appeal than that of any other opera, so a few words on the reason may not be out of place.

Though *Faust* may be considered as the last of the supernatural-romantic librettos, it is certain that the human interest contained in it is the strongest element of its attraction. It would be easy to maintain that the hero—if we may use the term—is the Devil himself, in the guise of Mephistopheles, yet the deepest impressions that remain with us are not of the supernatural; it is the poignant human tragedy of Marguerite that moves us, her innocent girlishness, the awful consequences of her betrayal, her unwavering fidelity to her lover, and her final redemption through the power of love. Vividly, too, do we realize the typical figures that surround her —Valentine, the rough soldier-brother, Siebel, her boyish lover, even the slight comedy-sketch of old Martha, all these appear to us as actual human beings, though placed in a romantic setting. Faust, on the other hand, is, dramatically, rather a shadowy character, except in the first Act, and Mephistopheles, although he dominates the play, a towering figure of evil, is so skilfully handled that he is able to take his place, for the most part, among the human personalities with hardly a touch of the grotesque absurdity which ruins most of the operas into which a supernatural element is introduced. It is finally the tragedy of Marguerite that enthrals us : the Germans do well to call the opera not *Faust* but *Margarete*, since of the spirit of Goethe's masterpiece there is hardly a trace. The psychology of Gounod's Marguerite is the invention of the librettists and the composer rather than of the great German philosopher. In any case the result is admirable ; *Faust* is one of the few operas which, while touching our deepest emotions, sets us at the same time pondering over the eternal truths of life and death.

Act I. The place is Nuremberg, the time the Middle Ages ; Faust is in his study. Though it is long past midnight, the aged scholar is still poring over his parchments or examining his crucibles. But even these have ceased to interest him ; he is tired of life, of a life misspent in a struggle to solve, by all means lawful and unlawful, the riddle of the universe, the secret of the soul of man. The secret of his own soul is shown us plainly in the gloomy, heavily dragging phrases of the orchestra : this man is weary to the verge of despair.

The gloom is broken by the sound of cheerful voices from without. Faust flings back the curtain from the window—a new day is dawning, another day to be endured ! The labourers go gaily to the fields, singing their songs of joy—the earth is fair, the skies are blue, praise God for all ! These sights and sounds of innocent happiness are too much for Faust : for him life has nothing more to offer ; he will die, and by his own hand. Into a crystal goblet he pours a swiftly working poison, and is about to drain it, when the joyful voices of simple men rise once more in chorus : "The earth is fair, and life is sweet—praise God for all ! " Roused to fury, the old man breaks out into a terrible cursing ; he curses all things, human and divine ; Heaven holds no hope for him—yet he knows on whom to call ! "Satan ! Satan ! Appear ! "

A crash and a flash! and into the room steps a courteous stranger, richly dressed, with plumed *chapeau*, and a sword at his side—the Devil himself, in fact, but with horns and hoofs well out of sight. Even Faust, versed as he is in the Black Art, recoils at first. " Begone! " he cries. But the Devil knows his own. " Ask what you will," he says, " I will give it into your hands! Speak! Is it riches—power—or glory? " " All these I despise! " Faust answers. " 'Tis pleasure I long for—and youth, to enjoy it! "

Nothing easier! He has only to sign his name to a certain little roll of parchment : Faust shall taste again all the joys of youth and life, and on earth the Devil will be his most obedient slave; but, after death—well, things will be very different down below!

As the wretched man still hesitates, the Tempter plays his strongest card. " Behold! " he cries, " where youth and beauty await thee! " Through clouds of enchanted vapour there appears a vision of Marguerite in all her innocent loveliness; she is seated at her spinning, and the sound of her wheel mingles, in the orchestra, with the seductive phrases of the great love-duet of the third Act. Faust hesitates no longer—the fatal deed is signed; he casts off the burden of old age, and emerges a handsome, gallant stripling, ready for all the delights that life and the Devil can offer him. They mingle their voices in a repetition of Faust's earlier confessions of his desires : *Je veux le plaisir*—

> 'Tis youth that I long for,
> The beauty of woman,
> Her ardent caresses,
> The love in her eyes!

and the pair go off arm-in-arm in quest of Marguerite.

The music of this Act is well on the way toward " the

music of the future," as the term was understood in those days and long afterward ; that is to say, in place of set airs and formal closes, the action is carried on mostly in a sort of melodious recitative—you may call it ' *melos* ' if you choose—helped by an orchestral accompaniment of high dramatic significance. We find very few real ' tunes,' and these are quite appropriate to the situation, *e.g.*, the snatches of the Peasants' Chorus ' off,' and Faust's impetuous expression of his love-longings in the air *Je veux le plaisir*, that is so aptly repeated for the closing duet. In addition to this the orchestra introduces, during the vision of Marguerite, the broad melody of the great love-duet of Act III.

A word as to the overture. After a short introduction, highly expressive of the scene on which the curtain rises, we pass abruptly to a bold and arresting melody, the significance of which is not apparent. This form of the overture dates from the production of the opera at Her Majesty's Theatre in 1864, in an English version, and the melody in question is the first part of the famous air " Even bravest heart may swell "—better known as *Dio possente*—which was written for Charles Santley, the original English exponent of Valentine ; " *Avant de quitter ces lieux* " is the first line of the French text.

Act II. A fair in full swing in the market-place This lively scene is the choristers' opportunity ; seldom indeed are the different sections of an operatic choru given such a chance of separate distinction. First th basses, the thirsty students, the swaggering soldiers, a equally bent on deep potations and amorous adventure next, the richly dressed burghers, the old men with thei high-pitched cackle, content to sit apart and watch th game of life go on around them.

Now come the young sopranos, giddy and tittering

quite ready to meet their gallants half-way, be they soldiers or students ; last of all the contraltos, not so young as they used to be, and shocked at the forwardness of their younger sisters.

Each of these groups has its own individual share of music and action, and finally they all combine in a masterly blending of the various characterizations. The climax is reached in a hand-to-hand scuffle between the younger and the elder women, in which the men also take part, and the crowd surges off the stage, to make room for Valentine, Marguerite's soldier-brother, Wagner, his comrade-in-arms, and the boyish Siebel. Valentine, who is off to the wars, is distressed at leaving Marguerite at an age when a brother's protection is most needed. He hangs round his neck a sacred medal which she has given him for a talisman in the hour of danger, and commends her to the care of Heaven in the famous air *Dio possente*, already referred to.

Siebel is allowed only a few bars in which to constitute himself Marguerite's watchful guardian, and Wagner bids them brush all such gloomy thoughts aside, for " *Toujours gai* " is the soldier's motto. He starts a lively song, but is cut off, after only a few bars, by the entrance of Mephistopheles, who at once dominates the scene. With a certain air of insolent courtesy, he proposes to entertain them with a song of his own—it is the song of the Golden Calf, (*Le veau d'or*) ; Gold is the lord of rich and poor— monarchs and people all adore him ! There is but one god, Gold—and Beelzebub is his servant ! Beelzebub, or Mephistopheles, the Master of Evil, stands there in the midst of them, and sways them all to his mood. In this song Gounod was inspired to write as fine a piece of grotesque *diablerie* as is to be found in any opera ; the brutal, assertive melody, the weird chromatic changes in the harmony, the reiteration of the buzzing figure for the strings—was not Beelzebub the Lord of Flies ?—all combine to produce an impression that is absolutely original and unique. When properly rendered the effect of this number is nothing less than terrifying.

Mephistopheles now proceeds to assert his uncanny influence in various ways. He seizes Siebel's hand, to tell his fortune ; knowing the secret of his devotion, he banters him. " Strange, indeed ! Henceforth each flower you pluck shall wither—so no more love-posies for Marguerite ! " Grumbling at the wine they offer him, with his magic art and a flash of red fire he conjures a rare vintage from an empty cask, and drinks to the health of Marguerite. Valentine, angry at the introduction of his sister's name, challenges him to a duel—but the soldier's well-tempered blade is not proof against Satanic power— it snaps in twain. The people, now thoroughly aroused, and led by Valentine, advance on Mephistopheles with their sword-hilts held aloft, thus confronting the Prince of Darkness with the sign of the Cross. Against that sign not Hell itself has power ; writhe as he may within the charmed circle, Mephistopheles cannot break through until they retire.

[The musical treatment of this scene is a striking example of economy ; the rough vigour of the first short chorus, the solemnity of the second, based on the ecclesiastical chant intoned by Valentine, produce an overwhelming effect by the simplest means and in the shortest time.]

Faust now joins Mephistopheles ; the orchestra, by its reference to the youth-and-pleasure motive of Act I, shows us what is passing in his mind—he is all impatience to see in the flesh the maiden of his vision. Nor has he long to wait. To the strains of the gayest and lightest o waltzes the stage is filled with a crowd of revellers, who sing what may best be described as a vocal accompaniment to the dance-rhythms, with a delicious effect of spontaneity. At last she comes—the damsel of the spinning-wheel! There is a lull in the dance—the crowd make way as Marguerite appears, with downcast eyes, and attended by old Martha, who, since the mother's death, has been her not too judicious guardian. In a moment Faust is at her side: " Pardon if I presume, O fair and gentle lady! Will you not take my arm and let me walk with you ? " " Nay, Sir, I am no lady—you must not call me fair—nor do I need an arm to help me on my way! " And Marguerite is gone. Nothing could be simpler, nothing more commonplace than these words, yet Gounod's genius has clothed them in the light of romance. This short passage makes an ineffaceable impression, commensurate with its dramatic importance ; if dialogue is to be carried on in measured melody, it could not be better done than in this instance.

In this chance meeting of a moment poor Marguerite's fate is decided ; while Faust's ardour is only increased by the modesty of her refusal, Mephistopheles jeers at him for a timid wooer, and urges him to instant pursuit. Meanwhile the chorus resume their dance with a new zest, and the Scene ends, as it began, in a whirl of gaiety.

Act III. This is the lovely Garden Scene which after nearly three-quarters of a century still keeps its colour and its fragrance. The short but striking prelude seems to tell us whose garden it is ; the time is evening, toward the moth-hour, the dew is gathering, and the air is filled with

> A rosemary odour, commingled with pansies—
> With rue, and the beautiful Puritan pansies.

And a yet more poignant perfume hovers there, ready

soon to descend and fill all the scene with a sense of enchantment. Marguerite's modest dwelling is just shown, with its low windows and little porch; there is another door opening through the high garden-wall into the street; and a small statue of the Virgin under a wooden canopy, with a shell for holy water.

The peaceful prelude changes to a livelier measure as Siebel enters from the street; it is his boyish delight each evening to place a nosegay near her door for Marguerite's acceptance, and then retire—for he is one who worships from afar. Ah—what is this! The flowers are withered in his grasp, as the Dark Stranger had foretold—undaunted, he dips his fingers in the holy water at the shrine where his beloved comes each evening to pray. Thus armed, he tries again. Joy! the curse is lifted, and full of triumph he plucks another posy for his offering.

[Siebel's Flower Song, *Faites-lui mes aveux*, one of the most hackneyed of airs, still keeps its fresh perfume; its effect on the stage is often marred by the custom of assigning the part to a heavy voice, in view of the sustained *legato* of the song in Act IV, *Si le bonheur*. But this Flower Song must be light and buoyant as a butterfly.]

Mephistopheles now enters with Faust, who seems at once to yield to the influence of the tranquil surroundings; he would be alone—and so Mephistopheles leaves him, after sarcastically calling attention to Siebel's innocent posy. Faust's better nature is in the ascendant, he feels he is in the presence of something pure and holy; this is the shrine that holds his beloved; the trees, the flowers, the humble cottage—oh! what peace, what wealth is hidden here!

[*Salut, demeure chaste et pure*, as a piece of expressive lyric beauty, is unsurpassed by any tenor solo in French opera; it demands the most perfect *bel canto* for its right delivery, and a fine bowing for the lovely violin obbligato.]

Mephistopheles returns with a casket of jewels, which he places at Marguerite's door, side by side with Siebel's freshly gathered flowers. Sounds are heard from the cottage, and the two intruders retire.

Marguerite enters; her thoughts are all of yesterday's meeting at the fair; who could he have been? Ah, if she only knew his name! With a sigh she seats herself at the spinning-wheel.

Gounod has avoided any 'spinning-wheel' music here; the interest lies in the song that Marguerite sings of the King of Thule, whose love was " faithful to the grave," a melody of rare beauty, with a sound as old as the hills. She is not thinking of the song, or its meaning—she sings mechanically, breaking off now and then to refer to the one subject which absorbs her: " His air was so courteous, his words were so kind. 'Tis only noble lords who speak like that."

She leaves her wheel; she takes up Siebel's humble bouquet—and drops it, for she has seen the glittering casket, and the spell of the ' Calf of Gold ' begins its subtle work. Trembling and eager she takes out the incredible treasure of diamonds and pearls, she decks herself a necklace, rings, and bracelets—mirror in hand, she laughs to see herself so lovely—she is no longer Marguerite, but " a king's daughter, to whom all must do reverence."

Such is the theme of the famous Jewel Song, *Ah, je ris*; is just a brilliant vocal waltz, a form which has been much abused, but which in this place seems very proper for the outpouring of a young girl's innocent vanity, and the natural pleasure she finds in her own beauty for the sake of the beloved.

The quartet that follows is a masterly blending of liveliness and tender romance. A vein of comedy is skilfully introduced in the absurd coquetries of old Martha with the Prince of Darkness, who seems to her the Perfect Gentleman. Mephistopheles brings the news of her husband's death, whereupon she loses no time in trying to capture him for her ' second.' Her ridiculous advances and the Devil's sarcastic encouragement are vividly reflected in the music, and make a capital foil for the love-passages between Faust and Marguerite. Arm-in-arm the two couples wander through the garden, twice the four voices are blended with wonderful effect in short lyric passages of restful beauty. Faust's passion grows with the rising moon, and Marguerite in her guileless innocence cannot help responding.

Mephistopheles, having shaken off his partner, has the stage to himself; in a brief but powerful number in which the orchestra is the predominant musical agent, he lays his evil spell upon the garden, and calls upon the demons of earth and air to put forth all their powers for the seduction of innocence—of the innocent pair, we may almost say, since Faust is for the present under the influence of Marguerite, his better angel.

The great love-duet begins—the loftiest expression in the older operatic form of sublimated sensuous passion : the heights of lyrical beauty are reached in the two movements, *Laisse-moi contempler ton visage* and *O nui d'amour !*

The two are alone in the moonlit garden ; it is late and Marguerite wishes to retire to rest, but Faust detains her, and she, like him, " could say good-night until to-morrow." But her lover's rising passion frighten the innocent girl, and she breaks away from his too ardent embrace : " To-morrow ! " she pleads, " ti to-morrow!"—and Faust is once more subdued by her virginal purity; he lets her go, with one last avowal of their love, and the cottage door closes upon her. But Mephistopheles will not let his prey escape him; he hurries to his side, to jeer at such a futile wooing. Faust still struggles to free himself, but the Tempter holds him fast, and points to Marguerite's window, which slowly opens. The girl leans out into the cool of the night—in the first ecstasy of love, she feels herself a part of all the loveliness around her; all things seem to whisper her own delicious secret: "He loves me!" And to-morrow—"Oh, happy dawn, hasten thy coming, and bring him back to me!" Her wish is hardly uttered before Faust has her in his arms, and Mephistopheles ends the scene with a peal of fiendish laughter.

Act IV. The two big episodes in this Act are the Death of Valentine and the Church Scene; this is the order in which Gounod designed them, though the former more spectacular Scene, with its Soldiers' Chorus, is often saved for the end. In any case the Act should open with a short scene between Marguerite and Siebel at the public fountain; the poor girl's betrayal and desertion are by this time known to all, and her former companions, as they pass by on the other side, jeer at her with mocking songs of "The lord who loved and rode away." Forsaken by all, she can still rely on the boyish devotion of Siebel, which he now expresses in the familiar ballad, *Si le bonheur* (written specially for the English production of 1864).

But Marguerite will hear no word against Faust; she still loves him, and expects his return; she will go to church now, to pray for him—and for their child. Shouts and cheering and the measured tramp of feet announce the return of the soldiers. [Here comes the famous

Soldiers' Chorus, as noisy and as effective a piece of stage-music as may be found in opera.]

Valentine enters, all impatience to see his sister once more ; to his questions as to her welfare Siebel returns such dubious and evasive answers that the soldier's suspicions are at once aroused, nor are they quieted by the arrival of Faust and his diabolical companion. Valentine conceals himself. Faust is conscience-stricken and depressed, but the Tempter is in his gayest mood ; under the garden-wall of Marguerite's cottage he sings a mocking serenade, *Vous qui faites l'endormie*, which bears unmistakable reference to her misfortune. Valentine at once guesses the truth, and, furious with indignation, challenges one of the two to mortal combat. [Here follows the famous trio, in the course of which Valentine throws away his sister's sacred talisman, and thus delivers himself wholly into Satan's power.] Faust and Valentine fight, the latter is mortally wounded, and Mephistopheles hurries his companion away.

The neighbours, led by old Martha, come running to the spot—it is night and they have their lanterns—they raise the wounded man and render what little aid they can, when Marguerite, distracted with grief, rushes to his side, only to be met by repulse and reproaches : it is her sin, her shame, that have brought about his death—a life of infamy is all that now remains to her. In spite of her piteous entreaties he casts her off, and, though all beg him to have mercy, he curses her again and again "In heaven, perchance, thou mayest find pardon, but on earth—be thou accursed ! "—and with these words he dies.

It is impossible to deny the theatrical effectiveness of this Scene and the sincerity of its musical treatment, but it must be admitted that the death agony is too long drawn out; nevertheless, it is one of the greatest of opportunities for a dramatic singer, and there are very few operatic baritones who do not desire to die the death of Valentine.

The Church Scene. This should be a side-chapel in some vast cathedral, remote from the choir and the organ which dominates the music of the Scene. The broken-hearted Marguerite prostrates herself before the altar, in a piteous appeal to the Divine clemency. At once the Tempter is at her side—visible to the audience, he is invisible to her—he will not suffer her to pray! A whirring as of leathern wings is heard from the orchestra —the name of Marguerite is howled by demon voices; blended with the solemn roll of the organ are heard the Archfiend's jeering words. He recalls those days of girlish innocence when the angels hovered round her as she knelt, and bore her prayers to heaven; those days are gone for ever: " 'Tis hell that now awaits thee! Eternal ruin! Eternal pain! "

The cathedral walls are shaken by the full blast of the organ as the choir gives out the tremendous words of the *Dies iræ*, the old Latin hymn for the burial of the dead :

> Day of wrath, oh day of mourning !
> See, the last dread fires are burning,
> All the world to ashes turning.

Her anguish increased tenfold by the religious chant, she pours out her soul in a long and fervent prayer; but it is the Tempter's hour—he stands before her now in visible form, and thunders out the awful words : " Marguerite! thy soul is lost—lost for evermore! " With a wild cry of terror she falls to the ground, and the people coming out of church find her senseless on the chapel floor.

Act V. The Prison Scene. Faust's desertion, Valentine's death, and the constant assaults of the Tempter have turned Marguerite's brain ; in a moment of frenzy she has destroyed her own child, and is now in prison awaiting execution.

The chromatic wailing of the prelude is interrupted by the sound of galloping hoofs ; Mephistopheles has come, with Faust, in the hope of securing Marguerite's soul as well as that of her lover ; should he succeed, the horses that wait in the courtyard below will bear all three straight to the Bottomless Pit. He has put the jailer to sleep, he has the keys of the prison—but the dawn is near and they must be gone ere it is light. Faust awakens Marguerite from her troubled slumber. Ah, how sweet sounds the voice of the beloved ! She gazes in ecstasy on the dear familiar face—once more she is in his arms ! But her mind is wandering—she is back once more in her cottage garden, nay, in love's enchanted garden of myrtles and roses ; Faust, too, is swept away by the flood of old emotions, and they seem to live again those first hours of ecstasy. Marguerite recalls the very words of their first chance meeting, and the orchestra plays the broad melody from the love-duet, *O nuit d'amour*. Her lover has indeed come back to her—for the time he is wholly hers once more.

Alas ! the dawn is here, the fatal hour is close at hand ; wild with fear for his beloved's safety, Faust urges their instant flight, but some instinct seems to fight with her desire to go with him—her guardian angel holds her back "It is too late ! " she cries ; " here must I stay and wait for death ! Farewell, beloved ! "

Now Mephistopheles will permit no more delay "Hasten ! Hasten ! " he commands, " you and I at least must be gone. Come, and leave her to her fate !

Marguerite at last awakens to realities—she sees the Archfiend stand before her, dreadful and menacing—in terror she turns for aid, not to her lover, but to Heaven. *Anges purs ! Anges radieux !*—three times, with ever-soaring voice and ever-increasing exaltation, she calls on the heavenly powers to protect her and guide her home. Her prayer is answered ; as Mephistopheles hurries his victim, Faust, away upon his last awful journey, a celestial chorus is heard, and angels come to earth to bear the pardoned soul of Marguerite to Heaven.

ROMÉO ET JULIETTE

Music by GOUNOD. Words by BARBIER and CARRÉ, from
SHAKESPEARE.
Paris, 1867 ; London, 1867 ; New York, 1867.

THERE is, or was, a legend to the effect that Gounod, the composer of *Roméo et Juliette*, *La Reine de Saba*, *Cinq-Mars*, etc., did not write *Faust*, the opera that made his reputation ; the man who was capable of that masterpiece would never have followed it up by works so vastly inferior ; *Faust* was the work of some obscure genius whom Gounod bribed to remain in the background, while he himself took the credit. This absurd story is obviously a malicious invention, yet it suggests a not unjust estimate of the composer's work as a whole. No other Gounod opera can stand worthily beside *Faust* ; written nearly three-quarters of a century ago, it still remains one of the most popular operas all the world over, and, hackneyed as it is, its freshness comes as a perpetual surprise. Outside of Paris, where it is still a favourite, *Roméo* languishes rather sadly, if indeed it ever had much independent vitality. It is a deliberate attempt to repeat the success of *Faust* on the lines of the old model, and the inevitable comparison is too damaging to the later work. Moreover, the libretto can hardly be said to favour such treatment ; the deathless lovers lend themselves well to the scheme, but there is no dramatic equivalent for Mephistopheles or Valentine, the Nurse has not old Martha's happy touches of comedy, while, to supply the place of Siebel, a new character, Stephano, had to be added to the *dramatis personæ* of Shakespeare.

In the love-scenes, of course, Gounod could hardly fail ; if the duets for Romeo and Juliet have not the real ecstasy we find in *Faust*, they are still full of that sensuous charm which the composer had almost always at command. But throughout the score the constant recurrence of methods, forms, and devices which we remember as having been used more successfully in the older and greater work is apt to weary us.

This opera must always depend more than others on interpreters of the two leading parts ; there have been many favourite Juliets, but by those who had the good fortune to hear him the late Jean de Reszké will always be remembered as the one and only Romeo.

Act I. A short symphony is followed by an unaccompanied choral Prologue, during which the curtain is raised to show us, in a dim light, the chief characters of the drama, who recite the gist of the plot, much as Shakespeare gives it at the beginning of his play. After another short orchestral passage, based on the theme which precedes the Scene in Juliet's chamber, the opera begins with the festivities in the house of Capulet. Juliet soon appears on her father's arm, and in a brilliant waltz-measure gives us a foretaste of the more elaborate show-piece with which she is always associated. After some dancing, and a good deal of singing for old Capulet, who for musical reasons is given an undue dramatic prominence throughout the opera, the stage is emptied for the arrival of Romeo and his friends. For Mercutio's sake a musical version of the Queen Mab speech is dragged in by the heels ; at the start it sounds suspiciously like a pale parody of Mephistopheles' "Calf of Gold" but develops into an agreeable patter-song, and serves at least to lend variety. Juliet's popular waltz-song, *Dans ce rêve qui m'enivre*, is but a disappointing reminder of

Marguerite's Jewel Song, and suffers badly by the comparison. But the first meeting of the lovers has inspired Gounod with a really charming duet ; this ' madrigal,' as he fitly calls it—*Ange adorable*—is not too unworthy of the honied conceits of Shakespeare's famous lines : " If I profane with my unworthy hand," etc.

Another line in the play, " My grave is like to prove my marriage bed," has been turned to good account ; it is made the occasion for a very effective *adagio* passage in the orchestra, during which Juliet, who has just learnt that her lover belongs to the hated house of Montague, gives way to a presentiment of coming misfortune. After this welcome point of repose the Act ends with more vocalism for old Capulet and the resumption of the dance.

Act II. The Balcony Scene. Conscious of the difficulty in sustaining the requisite lyric ecstasy for even a short Act's duration, Gounod has been at some pains to ensure variety. Not much of Shakespeare's text is utilized, but the mocking chorus of Mercutio and his friends outside enables Romeo, who is safe within the garden, to give point to the line, " He jests at scars who never felt a wound." The famous passage " But soft ! what light through yonder window breaks ? " has produced nothing better than a rather commonplace cavatina, *Ah, lève-toi, soleil !*

After the first colloquy, carried on in a melodious recitative, contrast is obtained by the intrusion of Capulet's servants, led by Gregory ; they have found the ladder by which Romeo entered the garden, and suspect a Montague to be somewhere in hiding. The Nurse (Gertrude) reassures them, and they depart after a little good-night chorus.

The long love duet is then resumed and runs a rather

undistinguished course; its climax is reached at the words :

> Parting is such sweet sorrow
> That I could say good-night until to-morrow !

a piece of cloying melody, well calculated to melt the hearts of the average audience. To the singers, of course, the whole Act is a blissful holiday; but the musician with memories of the Garden Scene in *Faust* must always feel a little sad.

Act III. There are two Scenes, of which the first, in Friar Laurence's cell, is a sorry bid for popular applause. How effectively Gounod could combine the organ with his orchestra we know from the Church Scene in *Faust*; some faint echo of that great and genuine success has been attempted, at the cost of adding some business for which Shakespeare is not responsible. In the play, when the lovers seek the friar's counsel, that worthy man takes them with him to find the priest who shall make them man and wife; in the opera he plays the priest himself, and goes through the form of a mock-marriage in his own cell. Juliet has brought the Nurse with her, so all is ready for the grand quartet, and with the aid of the organ we are treated to an absurd piece of sentimental religiosity which it is hard to bear with patience.

Scene II, a street in Verona, is given over to duels and general brawling. Here, too, the librettists have had recourse to their own invention; in order to avoid mono-tony, and also to secure a soprano for the *ensembles*, they introduce a new character in Stephano, Romeo's page. His graceful canzonet, *Que fais-tu, blanche tourterelle*, is meant as a provocation to Gregory, the Capulets' servant, who is quite ready to teach the stripling a lesson, when the serious combatants arrive on the scene, and vents follow exactly in the order of the play. The fiery

Tybalt challenges Romeo, who at first refuses, for Juliet's sake, to fight him ; Mercutio takes up the challenge and is slain ; Romeo then kills Tybalt ; there are two short *ensembles*, in which the quarrel becomes general ; lastly, the Duke of Verona appears and sentences Romeo to banishment. There is really nothing in the Scene that calls for musical comment.

Act IV. Gounod's masterpiece is known in Germany not as *Faust*, but as *Margarete*, owing to the prevalent feeling that the opera is merely a perversion of part of Goethe's great philosophic drama. An Englishman may be pardoned for raising a similar objection to the operatic treatment of the exquisite Scene in Juliet's chamber.

> Wilt thou be gone ?   It is not yet near day.
> It was the nightingale, and not the lark,
> That pierced the fearful hollow of thine ear.

For us that is the inevitable opening. In Gounod's score, before these lines are reached, we have a long duet in sickly thirds, of an intolerable sentimentality, set to such words as, *Nuit d'hyménée, O douce nuit d'amour !* and though the sweet dispute about the lark and nightingale does indeed exalt the music to some show of passion, it soon relapses into the commonplace.

After the parting, Juliet's father enters, with Friar Laurence, to bid his daughter throw off her mourning for Tybalt and prepare without delay for her wedding with the County Paris. As soon as he is gone, she turns for help to the Friar, who gives her the potion that will save her from that hateful union, and in the long solo *Buvez donc ce breuvage*—most grateful music for a *basso cantante*—explains to her its nature and the manner of its action.

Scene II. The wedding festivities. A processional march leads to an elaborate choral Epithalamium, chiefly unaccompanied. To this succeeds the ballet, with a chorus that reminds us pleasantly enough of the *Kermesse* in *Faust*. Room is then made for a grave solo in which old Capulet endeavours to cheer his drooping daughter. The orchestra prepares us for what is coming by repeating the ominous throbbing phrases of the *adagio* in the first *finale*. Juliet secretly drinks the potion and falls in a deathlike swoon.

Act V. The tomb of the Capulets. This last scene had, of course, to be altered in accordance with operatic requirements ; there must be a final duet for the lovers, and, consequently, Romeo is not allowed to die before Juliet has recovered from her trance.

After the orchestra has played a simple chorale by way of intermezzo, there is a short explanatory scene for Friar Laurence, and then another instrumental piece entitled, with but slight justification, ' Juliet's Sleep.' Perhaps the best of the music is the broad *andante* to which Romeo sings the equivalent of Shakespeare's words :

> Death, that hath sucked the honey of thy breath,
> Hath had no power yet upon thy beauty ;
> Thou art not conquered !

This motive has been already used on two occasions, at the end of the Prologue and again in the Scene in Juliet's chamber ; it seems intended to indicate that Romeo and Juliet were united in those true nuptials over which Death has no power.

The duet for the lovers is an exasperating imitation of the last Scene in *Faust*, only here it is the tenor, not the soprano, who wanders in his wits. Romeo, forgetting that he has taken the fatal poison, urges Juliet to fly with him, and, as he grows weaker, repeats, in the very manner of Marguerite, some snatches of the Scene of the bridal chamber. Juliet stabs herself, and the two breathe their last prayer in unison.

Gounod's is not the only setting of Shakespeare's tragedy ; Zingarelli wrote a *Romeo* as far back as 1796, and an opera by Bellini on the same theme, entitled *I Capuleti ed i Montecchi*, composed in 1830, had a long career of success. There is a touch of irony in the fact that Wagner's niece, Johanna, who had created the character of Elizabeth in her uncle's *Tannhäuser* in 1845, chose for her London début in 1856 the part of Romeo in Bellini's opera.

But *Romeo and Juliet* as a libretto is no longer possible ; with *Tristan* to set the standard, no composer will care again to handle a subject which must depend for its interest on a prolonged love-duet.

CARMEN

Music by BIZET.   *Words by* MEILHAC *and* HALÉVY
from MÉRIMÉE.
Paris, 1875 ; *London,* 1878 ; *New York,* 1879.

THE two most popular French operas are, beyond question, *Faust* and *Carmen,* but their
popularity is the only thing they have in
common ; in most essentials they present a striking
contrast. The plot of Gounod's opera, though but a
faint and fragmentary echo of Goethe's mighty creation,
has a certain ethical and philosophical basis ; the atmosphere both of words and music is of the romantic-senti-
mental order, yet no one will deny that a first hearing of
Gounod's *Faust* inclines the unspoilt mind to thoughtful-
ness. It is idle to look too closely into the ethics or
psychology of *Carmen* ; the best way is to give oneself
up to the fascination of the realistic drama so boldly
presented and clothed with music of such unfailing beauty
and sincerity. *Carmen* is a rush of colour and action,
of sensuous rhythm and delicious melody, but it is something greater than this—the music attains to heights of
tragic expression which few composers have ever surpassed.

Faust saw the light in 1859, *Carmen* in 1875 ; each
opera is undoubtedly its composer's masterpiece, yet how
different were their immediate rewards ! Gounod was
41 when he wrote *Faust* ; he lived to see it take its place
as the most popular opera in the repertory, and died in
1893, full of years and honour. *Carmen* was produced
when Bizet was 37 ; he died three months after, broken-

hearted at its failure. But if Paris rejected it, other capitals were quick to recognize a work of so rare a quality; it reached London in 1878, New York a year later; but not till 1883 was tardy justice done to it in the city that had shown herself so unworthy of its first production.

It is difficult for us to conceive how *Carmen* could have failed with any audience—only political rancour and the prejudices of musical pedantry can account for it. Its score is full of arresting melodies, its libretto must rank with the very best. MM. Meilhac and Halévy took the well-known tale by Prosper Mérimée, and, with many a deft alteration and addition, managed to build a drama that well preserves the spirit of the original. Nevertheless, the story of *Carmen* hardly attains to the importance of a plot; it is rather " a streak of life," actual, crude, and highly coloured; we recognize it as the begetter of *Cavalleria Rusticana*, *Pagliacci*, and many another degenerate offspring. The gipsy-heroine is hardly more than a splendid animal, irresistible in her sensuous beauty, superb in her physical courage, knowing no law higher than her own desires: Carmen's amours, we are told, are rarely of more than six months' duration. At the beginning of the play we find her making a fresh conquest, of a young soldier, Don José, who forsakes his sweetheart, Micaela, and sullies his military honour, at her call. He is even imprisoned, on her account; immediately after his release Carmen's fancy for him burns itself out; she flings herself into the arms of Escamillo, a handsome bull-fighter, and so drives her former lover mad with jealousy. The last scene is at the entrance of the bull-ring in which Escamillo is winning fresh victories; as Carmen is about to pass in to share his triumph Don José intercepts her and stabs her to death. The crowd pour out of the arena, and the last tableau shows us the lifeless body of Carmen between her two lovers, one of whom is doomed shortly to die, the victim of a heartless woman's caprice.

Act I. We are in Spain before the curtain rises. The overture starts off with a clash and blare of rhythmical jingle that sets us at once in the midst of the arena where a crowd is assembled for the bull-fight, the national pageant of the Spanish people. We are made a part of the coloured scene, the shouts of the fighters, the hoof-beats of the animals, the ever-growing excitement; then, without preparation, we seem to pass into a lurid dark-ness as the brass gives out a sinister theme that is partly the voice of judgment, partly a wail of despair, that speaks unmistakably of some dreadful doom to come. The overture ends in a discordant crash, and the curtain rises at once on a square in Seville, all brightness and animation (*Sur la place*).

> See, the square is like a fair,
> And high and low come and go!
> Droll is the sight, a motley show!

There is a lofty bridge, reached by a flight of steps, up and down and over which the people go; there is also a cigarette factory, and, to the front of the stage, a guard-house, with Captain Morales and his men on duty.

The crowd having cleared away, a young girl comes timidly down the steps and stands in hesitation, a country girl, it is plain, not used to cities and their ways. Still, she can speak to the Captain; she is looking for a corporal, José by name—does the Captain know him? He does —José will come on duty shortly, when the guard is changed. Micaela hurries away, preferring to put herself beyond the reach of the soldier's too gallant attentions.

The sound of fifes and drums is heard, and a little band of urchins marches solemnly across the stage, in droll imitation of the relieving guard that now arrives. José is informed of his pretty visitor : it must be Micaela, he says, his old playmate and sweetheart. At this moment a noisy bell is heard, and from the gates of the cigarette factory issues a stream of bold-eyed beauties, enough to unsettle a whole company of brigadiers. Lining up in the centre of the stage they lose no time in showing off their charms, while they sing a chorus of truly delicious quality, in which the melody seems to soar and mingle with the wreaths of smoke from the cigarettes the girls are holding.

A vivid flash from the orchestra, and Carmen appears on the bridge, hurries down the steps, and challenges the world to produce her equal in the way of seductive womanhood. The type was new to the stage of 1875 as *La Traviata* had been in 1853, but whereas Violetta, the soulful courtesan, almost set a fashion in operatic heroines, the full-blooded wanton of Mérimée and Bizet has found no imitators. Carmen stands for wild, untrammelled freedom : she must be free, above all in the matter of love, to bestow her favours where, when, and for just as long as she pleases.

The amorous soldiers are naturally all desirous of her flaming beauty : " Tell us, Carmen," they cry, " when are you going to choose a new lover ? " She surveys them coldly, with a slight contempt : " As I don't know myself, how can I tell you ? To-morrow, maybe— perhaps not at all ! But one thing is sure—not to-day ! "

Then follows the most famous of all operatic songs begotten in the last fifty years, known as the *Habañera*, the name of the slow, swinging dance to which Carmen moves about the stage, *L'amour est un oiseau rebelle* :

> Love must ever be wild and free,
> A mountain-bird that none can snare.

She sings of the waywardness of love, how none can tell the season of his coming nor the reason for his going; love cannot be lured, cannot be bound; 'tis not the man who tells his love that is always the chosen one—the maid will sometimes give the preference to one who never speaks a word. The refrain—" You love me not—but I love you! And when *I* love—why, then, beware! "— is evidently directed at José, who sits stolidly astride a chair, busy with some trifling task, and pretending to take no notice. At the end of her song Carmen takes a crimson flower from her dress, flings it with sure aim in the soldier's face, and runs off the stage, followed by her companions, amid peals of laughter.

That flower has given José his death-wound, though he knows it not; he stops to gather it and hide it near his heart just as Micaela returns, all modesty and maidenly affection. She brings him a letter from his mother, and the music takes on a great tenderness that speaks of happier days, and of the simple village pleasures they had known together in childhood.

Micaela's solo, and the duet that follows, *Ma mère, je la vois*, are delicious passages of a quiet lyrical quality in happiest contrast to what has gone before. Micaela cannot stay long, but it is clear that José's love for her has been revived by her visit. When she is gone he takes the crimson flower from his tunic and is about to throw it away when shrill cries are heard from the factory, and the girls come tumbling out in wild confusion. Carmen, it appears, has had a quarrel with another girl and has drawn her knife upon her; the chorus is divided into two parties, one laying the blame on the gipsy, the other defending her, with such vehemence that it ends in a free fight, in which the soldiers have to interfere. Meanwhile the Captain, who is accustomed to Carmen's dangerous outbursts, sends José with a couple of men to arrest her. The gipsy is dragged out, a prisoner, but unsubdued; to all questions put to her she answers merely with a jaunty "Tra-la-la!" sung as it were for her own amusement. Her hands are now bound behind her back, and she is given over into Don José's custody, while the others retire. Now is Carmen's opportunity; she has already taken the measure of the young corporal, and at once sets to work to enslave him. The charm works quickly; there is no need of a *pas de fascination*—the mere sound of her voice, a glance from under those dark lashes, is sufficient. She moves to the other side of the stage singing softly to herself, though the words are a spell to steal José's heart and senses away. *Sur les remparts de Séville*, sings Carmen, "I have a friend called Lillas Pastia; he keeps a tavern where the wine is good, and where one can sing and dance most gaily. It is there I am going—and I know who's going with me! None of your haughty glittering officers—no! he is just a poor corporal—but he loves me, and that is enough!" José is an easy conquest for so accomplished a charmer; at the end of the second verse she sidles up to him and makes a gesture with her tied hands. José, no longer master of himself, cuts the cords, and Carmen, free once more, dances wildly about the stage to the tune of the *Seguidilla* she has just been singing. But this is no time for dancing; José arranges the cords around her wrists so that she may still seem to be a prisoner; and only just in time, for now the Captain and his men return with a written warrant for her imprisonment, and a crowd has gathered to see the fun. Carmen is being led off between two guards when she makes an unexpected dash for liberty, up the steps and across the bridge, where she turns to fling the rope that had bound her into the midst of the astonished people, who have certainly had better entertainment than they had bargained for.

The construction of this Act compels our admiration. It is a vivid panorama of fresh and unexpected incidents, where nothing is forced, but all is knit together in a most natural sequence. Against the picturesque background the crimson-lipped gipsy stands out in bold relief, the others being merely accessory; although Micaela, the timid country girl, assumes some importance as an excellent foil to the flamboyant figure of Carmen. Micaela is an invention of the librettists; although apt to be dramatically tedious, the character is useful not only by way of contrast, but also as serving to develop the rather colourless psychology of José. Musically she is of the highest importance; on the two short scenes in which she appears Bizet has lavished his most exquisite melodies, so graceful, so appealing, that great singers have not disdained to appear in what is only a subordinate part. As to the rest, there is not a dull or negligible page in all the score, while the *Habañera* and the *Seguidilla* have definitely helped to raise the level of popular taste in operatic melody.

Act II. At the not too reputable tavern " close by the ramparts of Seville " we find Carmen in all her glory, among the gipsies, soldiers, smugglers, for whom the obliging host, Lillas Pastia, provides good accommodation. There has been feasting and drinking, and some of the gipsies have already begun to amuse the company with song and dance. Carmen cannot resist the familiar lure; leaping to her feet she rattles her tambourine and works up the frenzy as only she can do; this number, *Les tringles des sistres tintaient*, reaches almost the limit of rhythmical excitement.

She has good reason for her high spirits; José will

soon join her here; for eight weeks he has been in prison for conniving at her escape, and has only that day been released. Carmen's vanity is gratified at the thought of her conquest, and she thinks tenderly of the lover who has suffered for her sake.

But now the shouts of those outside announce the coming of one whom we may consider the real hero of the play: "Long live Escamillo!" is the cry, "Long live the Toreador!" A magnificent personage swaggers on to the stage, obviously conscious of his right to the applause that greets his appearance; one of the best bull-fighters in Spain, the idol of the people, there is no tavern that would not feel honoured by a visit from Escamillo.

It would be difficult to imagine a more vivid musical impression of such a figure than that which Bizet has given us in the famous Toreador's Song, *Votre toast*, with its picturesque description of the crowded arena, the exciting contest, and the daring spirit of the fighters. Of one thing only a Toreador is, and must be, afraid— the fire that flashes from a woman's eyes. Escamillo is at no pains to hide his admiration for Carmen, nor can she help being attracted toward him for the moment; indeed, they are a handsome pair of animals, and would be well mated, one thinks. The bull-fighter soon takes his departure—but that short encounter is enough; their eyes have mingled, and destiny has bound them fast together.

José still tarries. Carmen, however, is not alone, and the time is filled by some lively argument between her, Mercedes and Frasquita, her two friends, and the two smugglers Remondado and El Dancairo. The men are eager to be off on the adventure of the night, and insist that the girls shall accompany them—women's help is invaluable on such occasions! The quintet that follows is a little masterpiece of sparkling humour, *En matière de tromperie* :

> When there is cheating to be done,
> One thing is clear, clear as the sun,
> Women can always give good aid,
> Women are cheats, born to the trade !

The girls must come along, say the smugglers, in order to throw dust into the eyes of the excisemen ; her two companions are all for the adventure, but Carmen refuses to budge. She is quite frank with her reason—she is in love, head over heels in love, and she is expecting her lover shortly.

So the others go off with mocking laughter, just as a man's voice is heard singing a snatch of a song outside : " Halt there ! Who goes there ? " " 'Tis a Spanish Brigadier ! " It is José, and for the time being Carmen wants nothing more—he is sufficient for her passionate nature ; she lavishes all her love upon him, she will dance for him as no one has ever seen her dance before— dance for him alone !

José sits entranced as Carmen moves slowly round to a measure that is full of seductive grace, to the accompaniment of castanets and the sound of her own voice. She has become thoroughly absorbed into the spirit of the dance, as her lover is lost in watching her, when the call of a distant bugle breaks the spell—it is the signal for José to return to barracks. All the soldier in him responds to that sound—he rises to go. Carmen at first can hardly believe he is in earnest, she throws herself into the dance with greater vigour than before ; but the martial music grows more and more insistent, and at last José calls upon her to stop—for he must leave her.

The dancing gipsy is instantly transformed to a figure of sullen anger—she turns on José with violent reproaches :

" So this is my reward—and all my trouble wasted on a man who loves a bugle better than me ! Go then ! You shall not deceive me twice ! No, no ! you never loved me ! "

Never loved her ! The distracted lover takes from near his heart the crimson flower she flung him at their first encounter—he had treasured it ever since, his consolation, his pledge of hope. Does not that mean love at first sight, and love for ever ? José's Flower Song, *La fleur que tu m'avais jetée*, has become a favourite with the public, but hardly with the race of operatic tenors— in spite of its great lyrical charm, it is not easily made effective on the stage.

Carmen, relenting, now suggests that he shall fly with her " over the hills and far away," to share the roving life of absolute freedom for which she is best fitted. [The music of this passage may well be compared with the soprano air *Là tra foreste vergini* in *Aïda*, Act II, Scene 1, where the situation is very similar.] The handsome gipsy brings all her fascinations into play, and José is almost vanquished, but in the end the soldier in him triumphs, and he prepares to go. Defeated, humiliated, Carmen becomes a flaming fury. Reaching for his helmet, sword, and belt, she flings them noisily at him : nay, he shall not stay another minute, she herself will drive him away !

A knocking is heard at the door, and Morales breaks into the room. Although it has hardly been made clear hitherto, the Captain has long been under the spell of Carmen's opulent beauty ; on this occasion he expected a *tête-à-tête* with her, and is naturally enraged to find a common soldier preferred before him. There is a quarrel, and José is betrayed into drawing his sword on his superior officer. Carmen calls in her friends to part the two men, and Remandado and El Dancairo make Morales their prisoner. As for José, it is plain that his career as a soldier is at an end ; there is nothing now to prevent him from following Carmen and the smugglers, who welcome the new recruit, and so he is borne off, an incongruous figure among that lawless crew, to their haunts in the mountain fastnesses.

Act III. The action here requires careful watching, as so many small incidents occur which, while essential to the understanding of the plot, do not always succeed in making the right impression.

The scene is wildly picturesque ; a rocky hollow in some high mountain pass, the smugglers' secret haunt, accessible only by two narrow defiles carefully guarded. It is hardly dawn as yet, and men and women are still asleep among the packs and bales that strew the ground ; they wake to join in a chorus which is singularly happy in expressing the fresh out-of-door atmosphere of the scene ; to its swinging rhythm many of them move away to their different tasks, and we are aware of Carmen with her two girl friends, Frasquita and Mercedes, and of José, a restless, gloomy figure. He, the seasoned soldier, is badly out of place among this vagrant company ; his moody fits have already gone far to kill the gipsy's passion for him, to say nothing of the fact that the more imposing figure of Escamillo has taken full possession of her heart. She taunts her lover with his dejected air, and hints that it might be better for him to go back to his old way of life. That his mistress can even suggest that they should part fills the infatuated José with a blind jealousy, and he threatens to kill her ; but Carmen is not afraid. She is a born fatalist—when her time comes she must die, and not before ; it is all written in the book of Fate—each must abide the appointed hour.

Yet when Frasquita and Mercedes decide, half in jest,

to tell their fortunes by the cards, Carmen feels impelled to follow their example. The two young girls make merry over the bright fortunes they find predicted for them, but when Carmen begins to lift the veil all is darkness and horror—she draws a spade, the symbol of death. " Yes ! 'tis death ! " she cries. " First come I—afterwards he—both of us doomed to die ! "

This trio of the cards, *Coupons ! mêlons !* is one of the fine dramatic strokes of the opera. The graceful duet for the two young girls sparkles and ripples its vivacious course, to be succeeded by the tragic gloom of Carmen's solo, the latter part of which is overlaid by the return of the lighter melody. The situation is unique in opera, and Bizet may be said to have exhausted its musical possibilities.

All now go off, with the exception of José, who is set to guard the pass on the opposite side to that by which the others have left. On the empty stage Micaela now makes an entry even more timid and furtive than in the first Act. She has come to seek her lover, and she knows well in what company she may expect to find him.

The character of Micaela is too vague and colourless to raise much sympathy—we even find her a little tiresome —but the music assigned to her must always rank among the best things in French opera. The present solo, *Je dis que rien ne m'épouvante,* is one of the loveliest of romantic lyrics, and there have been performances of *Carmen* in which some fresh-voiced *débutante* has made it the outstanding success of the opera. It has no dramatic significance ; the young girl merely expresses her resolve to overcome her natural fears, and her pious trust in Heaven's protection—but it has the lovely effect of a momentary patch of liquid blue in the midst of a stormy sky.

Though there is no one in sight, Micaela is soon frightened into hiding by the sound of a carbine shot ;

it is José, who has fired at a figure he sees descending the rocky path that leads to the encampment. But the man still advances—it is Escamillo. He boldly tells José his business : he has come to try his luck with Carmen—he hears she has grown weary of her latest lover. A fight with knives ensues, which would have ended fatally for Escamillo had not the gang of smugglers returned in time to separate the two men.

The resourceful Toreador manages to make his peace, and invites them all to witness his triumph at the coming bull-fight at Seville. All joyfully accept the offer, and it is plain from Carmen's manner that Escamillo is, for the present at least, the man of her choice.

The Toreador goes carelessly on his way. Micaela is discovered and dragged from her hiding-place ; her love for José gets the better of her fears, and before them all she earnestly entreats him to return with her to their native village, where his old mother is lying at the point of death. From such an appeal José cannot turn away ; he is about to let Micaela lead him off when Escamillo's voice is heard outside singing the gallant refrain of the Toreador's song. Carmen, fascinated, is actually hastening after her latest lover when José stops her—there is murder in his look as he points his ugly knife at her heart. Carmen turns back with a mocking laugh, but in those eyes she has read her fate more plainly than any cards can tell her.

Act IV. A short scene suffices for the tragic *dénouement* ; Carmen herself plays into the hands of Fate, as if desirous of hastening the inevitable end.

We are again in Seville, and ready for the bull-fight. The great square, at the back of which is the entrance to the arena, is filled with the gayest of crowds, joyfully impatient for the coming show. As the ceremonial procession passes up the steps and through the gates the excitement grows and grows, until the climax is reached at the entrance of Escamillo, victorious in love as in the combat. For Carmen is with him; they are all in all to each other now; it is her applause that will nerve him for the most splendid triumph of his career, and it is she who will share in its reward.

It requires skilful stage management to make possible, in the midst of such a crowd, the intimate leave-taking which follows between the lovers, yet it is one of the most valuable dramatic touches in the play. This tender, passionate good-bye is only for a brief moment, as Escamillo thinks; but Carmen knows that it is farewell for ever—the cards can never lie—and with this last good-bye she feels that her good days are done. In this short passage a great actress can win more sympathy for the heroine than in all the rest of the play.

[The little duet *Si tu m'aimes, Carmen*, is one of the 'points' of the opera; the few bars of formal melody are perhaps the only banal thing in the score, but they are undeniably effective, and never fail to grip the house.]

Escamillo passes in to the scene of his glory—Carmen remains. Her smuggler friends surround her, and Frasquita takes her aside to warn her of her danger: she implores her to save herself while there is yet time; she has seen José lurking in the crowd, and there is murder in his face. But Carmen is unmoved: she is a fatalist and does not know fear. She bids them all go in to the show: for herself, she will remain, to face her destiny. The crowd disappears through the gates; Carmen waits till she is alone on the stage, then prepares to follow them. She is already up the steps and at the gates—but Fate is there before her; José bars her path, desperately in love, and half mad with jealousy.

Carmen rises to her greatest height; coldly, boldly, she tells him the truth. Her love for him is dead. She is not afraid of him, he may kill her if he will, but never again will she be his.

José strives to keep down the madman within him; piteously he implores her to fly with him, to follow him (as once she had besought him) to some ideal retreat " over the hills and far away "—there his devotion, his worship, will win back her love; there they will be happy once more together. Shouts of wild excitement are heard from the bull-ring—Escamillo's triumph is at its height. Carmen makes a rush toward the gate, when José again intercepts her, this time with his knife drawn : " Back ! " he cries, " you shall not go to your new lover ! Confess ! 'tis Escamillo you love ! "

" Yes ! " is the fearless answer, " I love him, and would gladly die for him ! *Viva ! Viva Escamillo !* "

But her end is near ; José is a madman now ; there are still a few moments of horror as he pursues Carmen from corner to corner of the stage, waiting his best opportunity to strike. At last she makes another wild attempt to escape through the gates ; she is already up the steps when José stabs her brutally between the shoulders, and Carmen staggers backward, falling lifeless in the middle of the stage, just as the people pour out from the arena, shouting for the victorious Escamillo.

José, a soldier to the end, gives himself up to an officer, then falls grief-stricken beside the body of his victim ; his is the last voice we hear : " Carmen, Carmen, I love you ! Speak to me, Carmen ! "—and the curtain falls to the impressive theme of doom which we heard in the overture and which throughout the opera has served to invest the rather brazen figure of the heroine with the dignifying shadow of tragedy.

SAMSON ET DALILA

Music by SAINT-SAËNS. *Words by* F. LEMAIRE.
Weimar, 1877 ; *New York*, 1895 ; *London*, 1909.

THE custom which once forbade the representation of Biblical subjects on the English stage must account for the fact that Saint-Saëns' best-known opera was over thirty years old before it was seen at Covent Garden, though it had previously been heard in the concert-room. It is still very popular, largely on account of Dalila's famous air *Mon cœur s'ouvre à ta voix* ; in fact it is the musical presentment of the Philistine enchantress that gives distinction to the opera. For the rest, the score is what we might call ' safe '—always musicianly, with plenty of solid choral-writing, picturesque orchestration, and a flow of graceful *cantilena* for the solo voices, thoroughly typical of the French school as influenced by Gounod.

The drama is extremely simple, admitting of little action outside the three chief incidents—the slaying of Abimelech by Samson, his betrayal by Dalila, and the final tragedy in the Temple of Dagon. The background is the racial struggle between Israelites and Philistines, but the central interest lies in the age-old story of the strong man, unconquerable in fight, vanquished at last by a beautiful woman—" terrible as an army with banners."

Act I. Gaza, a stronghold of the Philistine. " At that time the Philistines had dominion over Israel " ; thus much we learn from the Book of Judges ; otherwise the events of this Act are without Scriptural authority.

Before the rise of the curtain an invisible chorus of Israelites is heard bewailing their bondage, and imploring Jehovah's aid to free them from the Philistine yoke. When the scene is disclosed, a dejected crowd is dimly seen—for it is night—still engaged in lamentation and prayer. The choral work here, with its fugal passages, has that flavour of oratorio which is characteristic of this opera.

Samson comes forward to reproach his countrymen for their want of faith, and urges them to renew the struggle against their oppressors. He has hard work to rouse them from their dejection, but after his vigorous solo *Implorons à genoux* the crowd is caught by the fire of his inspiration : " It is the Lord who speaks through him ! Let us follow Samson, and Jehovah be our guide ! "

The ringing shouts of " Jehovah ! " bring on to the scene Abimelech, the Satrap of Gaza, with a guard of Philistine soldiers. He taunts the Israelites with their helpless position. What avails it to call upon their God Jehovah ? Did he deliver them in the day of battle ? Let them rather turn to Dagon, who is above all other gods ! At this blasphemy Samson asserts himself as the inspired leader of Israel ; he sees the heavens opened, and Jehovah's armies gathering to their aid. " The hour is come ! " he cries. " Lift up thy head, O Israel, and break the chains that bind thee ! " The crowd are now ready to follow wherever he may lead. Abimelech, seeing the danger, draws his sword on Samson, who disarms him and kills him with his own weapon ; still brandishing his sword, he scatters the panic-stricken Philistines right and left, and leads the Israelites off to victory.

The High Priest of Dagon, attracted by the uproar, comes from the temple and tries in vain to rally his demoralized people, whose only thought is to flee to a place of safety; he then proceeds to deliver a solemn curse on Samson, the Israelites, and the God they worship, and so departs, with the body of Abimelech borne before him.

There are situations in Italian Opera where the flight of time must be disregarded. As the dead Satrap is carried out, the Israelites return victorious: it has taken little more than the length of a High Priest's curse for Samson to destroy the army of the Philistines. The night is over, a splendid sun has risen—in the orchestra as on the stage—when the basses intone, unaccompanied, a solemn hymn of thanksgiving for victory, *Hymne de joie, hymne de délivrance*, which by its monotonous cadence and compass limited to five notes gives an effective touch of Eastern colour; this is relieved by a bass solo for a Hebrew Elder, and the short but impressive scene ends with the resumption of the chant.

But all sober thoughts are swept away before the flood of beauty which fills the stage as the portals of Dagon's temple unfold, and Dalila advances with her flower-maidens, bringing garlands of roses to crown the victors' brows. We are left in some doubt as to Samson's previous relations with the Philistine woman; she addresses him as "*Mon bien-aimé*," and it is plain that he is already in her toils, but no reason is suggested for his determined rejection of her present advances. She has come, she says, to greet the conqueror—the conqueror of her heart: in phrases suggested by the Song of Songs she offers him the honied wine of her love, and hints at the bliss in store for him at her home in the Valley of Sorek—let him follow her thither!

But Samson resolutely turns his face away and prays Heaven to keep him from the snare, while the Hebrew

Elder is at his side to strengthen his resolve by solemn warnings.

The weakness of the drama at this point is obvious. After the apparent failure of her effort there is really nothing more for Dalila to do ; any direct encounter with Samson at this point would be premature: she merely sings at him, and he continues to avoid her. Saint-Saëns has to fall back upon a ballet, in which the temptress bears a part, and the Act closes with a seemingly artless ballad, *Printemps qui commence*, and the return of Dalila to the temple with many a backward glance at Samson, who plainly shows by the trouble in his face that all his struggles have been in vain.

Act II. Outside Dalila's dwelling in the Vale of Sorek. A sultry night ; the air is heavy with the scent of flowers, and there is a presentiment of coming storm. [Saint-Saëns is as careful as Dickens to enlist the sympathies of Nature for the emotional situation.]

Dalila is seated on a couch beneath a vine-covered trellis. In the previous Act we may have taken her for merely a splendid courtesan, anxious to make a conquest of the hero of the hour ; but her character is developed on quite other lines—she is now seen to be of the race of Jael and Deborah, an instrument of the gods for her country's welfare. The armies of Philistia have fled before the power of Samson ; she, Dalila, ere this night be over, will make him bond-slave to her beauty and deliver him helpless into their hands. In the air *Amour, viens aider ma faiblesse*, she invokes the God of Love to strengthen her, and she has no fear for the issue.

The High Priest of Dagon now arrives, despondent and anxious ; the town of Gaza is in the hands of the rebel Israelites — all resistance has broken down — the nation's only hope is in Dalila. The High Priest is aware that Samson was at one time in thrall to her charms; if her influence has waned, can she not renew it? Let her but discover and destroy the secret sources of his giant strength, and she may demand of her country what reward she pleases.

But Dalila is not moved by the promise of riches; all she desires is to revenge herself on Samson. "For know," she cries, " that, like you, I abhor him ! " Hitherto she has exhausted all her store of flattery and fond caresses to win his secret from him, but in vain ; to-night she will try a surer way to victory—even Samson himself will not be able to hold out against her tears !

Dalila, left alone, looks out into the pitchy darkness, and listens anxiously for footsteps ; but there is no sound except the rising wind which foretells the coming storm, and she goes into the house.

Distant lightning shows up the blackness of the night as Samson enters, his heart in wild commotion. He is drawn hither against his will—he feels that for him the place is accursed ; even now he would retreat, but Dalila comes flying from the house and smothers him with her caresses.

Still Samson holds her off—he must not stay with her, he has only come to say farewell ; the Lord has chosen him to be the deliverer of his people, and he must obey the call.

Dalila knows the strong man's heart only too well: Samson has strength to resist her blandishments, her merely sensuous appeal, but, with the outbreak of her tears, the victory is in her hands.

The lightning is nearer now, more frequent, and more vivid, but the storm has to wait while the temptress draws her captive to the couch beneath the vines and sings the song on which the existence of the opera depends,

Mon cœur s'ouvre à ta voix. The words are nothing, but as an expression of purely voluptuous allurement the music could hardly be surpassed. It is difficult, indeed, to realize that Dalila is merely acting a part—if this be only a feigned emotion, in what form would this woman voice her real passion, as

Vénus, toute entière à sa proie attachée?

But not even her tears can wrest his secret from Samson. He dare not disobey the word of God: is not the storm now breaking a sign of His wrath? With a cry of rage, with words of bitter scorn, she leaves him, and sweeps into the house. Samson can endure no longer: raising his hands to heaven as if entreating pardon for his weakness, he follows after her, while the storm bursts in all its fury.

Toward the end of the descriptive orchestral passage which ensues, some Philistine soldiers are seen stealthily approaching the house; there is a crash of thunder as Dalila appears on the terrace, holding aloft the hero's shorn locks, the symbol of her victory. She calls to the soldiers to enter and finish the ruin she has begun: Samson, against whom no man living could stand; Samson, the slayer of thousands, lies blinded, bound, and helpless at a woman's feet.

Act III. This Act is, musically, the most satisfactory of the three; the interest is worked up by a steady crescendo to the climax—there is nothing superfluous; Saint-Saëns, relying largely on chorus and ballet, is at his best.

Scene I shows us Samson in prison, yoked like a beast of burden to the pole of the mill, around which he is laboriously plodding. Blinded, shorn of his strength, he compels our sympathy throughout. No insult, no humiliation, is spared him as the Act proceeds: he bears them all with the patience of Job; he is a penitent, who desires nothing better than to suffer.

The Israelites, his fellow-captives, are heard, without, reproaching him for betraying his country's cause: his only answer is to pray for their deliverance, and to offer his life as atonement for his transgressions.

So in *Scene* 11, in the Temple of Dagon, whither the helpless giant has been summoned to make sport for the Philistines, Samson is proof against all provocation— nothing can distract him from his fervent prayers.

Some of the music here is a repetition of what has gone before. The elaborate ballet, with its Oriental colour, is preceded by the strains in which the flower-crowned maidens sang of spring on their first appearance; when Dalila offers Samson the wine-cup and mockingly invites him to drink to the memory of their past delights, she plays with the very phrases of the great love-song in the previous Act. But nothing, not even the blasphemous insults of the High Priest, can move Samson to reply: he continues to pray, with growing fervour, that it may please Jehovah to give him back his strength, to be used for His honour and glory.

The coming catastrophe is finely imagined, and gives the composer his greatest opportunity. It is the hour of the morning sacrifice to Dagon, and an occasion of special thanksgiving for Samson's overthrow and the triumph of Philistia. The High Priest and Dalila lead off the hymn with broad, impressive phrases, sung in canon, *Gloire à Dagon vainqueur!* Glory to Dagon, who giveth his servants the victory! Let the name of Dagon be exalted above all other gods! All the people join in prayer and adoration: Samson too must do homage to Dagon and pour a libation in his honour: let him be brought forward that he may be seen of all! By the High Priest's command he is led to take his stand between the two massive pillars of stone that support the central dome.

Meanwhile the attention of all is turned to the ritual of the sacrifice. The Priest pours wine upon the altar fires, which, after dying down, are seen again to leap heavenward, and with a brighter flame—it is a sign that the god himself has descended. The worshippers are moved to tense excitement—Dalila and the High Priest join in a shrill, inarticulate cry—we almost expect the ' knives and lancets ' of the priests of Baal. " Glory to Dagon, who is god above all other gods ! "

But it is a vain thing that the people have imagined. Samson has never ceased from praying, and at last his prayers are answered—he feels his strength return. Unnoticed by any, he clasps either pillar with a mighty arm —they sway, they crash, and all is over—Samson once more has slain his thousands, and himself lies buried with them, beneath the ruins of Dagon's temple.

LES CONTES D'HOFFMANN

Music by OFFENBACH. *Words by* BARBIER.
Paris, 1881 ; *New York*, 1882 ; *London*, 1910.

*T*ALES OF HOFFMANN—for it is in its English form that it is best known in this country—is one of the surprises, the oddities, of operatic history ; it is the only regular ' opera,' in the conventional sense, of a composer whose immense, if ephemeral, reputation was gained in a very different field. Jacques Offenbach (1819–1880) might well be described as the King of *Opéra bouffe.* Throughout the Second Empire he dominated Paris, without a rival in his own peculiar realm. Nearly eighty operettas stand to his credit, all of the lightest possible texture, but exactly calculated to please the taste of that frivolous, cynical period. Some critics have compared them to the sparkling exhilaration of champagne, to others they have seemed merely a carrion corruption. Nor was their fame confined to the Gay City ; *Orphée aux Enfers, La Belle Hélène, La Grande Duchesse,* went the round of the European capitals. Works of this calibre however, are naturally short-lived, and not long after the composer's death Offenbach's name ceased to be one to conjure with. So far as England is concerned, partially successful revival of *The Grand Duchess* towards the end of the last century rang down the curtain When, therefore, in 1910, an opera entitled *Tales of Hoffmann* was staged at Covent Garden, the younger generation was, not unnaturally, puzzled. " Who is this Offenbach ? " many might easily ask, and, with still more reason, " Who was Hoffmann ? " The title it must be confessed, is a clumsy one, and requires explanation.

E. T. W. Hoffmann was a real personage, a shining light of the Romantic Movement in Germany at the beginning of the 19th century ; part musician, part author, he wrote an opera, *Undine*, to which Weber gave enthusiastic praise ; but he is best known for his fantastic romances, which may be compared with Poe's *Tales of Mystery and Imagination*. Both Hoffmann and Poe were in high favour with the literary circles of Paris, and in 1851 MM. Barbier and Carré produced at the Odéon a play called *Les Contes d'Hoffmann*, which seems to have made an indelible impression on Offenbach, then a young man of thirty. When in later life he determined to show the public that he was capable of something far better than the flummery with which he had so long delighted them, he turned to Hoffmann for the subject of a three-act opera, to which he devoted many years of loving care. He left it still unfinished at the time of his death (1880), but E. Girard supplied what was wanting, and *Les Contes d'Hoffmann* was produced at the Opéra Comique in 1881.

It was given in New York, without much success, in 1882, and revived in 1907. Introduced to London in 1910, it has been ever since one of the most popular operas, and has meant the resurrection of a composer whose life's work was almost forgotten in this country.

Offenbach called his work a Fantastic Opera, and the epithet is of the greatest importance toward a right appreciation of the very strange libretto. Between a Prologue and an Epilogue are unfolded three distinct stories, entirely disconnected, except as forming episodes in the life of the same person. The authors hit upon the original idea of taking the actual Hoffmann, the fantastic writer, as the central figure of certain weird adventures, such as he himself delighted to imagine. These adventures, concerned with three different love affairs, he relates to his boon companions as they sit drinking round the tavern table—or is supposed to relate, for the various scenes are really enacted for our benefit on the stage.

Hoffmann himself is the only character who appears in all the scenes, though Nicklaus his friend and fellow-student (a part assigned for the sake of vocal balance to a mezzo-soprano) bears him company up to the end of Act II. It will be noticed, however, that in each Act there is one mysterious figure for whom it is not easy to account, and that there is a strong family resemblance between the three : Coppelius, maker of magical glasses, Dapertutto, dealer in men's shadows, Dr Miracle with his unholy spells—all these do, in fact, represent the same personality, *i.e.*, the Devil himself, or, if you prefer, Hoffmann's Evil Genius, the cause of his disasters. The action of the piece is fantastic in the highest degree, and puts perhaps too great a strain upon our powers of make-belief, but the underlying idea is perfectly clear. *Tales of Hoffmann* is a somewhat cynical exposure of the vanity of love's young dream ; the hero's first love turns out to be merely a mechanical doll, his second a heartless courtesan, while the third is snatched from him by the hand of death—and Hoffmann turns for consolation to his old friend the punch-bowl.

The Prologue introduces us to a beer-cellar in Nuremberg, kept by one Luther, and attached apparently to an opera house : the students present are discussing a performance of *Don Giovanni*, of which they have just heard the first Act ; indeed, the entrance of Hoffmann (with Nicklaus his friend) is heralded by the first bars of Leporello's air in that opera, *Notte e giorno faticar*. The

appropriateness of the quotation lies in the fact that the
real Hoffmann is known to have had an intense enthusiasm
for Mozart ; he actually adopted one of the composer's
names, and was in the habit of signing himself ' Amadeus.'

The stage is filled by a crowd of noisy young Bohemians,
intent upon spending a merry evening. Hoffmann, though
moody and quarrelsome at first, dominates the assembly—
he is ' the master,' ' the poet.' After they have coaxed
a song from him—the ballad of the little dwarf Kleinzack
—no one thinks of returning to the theatre for the rest
of *Don Giovanni* ; they all settle down, pipe and glass,
to enjoy Hoffmann's account of his adventures with the
three goddesses who, from time to time, have reigned in
his heart—Olympia, Giulietta, and Antonia.

Act I. The delicious minuet that serves as *intermezzo*
prepares us for a gay gathering at the house of Spalanzani,
a somewhat shadowy personality, with a mania for experi-
menting in certain curious bypaths of what he is pleased
to call ' science.' " Science, my friends ! " he repeats
grandiloquently, " science is everything ! " At any rate
it has enabled him to invent a wonderful automaton, a
beautiful doll as large as life, that can walk, dance, sing,
and say a good deal more than "Yes !" and "No !"—
so well equipped, in fact, as to pass for a human being
except under the closest inspection. This very evening
he is to present his creation to his friends as, " Olympia,
my daughter ! " He has just placed his ' child ' on a
couch in a curtained recess and left the room when
Hoffmann enters, lifts the curtain, and at once falls in
love with the beautiful sleeper. Now comes on the
scene the mysterious Coppelius (' Mephisto No. 1 ' we
may call him), a purveyor of scientific instruments, and,
especially, of magic spectacles which enable the wearer to
see things in a particularly rosy light. [The capital song,

" I have glasses that sparkle and shine," has unmistakable affinity to the more genial aspects of Gounod's Mephistopheles.]

Hoffmann falls into the snare, and Olympia, seen through those wondrous glasses, at once becomes the loveliest vision in all creation.

Spalanzani now returns. Coppelius has a bone to pick with him : Olympia, he says, belongs as much to himself as to her actual inventor, for did not he, Coppelius, provide the eyes, which constitute the most irresistible of her attractions ? Spalanzani had anticipated this claim ; to meet it he gives Coppelius a cheque —which he knows to be worthless—on Elias the banker. To the strains of the lovely minuet the guests now arrive, prepared to pay homage to the fair *débutante*, though whether they are initiated into the secret is not apparent. Spalanzani leads in Olympia, whose sparkling eyes and elegant figure win instant admiration, while her mechanical bowings and an occasional squeaky " Oh ! " and " Yes ! " are sufficient to satisfy the requirements of society. When to a harp accompaniment she ' obliges ' with a high-pitched and tinkly solo, " Every grove," the wonder knows no bounds. Whatever conclusions the company may arrive at, we cannot fail to notice the careful way in which Spalanzani directs his ' daughter's ' movements, nor to hear an alarming whirring noise at such times as he contrives secretly to wind up the run-down machinery. Hoffmann, however, has no misgivings ; thanks to the magic spectacles, Olympia is living flesh and blood to him, the loveliest creature he has ever seen.

The guests go in to supper, and the amorous youth is left alone with his beautiful doll. His most impassioned pleadings elicit nothing more than a colourless " Yes ! " or " Ah ! " but when at last he ventures to squeeze her hand, some fresh machinery is set in motion ; the fair automaton runs aimlessly up and down the stage and glides through the curtains into another room, to which Hoffmann follows her.

The mystery-man, Coppelius, now returns in a furious rage ; he has discovered that Elias' bank has failed, and Spalanzani's cheque is worthless. Vowing vengeance, he rushes from the room.

The guests return from supper, and the dance begins ; Hoffmann leads out Olympia for the valse. It is soon plain that all is not well with the dancing doll—something has gone wrong with the works ; Olympia gets out of all control, and dances wildly hither and thither, off the stage and on again, dragging her partner along with her, until Spalanzani manages at last to stop her. Hoffmann sinks exhausted on a sofa ; his magic spectacles are broken, and there is no more spirit in him. Olympia has still vitality enough to execute a few more weird gyrations before she dances off the stage for the last time. Almost immediately a tumult springs up in the orchestra ; there is a cry behind the scenes : " The man with the glasses is here ! " and a noise is heard as of machinery being shattered into a thousand pieces. Coppelius has had his revenge. Hoffmann, already half disillusioned, realizes the truth at last—and the company offer him as much sympathy as is usual on these occasions :

> Ha ! ha ! ha ! the farce is over !
> To a doll he played the lover !

Act II. This scene is in most effective contrast to what has gone before. Instead of the mechanical doll and her rather tawdry surroundings we have Giulietta, the splendid courtesan, her voluptuous charms enhanced by all the beauty of a moonlight *fête* in Venice. The shimmer of lamps and torches is reflected in the waters of the Grand Canal, which lap, lap ever against the marble walls of her palace. The music, too, takes on a richer colouring. Austere indeed or wholly insensible must he be who does not yield to the seduction of the *barcarolle*, " Lovely night, O night of love ! " ; on its own level it is one of the perfect things in the music of the theatre, a piece of beauty which no amount of familiarity has yet been able to deflower. Played before the curtain rises, it is first sung by Giulietta and Nicklaus, who land from a gondola. Hoffmann, it seems, is in one of his cynical moods and rather contemptuous of the softer passions ; his spirited drinking-song, " When love is but tender and sweet," is a protest against such follies. Nicklaus, however, who knows his friend—and Giulietta—warns him against remaining in such dangerous company, but Hoffmann is rooted in his false security, and trouble soon begins.

Enter 'Mephisto No. 2,' in the guise of one Dapertutto (' Mr All-over-the-place,' ' Mr Ubiquitous '—what you please) ; he has overheard the young man's boasts, and marks him for an easy victim. Dapertutto, perhaps the most fantastic figure in the play, deals in human souls ; those of women, he knows, can always be snared by the glitter of diamonds—Giulietta's has long been his ; men's souls he catches by means of a certain magic mirror in his possession ; let a man but look therein, he is deprived at once of his reflection, his shadow, and his soul.

Hoffmann is to be the next victim, and it is Giulietta who is to hold up the mirror for his undoing, and add his soul to Dapertutto's collection : that mysterious personage explains his intentions in the solo " As jewels divine," in which he makes effective play with a hand-mirror and a splendid diamond which he has brought as an inducement for his fair accomplice. Giulietta has already been successful in the case of one Schlemihl—the name is taken from one of Chamisso's best-known stories—a sketchy character introduced to strengthen the slender thread of the plot ; it is an easy matter to captivate the amorous Hoffmann, to awaken Schlemihl's jealousy, and then to play off one against the other. Schlemihl, she tells Hoffmann, has a key to her boudoir—her new lover may have it if he can secure it. For such a prize what will he not do ! He challenges the other to a duel in which, thanks to the sword provided by 'Mephisto No. 2' (in imitation of his great original in Gounod's opera), he kills his rival. Snatching the key from the lifeless body, he rushes to Giulietta's room—to find it empty. The air is filled with the sound of many voices, chanting the lovely *barcarolle*, but the ' night of love ' is not for Hoffmann ; leaning from the balcony, he sees a gondola move slowly away—in it is Giulietta, reclining in the arms of some more favoured lover. Our poor hero has lost his shadow, his soul, his mistress—it is fortunate that Nicklaus, his friend, is at hand to drag him away and so save him from being arrested for the murder of his rival.

[Quite apart from the famous *barcarolle*, which dominates it, the music of this Act is well worthy of close attention ; it is surprisingly fresh, vigorous, and original, while the duet (No. 10) and the following septet attain to a distinction beyond the reach of many a composer with a reputation far greater than Offenbach's.]

Act III. In this Act the spirit of romantic fantasy runs wild. The mysterious personage whom we have seen in Act I as Coppelius, and as Dapertutto in Act II, throws off all disguise, and as Dr Miracle is obviously our old friend Mephistopheles himself.

The curious blend of the weird, the pathetic, and the picturesque from which the scene is woven has certainly called forth the highest powers of the composer. If it fails of its right effect, as is too often the case, it is because of the difficulty in finding singers at once able and willing to bring to the music that serious artistic treatment which it undoubtedly deserves and demands.

The story is of a certain Antonia, daughter of Councillor Crespel, a widower; her mother, it appears, was a prima donna of renown, from whom the girl has inherited voice and ambition, but not the strength to follow in her footsteps. Antonia is consumptive, and it is her father's unhappy duty to dissuade her as much as possible from the exercise of the talent she undoubtedly possesses. Hoffmann, with whom she is in love, joins his influence to that of her father, and she promises to sing no more; but Miracle, the Devil as Doctor, contrives that she shall break her vow. By conjuring up a phantom of her dead mother he induces her to give one more exhibition of her powers; the effort is too much for her, and she sinks lifeless to the ground.

A delicate art is needed to maintain the atmosphere of pleasing if rather morbid fantasy proper to this scene. Antonia is discovered seated at a harpsichord in a music-room "oddly furnished," to quote the stage directions; there are violins on the wall, and a large portrait of Antonia's mother. Her opening romance, " Thou art flown," has a curious quality of faded beauty well in keeping with the sad state of the consumptive girl, whose thoughts are partly of her mother, partly of Hoffmann, her long-absent lover. Her father enters and gently reproves her; she knows that all singing is forbidden because of the danger to her health. Antonia promises obedience and leaves the room dejectedly. Crespel

full of fears for the future, gives orders to his servant
Franz that no visitors are to be admitted that day, and
goes out. [This Franz, stupid and almost stone-deaf,
gives the one touch of humour to this scene; it seems a
pity that the amusing solo, " Night and Day," which
Offenbach has assigned him is always omitted in the
English performance.]

Thanks to Franz's stupidity, Hoffmann finds his way
into the room, and his duet with Antonia, " 'Tis but a
song of love," is one of the outstanding attractions of the
opera. At its close Hoffmann, who is not yet aware of
the girl's unhappy secret, is alarmed to see her in evident
distress after the exertion of singing, but his inquiries
are cut short by the voice of Crespel, and he conceals
himself in the room as the father enters. The stupid
Franz now announces the arrival of Dr Miracle, and the
atmosphere of sentiment is changed to one of weird
mystification.

Crespel, it is plain, is haunted by the fear of this so-
called Dr Miracle—" No doctor ! " he cries; " say, rather,
assassin and gravedigger ! He killed my wife, and
would kill my daughter ! Already I hear the clinking
of his deadly flasks ! " And with the conventional
" Ha ! ha ! ha ! " the Devil-Doctor makes a sudden and
glittering appearance on the stage. As in Act I our
Mephistopheles carried magic spectacles, and in Act II
the fatal mirror, as symbols of his uncanny powers, so
here he brandishes certain glass phials of sparkling fluid
which he clinks together with an air of triumph. In this
scene, indeed, the Satanic nature of this personage is
fully emphasized : he comes and goes at will through
walls and floors, is invisible at times to all but the audience,
and is constantly attended by a green light which throws
his sneering features into horrible prominence.

He has come, he says, to begin the cure of Antonia; will his good friend Crespel take him to her room? Crespel will throw him out of the window if he stirs a step in that direction! "Never mind!" says the amiable Doctor, "I will treat your daughter from a distance!"

Placing two armchairs in the middle of the room he seats himself in one and begins to put forth his spell of waving hands in the direction of Antonia's room: Crespel and Hoffmann (still in hiding) seem fixed in their places and look on with horror as the door slowly opens: no material form is seen, but Miracle rises, takes an invisible Antonia by the hand, and seems to seat her in the chair beside him. He then goes through the pantomime of feeling her pulse, and questions her as to her symptoms: finally he commands her to sing, and, from the wings, Antonia's voice is heard in a chromatic cascade of two octaves. The Doctor now apparently dismisses his patient, and, shaking his head over her sad condition, turns to the father, jingling in his face the glittering phials with which he proposes to effect a cure. Crespel indignantly turns him out of the room and locks the door. But the Devil is not so easily disposed of; in a minute he is back again, entering through the wall this time, and jingling his phials as before in the face of the infuriated Crespel, who once more drives him away and himself accompanies him.

Hoffmann now comes from his hiding-place and Antonia from her apartment. Her lover, at last awake to the danger that threatens her, exacts from her a solemn promise to sing no more; fearing her father's return, he hurries away, and Antonia sinks exhausted into a chair. In a moment the Tempter is at her side; invisible to his victim, we see Mephisto, with glittering eyes, gleaming teeth, and a face of sickly green, as he bends over Antonia

and pours poison into her soul. What! sing no more!
Beauty, youth, such wonderful talent, are all to be
wasted—buried in dull domesticity ? Let her think of
the career that is hers for the taking—to be the greatest
singer of the day ! Think of the joys of such a life as that
—the artistic triumphs, the applause of the crowded
theatre—and then the diamonds ! But Antonia is proof
against such allurements ; she will be true to Hoffmann
and to her promise, and she turns toward her mother's
picture, imploring her help. This is Miracle's great
opportunity. By his magic art the picture comes to life,
and a voice is heard, her mother's voice it seems, urging
her daughter to follow her on the path of glory:
" Sing on, sing on ! " it seems to say. Antonia yields to
the illusion; to Miracle's wild accompaniment on the
violin she gives out her voice in all its power and to the
full extent of its compass ; the strain is more than she
can bear—she falls, dying, on the stage, while Mephisto
vanishes through the floor with a peal of fiendish laughter.

[This number, " Dearest child, 'tis thy mother," is
perhaps the most distinguished achievement in the whole
opera ; Antonia's feverish ecstasy, the insidious persistence
of the Tempter, the effective melody of the ghostly
mother's voice, combine in a trio which, while making
the strongest possible popular appeal, must inspire all
musicians with admiration and respect, mingled with
regret that so singular a talent should have found in this
opera the sole opportunity for its proper exercise.]

To compensate the unlucky hero for his three disastrous
adventures in the field of love, the original libretto has a
short scene (*Intermezzo* and *Romance*) in which the Muse
appears, to console the wild poet with the assurance that
she alone is his true mistress, who will always be faithful
to him. This number, however, is never given to-day.

In the short *finale* Hoffmann is shown once more in
Luther's cellar with his fellow revellers. Olympia,
Giulietta, Antonia, have diverted them all exceedingly,
but it has been thirsty work for narrator and listeners
alike, and ' the master ' calls loudly for a steaming bowl
of punch, which is brought in to the noisiest of welcomes.

> If any pain or care remain,
> Let's drown it in the bowl !

is the prevailing sentiment ; yet Hoffmann has fallen
back into his sad reverie before the curtain falls.

MANON

Music by MASSENET. *Words by* MEILHAC *and* GILLE.
Paris, 1884; *London,* 1885; *New York,* 1885.

THE story from which the libretto is taken was written by Antoine Prévost, a renegade monk, in the first half of the 18th century. Massenet is not the only composer who has been attracted by it. A setting by Auber (1856) is still recalled by virtue of a single number, the " Laughing Song " (*L'éclat de rire*), which prima donnas seem determined to keep alive, while Puccini's *Manon Lescaut* (1893) has been placed by competent judges among his best work. The Abbé Prévost's story has always had a great popularity in France ; indeed, it ranks as a classic, the peculiar merit claimed for it being the success with which it points " the contrast of unworthy conduct and exalted sentiment " ; but the ' book ' of an opera can scarcely be expected to deal in such fine distinctions, and in *Manon* we have merely the story of a very charming wanton,

> Fond of a kiss and fond of a guinea,

who, after throwing over her true love for a richer man, succeeds later in inducing him to forsake the religious life to which he had dedicated himself, and, after many adventures, dies in his faithful arms.

Act I. The curtain rises on the courtyard of an inn at Amiens. It is a really old-fashioned coaching hostelry, with galleries and ample stables, promising good accommodation for man and beast. The court is filled with a noisy throng—swaggering Guardsmen, elaborately dressed beaux, coiffed girls in flowered gowns—all awaiting the arrival of the stage-coach from Arras, an event which never fails to afford infinite entertainment to the townsfolk. Prominent in the crowd is Lescaut, a Guardsman —bluff and careless and not over-subtle—who is expecting his young cousin Manon.

Intending passengers, with porters carrying their luggage, come on the scene just as the coach arrives.

Among the passengers who alight Lescaut notices a young and extremely pretty girl standing apart from the crowd and, hazarding that it is his cousin, introduces himself. She is delighted to find a friend among so many strangers, but his clumsy elegance embarrasses her, fresh from country ways. Her charming aria, *Je suis encore étourdie*, expresses her delight, mingled with shyness, at all the new and lovely things she has beheld that morning for the first time.

The coach takes in new passengers and departs, the townspeople gradually disperse, and Lescaut goes off to look after Manon's modest luggage, leaving her to gaze around in admiration at the gay life of the town, so different from the quiet surroundings to which she has been accustomed. Town manners, too, she soon discovers, are very different from those of the country, for an old *roué*, Guillot, coming out on to the balcony of a pavilion overlooking the courtyard, sees Manon and is instantly captivated by her beauty. He appears incredibly old to Manon, who is more amused than disturbed by his advances; but he is serious enough to suggest an elopement. Lescaut returns in time to hear the end of the whispered conversation, and takes the opportunity to give his cousin some rather pompous advice on the folly of talking to strangers (*Regardez-moi bien dans les yeux*).

Manon is soon left alone again, for Lescaut, excusing himself on the plea of momentary business, suffers himself to be drawn to the nearest tavern by some of his boon companions. She endeavours to follow her cousin's advice, but her romantic nature is spurring her to wild, ambitious dreams. Three gaily dressed ladies—the not over-virtuous friends of old Guillot—appear on the balcony and are greatly admired by the simple girl. Those dresses, those jewels, that brilliant, careless way of life— alas, they are not for Manon ! Her family have destined her for the grey austerities of the convent, to which she is even now on her way. [Manon's little snatch of song, *Hélas, Manon*, is an admirable example of Massenet's graceful way of expressing a sort of boudoir pathos, which charms but hardly touches us.]

However, Destiny now appears in the form of the handsome young Chevalier des Grieux. After a few platitudes about the joy of soon seeing his father again— notice the ' heavy father ' *motif* in the 'cellos !—he suddenly catches sight of Manon, and the fate of both is decided. [The orchestra here gives out a graceful theme in nine-eight time, expressive of nothing in particular, which will haunt us to the end of the opera, and may be labelled ' Des Grieux's love-*motif*.']

Not in any opera does the flower of love-at-first-sight —without the aid of a love-philtre—blossom so suddenly as here. Without a moment for reflection Des Grieux pours out his passion in spoken words, and then asks pardon for his boldness. " What is there to forgive," answers Manon, " when every word you say fills me with delight ? " She is just a simple village maiden, she explains, on her way to the gloom of the cloister. Nay, but that, says Des Grieux, will never happen now ; henceforth she is the mistress of his heart for evermore, and they must never part. Manon enters with enthusiasm into this proposal, and when the carriage ordered by old Guillot drives into the courtyard she sees in it the guiding hand of Providence. "How lucky!" she exclaims. "Let us take it and go to Paris!" And off to Paris they go!

The scene ends with a noisy quarrel between Guillot and the now tipsy Lescaut, each blaming the other for the mischief of the elopement; the others thoroughly enjoy the *fracas*, while from the balcony we hear the malicious tittering of the three gay ladies, Poussette, Javotte, and Rosette.

Act II.   The scene is the apartment in Paris to which Des Grieux has brought his simple country maiden. He is discovered writing a letter, the nature of which is suggested by the 'heavy father' *motif* in the orchestra. Manon peeps over his shoulder and will give him no rest until he consents to her reading it—aloud, of course, for our edification. Yes! it is to his father, extolling the charms of his beloved with all a lover's extravagance, and asking the parental consent to their union. Des Grieux is evidently very deeply in love, Manon apparently the same, though we, as onlookers, may have our doubts on that head. As the Chevalier is going out to despatch his letter, he notices for the first time a handsome bouquet of hothouse flowers, and questions Manon as to the sender. Ah! she cannot even guess; someone threw them in at the window!

The maid who now enters the room lets us into the secret; she comes to announce that two Guardsmen desire to speak with Des Grieux; one is a relation of Madame's (Lescaut, of course), the other, she whispers in her mistress's ear, "is a wealthy lord, who adores you!" Manon's instant exclamation "De Brétigny!" leaves us in no doubt as to the sender of the bouquet.

Lescaut and De Brétigny make a noisy entrance; the former has come, in the interests of the honour of his family, to demand of Des Grieux whether he intends to marry Manon; his behaviour is purposely offensive, and there is every prospect of a lively quarrel, but the reading of part of the Chevalier's recently written letter soon leads to a friendly understanding. Lescaut's motives throughout are not altogether clear, but it is plain that he has come in order to back up De Brétigny in the plot of which we are now to learn.

Lescaut, under pretext of reading the letters in a better light, manages to draw Des Grieux to the window, thus leaving Manon and De Brétigny together. There is obviously a very good understanding between the two already, and the object of his present visit is frankly this—to induce her to forsake her present love for the sake of the far greater luxury she would enjoy under the protection of a great nobleman like himself. As a cogent argument in favour of his proposal, he informs her that the Chevalier's father has arranged to seize and carry off his son that very night.

The effect of this announcement on Manon is difficult to determine. Although she is insistent all through the scene on expressing her devotion to Des Grieux, she makes no attempt to acquaint him with the plot of which she has just heard—though she seems to waver, her mind is apparently made up, she is not proof against the 'guilty splendour' that De Brétigny is able to offer her. When Des Grieux has at last gone out to send off his letter, Manon sings the most pathetic little song imaginable, *Adieu, notre petite table!*—nothing less than a farewell to the little supper-table laid for two, at which she and her lover are about to take their last meal together.

Des Grieux, on returning, has a rather sickly but very

' favourite ' number, in which he paints a picture of
Manon, as he would like to see her, installed in a ' home,
sweet home ' cottage, with the regulation birds and all
the usual accessories.

But Fate will have its way. There is a knocking without
—and Manon, visibly affected and affectionate, lets her
lover go out of the door through which she knows he
will never re-enter. She runs to the window, however,
to see him driven away, and then falls into a chair
" overcome with grief."

[The amount of spoken dialogue introduced into this
Act is thoroughly justified, but no device can make us
accept the dramatic development. It is an attempt
to depict the conflict between the worse and better
instincts in Manon's character; but a psychological problem which requires page after page of good prose for
its proper unfolding can hardly be compressed into one
short Act of an operatic libretto. The incidents we have
just witnessed, so far from winning sympathy for our
heroine, merely convince us that she is *capable de tout*.]

Act III. *Scene* I. Massenet can always be relied on for
a courtly dance-measure in the olden style, and the minuet
which forms the *entr'acte* with the gavotte which follows
are two of his most charming examples.

The scene is a delightful one. We are in the Cours-
de-la-Reine in Paris, on the day of a popular fête. There
are booths, a dancing pavilion, shouting hawkers, and
flocks of people. Enter the gay companions of old
Guillot—Poussette, Javotte, and Rosette. They sing a
little puff of a trio, and are gone in a moment. Lescaut
comes next, followed by a crowd of hawkers. It appears
that he is in love, for he delivers, with ludicrous sentimentality, a song in praise of a charmer. *O Rosalinde* is an
excellent piece of fooling.

De Brétigny now appears. He has succeeded in retaining the affections of Manon, but it is clear from the conversation between him and Guillot that the latter will make an attempt to outbid him; for he who would hold Manon must not deny her any fancy, however costly.

Manon herself now comes on the scene, and the admiring crowd, surging round her, hazards that this must be a duchess at the very least. She has indeed changed from the simple country miss that alighted from the Arras coach; she is now a great lady, sumptuously attired, and fully aware of her powers of fascination. And yet, despite her paint and powder and profusion of jewels, she is a pathetic figure. Indeed, the only real merit of the book is the portrait of this butterfly creature, capable of a great love, yet led through the most polluted places in her insatiable quest after pleasure and jewels, ever more dazzling jewels. There is a hint of this in the famous vocal gavotte which she now sings : *Obéissons quand leur voix appelle. Carpe diem !*—snatch at the passing hour while youth is yours.

Enter the old Count des Grieux, who engages De Brétigny in conversation. Manon, drawing near, overhears that her former lover is about to renounce the world and enter the seminary of Saint-Sulpice. She contrives to manœuvre De Brétigny out of the way and introduces herself to the Count. The old gentleman then commits a fatal mistake. Thinking that he has taken the full measure of her he insinuates that his son is no longer thrall to her charms, and has in fact quite forgotten her.

Forgotten her !—that is clearly impossible, reasons Manon, and impulsive as ever she captures Cousin Lescaut there and then and bids him take her to Saint-Sulpice at once.

The spoken dialogue at the close of this Scene has been accompanied by the graceful minuet which we have already heard, but as the main characters depart the people renew their song and dance to the loud strains of the gavotte.

Scene II.   The seminary of Saint-Sulpice.   There is no doubt as to where this scene is laid, for the music is charged with operatic ecclesiasticism.   Two *dévotes* are speaking rapturously of Des Grieux' eloquence as a preacher, and they reverently withdraw as the young seminarist enters with his father.   The latter is under no illusion as to his son's vocation; he bids him go and marry a girl worthy of his rank and station; but the boy is resolute, and so with a few words of kind irony the father leaves him.

Fuyez, douce image, sings the unhappy lover, striving hard to efface the memory of Manon from his mind. But he is destined to succumb.   No sooner has he left the scene than Manon herself appears, treading warily and much oppressed by the gloom of her surroundings.   From within the building comes the chant of the *Magnificat.*   A flood of religiosity invades Manon, and quite oblivious of the irony of her request she fervently prays to Heaven for the return of her lover.

Then Des Grieux, re-entering, comes face to face with her.   He is struck dumb by this unexpected apparition ; she is tearfully suppliant.   Though adamant at first, he is no proof against her enchantments and flees to her arms in the end, throwing all his clerical ambition to the winds.

It is strange that other librettists omit this Scene, which is the strongest in the whole opera.   Massenet, however, has made full use of the dramatic possibilities of the spectacle of earthly love, in arms, forcing the priestly citadel, and reclaiming the object of its desires.

Act IV. *Scene* 1. After a Prelude of a few bars the curtain rises on a fashionable gaming-house in Paris. Here we find a great many of our old friends—Lescaut, of course, and Poussette, Javotte, and Rosette, who though scarcely deserving of such considerate treatment, are nevertheless blessed with the most charming trios throughout the piece. There are also present gay gentlemen of fashion, old *roués*, professional sharpers, and hangers-on of every description, grouped about the tables.

After a terse chorus of sharpers (which might have come from *Rigoletto*) and some concerted music between Lescaut and the three merry ladies, Manon and the retrieved Des Grieux appear.

The Chevalier is in very low spirits ; and well he might be, for in his blind love for Manon he has allowed himself to be drawn into very unsavoury company. But Manon is the same as ever. The clink of gold is as music in her ears, and she easily persuades her lover to try his luck at the tables, for, as a matter of fact, their own supplies are running low and Manon cannot bear poverty. The young man begins to play with old Guillot for heavy stakes, while Manon, aided by Poussette, Javotte, and Rosette, spurs him to fresh efforts by her song. With all the luck of a beginner Des Grieux manages to win heavily until old Guillot, in a rage, swears that he is cheating. A general hubbub ensues, and the old gentleman leaves the room vowing that he will be avenged. He is back in no time with the night-watch and bids them arrest the young sharper and his female accomplice. Des Grieux is overcome with shame at the charge, and the sudden entrance of his father completes his disgrace. The music now swells to a climax, reinforced by all the voices. Manon and the young man are both taken in charge by the officers, and we learn what their fate is to be. The Count's influence will procure his son's release, but Manon will go . . . "to where many of her sort have gone"—she will be deported to the West Indies.

Scene 11. A short and mournful Introduction ushers in the last Scene. It is a lonely place on the road to Havre, along which the convict-gang will pass on their way to the ship. The whole scene is one of utter dreariness and hopelessness. Huddled by the roadside sits Des Grieux, bemoaning the terrible fate that has overtaken his Manon. Even at this last hour he entertains a wild hope of falling upon the escort with a body of men procured by Lescaut, and rescuing the unhappy girl. But even that hope is shattered; Lescaut, appearing, announces that his men have deserted him.

The soldiers' marching-song is heard in the distance; Des Grieux, driven almost to madness, proposes to attack them single-handed, but is persuaded in the end by Lescaut to hide behind some bushes and await developments.

The marching-song draws nearer and nearer, till the soldiers debouch on the scene, escorting a motley crowd of prisoners, and plainly ashamed of their inglorious charge. From his hiding-place Des Grieux, to his terrible distress, learns that one of the women, Manon in fact, is already half dead.

It is now time for Lescaut to act. Accosting the sergeant, he easily bribes him to allow Manon to be left behind, on the condition that she is brought in to a neighbouring village before nightfall. Convicts and escort are soon on their way again, and their song gradually fades in the distance.

Once again are the two lovers united; she exhausted and remorseful, Des Grieux deliriously happy at holding her once more in his arms. He beseeches her to cease reproaching herself; the past is past and a future full of happiness is before them. But Manon knows that she is dying. With fast-waning strength she recalls the various stages of their love—the coaching inn, Paris, and Saint-Sulpice—the orchestra, meanwhile, playing softly the love-music of their first meeting.

Her whole nature seems to be purified of all its dross and tinsel by the swelling torrent of love which she draws from her lover's embrace. She can even smile at her own foibles : on Des Grieux' bidding her look up at the evening star which has just appeared, she smiles and says : " Yes ! the sky is hung with jewels—and thou knowest how I always loved them ! "

But the end has come. With one last kiss she cries, " I die ! Better so, better so," and sinks back lifeless in the arms of her lover. A single phrase of her air in Act I, *Hélas, Manon,* is heard in the orchestra before the curtain falls on the sad story of Manon Lescaut.

THAÏS[1]

Music by MASSENET. *Words by* L. GALLET, *from* ANATOLE
FRANCE'S *romance.*
Paris, 1894 ; *New York,* 1908 ; *London,* 1911.

W E have here a striking example of the difficulty
inseparable from any attempt to turn a piece
of literature into an opera libretto. Egypt in
the fourth century of our era ; the contrast between the
unbridled luxury of Alexandria and the austere asceticism
of the Cenobites or monks of the desert ; a story of a holy
man who succeeded in converting the most celebrated
courtesan of the age, but nearly lost his own soul in the
effort—such are the picturesque elements from which
Anatole France evolved his famous romance of *Thaïs.*
Massenet was right in seeing in it an excellent subject for
operatic treatment, but the delicate irony of the original
has necessarily evaporated in the course of adaptation,
nor was the composer's talent of the calibre necessary to
recreate in music the spirit of Roman Egypt. Still, he
has written a picturesque opera containing much that is
attractive ; there is plenty of easy-flowing melody, and
his orchestral episodes, though often simple to the point
of *naïveté*, are frequently effective.

Act I. After a short orchestral Introduction, descriptive of the quiet life of the Cenobites, the curtain rises
on the Thebaïd, the desert home of those Christian
ascetics. The old Palemon and twelve of his brother-
monks are seated at their evening meal. After a short
while the conversation turns to Athanaël (the ' Paph-

[1] This analysis is contributed by Mr Peter Latham.

nuce' of the novel), and one gathers that he is absent upon a journey. Almost immediately, however, he appears, walking slowly as though overcome by fatigue. He is greeted by the brethren and offered food, but he pushes it away, saying that his heart is too full of sorrow for him to eat. He has been to Alexandria and found it entirely given over to wickedness under the influence of Thaïs.

" Who is this Thaïs ? " ask the monks.

" A vile priestess of the cult of Venus," replies Athanaël. He had known her, he goes on, in his unregenerate days, when only the grace of God had kept him from sinning with her. But now—if only he could win her soul for Christ !

Palemon gives him some wise advice against meddling with the affairs of the outside world, and the brethren, after their evening prayer, separate for the night.

Athanaël is left alone on the darkened stage, asleep in front of his cell. In his dreams he sees a vision of the theatre at Alexandria, the crowd, and Thaïs herself, representing the wanton goddess whom she serves. Starting up in horror he utters an impassioned prayer : he understands ; it is God's Will that he should return to Alexandria and rescue Thaïs. Raising his voice he summons the monks, tells them of his resolve, and, disregarding the advice of Palemon, starts off again into the desert. The rest fall on their knees in prayer.

In the second Scene we are overlooking Alexandria from the terrace of the house of Nicias the philosopher. After an orchestral Prelude representing the splendour and magnificence of the city, we see Athanaël slowly approaching. The servant is at first disinclined to admit him, but soon, struck by his bearing, goes off to tell his master.

Athanaël, left alone, apostrophizes the city of his birth. "Alexandria," he says, "from thy love I have turned away my heart. For thy riches I hate thee! Ye Angels, purify with the beating of your wings the tainted air that surrounds me."

Nicias appears, accompanied by two beautiful slaves, Crobyle and Myrtale. He had known Athanaël well before the latter became a monk, and now hastens forward to welcome him. Athanaël soon acquaints him with the reason of his visit, and asks him if he knows Thaïs and where she may be found. Yes, Nicias can tell him; she is his mistress, and is to be one of his guests that very evening. He willingly agrees to Athanaël's suggestion that he, too, should be of the party, and to his request to be provided with suitable garments. But let him beware of offending Venus!

There follows an amusing scene as Crobyle and Myrtale deck out the monk in some of their master's finery, laughing the while and paying him mocking compliments. Nicias joins in, urging him to take their jesting in good part, and Athanaël completes the quartet with earnest prayers for strength.

No sooner is the toilette finished than the guests begin to arrive. They enter, Thaïs among them, to the strains of a *bizarre* march, are greeted by Nicias, and pass on to the banqueting-hall. Nicias and Thaïs are left alone, and in a short and delicate scene they agree to enjoy the evening to the full as to-morrow they are to part for ever. Athanaël soon returns and exhorts Thaïs to penitence, but she is in no mood to listen to such talk, and in an air full of grace and lascivious charm she tells him, "There is no truth but in loving—open your arms to love!" Athanaël will accept no rebuff, and tells her he will seek her again in her own house; Thaïs and Nicias, who have now been joined by the other guests, drown his voice in a repetition of the previous air, and with a gesture of horror he flies from the scene.

Act II. The house of Thaïs. She is seen surrounded by a gay company of actors and actresses, but soon dismisses them. Left alone, haunted by a fear that her beauty is on the wane, she turns for reassurance to her mirror, and in a dainty song implores Venus for the gift of everlasting youth. But she cannot stifle the inward voice that cries: " Thaïs, Thaïs, you too will grow old ! " Turning round, she perceives Athanaël, who has entered quietly. Breathing a prayer against temptation he starts on his task of conversion. At first he fails to make any impression and himself almost falls a victim to her charms, for she takes him for a magician and is ready to offer herself to him in return for the secret of that eternal life of which he speaks.

" First," he cries, " leave the living death which you call life, and which destroys you, body and soul ! Arise, arise ! flee to the desert ! "

Terrified at last, she begs him to do her no harm, but he only renews his appeal, and at length she begins to yield. At this moment, however, the voice of Nicias is heard calling for admittance, and all her self-control gives way to an outburst of petulant anger. She will not surrender to the pleading of either man. " Tell him," she says to Athanaël, " that I am not for him—nor will I follow you ! I am Thaïs—Thaïs I will remain—Thaïs, who believes neither in him, nor in you, nor in your God ! " She breaks down in hysterical laughter and tears as the curtain falls.

Athanaël, in no way discouraged, but taking her rejection of her former lover as a good omen, resolves to wait outside on her threshold until the morning light.

The music that follows suggests the gradual change that takes place in Thaïs' mind. The storm that has arisen does not die down immediately, but presently she becomes calmer, and, her thoughts recurring to what Athanaël has said, she resolves to do as he wishes. Her conversion is symbolized by the well-known " Meditation," which has established an independent fame as a concert-piece.

Scene 11. An open place in front of Thaïs' house. From across the way comes sounds of music and revelry ; it is Nicias and his nightly crew. The moon is low in the west, and a lamp by Thaïs' door throws a flickering light on the figure of Athanaël stretched on the pavement. After a few moments Thaïs appears and, recognizing Athanaël, tells him she is willing to obey him. What are his commands ? Not far from Alexandria, he tells her, there is a community of holy women ; thither he will take her. But first she must prove the sincerity of her resolve—she must burn her house and all that it contains. This she will do ; she pleads only for a little statue of Eros ; it is so beautiful ; may it not be spared ? But Athanaël, hearing that it is a gift from Nicias, dashes it angrily to the ground, where it is shattered to fragments. He and Thaïs then enter the house to set it alight.

No sooner have they disappeared than Nicias and his friends come out from the house opposite. They are in high spirits and express their determination to keep up the revels till long after sunrise.

Here, appropriately enough, Massenet has inserted the ballet which at that time was essential to any work that aspired to a performance at the Paris Opéra. On other stages, however, this is often omitted and the play goes straight on.

Athanaël reappears at Thaïs' door and is recognized by ther evellers. At first they misconstrue his appearance at such a place and such a time, but very soon his words and the appearance of Thaïs in a rough dress ready for the journey reveal to them the true state of affairs. At the same moment a wisp of smoke from the house shows that Athanaël has been as good as his word. At once a shout of protest is raised : Thaïs must not be allowed to leave them ; as for Athanaël, to the gallows with him ! The group of revellers, now enlarged to a crowd by the advent of a number of people who have been attracted by the noise, becomes more and more angry, and stones are thrown ; it is Nicias who, by the ingenious device of scattering the contents of his purse upon the ground, succeeds in distracting their attention, and, lit by the flames of the burning house, Thaïs and Athanaël make good their escape.

Act III. takes us to an oasis in the desert. The sight of some women who come in silence to draw water from the well suggests that the religious house mentioned by Athanaël is not far off. The music portrays alternately the cool waters of the oasis and the heat of the sun through which Thaïs and her guide are struggling on their toilsome journey. Presently they appear, Thaïs half-dead with fatigue, and Athanaël pitilessly urging her onward ; only when she stumbles and he has to catch her to prevent her falling does he consent to call a halt. And now a sudden change manifests itself in him. From hurling curses on her past iniquities he turns to blessing her present attitude—their journey's end is near, he says, but for a while she must rest. He departs to fetch some water and gather fruit, and on his return they join in a duet of pious rejoicing as they eat their meal. Immediately after, voices are heard intoning a Paternoster, and the holy women appear, led by their abbess, Albina. Athanaël briefly explains to her the situation, and with a few tender words of farewell entrusts Thaïs to her care. " Farewell," replies Thaïs, " farewell for ever ! " Athanaël starts. " For ever ? " he exclaims. But the procession has already moved away. Once more we hear the music of the " Meditation " as Athanaël, left alone, gives way to words of passionate regret in no wise suitable to his monkish habit.

With *Scene* ii we return to the Thebaïd. A storm is threatening, and the monks, having supped, are already preparing to disperse to their cells, when Athanaël appears. Since his return from his journey he has neither eaten nor drunk, in a vain attempt to drive out by his austerities the pride he feels at his success and the vision of Thaïs by which he is haunted. Flinging himself at the feet of Palemon he confesses his temptation and invokes his aid. But Palemon has no counsel to give him—he must fight his own battle. He sleeps, and in a vision he sees Thaïs as she appeared to him at Nicias' banquet. Suddenly she disappears, and he hears a voice —" Thaïs of Alexandria is about to die ! " Rising in a frenzy of passion and despair he abjures his hopes of Heaven and rushes off into the gathering storm.

Scene iii. The music calms down and it is to the quiet strains of the " Meditation " that the curtain rises for the last time on the garden of Albina's convent. In the middle, under a fig-tree, lies Thaïs, dying. Round her are assembled the nuns praying for her soul. Albina speaks of her virtues : " For three months she has watched, wept, prayed, without ceasing—cruel penances have marred the beauty of her body, but her soul is washed clean of every stain."

Soon a tumult in the orchestra heralds the arrival of Athanaël. Albina greets him, but at the sight of Thaïs he forgets all else and throws himself down by her bed

She opens her eyes, recognizes him, and speaks of their journey together, while the orchestra once again plays the melody of the " Meditation." But it is only earthly love that he now desires, and in strangled accents he begs her to live—for him. Thaïs is deaf to all his appeals. She is beyond earthly things, and in great soaring phrases sings of the angels whom she sees coming to take her soul. The heavens open, and, stretching out her arms toward the celestial vision, she expires. Athanaël gives a wild cry, " She is dead ! " and the curtain falls.

CAVALLERIA RUSTICANA

Music by MASCAGNI. *Words by* TARGIONI-TOZZETTI *and*
MENASCI.

Rome, 1890 ; *London*, 1891 ; *New York*, 1891.

AT the time of its production this short, realistic
opera, with its straightforward story of love and
revenge, its swinging rhythm, and the irresistible
Intermezzo, had an enormous success, and great hopes
were entertained of the composer's future. These have
never been fulfilled. Although he has written many other
operas, Mascagni is known the world over merely as the
composer of *Cavalleria Rusticana*.

The plot of the opera is taken from a Sicilian tale by
Giovanni Verga, out of which the librettists have woven
a sordid but effective drama of love, hate, jealousy, and
revenge. Turiddu, a Sicilian peasant, on returning from
army service, finds that his old love, Lola, has married
a young carter, Alfio. He consoles himself by making
love to Santuzza, and his advances meet with more than
adequate response. As is the way of human nature,
however, Turiddu tires of his easy conquest and hankers
after his old allegiance. Lola, delighted to have an
opportunity of revenging herself upon Santuzza, of
whom she is wildly jealous, encourages him. Santuzza,
when it dawns upon her that Turiddu is tired of her and,
crowning insult, is making love to Lola again, very
naturally enlightens Alfio. Alfio kills Turiddu, and the
curtain falls upon general woe and lamentation.

Very effective is the temporary interruption of the
orchestral Prelude by a tenor solo sung behind the

curtain by Turiddu, *O Lola, bianca come fior di spino* ; this was an absolutely new idea at the time, and one which the composer's rival, Leoncavallo, did not hesitate to imitate two years later in *Pagliacci*.

The curtain rises to disclose a picturesque market square in a Sicilian village bathed in sunlight. On the right a church lends an air of additional peace to a naturally tranquil scene. The natural complement of the church, the village inn, stands on the left-hand side next to a little cottage.

Festivity is in the air—for it is Easter Day—as one may gather from the little parties of men and women, gaily dressed, who hurry across the square to church, and from the joyous ringing of the bells. To complete the picture, a band of peasants passes by, singing the praises of youth and spring—it is well-nigh impossible to believe these happy surroundings are to be the setting of a tragedy. But now Santuzza, entering, makes her way over to the tavern where Lucia, Turiddu's mother, lives. Her suspicions at once begin to darken the scene. At first only vague, they are strengthened by Lucia's innocent report of her son's doings ; she says that he went the night before into a neighbouring hamlet for wine, but Santuzza replies that he was seen that very night in the village. Their conversation is interrupted by the entrance of Alfio, a cheerful young carter, with a crowd of peasants. He sings a rollicking song of the road, *Il cavallo scalpita*, which certainly clears the atmosphere. When the crowd have melted away, Alfio, friendly and talkative, unwittingly discloses the fact that he saw Turiddu near his cottage that morning, thus confirming Santuzza's worst suspicions. But now the organ sounds, so, bidding them go to Mass without him, Alfio departs.

The action is interrupted by the entry of the chorus,

who, ranging themselves across the stage, sing the *Regina Cœli* to a strain which is repeated in the first part of the famous *Intermezzo*. This is followed by the Easter Hymn *Inneggiamo, il Signor non è morto*, led by Santuzza. The hymn finished, the peasants again enter the church, leaving Santuzza and Lucia alone. The former relates the story of Turiddu's faithlessness in the aria *Voi lo sapete, o mamma*, almost breaking down in the agony of her emotion. Lucia, failing in her attempts to comfort, goes into church to pray for her.

The inevitable collision between Santuzza and Turiddu now occurs. In reply to his protests that he did, indeed, go to Francofonte, the village, for wine, Santuzza retorts that he was seen at dawn stealing from Lola's, or rather Alfio's, cottage. She has evidently hit upon the truth; able at last to give expression to long suppressed grievances, Santuzza works herself into a pitch of frenzy. The more Turiddu urges he has ceased to care for her, the more violently she affirms her love for him. Then comes a dramatic moment. Lola is heard without, singing a charming *stornello*—one of those short snatches of song so popular in Sicily—*Fior di giaggiolo*. On her entry she understands the situation at a glance, and takes a malicious pleasure in aggravating it. Lola feels quite sure of her position—she can safely jeer at her discarded rival. What! Santuzza! neighbour Turiddu! still lingering to gossip! Why are they not at Mass? " Lola," says Santuzza, " this is Easter Day—our Lord is risen—He is with us, and sees all things. Only those whose conscience is clear dare go to Mass to-day." " Then," replies Lola, " I thank the Lord that *I* dare ! " and with a toss of the head and a challenging glance to Turiddu, she enters the church.

The unequal combat between the other two is renewed

in the duet *No, no, Turiddu*, which works up to a climax where the exasperated man flings Santuzza brutally to the ground, and hurries to join Lola in the church.

Crushed, exhausted, the girl does not stir until the arrival of Alfio puts new life in her—the life of hate, the desire of revenge. She has only to tell the young Sicilian the bare facts of Lola's relations with Turiddu, and the tragic sequel becomes inevitable ; Alfio is changed to a madman, thirsting for vengeance without delay (*Ad essi non perdono, vendetta avrò*).

Now follows the famous *Intermezzo* which from the first made such a sensational and universal success as has not since been equalled. Yet it is doubtful whether its real merit is generally appreciated. To countless thousands, who may or may not have seen the opera, it appeals as a series of luscious melodic phrases with a rhythmic swing that is irresistible—in fact as ' a rattling good tune.' But it is much more than this—the *Intermezzo* is an essential part of *Cavalleria Rusticana*, and loses half its value when detached from its proper environment. The manner of its introduction is masterly. We have been listening to a tale of passion and wrong, of fiery love and hate—a broken-hearted girl has just left the stage, and a jealous madman crying out for blood— we know that tragedy is close at hand. Now the stage is empty, but the curtain is not lowered ; we are left to the contemplation of the inanimate scene before us while the *Intermezzo* is being played.

It has been said that the function of the orchestra in Wagnerian music-drama is, like that of the chorus in Greek tragedy, to afford a running commentary on the action of the piece ; that is undoubtedly Mascagni's intention in the *Intermezzo*. We see before us the quiet village, the small white houses glowing golden in the sunlight under a pure Sicilian sky. There is the tavern, for refreshment and good-fellowship—there is the church for prayer and adoration, where all the homely joys of every life are blessed and sanctioned, and where the weary body is brought to welcome rest at last. As we gaze and listen we pass into a dream of peace and beauty—it is a scene where " all but the spirit of man is divine "—and we wake to realize what a sorry mess man is prone to make of it.

It is a sense of this violent contrast that Mascagni's music should convey to us. At the same time it is obvious that the art of the scene-painter is here raised to a quite unique importance ; not the most elaborate and costly setting for *Parsifal* or *The Ring* can ever have a tithe of the artistic significance contained in this simple picture which we absorb, as it were, through two senses while we listen to the *Intermezzo*.

Mass is over and the people come out of church, Turiddu with Lola at his side ; he invites them all to join him at his mother's tavern across the square. His drinking-song, *Viva il vino spumeggiante*, is barely ended when Alfio comes up ; one look at his face is enough to drive the women off the stage. Turiddu offers him a cup of wine ; Alfio dashes it aside and challenges him to a duel, which is accepted in the Sicilian fashion, by an embrace and a bite of the ear. Alfio goes off while Turiddu remains to take a pathetic farewell of his mother; he is leaving home for a time, he tells her, and commends Santuzza to her care, if he should not return. [Musically this is one of the most effective moments of the opera.] The poor woman is not left long in bewilderment—Santuzza enters and falls weeping on her neck ; the others wander back in twos and threes, uneasy with a presentiment of coming trouble. The orchestra prepares us for the climax with a succession of arresting chords and a mutter of drums; then shrieks are heard outside, and a woman rushes on with the cry, "Turiddu is dead! Someone has killed poor Turiddu!" The curtain falls on the horrified crowd closing round the senseless forms of Santuzza and Mother Lucia.

Cavalleria Rusticana has held the stage for thirty-five years, and its popularity to-day is hardly diminished; it has outlived the excessive laudation with which it was first received, as well as the many severe criticisms that have since been passed upon it. Like the story, the music is generally too melodramatic, occasionally violent, in its method, and truth of expression is often sacrificed to the impulse of a too insistent rhythm. Yet when the composer can resist this tendency—as, for example, in Santuzza's song, *Voi lo sapete, o mamma*, and Turiddu's farewell to his mother—he is truly and powerfully dramatic. His gift of fresh, spontaneous melody never fails him; above all, from first to last he is passionately sincere. Of the many Italian operas written since the death of Verdi, *Cavalleria Rusticana* is the one that would seem to have the best chance of survival.

PAGLIACCI

Words and Music by LEONCAVALLO.
Milan, 1892 ; *London*, 1893 ; *New York*, 1893.

LEONCAVALLO'S tense and vivid musical drama shares with Mascagni's *Cavalleria Rusticana* the distinction of having founded the modern Italian school of *verismo* (realism), which Mr Krehbiel trounces so soundly in his *Second Book of Operas*. The composer has told us that the plot was suggested by incidents in real life which had deeply impressed him as a boy. The realistic note is boldly insisted upon at the very outset by the famous Prologue, which, though imitating Mascagni in the interruption of the orchestra by a vocal solo, contains an idea that is quite original.

As a rule the Prologue to a play is either a short *résumé* of the plot, or an apologetic reminder of the fact that, after all, it is 'only play-acting.' But here, when the Clown suddenly thrusts his whitened face through the curtain to beg a word with us, it is something very different that he has to say. " Our story," he declares, " is a true one—the incidents are real, and, what is more, we people on the stage are real men and women, with passions like yourselves ; often we are cast for parts for which we are but little in sympathy at the moment—so be sorry for us, since, as you know, it is hard to have to play the clown when one's heart is breaking. And one thing more : the saying that 'all the world's a stage' may also be read backward, if you please ; sometimes the real tragedies of life are played out on the stage, as you will shortly see Up with the curtain ! "

People are accustomed to enjoy the fine dramatic stuff of the Prologue to *Pagliacci*, much as they do the " Star of Eve " song in *Tannhäuser*, without troubling to understand its precise meaning: that meaning is certainly not quite clear, but the above paraphrase, we think, conveys its true intention.

The opera is a play within a play; the incidents of the First Act result in the crude farce that is presented in Act II being turned into an actual tragedy. *Pagliacci* is the Italian name for those strolling players, or mountebanks, who are a feature of village festivals all over Italy; the little play around which Leoncavallo's tragedy turns is a typical example of the entertainment they have to offer. The characters are the conventional ones that have been handed down for centuries—Columbine, Harlequin her lover, Pagliaccio (or First Clown, we may here call him) her husband, and Taddeo (Second Clown). Harlequin makes love to Columbine, Taddeo catches them at it, and runs to fetch Pagliaccio; in the regular sequel the husband's part is to be held up to ridicule, and chased off the stage by Harlequin, but in the opera this little knockabout show is not allowed to run its natural course, and the end is very different. However, all this occurs in the Second Act, to which the First is in the nature of a prelude.

Act I. A blazing afternoon in an Italian village. It is the Feast of the Assumption, so there can be no question of work for anyone; the peasants are all out to welcome the troupe of *pagliacci*, whose theatre is seen set up already in a field, with a hunchback to guard it. This is Tonio, who has just sung the Prologue; in the little play he takes the part of Taddeo. The others now arrive, almost mobbed by the excited people, who have to be called to silence by the loud beating of a drum; the drummer is

Canio, the proprietor of the show, and the Pagliaccio of the little play. With him are Nedda the Columbine, who is his wife off the stage as well as on, and Beppe, who plays Harlequin. Canio invites them all to come and see the show at seven that evening, and, as the church bell rings, the peasants troop off to Vespers, singing a very charming chorus, *Din don ! suona vespero.*

By this time an incident has occurred that throws light on the relations between Canio and his pretty wife, Nedda. On her arrival Tonio has stepped forward to help her to descend from the cart in which she is seated, but Canio sends him back with a box on the ear, and lifts his wife down himself. The peasants roar with laughter, regarding it as a foretaste of the fun to come, but Tonio slinks away muttering threats of vengeance, and Nedda has seen a look in her husband's face which frightens her. Canio goes off to the tavern with some villagers, and Nedda believes herself to be alone.

We soon learn that her husband has good cause for his jealousy ; she is afraid of him ; but, light of heart as she is light of love, she can give herself up wholly to the charm of the glorious sunshine. A passing flight of birds attracts her fancy, and she addresses them in the popular ' ballatella,' *Stridono lassù.* These " feathered *zingari* of the air," whither do they journey ? What seek they ? They know not ; only their vague desires lead them to wander, and Fate directs their course : in them she sees a symbol of herself.

The words of this song are contrived with considerable skill to fit the situation ; the melody, unfortunately, is frankly banal, though helped by some graceful and effective orchestration.

Tonio, who has been in hiding, now comes forward to plead his cause with Nedda. The hunchback is madly in love with her, and in spite of her contemptuous refusal his passion grows more and more violent until, at last, she is obliged in self-defence to strike him with a whip. The blow is her own death-warrant.

The music is not adequate to the strong situation. Tonio's monologue, *So ben chè difforme*, was the favourite ' sob-stuff ' of sentimental baritones for many a year; the English version, though not very close to the original, conveys a just impression of the quality of the music :

> I know that you hate me, and laugh in derision—
> For what is the Jester ?   He plays but a part;
> Yet he has his dream and his hope and his vision—
> The Clown has a heart !
> And ah, when you pass me, uncaring, unseeing,
> You know not my sorrow, so cruel and sweet;
> I give you my spirit, my life, and my being,
> I die at your feet !

After the maddened hunchback is gone, Nedda's accepted lover appears—Silvio, a young farmer, who has been for some time smitten with the pretty Columbine, and has now come to urge her to fly with him. Their long duet is effectively varied, but the leading love-*motif*, with its perpetual triple rhythm, is too much in the vein of the solo we have lately had from Tonio, and it must be remembered that both the parts are for baritone.

The lovers have just agreed to meet at midnight when Canio, guided by Tonio, rushes on in time to hear his wife's words : " To-night, and for ever, I am thine," but the man to whom they are addressed is already out of sight. Canio goes in frenzied pursuit, but returns baffled. Nedda, of course, will not disclose her lover's name : maddened by her refusal, her husband rushes at her with a knife, and is stopped only just in time by Beppe and Tonio. The latter persuades Canio to postpone his vengeance till after the show ; Nedda's lover will probably be among the spectators, and means may be found to make him betray himself. Meanwhile all must go and dress for the evening performance.

Canio is left alone on the scene ; yet he too must follow the rest, plaster his face with white and red, and put on the comical garments of the Clown. The people pay him to make them laugh, and he must laugh with them —laugh, though his love is faithless, laugh, though his heart is broken.

This soliloquy, known as *Vesti la giubba,* is in a way the complement of the famous Prologue ; both are excellent examples of the purely emotional type of music by virtue of which this opera makes its strong popular appeal.

Act II. Our mountebanks are preparing for the little crowd that is hurrying up from all sides to see the show. Tonio beats the big drum and does the shouting, while Beppe looks after the women and tries to keep them from quarrelling. When enough people have assembled, Nedda goes round from bench to bench to take the money ; Silvio is already in the front row, and as he pays for his place he reminds her of their assignation for to-night. So all is ready for the tragedy which we know must follow.

But, first, the unsuspecting peasants must enjoy the fun for which they have paid—the curtains of the tiny stage are parted, and the simple farce begins.

The music now takes on a welcome change. Instead of long, cloying phrases of violent passion or clammy sentiment, we are glad to listen for a time to clean dance-music and airs with an old-fashioned grace. Columbine (Nedda) is alone on the stage, but not for long ; though her husband, as she tells us, is away for the night, someone else is evidently expected. The minuet which serves for her short solo stops as the sound of a guitar is heard outside. Columbine listens with rapture to the voice of Harlequin (Beppe), who sings a serenade which belongs to that delightful world of music from which passion is excluded. But she does not admit him yet. Taddeo (Tonio) has first to appear—he has been to market, and proceeds to lay his basket and his heart at Columbine's feet. The first part of the scene is pure burlesque, but when Columbine, weary of his nonsense, tells him to be off, we get a dramatic surprise. In order to remind us that it is really Tonio, not poor Taddeo, with whom Nedda has now to reckon, the music of the scene in Act I where the hunchback pleads and is rejected in similar fashion is repeated note for note. But when Harlequin jumps in at the window, we are back again in the world of unreality—he kicks poor Taddeo out of the room, and the audience roars with laughter.

Harlequin and Columbine now sup together to the strains of an intimate little gavotte, and all goes merrily until Taddeo rushes in to warn them that Columbine's husband, Pagliaccio, has returned before his time—he knows all, and is on their track. The spectators are delighted at Taddeo's droll manner, and the way in which the plot is developing.

Harlequin leaps out of the window, and Canio, as Pagliaccio, enters just in time to hear his wife call after her stage-lover the very words she had used in the real situation in the First Act: "This night, and for ever, I am thine, love!" He strives hard to keep within the spirit of his part, but the question which he has to put to Columbine: "Who has been with thee? Tell me his name!" and her stubborn refusal force him back into the world of reality. He will act no more: "No!"

he cries, " I'll play the Clown no longer ! I am a man again, and my poor bleeding heart calls out for blood— blood to wipe out your shame and mine, accursed woman ! "

The spectators are quite carried away by excitement, and wildly applaud what they consider a splendid piece of acting. Nedda, as Columbine, makes a brave effort to get back to the play ; to the tune of the recent gavotte she assures him, coquettishly, that the man who has just left her was only Harlequin—poor, harmless Harlequin !

But the tension is too great—the storm of passion breaks loose. After one more terrible " Tell me your lover's name ! " and one last cutting " No ! " from Nedda, the audience wake up to the truth—there is murder in Canio's words and looks.· Some of the women leave in terror. Silvio is on the alert ; he has drawn his knife, but is held back by those around him. Nedda tries to escape into the audience, but Canio is too quick for her—she falls to the ground, his knife between her shoulders. In her death-agony she calls instinctively on her lover : " Help, Silvio ! "

So Tonio was right ! In an instant Canio has leapt from the stage and stabbed Silvio to the heart.

It is all over. The knife drops from his listless hands as the poor Clown turns, in dazed fashion, to the audience and addresses them for the last time : " The play is finished."

Pagliacci and *Cavalleria Rusticana* were for a long time the Tweedledum and Tweedledee of the operatic world ; dispute would grow hot as to their relative merits. Leoncavallo's work is obviously the more subtle conception of the two, and shows a far greater talent for orchestration: moreover, we must not forget that Leoncavallo was fortunately able to write his own words, and the ' book ' of *Pagliacci* is no mean achievement.

In *Cavalleria Rusticana*, on the other hand, Mascagni excels by a constant flow of broad, spontaneous, vocal melody, in which his rival was conspicuously lacking, and this, when combined with a strong libretto, such as we have here, is the best guarantee of a long life for any opera. At the present time it seems probable that both these works, in spite of their many weaknesses, will survive all the many imitations that have succeeded them.

LA BOHÈME

Music by PUCCINI. *Words by* ILLICA *and* GIACOSA,
from MURGER'S *romance.*
Turin, 1896 ; *London*, 1897 ; *New York*, 1898.

LOVERS of Henry Murger's *Scènes de la vie de Bohème*, a series of brilliant sketches of student-life in Paris's *Quartier Latin* toward the middle of the last century, were inclined to look askance at any attempt to consolidate such slight material into a four-Act opera libretto.   The book, while possessing a fantastic charm and a definite literary quality, was entirely lacking in dramatic interest, and yet Puccini was assuredly justified in his choice ; the subject was well suited to his picturesque methods, and with the aid of two skilful librettists [1] he has contrived a very pretty entertainment. Of all his operas *La Bohème* is the most pleasing, and will probably prove the most enduring.

The work is divided into four short Acts ; each one is prefaced in the vocal score with a quotation from the novel; the *leit-motif* to the whole, in a literary sense, is to be found in the phrase, " A gay life but a terrible one," which the librettists have taken from the French writer's admirable preface.   Certain incidents susceptible of musical or dramatic treatment have been detached from the lengthy original, and are connected by a sufficiently coherent thread of interest.   The music is beautifully orchestrated at all points, and catches exactly the spirit of each scene, grave or gay.

[1] My thanks are due to Messrs G. Ricordi and Co. for permitting me to use their text of the opera.

Act I. (*In the Attic.*) The curtain rises almost immediately and discloses a typical Bohemian studio of a poverty-stricken aspect. Though it is Christmas Eve, there is no fire in the stove. Two of the 'faithful,' Rudolf the poet and Marcel the painter, are seen ; the one looking pensively out of the window, as is the way of poets, and the other at work on his masterpiece, " The Passage of the Red Sea." We hear a vigorous phrase in the orchestra which stands for the whole of the Latin Quarter brood, with their " gay and terrible" life : it often reappears in the course of the opera.

Marcel complains of the cold, and Rudolf answers with a charming phrase from his big aria in the scene with Mimi later in this Act. Naturally the conversation soon turns to love, but even this fiery topic does not suffice for warmth, so Rudolf, in a fit of abnegation, sacrifices the manuscript of his latest tragedy to provide fuel. While they warm themselves, Colline, a philosopher, enters, frozen with cold, and in no good humour : he throws a large bundle of books tied up in a handkerchief on the table—volumes which he has been unsuccessful in pawning. A trio follows, as more of the manuscript goes to feed the flames, when, unexpectedly, two boys come in bearing food, wine, cigars, and fuel for the fire, which they set down before the astonished eyes of the three. Schaunard, a musician, who completes the Bohemian quartet, enters triumphantly ; he has been playing to an English *milord*, who naturally is fabulously wealthy, and the musician, faithful to tradition, has incontinently spent his reward. But he refuses to allow his comrades to eat indoors on the night of the Christmas vigil, and puts away the provisions in a cupboard. " You may drink here," he says, "but you must dine in the Latin Quarter!" As they are filling their glasses a knock is heard : it is the landlord, a person of benevolent aspect, come to collect the rent. The quartet manage with wine and jest to divert him from his purpose, and finally bundle the befuddled old man out of the room. The whole of this scene is treated with the greatest vivacity. Marcel, Colline, and Schaunard now propose going out ; the poet has an article for a new journal to finish ; he promises to join them later.

Rudolf has not been long at work before there is a timid knock, and a female voice is heard, complaining that her candle has been blown out. It is Mimi, the little seamstress who lives on the floor above ; immediately on her entrance she is seized with a fit of coughing, and—how the word dates her !—' swoons ' ! Rudolf, helpless after the manner of his sex, sprinkles a little water on her face, and she revives on hearing him comment audibly on her charms. Whether this determines her subsequent manœuvres it is hard to say, but she makes for the door, only to find that she has left her key behind : her candle again goes out : then his : and the two are left in darkness hunting for the key. Rudolf finds it but secretes it in his pocket, and perjures his immortal soul in emphatic denial of its whereabouts. Soon, as will have been guessed, the hands of these two young people touch and Rudolf gives voice to the famous aria *Che gelida mannina.* Mimi, who, for a prima donna, has listened with commendable silence, now feels it is time the poet gave way to her, so she follows with the equally famous aria, *Mi chiamano Mimi.*

The moon (ah, faithful, punctual moon !) has risen and brightens the room : in the courtyard Rudolf's friends are calling out to him to come down : their voices fade into the distance, and Rudolf, turning from the window, sees Mimi encircled by the moonlight.

The theme of the poet's big song is played very softly on the orchestra and marks the beginning of the short scene which Caruso and Melba used to make so memorable.

Mimi tells Rudolf to go off and join his friends, but coyly suggests that she too might come. The infatuated poet does not, apparently, read in this request the sign-manual of the coquette ; so they go out into the night together.

Act II. (*In the Latin Quarter.*) "Christmas Eve: a square flanked by shops of all sorts ; on one side a café. A vast motley crowd : soldiers, serving-maids, children, students, work-girls, gendarmes, etc. Shop-keepers are crying their wares." Such are the stage directions. Rather apart from this bustling scene Rudolf and Mimi are walking up and down together, and the other Bohemians can be recognized here and there. Puccini has built up an excellent concerted piece at the beginning of the Act, a Scene which is a pleasure both to eye and ear.

Mimi displays a distinctly acquisitive instinct, and makes straight for the milliner's, where the unfortunate Rudolf has to purchase a bonnet for her : then she artlessly admires a necklace in a jeweller's shop, but this time the poet will not be drawn.

Presently Colline, Schaunard, and Marcel come out of the café carrying a table, and are at once noted by the eagle-eye of Mimi, who insists on joining them : she is formally introduced by Rudolf.

A charming little interlude is provided by the entrance of Parpignol the toymaker, with a gaily painted little barrow festooned with foliage and flowers and painted lanterns, followed by a crowd of merry urchins : unfortunately for the young rascals their mothers are in the vicinity, so they are bundled off to bed.

An extremely pretty girl, followed by a pompous, over-dressed old gentleman, now comes in : this is Musetta, a lady of light virtue but great charm, with her latest admirer, whom she treats like a dog. She is well known to the Bohemians and particularly to Marcel, an early flame of hers : the oddly matched couple sit down at a table opposite to the others, and the lady proceeds to give an exhibition of histrionics, mainly with the idea of attracting Marcel's attention : the poor man is doing his best to resist the fascination of the heartless little wretch, but when she sings the best-known tune in the opera, *Quando men vo soletta per la via,* he has to be restrained by force from rushing over to her. Alcindoro, the aged beau, is scandalized ! Colline, as befits a philosopher, and Schaunard also are deeply interested in the psychology of the scene, and their comments as well as the conversations of Mimi and Rudolf are all woven into the texture of the music with great skill.

Finally Musetta hits on an old ruse—the manœuvre of the tight shoe—and screams the place down until Alcindoro rushes off to buy another pair : as soon as he disappears, Marcel and Musetta embrace with much fervour.

But we are not done with excitement yet : drums in the distance herald a tattoo, and the people run here and there, not knowing from which direction the soldiers will come. They enter on the left, headed by a gigantic drum-major, dexterously wielding a baton. The Bohemians calmly tell the waiter that Alcindoro will settle *both* the bills, and prepare to leave, in such a way as to draw the attention of all around them. Musetta, being without her shoe, cannot walk, so Marcel and Colline must carry her : they are given an ovation by the crowd, who proceed to follow after the soldiers. Alcindoro now returns and is confronted with the two bills—one of a prodigious length. He subsides into a chair as the curtain falls. So ends what is one of the merriest scenes in the whole range of modern Italian Opera.

Act III. (*The Barrière d'Enfer.*) A cheerless dawn over a snow-covered landscape toward the close of February—conditions that temporarily justify such a description as the ' gateway of hell ' for the toll-gate on the Orleans road leading to Paris.

Marcel and Musetta now live together in a tavern near by and earn their living, one by painting signboards, and the other by teaching singing. A light burns in the tavern, from which sounds of joviality are heard coming even at this late hour : Musetta strikes in with a few bars of her waltz-song.

The coldness and dreariness of the scene are cleverly painted in the music. Men and women on their way to work pass through the toll-gate, and as the light grows Mimi comes in looking anxiously about her : she is seized with a violent fit of coughing, but, recovering herself, asks a serving-woman who has come out of the inn to tell Marcel she is there. As she waits, a bell in a convent near by rings for Matins. Marcel is very surprised to see her ; he tells her how Musetta and he have been earning their living, and diffidently adds that Rudolf is asleep in the tavern. Poor Mimi bursts into tears, she declares that she cannot go to him, for though he loves her he is madly jealous—with cause, one suspects. Marcel suggests a separation and promises his help. Mimi is again shaken with coughing, and then, as Rudolf is waking, Marcel advises her to hide behind a tree and hear what passes. Rudolf comes out and at once says he wants a separation from Mimi on account of her heartlessness and constant flirtations : then suddenly the poet retracts his hard words, and works himself into a passion of tender solicitude—he loves her still, and fears she is dying from the awful cough which never leaves her. This upsets the poor girl behind the tree so much that she forgets her concealment and betrays her presence by her sobbing. The lovers are swept into each other's arms ; and Marcel, whether from tact or necessity, rushes into the tavern.

Releasing herself from Rudolf's embrace Mimi sings the beautiful little aria which is founded on her song in the First Act : very softly a solo violin rises above the rest of the orchestra with one of the phrases heard under such different conditions before, and then the music swells into a passionate climax which merges into the final quartet. The two sing tenderly of past joys, but their reminiscences are rudely broken into by a sound of breaking plates and glasses from the tavern : Musetta runs out pursued by Marcel : she has been caught flirting ! The two have a pretty quarrel, unheeded by Mimi and Rudolf. Calling each other by abusive names they go back into the inn ; the other two, oblivious to all the world in the new joy of reconciliation, move away arm in arm and are heard singing in the distance as the curtain falls.

Act IV. (*In the Attic.*) The scene is the same as in the First Act : Marcel and Rudolf are pretending to work—a usual state of affairs—but are really trying to draw information from each other about their respective mistresses, who, it seems, have once more deserted them. Rudolf has seen Musetta in a *coupé*, Marcel has caught a glimpse of Mimi in a carriage, apparelled like a duchess. Both men pretend not to care, but the duet which follows shows that they are longing for reunion. Rudolf even gets maudlin over Mimi's rose-pink bonnet, which he fondles as he sings.

Schaunard and Colline coming in now, with four rolls and a herring, reveal the poverty-stricken condition of the commissariat : the four try to imagine their poor fare is, in reality, a fine dinner. To keep up their spirits they indulge in some rather obvious foolery which takes the form of a mock dance and fight : when this is at its height the door suddenly opens and Musetta enters in a state of great agitation : Mimi, she says, is there, but scarcely strong enough to climb the staircase. The poor little consumptive is brought in by Rudolf, and, with the help of the others, is put into the bed. Musetta relates how she had found her (having left her old viscount) almost dying—but longing to be near Rudolf. The orchestra plays the tune of her first song, which colours the whole scene. The Bohemians are in a fix—no food, no warmth for the dying girl, who for the moment is better and glad to be with her friends.

Musetta determines to pawn her ear-rings and Colline his coat, to which he bids an emotional farewell. They all go out leaving Mimi and Rudolph alone : the orchestra now plays a phrase of the poet's song and, as the scene progresses, snatches of tunes before heard are played or sung with pathetic significance. Mimi, with the old instinct of coquetry still strong in her, bids Rudolf tell her if she is still pretty ; she recalls their first meeting, the ruse of the key, sings very softly his words, " Your tiny hand is frozen ! let me warm it into life ! " Then a sudden spasm shakes her, terrifying Rudolf ! But she recovers as the others come in, Musetta with the muff the poor little creature so longs for, and Marcel with a phial : the doctor will follow as quickly as he can. Childishly happy with the muff, Mimi gently falls asleep. Musetta, busied in preparing the medicine, murmurs a prayer for her companion, and the others whisper together in a corner.

Schaunard is the first to see that Mimi is dead ; he tells Marcel, but they dare not break the news to Rudolf, until their strange looks and sunken voices force him to realize what has happened ; he flings himself on Mimi's bed sobbing, while the others stand round, grief-stricken, as the curtain falls.

MADAMA BUTTERFLY

Music by PUCCINI. *Words by* ILLICA *and* GIACOSA.
Milan, 1904 ; *London,* 1905 ; *New York,* 1906.

PUCCINI had achieved two great successes in the operatic world with *La Bohème* (1896) and *La Tosca* (1900), and therefore might reasonably have expected to add to his laurels upon the first production of *Madama Butterfly* (1904). But the Italian public is not, like the British, a respecter of persons, however celebrated, and evidences of displeasure were manifest soon after the rise of the curtain at the Scala : these gave way later to hoots and hisses in the best Italian style.

The curious thing is that no one appears to know why these things occurred. Some put forward the unfamiliarity of the stage setting as a reason, others (which seems more probable) the inadequacy of the singers ; it has also been suggested that playing the opera in only two Acts provoked resentment.

Whatever the cause, when the work, revised, slightly shortened, and with Act II played in two parts, was given at Brescia only a few months after, it obtained a brilliant reception, and has since gone the round of all the opera houses with unvarying success.

The plot is drawn from a play by David Belasco which is actually a heavily sentimentalized version of Pierre Loti's *Madame Chrysanthème*. It is, for an opera, very simple and straightforward, and is founded on the time-honoured tradition that a sailor has a wife in every port.[1]

---

[1] My thanks are due to Messrs G. Ricordi and Co. for permitting me to use their text of the opera.

The situation before the curtain rises is quickly told. Pinkerton, a young U.S. naval lieutenant stationed at Nagasaki, has determined to make 'a Japanese marriage' with a pretty young *geisha*, Cho-Cho-San, with whom he fancies himself to be in love.

Having bought a house for the honeymoon, he has come to inspect it on the wedding day.

Act I. A Japanese house, terrace, and garden. Below, in the background, the bay, the harbour, and the town of Nagasaki.

A short and vigorous Prelude opens the First Act, during which, as well as at other times in the opera, fragments of Japanese tunes give effective touches of local colour. On the rise of the curtain we behold B. F. Pinkerton—radiant in the uniform of a lieutenant in the U.S. navy, with Goro, euphemistically described as a marriage-broker. This egregious personage is explaining, " obsequiously and with much bowing and scraping," cleverly suggested in the music, the many advantages of the house that Pinkerton has hired for his temporary ménage, and which is full of the most ingenious contrivances. The inspection over, Goro claps his hands, and two men and a woman enter and prostrate themselves before the embarrassed Pinkerton; they are Suzuki, Cho-Cho-San's hand-maid, the cook, and the servant. The first-named betrays a loquacity which fortunately has little opportunity to display itself in the course of the opera. As Pinkerton is frankly bored, Goro bundles them off. It is significant that the gallant sailor regards their charming soubriquets —Miss Gentle-Breeze-of-Morning, Ray-of-the-Golden-Sunbeam, and Sweet-scented-Pine-Tree, as foolish ; he is evidently a person of little artistic sensibility.

Presently the U.S. Consul, Sharpless, appears, breathless from climbing the hill.

[Pinkerton's aria at this point, *Dovunque al mondo*, addressed to Sharpless, is preceded by a few bars of the *Star-spangled Banner*, an air for which one may claim, without being ' a hundred per cent. American,' that it can at least hold its own with any melody in the opera.]

Pinkerton breaks off, to have a drink with the Consul before continuing the ingenuous exposition of nautical morality that constitutes the basis of his song, concluding with a toast, " America for ever ! " in which Sharpless, and the brass of the orchestra, join with much fervour.

Now that the social amenities have been observed, the Consul feels it his duty to warn Pinkerton of what may be the consequence of his impulsive action, but the heedless youth merely replies with a charming expression of his passion for Cho-Cho-San, *Amore o grillo*. The men drink again ; this time to Pinkerton's new friends and relations to be, though Pinkerton at the same time unashamedly toasts the *real* wife from America he will one day marry

Goro runs in to say that Butterfly and her friends are coming ; indeed, their shrill voices are already heard in the distance, one soaring like a lark above the rest—it is Butterfly. Her entrance, just as the climax of her song (*Ancora un passo*) is reached, is an effective moment, vocally and dramatically, while the brightly coloured kimonos and sunshades of the heroine and her companions make a charming stage picture.

Butterfly explains in the ensuing dialogue that her people were once wealthy but lost their money, so that she was compelled to earn her living as a *geisha*. Sharpless very naturally asks where her father is—her mother is with her—but the innocent question has a most depressing effect on the assemblage, which nervously fans itself as Butterfly answers shortly, " Dead." A rather humorous incident now takes place. "What might your age be ?" asks Sharpless. "Try to guess !" coquettes Butterfly. "Ten !" hazards the gallant gentleman. "Guess higher !" the lady replies. "Twenty, then !" "Guess lower !—Fifteen exactly ! I am old, am I not ?" she adds—a statement which may be variously interpreted !

The High Commissioner, the Official Registrar, and a crowd of relations now come on to the scene, excitedly discussing the two Americans, while refreshments are brought. Puccini manages the bustle of this scene cleverly, and it makes an effective concerted piece. Butterfly introduces her relatives ; then, taking Pinkerton on one side, she shows him her few girlish possessions (which she produces from her sleeves)—silk handkerchiefs, a fan, a mirror, a knife, held sacred because the Mikado had sent it to her father for the purpose of committing *hara-kiri*—thus is the mystery of this parent explained— and finally the souls of her ancestors ; but Pinkerton shows not the slightest sympathy with this rather pathetic little exhibition.

Butterfly tells him confidentially how she has become a Christian to please him, and, to prove her sincerity, incontinently throws away the souls of her unfortunate forefathers !

At length they are married : Cho-Cho-San is now Madame Pinkerton. The Consul takes his leave, and the relatives are drinking the health of the newly married couple to a delightful tune, *O Kami, O Kami,* when the peace of the scene is rudely interrupted by strange cries coming from the path up the hill. It is the Bonze, Cho-Cho-San's uncle, a High Priest of the Buddhist faith. "Abomination !" he cries to the frightened girls now huddled together, while Butterfly remains alone in a corner. "She has renounced her true religion!" After consigning Butterfly's soul to everlasting torment and inducing all the relations to disown her, the Bonze is bundled out by the enraged Pinkerton, the rest following with cries of "*Hou! Hou! Hou! Cho-Cho-San!*"

Pinkerton endeavours to comfort his terrified little bride. He scarcely realizes, being what he is—a very ordinary, unobservant young man—what her change in belief has meant to Butterfly. He, not Christianity, is now her religion. But the faith of her ancestors cannot easily be uprooted—and Suzuki, muttering her prayers before the Buddhist shrine, is a further reproach to her.

Twilight is beginning to fall as Pinkerton leads his bride toward the house. A beautiful theme wells up out of the orchestra, scored with Puccini's almost unfailing instinct for the right thing. Suzuki helps Butterfly into her white wedding garment and retires for the night; the two lovers are left alone.

From here to the end is a long love-duet (*Viene la sera*), broken only by sinister reminiscences of the Bonze's theme. The night gradually falls, the stars come out, and the music glows with lyric fervour. Finally the tune heard on Butterfly's first appearance takes possession of both orchestra and singers.

As the curtain falls Pinkerton vanishes into the house with Butterfly clasped in his arms.

Act II. *Part* 1. Inside Butterfly's house. After a few bars of prelude, in which the Bonze's theme is prominent, the curtain rises to disclose a barely furnished interior. The curtains are drawn, leaving the room in semi-darkness, but Suzuki can just be seen praying before the image of Buddha; from time to time she rings the prayer bell. Butterfly is standing rigid and motionless near a screen—it is three years since she entrusted her life and soul to the care of Pinkerton—and she is a mother.

Presently Suzuki draws up the curtains and slides back the partition giving on to the charming little garden. "How soon," asks Butterfly half jokingly, "shall we be starving?" They have only a few coins left, but Butterfly is confident Pinkerton will come back, in spite of Suzuki's scepticism. Did he not have locks put on the doors to keep out her relations and give her protection? She sings the theme of the first song with passionate emphasis, but Suzuki is still unconvinced. "Did ever a foreign husband yet return to his nest?" Butterfly, furious, seizes hold of her, cries: "Silence! or I'll kill you!" and then, calming down, she relates with much charm Pinkerton's last words to her—his promise to come back "when the robins nest again." The violins in the orchestra set up a realistic twittering followed by what is probably the most famous aria in the opera, *Un bel dì*, so often heard on the concert platform. As she finishes, Butterfly, overcome with emotion at the picture she has imagined of her husband's return, casts herself into Suzuki's arms.

Suddenly Goro and Sharpless appear in the garden and presently the Consul comes in. "Madame Butterfly?" he asks. "No! Madame Pinkerton," she answers: then, turning round, she recognizes him, claps her hands with pleasure, and orders Suzuki to bring cigarettes and cushions. Sharpless is anxious to explain the reason of his visit, which weighs not a little on his mind, but the little lady constantly interrupts and will not allow him more than a few words for some moments. At last he manages to say, "I've a letter from Mr Pinkerton," and shows it to her. The poor little creature is overjoyed: "I am the happiest woman in Japan," she cries. Then,

" When do the robins nest in America ? " she asks. The Consul is surprised at the apparently irrelevant question, so she explains. Then he understands too well and hesitatingly confesses his ignorance of ornithology—a word which puzzles Butterfly. She tells him how Goro—who was presumably in the habit of receiving a commission on marriage contracts—had come to her soon after Pinkerton's departure and tried to persuade her with arguments and presents to remarry, and that he is now pressing the claims of the wealthy Yamadori, a mentally deficient plutocrat! Indeed, at this moment the gentleman appears with his retinue and again presses his suit. Butterfly refuses him—she is already married, as she thinks. A discussion as to grounds of divorce follows. " In my country, the United States," the little Japanese ' wife ' says, " desertion does not give the right of divorce " ; and she appeals to Sharpless to support her. Goro whispers to the Consul, " Pinkerton's ship is already signalled." Yamadori takes his pompous farewell, and Sharpless settles down to the difficult task of reading Pinkerton's letter to Butterfly, a scene which has been delightfully treated by Puccini with the lightest of touches.

Inevitably Butterfly misunderstands the purport of Pinkerton's words to the Consul, " On you I am relying to act discreetly, to prepare her with tact and caution."

" He's coming," she cries and is enraptured. The Consul tries another way. He asks her what she would do if he never came back. " Two things I might do," she answers, while the orchestra gives out low chords of heavy portent—" become again a *geisha*—or die." Sharpless is much moved and, in his longing to help, urges her to accept Yamadori. This mortally offends Butterfly. She tells Suzuki to show him the door—then, repenting, runs into the room on the left, to return carrying her baby, which she exhibits to the Consul, proudly pointing out his American features.

The big dramatic aria, *Sai cos' ebbe cuore*, if sung as it deserves, is really touching. The poor little mother breaks down at the end and hugs the child passionately ; even Sharpless cannot restrain his tears. " The child's name is ' Trouble ' now," Butterfly says, " but it shall be ' Joy ' when the father returns."

The theme of *Un bel dì* is heard again in the orchestra. The Consul goes, but there is no rest for Butterfly, for Suzuki rushes in dragging Goro by the ear. She has found that he was going about the town saying that no one knows who the child's father is, a statement that makes Butterfly nearly kill him as she pushes him out of the house. Worn with emotion her thoughts fly to the child. She tells him his avenger will soon be here ; indeed at this moment a cannon-shot is heard from the harbour. Very softly the strings play the *Un bel dì* theme as Butterfly, running to the window with her telescope, reads the name of the man-of-war which has just come into harbour—"Abraham Lincoln." Now all her hopes are justified : " My love and my faith have triumphed ! " she cries ; " he's here ! He loves me ! "

The entrancing flower-duet, *Scuoti quella fronda*, follows, during which the two women deck the house so profusely with flowers that the garden is stripped bare. Then Suzuki brings in the baby, while Butterfly touches up her white face with carmine, dreading lest Pinkerton should find her changed. She puts on her white kimono so that he may see her as on her wedding day, and even the baby is dressed up in festal garments for the occasion.

Night has fallen. Suzuki brings in some Japanese lanterns, which she puts on the flower-strewn floor.

Butterfly intends to watch at the window for the husband who is coming back to her; she makes three holes in the paper screen through which they may peep; and so, like sentinels, the wife, the child, the faithful servant, take up their posts—Butterfly remaining rigid and motionless as a statue.

Puccini has secured a very beautiful effect for the end of this scene. The chorus, out of sight, hums softly a tune heard previously during the reading of Pinkerton's letter, supported by a very light and delicate orchestral accompaniment. It intensifies the pathos of the stage picture. Suzuki and the baby are already dropping off to sleep as the curtain falls—Butterfly alone stands upright and tragically awake.

Act II. *Part* ii. There is no change of scene. When the curtain rises Butterfly is standing, still motionless, by the window; the other two are fast asleep. As it is now daylight, Butterfly wakes up Suzuki and takes the baby in her arms; she is still confident of Pinkerton's return. With the baby clasped to her bosom she goes up the staircase singing a simple little lullaby, while Suzuki mourns for her "poor Madame Butterfly." The orchestra now announces the arrival of Sharpless and Pinkerton, who are soon heard knocking at the door; Suzuki cannot restrain her surprise when she lets them in, but they motion her to be silent and creep in cautiously on tip-toe.

She tells them how eagerly Butterfly has examined every ship that came into the harbour, and how, confident that Pinkerton is returning to her, she has decorated the house with flowers; how, too, she has been up all night watching. Then she catches sight of a figure in the garden. "Who is that," she says fearfully. Sharpless tells Suzuki that the strange lady is Pinkerton's wife—his real

American wife. A trio follows, in which Sharpless insists that the baby must be cared for. Pinkerton expresses futile remorse, and Suzuki wonders how she can ever break the news to Butterfly. When she is gone, Pinkerton, after giving Sharpless money for the deserted little wife, sings a most unconvincing "Farewell, O happy home; farewell, home of love," while Sharpless reminds him of his repeated warnings, only too well justified. So the contemptible creature goes out, leaving Sharpless to face the music.

Kate, the American wife, who has surely the most thankless part in all opera, comes in with Suzuki from the garden. Butterfly calls from the room above, "Suzuki, where are you?" and appears at the head of the staircase. The faithful maid tries to stop her mistress coming down, but Butterfly runs into the room, sure that Pinkerton is hiding somewhere. A sinister reminiscence of the Bonze's curse-theme comes out of the orchestra. Suddenly Butterfly sees Kate, who is crying quietly. The scene that follows is of almost unbearable poignancy, and Puccini has treated it only too convincingly. Butterfly, who is trying not to understand what is only too obvious, drags the admission from Suzuki that Pinkerton is alive but will come no more to her. Kate tells her, as kindly as possible, who she is—she was married a year ago—and asks if she may do something for the child. She is certainly more broad-minded than most wives would be in similar circumstances! "Can he have his son?" she asks. "Yes, if he comes here half an hour from now," replies Butterfly; so Kate and Sharpless go. Butterfly almost collapses, but under Suzuki's tender care gradually recovers; she tells the maid to shut out the sunlight so that the room may be in almost total darkness.

"Go and play with my child," Butterfly commands

poor Suzuki, who is very reluctant to leave her, so unnaturally calm is she. At length the maid goes, and Butterfly crosses to the shrine, lifts the white veil from it, throws this across the screen, and takes down the dagger hanging near the image of Buddha. This she kisses softly, while reading the words inscribed upon it :

Death with honour is better than life with dishonour.

As she points the knife at her throat the door on the left opens and the child runs in, holding out his arms toward his mother. She lets the dagger fall, and clasps him to her heart. "You! You! You!" she cries. "Though you must never know it, 'tis for you, my love, I'm dying !"

When her fit of sobbing is over Butterfly bandages the child's eyes, and gives him two American flags to play with, then seizes the dagger and goes behind the screen.

Tottering out with the white scarf round her throat, she gropes her way to the child, falls to the ground beside her son with just enough strength left to embrace him. Pinkerton is heard calling from outside, "Butterfly, Butterfly !" and rushes into the room with Sharpless, as Butterfly, pointing feebly to the child, who is still waving his little flags, draws her last breath.

Pinkerton falls on his knees beside her, and Sharpless, picking up the child, turns from the tragic scene.

The opera ends with an enigmatic chord which has no suggestion of finality in it. Can it be intended to indicate that Kate also will have to suffer for the most despicable of all operatic heroes ?

TOSCA

Music by PUCCINI. *Words by* ILLICA *and* GIACOSA,
from SARDOU'S *drama.*
Rome, 1900; *London,* 1900; *New York,* 1901.

WHILE *Tosca*[1] after a prosperous career of a
quarter of a century still holds a prominent
place on the operatic stage, Sardou's drama
from which it was taken seems to have fallen out of the
repertory, possibly because no actress has cared to follow
the great Sarah Bernhardt in the title part written
especially for her. In the case of the opera, however, it
is probably the sensational character of the drama rather
than the lure of the music that is the vital element, since,
apart from the two numbers *Vissi d'arte* and *E lucevan le
stelle*, so dear to patrons of the gramophone, Puccini's
score contains little of the melodic charm which has
secured for *Bohème* and *Butterfly* so wide a popularity.

Tosca may perhaps be described as a fashionable rather
than a popular opera; the feast of horrors it supplies is
not altogether to the general taste, whereas the central
character makes a very special appeal to a more sophisti-
cated audience. The part of Floria Tosca, the brilliant,
voluptuous *diva*, swayed by alternate fits of passion and
piety, capable of daring all things for her lover, demands
for its interpretation an artist who is at once beautiful,
distinguished, in the highest degree ' temperamental,' and
powerful enough to convey to us three of the biggest
thrills to be found in any opera.

[1] My thanks are due to Messrs G. Ricordi and Co. for permitting me to
use their text of the opera.

Apart from the commanding figure of the heroine, it is as a highly coloured melodrama that *Tosca* makes its effect. The scene is Rome in the year 1800, a time when the name of Bonaparte was a terror to the monarchy, and anyone suspected of Republican tendencies stood in deadly peril. The tragedy turns upon the rivalry between Scarpia, the Chief of the Police, and Mario Cavaradossi, a young painter of Republican sympathies, for the possession of Floria Tosca, the beautiful singer and faithful mistress of Mario. Scarpia, on discovering that his rival has given shelter to Angelotti, a fugitive political prisoner, condemns him to torture and to death. Tosca, to save her lover, consents to yield to the desires of Scarpia, who accordingly gives orders to his officer, in Tosca's presence, to arrange for merely a mock execution. When he turns to claim his share of the bargain at Tosca's hands, she stabs him to the heart, and hurries off to acquaint her lover with the news. She is allowed to be present while the firing party arrives, does its duty, and departs. But Mario does not rise. Bending over his body, the horrified woman realizes the truth—Scarpia's agents had understood their orders in accordance with that villain's real intention. Mario is dead.

Meanwhile Scarpia's body has been found, and the guard arrives to arrest his murderers. Before they can take her, Floria Tosca has thrown herself from the walls of the castle of Sant' Angelo.

Act I. There is no overture : after a few *fortissimo* chords, ominous in their harsh progression, the curtain rises on the interior of the Jesuit church of Sant' Andrea in Rome. Raised on a platform to the left is a large canvas, with the painter's materials at hand ; on the right a private chapel, guarded by an image of the Blessed Virgin.

Some hurried syncopation in the orchestra brings on the dishevelled figure of the fugitive Angelotti, still in the prison garb in which he has just escaped from Sant' Angelo. Making straight for the shrine of the Madonna, he searches eagerly and finds at last a key with which he unlocks the door of the chapel and disappears inside. (This key has been placed there by his sister, the Marchesa Attavanti, the holder of the chapel, who has assisted in his escape.)

The orchestra now passes to a swinging rhythm in six-eight time for the shambling entrance of the Sacristan, the only comedy character in the opera ; so anxious is Puccini to make the most of him that he even uses a special sign to mark the various bars at which the good man is to give a nervous twitch to his shoulders. The Sacristan is busy with a sheaf of brushes that he is cleaning for the painter, Mario Cavaradossi, but breaks off at the sound of the Angelus bell. His prayer is hardly over when Mario enters and resumes work on his canvas—a representation of the Magdalen. Glancing at the picture, the Sacristan is surprised to find that it is a portrait of a lady whom he has lately noticed kneeling long in prayer before the Virgin's shrine. Mario, it seems, struck by her beauty, has given his saint the blue eyes and golden hair of this lady—none other than the Marchesa Attavanti, who has come hither to invoke the aid of Heaven on her brother's behalf. Puccini has found room here for one of the few purely lyrical pieces in the opera ; Mario takes from his pocket a miniature of Floria Tosca, and in the aria *Recondita armonia* contrasts the blonde beauty on his canvas with the darker, more compelling charm of Tosca, to whom all his love is given. The Sacristan is shocked at such unsuitable reflections, and, after a muttered denunciation of the painter as a " dog of a Voltairean " and a foe to the Government, leaves him alone.

Angelotti, supposing the church to be empty, now comes from his hiding-place, and is greeted as a friend and fellow by Cavaradossi, who has hardly time to lock the door of the church and press food and wine upon him from the basket the painter had brought for himself when Tosca's voice is heard outside, and the fugitive retires again to the chapel, taking the basket with him.

Floria Tosca now makes her entrance, in the *directoire* costume, the long stick, and large sheaf of flowers so familiar to a former generation from the many portraits of Bernhardt in one of her most famous parts. The long-drawn phrases on the violins convey to us the softer, more gracious side of Tosca's nature, while the scene that follows serves rapidly to develop some other aspects of her character—a not too pleasing mixture of sensuous passion and sentimental piety. The flowers she brings are for the Virgin's altar; these disposed of, she lays amorous siege to the willing Mario in the long solo *Non la sospiri, la nostra casetta*; although her lover responds with equal warmth, her mood soon changes to furious jealousy on recognizing in Mario's painting the likeness of the Attavanti, whom she at once imagines to be her rival. It requires a passage of tender protest on Mario's part, *Qual'occhio al mondo*, and a lengthy duet to calm Tosca's suspicions; at last she leaves him to his work, with the parting words: "Paint your saint with black eyes, not blue—black, like mine!"

Angelotti now ventures out again, and it is arranged that he shall go at once to the painter's villa, where he can lie safely hidden for the time in a secret chamber leading from a well in the garden. A noise outside alarms them, and Mario hurries the fugitive away through a door at the back of the chapel.

The orchestra, which has been almost superfluous during the dialogue, now wakes up as the Sacristan enters, out of breath, with the report of the defeat of Bonaparte and all the Powers of Darkness ; he has counted on annoying Mario by his news, since, according to his peculiar theology, " To vex an infidel is deserving of a big Indulgence." However, he has to content himself with the sympathy of the crowd of choristers and altar-boys who now rush into the church and rejoice noisily at the good tidings—there is to be a *Te Deum* that very evening, for which they will be paid extra, while at the Farnese Palace will be given a grand new cantata, and Floria Tosca is to sing.

The excitement is at its height when the stern figure of Scarpia is seen at the door of the church ; the boys steal meekly away, leaving the Sacristan alone with the Chief of the Police. Once more the music sinks necessarily into abeyance during the close dialogue which follows. Scarpia has reason to believe that Angelotti is hidden in the church. He questions the Sacristan, notes the half-finished portrait of the Marchesa Attavanti, then searches her private chapel ; here he discovers a fan with the Attavanti coat of arms, and the empty food basket—the property, as the Sacristan tells him, of Mario Cavaradossi. He concludes that Angelotti has certainly been in the church, and that Mario and the Marchesa have together assisted him to some safe hiding-place.

With the re-entrance of Tosca the musical interest rises in a steady *crescendo* to the final climax. She has come, expecting to find her lover, to tell him of her unforeseen engagement to sing at the Palace that evening—Scarpia at once sees his way to profit by Mario's absence and Tosca's disappointment.

To the subdued ding-dong of bells the villain, like another Iago, proceeds to pour his poison into Tosca's jealous heart. With suave flattery he compliments her on her fervent piety—she, the darling of the stage, can always find time for her devotion ; many women, indeed, come to church, but not all of them to pray—nay (with a glance at the portrait), some come merely to wanton with their lovers! Tosca's suspicious nature at once takes fire—Scarpia has but to show her the fan with the Attavanti coronet to convince her of Mario's faithlessness. She bursts into a passion of jealous rage—it is obvious that on leaving the church she will go straight to her lover in the hope of surprising him with her rival. Scarpia conducts Tosca to the door with grave courtesy—and gives orders to his officer, Spoletta, to follow her instantly and report to him without delay. Meanwhile the church has been filling with a devout and eager throng ; as the Cardinal and his train proceed up the aisle to the high altar the boom of cannon is heard without, and the organ floods the building with the strains of triumph. Scarpia has good reason to exult ; Cavaradossi and Tosca, fate has thrown them both into his power—the one he destines for the scaffold, the other for his own amorous arms. The mingled lust and hate that make up his long soliloquy stand out clearly against the background of the solemn *Te Deum* which fills the church and in which he finally joins. The whole *finale* is an undeniably fine piece of theatrical effect—it was very fitting that it should be repeated on the occasion of its first performance.

Act II. In spite of the necessary predominance of the heroine, it is a question whether the figure of the villain of the piece is not the finer operatic achievement. In the

previous Act we have his character firmly outlined—
Baron Scarpia, Chief of the Police, a name to tremble at
—a man made up of lust and craft and inexorable hate;
here we see him expanding in the hour of his expected
triumph. He is seated in his apartment at the Farnese
Palace; through the open window come the sounds of a
gavotte, for, on the floor below, the Queen of Naples has
a grand entertainment to celebrate the defeat of Bonaparte; it is here that the new cantata is to be given, in
which La Tosca will take the leading part. (It will help
us to realize the period if we recall that, in Sardou's drama,
Paisiello is the composer of the music, which he conducts
in person.)

All promises well for Scarpia, both in love and war; the
Republican forces have received a check, and two of their
supporters, Angelotti and Mario Cavaradossi, will soon
be in his power; with the removal of the latter the path
is clear to the attainment of his great desire—Mario gone,
Tosca surely cannot long resist him!

Scarpia, it will be remembered from the first Act, by
arousing her jealousy, had driven Tosca to hurry to Mario's
villa in the expectation of finding him with the Marchesa
Attavanti, and had ordered Spoletta to follow and spy
upon her actions. That officer now returns with his
report. Tosca had stayed but a short time at the villa;
search has been made for Angelotti, but in vain; Mario
Cavaradossi, denying all knowledge of the fugitive, has
been arrested, and is now at Scarpia's disposal.

Having written a short note to be handed to Tosca
so soon as the cantata should be ended, the Chief of the
Police orders Mario to be brought before him. The *diva's*
powerful voice is heard from the royal halls below as
Scarpia sternly accuses the young painter of aiding
and sheltering Angelotti, an enemy to the State; Mario

haughtily denies the charge, and disclaims all knowledge of the fugitive's movements.

The cantata now over, Tosca hastens into the room, surprised but not yet alarmed to find Mario present. From her affectionate greeting to her lover Scarpia argues that she had found at the villa not the Marchesa Attavanti but Angelotti, and had assisted at his concealment—he resolves to try a plan by which he hopes to obtain from Tosca the information which Mario may still persist in withholding.

The scene that follows is without doubt the most gruesome, the most harrowing, to be found in the whole of opera ; whether the situation is fit for artistic treatment is a matter of question—it is certainly a potent attraction for a certain section of opera-goers, and a favourite with the singers. Though the tenor's opportunities are comparatively slight, it is a great scene for the soprano and the baritone, both of whom must have exceptional dramatic power to enable them to carry it through with success.

Mario Cavaradossi is led into an adjoining room, where, as Scarpia puts it, his deposition will be taken ; the latter then proceeds to question Tosca as to her knowledge of Mario's dealings with Angelotti. Her first answers are given with haughty indifference ; she knows nothing— it is quite useless to question either her or Mario. " We shall see ! " says Scarpia—then, with an awful change of demeanour, he tells her the truth. In the next room, behind those doors, lies her lover, bound hand and foot— round his head an iron band with terrible claws which, at the turn of a screw, can tear the tender flesh, make blood gush from his temples, or crush the skull, if nothing else will serve. As Scarpia pauses the victim's groans begin, and the wretched woman is thus made to share each pang of the beloved, yet remains powerless to soothe or help him. Nay, says Scarpia, her lover's fate is in her own hands ; will she not shorten his agony by confessing all she knows ? She will not, dare not—she has pledged her word to Mario.

The torture is renewed with greater violence—a door is opened that she may more plainly hear the sufferer's groans—she is even allowed to see and speak with him. Cavaradossi is heroic in his agony, he is resolved to keep the secret to the end, and exhorts Tosca to equal firmness —he can even shout defiance at his enemy. A fine musical climax is here attained in a passage between Scarpia— with his ever more thunderous demand, " Say, where is Angelotti ? Where have you hidden him ? "—and Tosca with her growing frenzy of denial and refusal. This is succeeded by a short lull, as the exhausted woman gives way to a fit of quiet sobbing, and Spoletta mutters a verse of the *Dies iræ*.

But Scarpia, impatient of further delay, gives orders for a still sharper turn of the screw—the appalling cry wrung from the tortured man is too much for Tosca's weakened resistance; indeed, she has hardly strength to gasp out : " The well in the garden—Angelotti is hidden there."

At a word from Scarpia, Mario is brought in, bleeding, unconscious, and is laid on the sofa. Tosca flings herself beside the senseless form, covering it with tears and kisses. On regaining consciousness Mario's first fear is whether, in his delirium, he may have betrayed the secret of Angelotti's hiding-place ; Tosca has hardly time to assure him to the contrary when Scarpia, with diabolical inten- tion, turns to Spoletta with the words : " *Go ! Search the well in the garden !* "

Mario knows that Tosca must have given the information ; he curses, but has scarcely strength to cast her from him, when a messenger arrives with tidings that galvanize the young Republican into new life. To-day's rejoicings have been premature; Napoleon has retrieved his fortunes by a decisive victory at Marengo. Now comes one of the finest moments in the opera. With a great shout of " Victory ! " Mario contrives to stagger from the couch, confront his enemy Scarpia, and hurl insults and defiance at him in his share of the short trio *L'alba vindice appar'*, a vigorous piece of vocal writing, doubly welcome after the prolonged melodrama which has been the only possible accompaniment of the previous action.

Mario is led away to execution ; Tosca makes a wild but futile attempt to cling to him—she is thrust violently back by the guard, and the door is closed. She is alone with the cruel and lustful Scarpia.

The rest of the Act, with the exception of Tosca's one lyrical passage, is really Scarpia's. With the suavity peculiar to the stage villain in his most deadly mood, he invites Tosca to join him at the table where supper is waiting—at least she will taste a glass of wine ? Fie ! so fair a lady should not so distress herself ! Doubtless in a little talk together they will be able to arrange some plan for setting Mario at liberty. Tosca only partly grasps his meaning. " How much do you demand for his release ? " she asks. " Name your price ! " But it is not money that will satisfy this man, who now shows her his real nature. He has always loved her, always desired her, but what he has seen to-day has increased his passion tenfold. In a fiery passage, *Già mi struggea l'amor della diva,* he tells her how her tears and caresses for her lover, her scorn and hatred of himself, have fanned the flame of his desire—he has sworn to possess her ! Horrified and desperate, Tosca answers with words of anger and loathing that serve merely to whet his lust. "I hate you! I hate you!" she cries, "villain and coward!" "What matter!" he replies; "love and hate are all one to me when once I have you safely in my arms!" He pursues her round the room, she shrieking wildly for help—when both are arrested by the throbbing of a drum; it is the guard escorting a party of doomed men to the scaffold. Mario, says Scarpia, has but an hour to live—but Tosca may save him yet. This prolonged passage of repose, where nothing is heard but the ominous tap of the drum, blending with the faint suggestion of a funeral march in the orchestra, is certainly one of the happiest ideas in the opera—it prepares us admirably for Tosca's famous solo, *Vissi d'arte, vissi d'amore*. Although the effect is pathetic, it cannot be said that the melody here is either novel or distinguished; in the second section, *Sempre con fè sincera*, good use is made in the orchestra of the suave theme that heralds Tosca's appearance in the church in Act I. The song is a wail of self-pity; Tosca, who, with all her faults, has done many deeds of kindness and preserved some fervour of religion, finds it hard that she herself should be left to suffer such cruelty from another.

At the end she kneels to Scarpia, imploring him to spare her lover's life. He is beginning again to press her for the only price he will accept, when Spoletta enters the room: Angelotti has been found, but has succeeded in taking his own life. "Then," says Scarpia, "let his dead body hang on the gallows!" "And the other— Mario Cavaradossi?" asks Spoletta. Scarpia looks at Tosca: "What say you now?" he whispers.

Her lover's peril is too imminent—Tosca signifies her willingness to pay the price, provided that Mario is at once set free. That, says Scarpia, is impossible—it is necessary that the mere form of execution shall first be gone through. He turns to Spoletta: "The prisoner Cavaradossi will not be hanged—he must be shot—but only blank cartridges are to be used, *as was done in the case of Count Palmieri*—a mock execution—you understand me?" Yes—Spoletta understands quite well what his master intends. Tosca is satisfied, the more as she herself will be allowed to be present, and will tell Mario what to do—furthermore, she demands a safe conduct for herself and Mario, who will leave Rome at once.

During the long passage of melodrama that accompanies the writing and sealing of the necessary passport Tosca manages to get possession of a sharp knife from the supper-table. Scarpia has finished writing, and advances on her with arms open to embrace her: "At last, my Tosca! Mine at last!" "At last!" she cries, "here is my kiss!"—and stabs him to the heart. Escaping the clutches of the dying man, she mocks him in his agony: "Yes! Look at me! I am Tosca—and there lies Scarpia, slain by a woman's hand!" She bends over him, listening greedily for the death-rattle: "Die, then, with God's curse upon you!"

Then her mood changes. Now Scarpia is dead Tosca must forgive him—nay, even say a prayer for his sin-stained soul. She takes two candles from the table and places them on either side his head—the large crucifix from the wall she lays upon his breast. But for these lights the stage is in darkness as Tosca leaves the room.

The torture scene of this Act, as given in the opera, though sufficiently harassing for most tastes, is but a modification of the horrors of Sardou's drama as produced at the Porte-Saint-Martin theatre in 1887. The realistic treatment then adopted was, in fact, too much for the first-night audience, and some considerable retrenchment of the blood-curdling details had to be made for subsequent performances ; the Fat Boy, it was felt, had gone too far in his desire to make our flesh creep. Of the critics, the judicious Jules Lemaître did not hesitate to utter a vigorous protest : " M. Sardou," he wrote in the *Journal des Débats*, " a soif de sang. Il est le Caligula du drame."

Act III. In a melodrama of this kind, which depends largely on a cumulative series of harrowing incidents, it is not always easy for the composer to find sufficient opportunities for the necessary periods of relief. In the preceding Act the audience has been kept on the rack even more continuously than the tortured Mario ; Puccini must have felt that we should all be glad of a rest, and he deserves our gratitude for the opening of Act III.

After a short but impressive theme has been given out by the horns, our eyes and ears are soothed on the rising of the curtain. We see a platform on the roof of the castle of Sant' Angelo, under a starry sky—in the distance, though hardly visible as yet, are the Vatican and the dome of St Peter's ; the quiet beauty of the scene is enhanced by the distant tinkle of sheep-bells, and some snatches of an antique song from a shepherd in the valley below. But now the dawn begins to break, and from far around comes the clear sound of matin-bells from church and convent. As the light grows, we notice the details of the stage setting ; we are aware of a sort of chamber in the wall in which are chairs and a table, with heavy registers upon it, and a crucifix above ; also in a corner of the platform the head of a stairway leading to the floor below. From this a gaoler presently appears, to prepare for the arrival of the firing party with the prisoner. He has just lit the lamp in front of the crucifix when Mario is brought in under escort.

He is informed that he has just an hour to live. The proffered services of a priest are rejected by this sturdy Voltairean—he has only one request, to be allowed to write a letter. The gaoler is bribed by the offer of a costly ring to supply him with paper and pen, and Mario is left alone.

But it is obvious that the tenor cannot be allowed to waste the precious moments in selfish silence—very soon the pen is laid aside, and Mario indulges in sweet, sad memories of his first meeting with her for whom the letter is intended—the beloved Tosca, whom he will never see again. The result is the well-known air *E lucevan le stelle*, a picturesque romance memorable for its sonorous climax on the words *e muoio disperato.*

Tosca now enters; too excited to speak, she merely thrusts the order for their safe conduct into his hands; but the necessary explanation is soon given in the vigorous movement *Il tuo sangue o il mio amore*, a fine piece of straightforward declamation with just sufficient support from the orchestra, which supplies an echo of the drum-taps and the funeral march that were the features of the scene described.

Tosca alternately shudders and exults at the thought of her fearful experience—" These hands of mine," she says, " were steeped in Scarpia's blood ! " This gives occasion for Mario's amorous outburst, *O dolci mani, mansuete e pure*, and a long duet follows, in which they picture the perfect happiness that awaits them in the future.

It is doubtful at first whether Mario is quite convinced —he seems almost to have a presentiment of the awful truth ; but Tosca's exuberant confidence prevails with him, and the two join in a fine outburst of hope and love triumphant, *Trionfal di nova speme*, to the melody given out by the horns at the beginning of the Act. But the hour will soon be over—there is still much to be arranged.

The poignant pathos of the remainder of this Act, achieved as it is by quite legitimate means, has a certain artistic value far superior to the crude horrors that have gone before. Tosca is excited to the point of gaiety; Mario has a part to act, and she will coach him in the "business"; as soon as the muskets go off, he must be sure to drop flat on the ground, just like a dead man— Tosca, the actress, is of course familiar with the trick, and can show him how an effective stage fall is managed. The two can even laugh together over their little piece of play-acting; yet, somehow, we feel that Mario is acting merely for Tosca's sake—he himself is certain what the end will be. The situation is finely conceived and really touches us to pity and terror.

The clock strikes four, and the sun is rising, when the firing party lead Mario to the spot where the sentence is to be carried out—" a mock execution, *just as in the case of Count Palmieri.*" Spoletta has not forgotten how that nobleman died.

Tosca waits impatiently for the farce to be ended; she has no misgivings—but must stop her ears when the muskets go off; she is delighted with the way in which Mario manages his fall: "Like a true artist!" she comments. Then, as the soldiers disappear down the stairway, she moves warily toward the spot where Mario lies—covered over with a cloth. She cautions him not to move yet— they might return! She listens at the stairs until the footsteps have quite died away—then she flies to her lover: "Mario! Mario! Get up! 'Tis time now!"

But Mario does not stir—neither did the Count Palmieri.

Tosca raises the cloth——

Fortunately she has but little time to suffer. The body of Scarpia has been discovered, and Spoletta with his men are heard approaching, on the track of the murderess.

As they pour on to the stage, Floria Tosca takes the only way—she mounts the parapet, and finds her death below the walls of the castle of Sant' Angelo.

LOUISE [1]

Words and Music by CHARPENTIER.
Paris, 1900 ; *New York,* 1908 ; *London,* 1909.

THIS work has probably had a greater success upon the English stage than any French opera since *Carmen*. No doubt this is largely due to the performance of Madame Edvina in the title-rôle, where she scored a triumph that will not be forgotten by those who witnessed the first London productions of Charpentier's work. But the piece itself contains novel qualities that account for much of its attraction, and at the same time make it difficult to fit into any definite category. *Louise* is one of the few operas that deal with contemporary life. This by itself might incline us to class it with Puccini's *La Bohème*, especially as in both cases the scene is laid in Paris, but Charpentier's libretto shows a more vivid sense of the picturesque side of Parisian life than is to be found in the work of the Italian composer. The style of the music, too, is completely different. Limpid, light, and unmistakably French, it nevertheless exhibits a closely woven texture into which are introduced constantly running fragments of tune that remind us in spite of ourselves of the Wagnerian *leit-motif*. And yet *Louise* is almost as remote from Wagner as it is from Puccini. Seldom or never do these fragments assume the supreme importance that is theirs in the work of the German master, where they are at once the structural framework of the opera and the elements from which long melodies and even complete tunes are evolved.

[1] This analysis is contributed by Mr Peter Latham.

Here they are rather bubbles that from time to time
float to the surface of the orchestral river. They have
no history, they are seen and they disappear, only to
reappear again. Or they are like the sounds that detach
themselves at intervals from among the dull murmurs of
a great city, sounds insignificant enough taken singly,
but containing in their sum the very spirit of the place
and its inhabitants.

Thus it is that in the short, epigrammatic Prelude we
are transported at once to Paris, Paris the gay and careless, the paradise of young artists, and the very home of
freedom. And thus, when the curtain goes up and shows
us Louise in the humble living-room of her parents'
house we are not in the least surprised to see a young man
standing outside his studio opposite and pouring out his
love with a passion and vehemence that in London would
bring a couple of policemen on the scene before he had
finished a dozen bars. This is Julien, and it soon appears
that Louise is not indifferent to his advances. She goes
to the window and there follows a duet, in the course of
which it becomes clear that, like other lovers, they have
their difficulties. Louise's parents, it seems, do not entirely trust unattached young artists. Her mother, in
particular, has assumed an attitude which the young
couple are inclined bitterly to resent. But what matter?
They have managed to meet none the less! Unfortunately the mother, entering quietly, has overheard the
last part of the conversation, and when Louise turns
from the window the situation is distinctly awkward.
The mother, naturally annoyed, mocks at her daughter's
transports and gives her a good scolding. Louise im-
prudently allows herself to be drawn into a discussion
which only make things worse. " Shameless girl ! "
exclaims the mother, " instead of hiding your face you

dare to boast of your lover!" "My lover!" cries Louise, "he is not that yet; but, really, one would think that you wished him to become it!" "Little wretch," says the incensed parent, "be careful that I don't tell the whole story to your father."

At this moment the father's step is heard on the stairs. He enters, a letter in his hand. Louise takes heart again, for Julien, before they were separated, had shown her a letter that he was sending to her parents, telling her that it contained a request for her hand. During the meal which follows the conversation comes mainly from the father, who is in philosophic mood. He is a poor man and has to work hard for his living. But are the rich any better off than he is? All a man wants is good health, a happy home, and a loving family. These he has got, and he asks no more. After dinner the matter of the letter is introduced. The father is inclined to be reasonable; his idea is to make some inquiries about the young man, and ask him in one evening. But the mother, stung by the memory that Julien has laughed at her, will not hear of it, and Louise, attempting to defend her lover, only receives a smack for her pains. Her father tries to comfort her. If they are thwarting her, they are doing it for her good; choosing a husband is not an easy business; she lacks experience, and love is proverbially blind. He has not yet made up his mind about Julien, but what he has heard of him so far has not been very encouraging. If he separates them now, Louise may live to thank him some day. She loves her father, does she not? Very well; he also loves her. But she must obey him.

Louise is in despair. In compliance with his request she takes the evening paper and starts to read to him. But her voice is stifled with sobs; she stops and breaks down in tears.

Act II opens with a graphic orchestral picture, " Paris awakes." The curtain then rises on an open space in front of the house at which Louise works. It is five o'clock in the morning. We need not concern ourselves with the sociological lessons which Charpentier wished to teach in *Louise*. All we need to know is that this very picturesque scene is designed to show the dangers of the girl's position. Freedom is all very well, but daughters who refuse to take good advice, however distasteful it may be, are apt to get into serious trouble and bring nothing but misery on themselves and those who love them.

Dotted about the stage are various figures typical of the Paris streets at dawn. To them enters the " Noctambule," a young man in evening dress. He plays no part in the general action of the play, and like the rest is rather a type than a character. He is the very essence of the gay night-life of Paris, the thoughtless, irresponsible ' Night Wanderer.' Blessed with the gift of youth and riches he goes about in the pursuit of pleasure, ignorant, or at least careless, of the suffering around him. A social parasite and an egotist to the core, he can be cruel in the satisfaction of his whims. Should they cause ruin to his victims, so much the worse for them. The attractive but rather sinister figure is thus the very embodiment of the temptations that beset Louise.

Gradually the light increases and these strange characters disappear. A band of Bohemians arrives, Julien among them. It soon appears that he is bent on carrying off Louise. She will come to work as usual, escorted by her mother, but the mother will leave her at the door and Julien will rush forward and persuade her to run away with him. One by one the Bohemians depart, wishing him good luck, and saying they will make Louise their Muse, a phrase that is explained later. All falls out as

arranged, but Julien finds it more difficult than he anticipated to persuade Louise to elope. She loves him, yes !
but she is frightened, and evading his ardent appeals
she slips back into the workshop. Throughout the scene
there is a constant stream of typical Parisian characters
passing across the stage at the back.

Scene ii shows the interior of the workroom. The
girls are all at work, chattering and gossiping the while.
Louise alone, sitting a little apart from the rest, sews
in silence. They suspect her of being in love, and start
to tease her, but are distracted by the sound of music
in the street. It is Julien with his guitar. At first they
are charmed and throw him coppers and kisses, to the
annoyance of Louise, who begins to wish she had gone
off with him as he suggested. But they soon tire of his
persistent eloquence and call to him to change his song.
Suddenly Louise gets up and puts on her hat. She is
not well and is going home. No, she requires no escort.
As soon as the door has closed behind her, the girls,
suspecting something of the truth, crowd to the window.
Louise appears in the street, and—walks off with Julien !
The girls turn back into the room amid peals of laughter.

Act III. The scene now changes to a little rustic
house and garden in the Butte Montmartre. In the background, over the hedge, Paris appears like a panorama.
It is evening, some time after the events of the preceding
Scene. A Prelude, entitled *Vers la cité lointaine*, prepares
us for the rising of the curtain, which shows us Julien,
a book in his hand, seated in a chair in the garden. Behind him is Louise, her face radiant with happiness.
She comes forward and tells him of her love and the joy
of surrender in a song, *Depuis le jour*, a lyric inspiration
of real beauty that has become as well known on the
concert platform as on the operatic stage. The dialogue

that follows is a good deal too long. The memory of the objections raised by her parents to her union with Julien leads Louise to ask if love should really be guided by experience. This gives him the opportunity for some shallow philosophizing, while the night falls, and in the distant city lights begin to appear. Turning toward it the lovers deliver an invocation praying it to protect them, its children. Paris seems to respond with a promise of freedom, and after an ecstatic outburst of passionate song they go slowly into the house.

A change in the music, which begins to glitter with strange orchestral effects, announces a fresh development. Outside in the road appears a Bohemian. He jumps the hedge, looks carefully round, and seeing that the coast is clear, beckons to another. They open the gate to yet three more who enter staggering under a huge burden. This turns out to consist of Venetian lanterns, streamers, and other decorations with which they hastily adorn the façade and door of the cottage. A fresh crowd of Bohemians, men and girls, arrives, followed by the good people of the neighbourhood, who have considerable misgivings about what is going to happen next. Finally the "Noctambule," dressed up as *Le Pape des fous,* comes in with mock dignity. The stage, which has assumed an exceedingly picturesque aspect, is now ready. A Bohemian who has climbed to the roof of the house points to Louise, who has appeared with Julien, and in a short speech announces that they have assembled to instal her as the "Muse of Montmartre." This they proceed to do. There is plenty of shouting and dancing and a *danseuse* executes a *pas seul,* after which, as representative of all the Bohemians, she presents Louise with a crown made of roses that the girls have brought with them. There are speeches from the *Pape des fous* and from an old Bohemian, and Louise, who has shyly signified her acceptance of their homage, is hailed with acclamations. Then comes the *dénouement*. There is a sudden interruption of the revels. The brightly dressed crowd parts asunder and there in the background is a single veiled figure, dressed all in black. It is Louise's mother. Timidly she starts to come forward. Some Bohemians make a half-hearted attempt to stop her, but the crowd quickly melts away and she is left alone with Louise and Julien. She has a message to deliver : Louise's father has been prostrated by grief at her elopement and is now very ill. Will she come ? The lovers are deeply moved, but Julien is distrustful. His fears are somewhat allayed, however, when the mother promises to let the girl return to him, and reluctantly he gives his consent. Louise embraces him and then slowly and regretfully follows her mother from the scene.

Act IV brings us back to the house of the parents. The houses opposite have been pulled down and a view of Paris has thus been opened up. Otherwise nothing is changed. Louise is visible in her room, at work. Her father is seated near the table in the living-room. He has almost recovered from his illness, but is sunk in gloomy thoughts from which his wife vainly endeavours to distract him. Gone now is his contentment with his lot ; he has loved his daughter and believed that she loved him, but the call of young blood has been too strong, and all his efforts for her sake have only resulted in estranging her from him. The memory of all they have done for her has been blotted out by the mere glance of a stranger. Curses on him ! The mother goes to Louise in the next room and begs her to come and soothe her father. Unfortunately she cannot resist the temptation to scold her, and allows it to slip out that they have no intention of letting her return to Julien, promise or no promise. The girl comes into the living-room, goes to her father, and meekly but coldly wishes him good-night. In a pitiful attempt to win her over he takes her on his knee and rocks her as he had done when she was a child. It is her loving parents who are with her ; all they desire is her happiness. But the inevitable answer comes at once : " If you desire my happiness you have only to make a sign." And so the useless discussion goes on once more, till at last, in answer to another appeal, her father exclaims, " Ah, she that speaks is not my daughter ! my only joy ! my hope ! my beauty ! " " My beauty ! " How sweet these words had sounded on her lover's lips. Distant echoes from the town seem to repeat the phrase, and forgetful of all else she turns to the window and invokes Paris, in the name of freedom, to come to her rescue. Her father, who is beginning to lose his temper, closes the window, but this only has the effect of directing her thoughts to Julien. To him she will return ! And with words of passionate love on her lips she makes for the door. Her father blocks the way and she turns back. But her resolution is unshaken : Julien will soon come and take back his love. This is too much for the old man ; in a transport of rage he flings open the door ! " Go then ! Go and enjoy yourself ! Go to the city ! They are waiting for you—go ! " Louise, terrified by his change of tone, hesitates. But he picks up a chair as though to throw it at her, and with a cry of fright she rushes from the room. Immediately his anger cools. He follows her on to the staircase and his voice is heard calling " Louise ! " But it is too late : she has gone. Slowly he comes back, and stops, listening to the sounds of the city. Then, raising his fist and shaking it, he cries despairingly " O Paris ! ! ! " as the curtain falls.

PELLÉAS ET MÉLISANDE

Music by DEBUSSY. *Words by* MAETERLINCK.
Paris, 1902 ; *New York*, 1908 ; *London*, 1909.

IT is exceedingly difficult to give a description of this amazing work that shall be at once just and sympathetic, or even to convey any definite impression of its quality, so remote is it from all other operas. Everything in it is different ; of drama there is the least possible allowance ; scene after scene passes in which the characters do nothing but talk, and their talk is of a strange, unintelligible nature. The dialogue is carried on largely in the language of every day, lapsing at times into a childish simplicity which can hardly fail to irritate, while we are often puzzled to understand exactly what bearing it has upon the situation. So with the scanty and disjointed action. Great emphasis is laid on incidents whose significance is not apparent ; the importance of the actors seems dwarfed at times by that of the scenic surroundings, which assume here and there almost the place of a protagonist ; the climax is already reached in Act IV, and the last Act, like the first, is almost wholly given over to vague dialogue.

As for the music, it is impossible in so short a compass to give any but the sketchiest outline of the methods by which Debussy works his lovely magic ; all is so new, so strange at first, that it may well bewilder, but we end by acknowledging that it lights up, interprets, and transcends the text with the sure intuition of genius in a way that no other composer has ever approached.

The vocal part consists largely of an unfettered recitative

that follows with remarkable fidelity the inflexions of the speaking voice, except in moments of exalted passion, where certain lyrical passages are introduced that seem to spring naturally from the situation.   This is obviously the only treatment possible for Maeterlinck's peculiar dialogue, and Debussy has applied it with perfect success ; there are passages in *Pelléas et Mélisande* which come very near to realizing the ideals of the Renaissance scholars who in 1600 set out to restore the methods of Greek Tragedy, though the apter comparison would be with the Gregorian Chant of the Roman Church, in the study of which the composer is known to have been deeply immersed.

But the real interest lies in the orchestra, and here again both structure and texture are so peculiar that it is hardly possible to give any idea of the music except by actual quotation.   Two striking features, however, must be noted.   First there are the startling harmonies, almost revolutionary it would seem in their novelty, yet based, as the composer maintained, on the fundamental principles of acoustics, combined with a reverential study of the voices of Nature.   The second feature is absolutely original ; in each Act, although the dramatic action may be interrupted by several changes of scene, the music forms a continuous symphonic poem, never admitting of a full close until the end.

After these very imperfect indications of what is to be expected of this unique musical drama, we will proceed to give some account of its development.

The story resembles in outline that of Paolo and Francesca. Golaud, who has been a widower for some years, takes a young girl, Mélisande, for his second wife ; she is drawn by an irresistible affinity to the love of Pelléas, his younger brother ; Golaud discovers the secret, and kills Pelléas.

The other characters are the aged King Arkel, grand-father of the two brothers, Geneviève their mother, and Yniold, the little son of Golaud. The whole atmosphere is unmistakably Poesque ; the scenery has its psychology as well as the men and women, on whom it exercises a powerful influence ; the domain of Allemonde, where the action takes place, is assuredly not far distant from

> . . . the dim lake of Auber
> In the misty mid region of Weir.

We will analyse the first Act in some detail, in order to show the general manner in which the drama is con-ducted.

Act I. *Scene* i. Golaud, while on a hunting expedi-tion far from home, comes upon a young girl, Mélisande, sitting by a well in a wood and sobbing bitterly. Drawn by her beauty and her distress, he questions her, but with little result—she will only say that she comes from a far land from which she has fled, and that she has lost her way. " From whom, then, hast thou fled ? Who hath done thee wrong ? " asks Golaud. " All men ! " is the reply.

At the bottom of the well he spies the glitter of a crown, evidently fallen from her head, and proposes to recover it for her. But no—she will not have it—it was the crown " he " gave her, she says, and offers no further word of explanation.

Mélisande is beautiful, and very young—Golaud's hair, as she frankly tells him, is already turning grey ; neverthe-less she lets him lead her out of the wood. We hear no more of the crown, nor of him who gave it to her. " Where are we going ? " asks the girl. " I know not," is Golaud's answer ; " I too have lost my way."

Scene ii. The interior of Arkel's castle, where we find

the aged, half-blind king with his daughter Geneviève, the mother of Golaud and Pelléas. She reads him a letter that Golaud has written to Pelléas announcing his return in three days' time, accompanied by the youthful Mélisande, his six months' bride. He has not informed them of his marriage—the girl is from a strange and far-off country, and he is doubtful as to the feelings of his family ; if they are willing to receive her, let them hang from the castle turret a light that may be seen from the ship on which he is returning. To Pelléas, who makes a very brief appearance, this task is assigned.

Scene III. Borne as it were on the stream of the orchestra we pass to the gardens of the castle. A gloomy region this, hidden in the midst of vast forests, so dense in parts that the sun is never seen ; only toward the sea is there any open sky. Geneviève and Mélisande are gazing toward the light, when Pelléas enters from that direction. The talk now is all of the sea. 'Tis to the sea, says Geneviève, that they must look for their light, but now even the sea is darkling. There will be a storm to-night, thinks Pelléas. As he speaks, the voices of sailors are heard, putting out to sea ; as the ship sails into the light Mélisande recognizes it as the one which had brought her to Allemonde—ah ! why should that ship put out to sea in the face of a tempest ?

The night falls suddenly. Geneviève turns to go home, leaving Pelléas to show Mélisande the way. He offers to lead her by the hand—but both her hands are full of flowers—then he must take her arm in his, so steep is the path, so dark the night.

" To-morrow," he says, " I may be going away ! "
" Ah ! " cries the girl, " why should you go ? "

So ends the first Act : the remaining four preserve a consistent similarity of treatment. It is plain that by this flat, bald dialogue, this languid trickle of action, something more is intended than is at first apparent. The truth is that all must be interpreted by the light of symbolism ; certain words, for instance, as light and darkness, forest and sea, must be understood in their symbolic values ; read in this way, each phrase, each incident, will be found to have its full significance. But such specialized discernment is not for all of us ; it is to the orchestra that we must turn for enlightenment, and few can fail to be impressed by the marvellous art with which Debussy succeeds in creating an atmosphere which conveys the very spirit of the scene, as well as the vague emotions of the shadowy figures before us.

It seems advisable in the case of *Pelléas et Mélisande* to depart from our usual custom of giving a detailed analysis of each Act—this would entail quoting passage after passage of the symbolist dialogue, which, when divorced from the music, is generally tedious. We must content ourselves with disentangling the thin thread of the drama from the many scenes which consist of little but talk.

Act II. *Scene* i shows us Pelléas and Mélisande sitting by the fountain in the castle grounds at midday. The girl is playing with her wedding-ring, which falls into the well and is seen no more. Some mysterious connexion is evidently intended between this scene and the opening episode of the opera where Golaud first meets Mélisande by the well, into which her crown has fallen.

Consequently in *Scene* ii we are not surprised to find that Golaud has been telepathically affected by Mélisande's action. He is lying injured, on a couch, tended by his young wife ; while hunting on the previous day he was thrown from his horse while the bells were sounding for midday, the precise time at which the ring was lost ;

as he fondles Mélisande's fingers he notices its absence
and demands an explanation. Mélisande lies to him:
she dropped the ring, she says, in a cave by the sea when
she was gathering shells, and it is still there. Golaud
sternly bids her go at once and recover it. She is afraid
to go alone? Then let Pelléas accompany her.

Scene iii. The entrance to the sea-cave. The two
stand hand-in-hand in the darkness, waiting for the moon
to light them—they have come, apparently, in order to
be able to describe the spot at which the ring is supposed
to have been dropped. When at last the moon shines
out it shows, within the cave, the forms of three old men
with long white hair, asleep. " There is famine in the
land," is Pelléas's comment. [While we faithfully record
such incidents, we must leave it to the reader's ingenuity
to explain them.]

Act III. *Scene* i. This is the first real love-scene in
the opera. Mélisande is combing her hair at the window
of her bower in the turret. Though it is near midnight
Pelléas happens to be passing by, and begs Mélisande to
reach him her hand that he may kiss it. As she leans far
out of the window the whole mass of her long hair—
" longer than myself," is her own description—falls over
Pelléas, hiding him for the moment in a cloak of rippling
gold. Passion awakes in him, and he requires many
words and images to express his lover's ecstasy while
he holds her captive by her hair. After Mélisande's
white doves have flown out from her tower—" never
again to return," she says—Golaud comes upon them
thus entangled. " Such children! Such children!"
he remarks—" laughing nervously," as the stage direction has it—and walks off with Pelléas.

Scene ii. The atmosphere here is that of " The House
of Usher." Golaud has brought Pelléas down to the

mouldering caverns underneath the castle—there are pools of stagnant water, and the whole place reeks of death. The elder man takes Pelléas by the arm and makes him lean over a projecting rock : " Do you see the gulf on the edge of which you are standing, Pelléas ? "

But Golaud's arm is shaking ominously—Pelléas rises : " It is stifling here," he says ; " let us go ! "

The change from the gloom to a sunlit terrace in the gardens gives Debussy occasion for one of his loveliest tonal pictures, which Pelléas accompanies by a vocal rhapsody on the beauty of the scene. Golaud then proceeds in the baldest possible language to tell his brother that he has noticed there is something between him and his wife. " I know, of course," he says, " that there is no harm in it—nothing but childish folly. But Mélisande is about to become a mother, and we must be careful not to upset her ; so, for the present, it will be best for you to keep away from her."

Scene iv.   This is the Scene which has given such great offence to many—and, indeed, it is difficult to defend it.

Golaud and his little son Yniold are seated below the window of Mélisande's room in the turret. Knowing that the child is often with Mélisande, he questions him closely as to what he has seen pass between her and Pelléas. At last, suspecting his brother to be even now in her room, he lifts the child up to the level of the window, to play the spy and report on what he sees.

" They are silent," says Yniold ; " they are standing apart, and both are looking at the light."

The Scene is frankly unpleasant, both in conception and detail—its object, apparently, is to establish Mélisande's innocence.

Act IV.   *Scene* i.   A short scene for the lovers in which

they agree to meet that evening for the last time—
Pelléas leaves on the morrow. Incidentally he mentions
the strange recovery of his father, who has been lying ill
for a long time in the castle; this event Pelléas looks
upon as the happiest of omens for the future.

Scene II. The aged King Arkel harps also on this
theme. In a long monologue for the benefit of Mélisande
he expresses his sympathy with her obvious unhappiness,
and hints that now sickness has at last been banished
from the castle all things else will take a turn for the
better. Unfortunately for his theory, Golaud enters at
this moment, his long-pent jealousy in flood at last. The
innocent testimony of the child Yniold, the memory
of Pelléas and Mélisande bound together in the meshes
of her long golden hair—these things have fermented in
his brain, and now the boiling torrent of passion is poured
out upon his young wife. Harsh words lead to brutal
action : seizing her by the long hair he drags her up and
down the stage until old Arkel interferes. " Absalom !
Absalom ! " shouts the madman, as he hauls the wretched
girl along. " Is he drunk ? " asks Arkel. " No ! " replies Mélisande, " but he does not love me any more—
and I am not happy ! "

Scene III. We are again by the fountain. The child
Yniold is provided with a solo in which he laments his
inability to move a boulder behind which he has lost his
golden ball; he is also interested in the distant bleating
of some sheep which are being driven to the slaughter-
house. [Here once more we appeal to the reader's
interpretative powers !]

Scene IV. The last meeting of Pelléas and Mélisande.
In the moonlight by the fountain, under shelter of the
linden-tree, they make the first definite mutual avowal of
their love. The language here is fortunately purged to a

great extent of symbolism, and goes no farther than the usual extravagance of lovers' talk.

> PELLÉAS.   Come into the light! Here 'tis too dark for us to see our happiness.
> MÉLISANDE. Nay, let us stay here! I feel I am closer to you in the darkness!

Alas! their time is short. A harsh grating sound is heard—it is the closing of the castle gates for the night. The lovers find a positive happiness in the thought that fate has decided for them. "All is lost now—yet all is won!" Their passion rises to the height of ecstasy —they know, they feel that someone is coming, that death is nearing, yet they only hold each other in a closer embrace.

Then Golaud steals behind them, unseen—his sword descends, and Pelléas falls dead beside the fountain's brim.

Act V. Mélisande's chamber. She has been delivered before her time of a little girl, and now lies at the point of death.

Golaud, filled with remorse, asks pardon of Mélisande, which she freely grants. But his worst torment comes from the doubt which he still entertains as to her relations with Pelléas. He asks her plainly, "Was her love for Pelléas a guilty passion?" Her simple "No!" fails to satisfy him: again he implores her, under the shadow of death, to tell the truth. She still persists in her former answer—how can he suppose the contrary? But Mélisande is soon past questioning, and Golaud's doubts are still unsolved, when she passes away with her little child beside her—seeming herself so small, so innocent, that, as old Arkel says, she might well be, not its mother, but an elder sister.

A more thankless task could hardly be imagined than

to attempt such a skeleton analysis of Maeterlinck's text, to which Debussy has only too faithfully adhered ; yet, vague, elusive, even meaningless, as it must seem at a first approach, it has the one supreme merit of having inspired the composer with a musical masterpiece. The talent of Maeterlinck is happily merged in the genius of Debussy. If we find the drama difficult of comprehension, it is to the orchestra, as we said before, that we must look for enlightenment. Here Debussy holds up for us the seer's crystal globe in which before us pass the thoughts and emotions of the characters, the scenes in which they move, and, behind all, the shadows of "vast, formless things" that weave their inevitable destinies. All is like

> Chases in arras, dreams in a career—

but, however fleeting the vision, Debussy has contrived that it shall be invariably lovely in colour and design.

It is probable that the opera of *Pelléas et Mélisande* will long outlive the play of that name; yet what lover of Debussy but must wish that the composer could have had for his partner, not Maeterlinck, the experimental symbolist, but that "august master of beauty," Edgar Allan Poe !

A CATALOGUE OF SELECTED DOVER BOOKS
IN ALL FIELDS OF INTEREST

AMERICA'S OLD MASTERS, James T. Flexner. Four men emerged unexpectedly from provincial 18th century America to leadership in European art: Benjamin West, J. S. Copley, C. R. Peale, Gilbert Stuart. Brilliant coverage of lives and contributions. Revised, 1967 edition. 69 plates. 365pp. of text.

21806-6 Paperbound $3.00

FIRST FLOWERS OF OUR WILDERNESS: AMERICAN PAINTING, THE COLONIAL PERIOD, James T. Flexner. Painters, and regional painting traditions from earliest Colonial times up to the emergence of Copley, West and Peale Sr., Foster, Gustavus Hesselius, Feke, John Smibert and many anonymous painters in the primitive manner. Engaging presentation, with 162 illustrations. xxii + 368pp.

22180-6 Paperbound $3.50

THE LIGHT OF DISTANT SKIES: AMERICAN PAINTING, 1760-1835, James T. Flexner. The great generation of early American painters goes to Europe to learn and to teach: West, Copley, Gilbert Stuart and others. Allston, Trumbull, Morse; also contemporary American painters—primitives, derivatives, academics—who remained in America. 102 illustrations. xiii + 306pp. 22179-2 Paperbound $3.50

A HISTORY OF THE RISE AND PROGRESS OF THE ARTS OF DESIGN IN THE UNITED STATES, William Dunlap. Much the richest mine of information on early American painters, sculptors, architects, engravers, miniaturists, etc. The only source of information for scores of artists, the major primary source for many others. Unabridged reprint of rare original 1834 edition, with new introduction by James T. Flexner, and 394 new illustrations. Edited by Rita Weiss. 6⅝ x 9⅝.

21695-0, 21696-9, 21697-7 Three volumes, Paperbound $13.50

EPOCHS OF CHINESE AND JAPANESE ART, Ernest F. Fenollosa. From primitive Chinese art to the 20th century, thorough history, explanation of every important art period and form, including Japanese woodcuts; main stress on China and Japan, but Tibet, Korea also included. Still unexcelled for its detailed, rich coverage of cultural background, aesthetic elements, diffusion studies, particularly of the historical period. 2nd, 1913 edition. 242 illustrations. lii + 439pp. of text.

20364-6, 20365-4 Two volumes, Paperbound $6.00

THE GENTLE ART OF MAKING ENEMIES, James A. M. Whistler. Greatest wit of his day deflates Oscar Wilde, Ruskin, Swinburne; strikes back at inane critics, exhibitions, art journalism; aesthetics of impressionist revolution in most striking form. Highly readable classic by great painter. Reproduction of edition designed by Whistler. Introduction by Alfred Werner. xxxvi + 334pp.

21875-9 Paperbound $2.50

VISUAL ILLUSIONS: THEIR CAUSES, CHARACTERISTICS, AND APPLICATIONS, Matthew Luckiesh. Thorough description and discussion of optical illusion, geometric and perspective, particularly; size and shape distortions, illusions of color, of motion; natural illusions; use of illusion in art and magic, industry, etc. Most useful today with op art, also for classical art. Scores of effects illustrated. Introduction by William H. Ittleson. 100 illustrations. xxi + 252pp.

21530-X Paperbound $2.00

A HANDBOOK OF ANATOMY FOR ART STUDENTS, Arthur Thomson. Thorough, virtually exhaustive coverage of skeletal structure, musculature, etc. Full text, supplemented by anatomical diagrams and drawings and by photographs of undraped figures. Unique in its comparison of male and female forms, pointing out differences of contour, texture, form. 211 figures, 40 drawings, 86 photographs. xx + 459pp. 5⅜ x 8⅜.

21163-0 Paperbound $3.50

150 MASTERPIECES OF DRAWING, Selected by Anthony Toney. Full page reproductions of drawings from the early 16th to the end of the 18th century, all beautifully reproduced: Rembrandt, Michelangelo, Dürer, Fragonard, Urs, Graf, Wouwerman, many others. First-rate browsing book, model book for artists. xviii + 150pp. 8⅜ x 11¼.

21032-4 Paperbound $2.50

THE LATER WORK OF AUBREY BEARDSLEY, Aubrey Beardsley. Exotic, erotic, ironic masterpieces in full maturity: Comedy Ballet, Venus and Tannhauser, Pierrot, Lysistrata, Rape of the Lock, Savoy material, Ali Baba, Volpone, etc. This material revolutionized the art world, and is still powerful, fresh, brilliant. With *The Early Work,* all Beardsley's finest work. 174 plates, 2 in color. xiv + 176pp. 8⅛ x 11.

21817-1 Paperbound $3.00

DRAWINGS OF REMBRANDT, Rembrandt van Rijn. Complete reproduction of fabulously rare edition by Lippmann and Hofstede de Groot, completely reedited, updated, improved by Prof. Seymour Slive, Fogg Museum. Portraits, Biblical sketches, landscapes, Oriental types, nudes, episodes from classical mythology—All Rembrandt's fertile genius. Also selection of drawings by his pupils and followers. "Stunning volumes," *Saturday Review.* 550 illustrations. lxxviii + 552pp. ⅛ x 12¼.

21485-0, 21486-9 Two volumes, Paperbound $10.00

THE DISASTERS OF WAR, Francisco Goya. One of the masterpieces of Western civilization—83 etchings that record Goya's shattering, bitter reaction to the Napoleonic war that swept through Spain after the insurrection of 1808 and to war in general. Reprint of the first edition, with three additional plates from Boston's Museum of Fine Arts. All plates facsimile size. Introduction by Philip Hofer, Fogg Museum. + 97pp. 9⅜ x 8¼.

21872-4 Paperbound $2.00

GRAPHIC WORKS OF ODILON REDON. Largest collection of Redon's graphic works ever assembled: 172 lithographs, 28 etchings and engravings, 9 drawings. These include some of his most famous works. All the plates from *Odilon Redon: oeuvre graphique complet,* plus additional plates. New introduction and caption translations by Alfred Werner. 209 illustrations. xxvii + 209pp. 9⅛ x 12¼.

21966-8 Paperbound $4.00

DESIGN BY ACCIDENT; A BOOK OF "ACCIDENTAL EFFECTS" FOR ARTISTS AND DESIGNERS, James F. O'Brien. Create your own unique, striking, imaginative effects by "controlled accident" interaction of materials: paints and lacquers, oil and water based paints, splatter, crackling materials, shatter, similar items. Everything you do will be different; first book on this limitless art, so useful to both fine artist and commercial artist. Full instructions. 192 plates showing "accidents," 8 in color. viii + 215pp. 8⅜ x 11¼. 21942-9 Paperbound $3.50

THE BOOK OF SIGNS, Rudolf Koch. Famed German type designer draws 493 beautiful symbols: religious, mystical, alchemical, imperial, property marks, runes, etc. Remarkable fusion of traditional and modern. Good for suggestions of timelessness, smartness, modernity. Text. vi + 104pp. 6⅛ x 9¼. 20162-7 Paperbound $1.25

HISTORY OF INDIAN AND INDONESIAN ART, Ananda K. Coomaraswamy. An unabridged republication of one of the finest books by a great scholar in Eastern art. Rich in descriptive material, history, social backgrounds; Sunga reliefs, Rajput paintings, Gupta temples, Burmese frescoes, textiles, jewelry, sculpture, etc. 400 photos. viii + 423pp. 6⅜ x 9¾. 21436-2 Paperbound $5.00

PRIMITIVE ART, Franz Boas. America's foremost anthropologist surveys textiles, ceramics, woodcarving, basketry, metalwork, etc.; patterns, technology, creation of symbols, style origins. All areas of world, but very full on Northwest Coast Indians. More than 350 illustrations of baskets, boxes, totem poles, weapons, etc. 378 pp. 20025-6 Paperbound $3.00

THE GENTLEMAN AND CABINET MAKER'S DIRECTOR, Thomas Chippendale. Full reprint (third edition, 1762) of most influential furniture book of all time, by master cabinetmaker. 200 plates, illustrating chairs, sofas, mirrors, tables, cabinets, plus 24 photographs of surviving pieces. Biographical introduction by N. Bienenstock. vi + 249pp. 9⅞ x 12¾. 21601-2 Paperbound $4.00

AMERICAN ANTIQUE FURNITURE, Edgar G. Miller, Jr. The basic coverage of all American furniture before 1840. Individual chapters cover type of furniture—clocks, tables, sideboards, etc.—chronologically, with inexhaustible wealth of data. More than 2100 photographs, all identified, commented on. Essential to all early American collectors. Introduction by H. E. Keyes. vi + 1106pp. 7⅞ x 10¾. 21599-7, 21600-4 Two volumes, Paperbound $11.00

PENNSYLVANIA DUTCH AMERICAN FOLK ART, Henry J. Kauffman. 279 photos, 28 drawings of tulipware, Fraktur script, painted tinware, toys, flowered furniture, quilts, samplers, hex signs, house interiors, etc. Full descriptive text. Excellent for tourist, rewarding for designer, collector. Map. 146pp. 7⅞ x 10¾. 21205-X Paperbound $2.50

EARLY NEW ENGLAND GRAVESTONE RUBBINGS, Edmund V. Gillon, Jr. 43 photographs, 226 carefully reproduced rubbings show heavily symbolic, sometimes macabre early gravestones, up to early 19th century. Remarkable early American primitive art, occasionally strikingly beautiful; always powerful. Text. xxvi + 207pp. 8⅜ x 11¼. 21380-3 Paperbound $3.50

ALPHABETS AND ORNAMENTS, Ernst Lehner. Well-known pictorial source for decorative alphabets, script examples, cartouches, frames, decorative title pages, calligraphic initials, borders, similar material. 14th to 19th century, mostly European. Useful in almost any graphic arts designing, varied styles. 750 illustrations. 256pp. 7 x 10.   21905-4 Paperbound $4.00

PAINTING: A CREATIVE APPROACH, Norman Colquhoun. For the beginner simple guide provides an instructive approach to painting: major stumbling blocks for beginner; overcoming them, technical points; paints and pigments; oil painting; watercolor and other media and color. New section on "plastic" paints. Glossary. Formerly *Paint Your Own Pictures*. 221pp.   22000-1 Paperbound $1.75

THE ENJOYMENT AND USE OF COLOR, Walter Sargent. Explanation of the relations between colors themselves and between colors in nature and art, including hundreds of little-known facts about color values, intensities, effects of high and low illumination, complementary colors. Many practical hints for painters, references to great masters. 7 color plates, 29 illustrations. x + 274pp.
20944-X Paperbound $2.75

THE NOTEBOOKS OF LEONARDO DA VINCI, compiled and edited by Jean Paul Richter. 1566 extracts from original manuscripts reveal the full range of Leonardo's versatile genius: all his writings on painting, sculpture, architecture, anatomy, astronomy, geography, topography, physiology, mining, music, etc., in both Italian and English, with 186 plates of manuscript pages and more than 500 additional drawings. Includes studies for the Last Supper, the lost Sforza monument, and other works. Total of xlvii + 866pp. 7⅞ x 10¾.
22572-0, 22573-9 Two volumes, Paperbound $10.00

MONTGOMERY WARD CATALOGUE OF 1895. Tea gowns, yards of flannel and pillow-case lace, stereoscopes, books of gospel hymns, the New Improved Singer Sewing Machine, side saddles, milk skimmers, straight-edged razors, high-button shoes, spittoons, and on and on . . . listing some 25,000 items, practically all illustrated. Essential to the shoppers of the 1890's, it is our truest record of the spirit of the period. Unaltered reprint of Issue No. 57, Spring and Summer 1895. Introduction by Boris Emmet. Innumerable illustrations. xiii + 624pp. 8½ x 11⅝.
22377-9 Paperbound $6.95

THE CRYSTAL PALACE EXHIBITION ILLUSTRATED CATALOGUE (LONDON, 1851). One of the wonders of the modern world—the Crystal Palace Exhibition in which all the nations of the civilized world exhibited their achievements in the arts and sciences—presented in an equally important illustrated catalogue. More than 1700 items pictured with accompanying text—ceramics, textiles, cast-iron work, carpets, pianos, sleds, razors, wall-papers, billiard tables, beehives, silverware and hundreds of other artifacts—represent the focal point of Victorian culture in the Western World. Probably the largest collection of Victorian decorative art ever assembled—indispensable for antiquarians and designers. Unabridged republication of the Art-Journal Catalogue of the Great Exhibition of 1851, with all terminal essays. New introduction by John Gloag, F.S.A. xxxiv + 426pp. 9 x 12.
22503-8 Paperbound $4.50

A HISTORY OF COSTUME, Carl Köhler. Definitive history, based on surviving pieces of clothing primarily, and paintings, statues, etc. secondarily. Highly readable text, supplemented by 594 illustrations of costumes of the ancient Mediterranean peoples, Greece and Rome, the Teutonic prehistoric period; costumes of the Middle Ages, Renaissance, Baroque, 18th and 19th centuries. Clear, measured patterns are provided for many clothing articles. Approach is practical throughout. Enlarged by Emma von Sichart. 464pp. 21030-8 Paperbound $3.50

ORIENTAL RUGS, ANTIQUE AND MODERN, Walter A. Hawley. A complete and authoritative treatise on the Oriental rug—where they are made, by whom and how, designs and symbols, characteristics in detail of the six major groups, how to distinguish them and how to buy them. Detailed technical data is provided on periods, weaves, warps, wefts, textures, sides, ends and knots, although no technical background is required for an understanding. 11 color plates, 80 halftones, 4 maps. vi + 320pp. 6⅛ x 9⅛. 22366-3 Paperbound $5.00

TEN BOOKS ON ARCHITECTURE, Vitruvius. By any standards the most important book on architecture ever written. Early Roman discussion of aesthetics of building, construction methods, orders, sites, and every other aspect of architecture has inspired, instructed architecture for about 2,000 years. Stands behind Palladio, Michelangelo, Bramante, Wren, countless others. Definitive Morris H. Morgan translation. 68 illustrations. xii + 331pp. 20645-9 Paperbound $3.00

THE FOUR BOOKS OF ARCHITECTURE, Andrea Palladio. Translated into every major Western European language in the two centuries following its publication in 1570, this has been one of the most influential books in the history of architecture. Complete reprint of the 1738 Isaac Ware edition. New introduction by Adolf Placzek, Columbia Univ. 216 plates. xxii + 110pp. of text. 9½ x 12¾. 21308-0 Clothbound $10.00

STICKS AND STONES: A STUDY OF AMERICAN ARCHITECTURE AND CIVILIZATION, Lewis Mumford. One of the great classics of American cultural history. American architecture from the medieval-inspired earliest forms to the early 20th century, evolution of structure and style, and reciprocal influences on environment. 21 photographic illustrations. 238pp. 20202-X Paperbound $2.00

THE AMERICAN BUILDER'S COMPANION, Asher Benjamin. The most widely used early 19th century architectural style and source book, for colonial up into Greek Revival periods. Extensive development of geometry of carpentering, construction of sashes, frames, doors, stairs; plans and elevations of domestic and other buildings. Hundreds of thousands of houses were built according to this book, now invaluable to historians, architects, restorers, etc. 1827 edition. 59 plates. 114pp. 7⅞ x 10¾. 22236-5 Paperbound $3.50

DUTCH HOUSES IN THE HUDSON VALLEY BEFORE 1776, Helen Wilkinson Reynolds. The standard survey of the Dutch colonial house and outbuildings, with constructional features, decoration, and local history associated with individual homesteads. Introduction by Franklin D. Roosevelt. Map. 150 illustrations. 469pp. 6⅝ x 9¼. 21469-9 Paperbound $4.00

THE ARCHITECTURE OF COUNTRY HOUSES, Andrew J. Downing. Together with Vaux's *Villas and Cottages* this is the basic book for Hudson River Gothic architecture of the middle Victorian period. Full, sound discussions of general aspects of housing, architecture, style, decoration, furnishing, together with scores of detailed house plans, illustrations of specific buildings, accompanied by full text. Perhaps the most influential single American architectural book. 1850 edition. Introduction by J. Stewart Johnson. 321 figures, 34 architectural designs. xvi + 560pp.
22003-6 Paperbound $4.00

LOST EXAMPLES OF COLONIAL ARCHITECTURE, John Mead Howells. Full-page photographs of buildings that have disappeared or been so altered as to be denatured, including many designed by major early American architects. 245 plates. xvii + 248pp. 7⅞ x 10¾. 21143-6 Paperbound $3.50

DOMESTIC ARCHITECTURE OF THE AMERICAN COLONIES AND OF THE EARLY REPUBLIC, Fiske Kimball. Foremost architect and restorer of Williamsburg and Monticello covers nearly 200 homes between 1620-1825. Architectural details, construction, style features, special fixtures, floor plans, etc. Generally considered finest work in its area. 219 illustrations of houses, doorways, windows, capital mantels. xx + 314pp. 7⅞ x 10¾. 21743-4 Paperbound $4.00

EARLY AMERICAN ROOMS: 1650-1858, edited by Russell Hawes Kettell. Tour of 12 rooms, each representative of a different era in American history and each furnished, decorated, designed and occupied in the style of the era. 72 plans and elevations, 8-page color section, etc., show fabrics, wall papers, arrangements, etc. Full descriptive text. xvii + 200pp. of text. 8⅜ x 11¼.
21633-0 Paperbound $5.00

THE FITZWILLIAM VIRGINAL BOOK, edited by J. Fuller Maitland and W. B. Squire. Full modern printing of famous early 17th-century ms. volume of 300 works by Morley, Byrd, Bull, Gibbons, etc. For piano or other modern keyboard instrument; easy to read format. xxxvi + 938pp. 8⅜ x 11.
21068-5, 21069-3 Two volumes, Paperbound $10.00

KEYBOARD MUSIC, Johann Sebastian Bach. Bach Gesellschaft edition. A rich selection of Bach's masterpieces for the harpsichord: the six English Suites, six French Suites, the six Partitas (Clavierübung part I), the Goldberg Variations (Clavierübung part IV), the fifteen Two-Part Inventions and the fifteen Three-Part Sinfonias. Clearly reproduced on large sheets with ample margins; eminently playable. vi + 312pp. 8⅛ x 11. 22360-4 Paperbound $5.00

THE MUSIC OF BACH: AN INTRODUCTION, Charles Sanford Terry. A fine, nontechnical introduction to Bach's music, both instrumental and vocal. Covers organ music, chamber music, passion music, other types. Analyzes themes, developments, innovations. x + 114pp. 21075-8 Paperbound $1.25

BEETHOVEN AND HIS NINE SYMPHONIES, Sir George Grove. Noted British musicologist provides best history, analysis, commentary on symphonies. Very thorough, rigorously accurate; necessary to both advanced student and amateur music lover. 436 musical passages. vii + 407 pp. 20334-4 Paperbound $2.75

JOHANN SEBASTIAN BACH, Philipp Spitta. One of the great classics of musicology, this definitive analysis of Bach's music (and life) has never been surpassed. Lucid, nontechnical analyses of hundreds of pieces (30 pages devoted to St. Matthew Passion, 26 to B Minor Mass). Also includes major analysis of 18th-century music. 450 musical examples. 40-page musical supplement. Total of xx + 1799pp.

(EUK) 22278-0, 22279-9 Two volumes, Clothbound $17.50

MOZART AND HIS PIANO CONCERTOS, Cuthbert Girdlestone. The only full-length study of an important area of Mozart's creativity. Provides detailed analyses of all 23 concertos, traces inspirational sources. 417 musical examples. Second edition. 509pp. 21271-8 Paperbound $3.50

THE PERFECT WAGNERITE: A COMMENTARY ON THE NIBLUNG'S RING, George Bernard Shaw. Brilliant and still relevant criticism in remarkable essays on Wagner's Ring cycle, Shaw's ideas on political and social ideology behind the plots, role of Leitmotifs, vocal requisites, etc. Prefaces. xxi + 136pp.

(USO) 21707-8 Paperbound $1.50

DON GIOVANNI, W. A. Mozart. Complete libretto, modern English translation; biographies of composer and librettist; accounts of early performances and critical reaction. Lavishly illustrated. All the material you need to understand and appreciate this great work. Dover Opera Guide and Libretto Series; translated and introduced by Ellen Bleiler. 92 illustrations. 209pp.

21134-7 Paperbound $2.00

HIGH FIDELITY SYSTEMS: A LAYMAN'S GUIDE, Roy F. Allison. All the basic information you need for setting up your own audio system: high fidelity and stereo record players, tape records, F.M. Connections, adjusting tone arm, cartridge, checking needle alignment, positioning speakers, phasing speakers, adjusting hums, trouble-shooting, maintenance, and similar topics. Enlarged 1965 edition. More than 50 charts, diagrams, photos. iv + 91pp. 21514-8 Paperbound $1.25

REPRODUCTION OF SOUND, Edgar Villchur. Thorough coverage for laymen of high fidelity systems, reproducing systems in general, needles, amplifiers, preamps, loudspeakers, feedback, explaining physical background. "A rare talent for making technicalities vividly comprehensible," R. Darrell, *High Fidelity*. 69 figures. iv + 92pp. 21515-6 Paperbound $1.25

HEAR ME TALKIN' TO YA: THE STORY OF JAZZ AS TOLD BY THE MEN WHO MADE IT, Nat Shapiro and Nat Hentoff. Louis Armstrong, Fats Waller, Jo Jones, Clarence Williams, Billy Holiday, Duke Ellington, Jelly Roll Morton and dozens of other jazz greats tell how it was in Chicago's South Side, New Orleans, depression Harlem and the modern West Coast as jazz was born and grew. xvi + 429pp.

21726-4 Paperbound $2.50

FABLES OF AESOP, translated by Sir Roger L'Estrange. A reproduction of the very rare 1931 Paris edition; a selection of the most interesting fables, together with 50 imaginative drawings by Alexander Calder. v + 128pp. 6½x9¼.

21780-9 Paperbound $1.50

AGAINST THE GRAIN (A REBOURS), Joris K. Huysmans. Filled with weird images, evidences of a bizarre imagination, exotic experiments with hallucinatory drugs, rich tastes and smells and the diversions of its sybarite hero Duc Jean des Esseintes, this classic novel pushed 19th-century literary decadence to its limits. Full unabridged edition. Do not confuse this with abridged editions generally sold. Introduction by Havelock Ellis. xlix + 206pp. 22190-3 Paperbound $2.00

VARIORUM SHAKESPEARE: HAMLET. Edited by Horace H. Furness; a landmark of American scholarship. Exhaustive footnotes and appendices treat all doubtful words and phrases, as well as suggested critical emendations throughout the play's history. First volume contains editor's own text, collated with all Quartos and Folios. Second volume contains full first Quarto, translations of Shakespeare's sources (Belleforest, and Saxo Grammaticus), Der Bestrafte Brudermord, and many essays on critical and historical points of interest by major authorities of past and present. Includes details of staging and costuming over the years. By far the best edition available for serious students of Shakespeare. Total of xx + 905pp. 21004-9, 21005-7, 2 volumes, Paperbound $7.00

A LIFE OF WILLIAM SHAKESPEARE, Sir Sidney Lee. This is the standard life of Shakespeare, summarizing everything known about Shakespeare and his plays. Incredibly rich in material, broad in coverage, clear and judicious, it has served thousands as the best introduction to Shakespeare. 1931 edition. 9 plates. xxix + 792pp. (USO) 21967-4 Paperbound $3.75

MASTERS OF THE DRAMA, John Gassner. Most comprehensive history of the drama in print, covering every tradition from Greeks to modern Europe and America, including India, Far East, etc. Covers more than 800 dramatists, 2000 plays, with biographical material, plot summaries, theatre history, criticism, etc. "Best of its kind in English," *New Republic*. 77 illustrations. xxii + 890pp. 20100-7 Clothbound $8.50

THE EVOLUTION OF THE ENGLISH LANGUAGE, George McKnight. The growth of English, from the 14th century to the present. Unusual, non-technical account presents basic information in very interesting form: sound shifts, change in grammar and syntax, vocabulary growth, similar topics. Abundantly illustrated with quotations. Formerly *Modern English in the Making*. xii + 590pp. 21932-1 Paperbound $3.50

AN ETYMOLOGICAL DICTIONARY OF MODERN ENGLISH, Ernest Weekley. Fullest, richest work of its sort, by foremost British lexicographer. Detailed word histories, including many colloquial and archaic words; extensive quotations. Do not confuse this with the Concise Etymological Dictionary, which is much abridged. Total of xxvii + 830pp. 6½ x 9¼. 21873-2, 21874-0 Two volumes, Paperbound $6.00

FLATLAND: A ROMANCE OF MANY DIMENSIONS, E. A. Abbott. Classic of science-fiction explores ramifications of life in a two-dimensional world, and what happens when a three-dimensional being intrudes. Amusing reading, but also useful as introduction to thought about hyperspace. Introduction by Banesh Hoffmann. 16 illustrations. xx + 103pp. 20001-9 Paperbound $1.00

POEMS OF ANNE BRADSTREET, edited with an introduction by Robert Hutchinson. A new selection of poems by America's first poet and perhaps the first significant woman poet in the English language. 48 poems display her development in works of considerable variety—love poems, domestic poems, religious meditations, formal elegies, "quaternions," etc. Notes, bibliography. viii + 222pp.

22160-1 Paperbound $2.50

THREE GOTHIC NOVELS: THE CASTLE OF OTRANTO BY HORACE WALPOLE; VATHEK BY WILLIAM BECKFORD; THE VAMPYRE BY JOHN POLIDORI, WITH FRAGMENT OF A NOVEL BY LORD BYRON, edited by E. F. Bleiler. The first Gothic novel, by Walpole; the finest Oriental tale in English, by Beckford; powerful Romantic supernatural story in versions by Polidori and Byron. All extremely important in history of literature; all still exciting, packed with supernatural thrills, ghosts, haunted castles, magic, etc. xl + 291pp.

21232-7 Paperbound $2.50

THE BEST TALES OF HOFFMANN, E. T. A. Hoffmann. 10 of Hoffmann's most important stories, in modern re-editings of standard translations: Nutcracker and the King of Mice, Signor Formica, Automata, The Sandman, Rath Krespel, The Golden Flowerpot, Master Martin the Cooper, The Mines of Falun, The King's Betrothed, A New Year's Eve Adventure. 7 illustrations by Hoffmann. Edited by E. F. Bleiler. xxxix + 419pp.

21793-0 Paperbound $3.00

GHOST AND HORROR STORIES OF AMBROSE BIERCE, Ambrose Bierce. 23 strikingly modern stories of the horrors latent in the human mind: The Eyes of the Panther, The Damned Thing, An Occurrence at Owl Creek Bridge, An Inhabitant of Carcosa, etc., plus the dream-essay, Visions of the Night. Edited by E. F. Bleiler. xxii + 199pp.

20767-6 Paperbound $1.50

BEST GHOST STORIES OF J. S. LEFANU, J. Sheridan LeFanu. Finest stories by Victorian master often considered greatest supernatural writer of all. Carmilla, Green Tea, The Haunted Baronet, The Familiar, and 12 others. Most never before available in the U. S. A. Edited by E. F. Bleiler. 8 illustrations from Victorian publications. xvii + 467pp.

20415-4 Paperbound $3.00

MATHEMATICAL FOUNDATIONS OF INFORMATION THEORY, A. I. Khinchin. Comprehensive introduction to work of Shannon, McMillan, Feinstein and Khinchin, placing these investigations on a rigorous mathematical basis. Covers entropy concept in probability theory, uniqueness theorem, Shannon's inequality, ergodic sources, the E property, martingale concept, noise, Feinstein's fundamental lemma, Shanon's first and second theorems. Translated by R. A. Silverman and M. D. Friedman. iii + 120pp.

60434-9 Paperbound $1.75

SEVEN SCIENCE FICTION NOVELS, H. G. Wells. The standard collection of the great novels. Complete, unabridged. *First Men in the Moon, Island of Dr. Moreau, War of the Worlds, Food of the Gods, Invisible Man, Time Machine, In the Days of the Comet.* Not only science fiction fans, but every educated person owes it to himself to read these novels. 1015pp.

(USO) 20264-X Clothbound $5.00

LAST AND FIRST MEN AND STAR MAKER, TWO SCIENCE FICTION NOVELS, Olaf Stapledon. Greatest future histories in science fiction. In the first, human intelligence is the "hero," through strange paths of evolution, interplanetary invasions, incredible technologies, near extinctions and reemergences. Star Maker describes the quest of a band of star rovers for intelligence itself, through time and space: weird inhuman civilizations, crustacean minds, symbiotic worlds, etc. Complete, unabridged. v + 438pp. (USO) 21962-3 Paperbound $2.50

THREE PROPHETIC NOVELS, H. G. WELLS. Stages of a consistently planned future for mankind. *When the Sleeper Wakes,* and *A Story of the Days to Come,* anticipate *Brave New World* and *1984,* in the 21st Century; *The Time Machine,* only complete version in print, shows farther future and the end of mankind. All show Wells's greatest gifts as storyteller and novelist. Edited by E. F. Bleiler. x + 335pp. (USO) 20605-X Paperbound $2.50

THE DEVIL'S DICTIONARY, Ambrose Bierce. America's own Oscar Wilde— Ambrose Bierce—offers his barbed iconoclastic wisdom in over 1,000 definitions hailed by H. L. Mencken as "some of the most gorgeous witticisms in the English language." 145pp. 20487-1 Paperbound $1.25

MAX AND MORITZ, Wilhelm Busch. Great children's classic, father of comic strip, of two bad boys, Max and Moritz. Also Ker and Plunk (Plisch und Plumm), Cat and Mouse, Deceitful Henry, Ice-Peter, The Boy and the Pipe, and five other pieces. Original German, with English translation. Edited by H. Arthur Klein; translations by various hands and H. Arthur Klein. vi + 216pp. 20181-3 Paperbound $2.00

PIGS IS PIGS AND OTHER FAVORITES, Ellis Parker Butler. The title story is one of the best humor short stories, as Mike Flannery obfuscates biology and English. Also included, That Pup of Murchison's, The Great American Pie Company, and Perkins of Portland. 14 illustrations. v + 109pp. 21532-6 Paperbound $1.25

THE PETERKIN PAPERS, Lucretia P. Hale. It takes genius to be as stupidly mad as the Peterkins, as they decide to become wise, celebrate the "Fourth," keep a cow, and otherwise strain the resources of the Lady from Philadelphia. Basic book of American humor. 153 illustrations. 219pp. 20794-3 Paperbound $1.50

PERRAULT'S FAIRY TALES, translated by A. E. Johnson and S. R. Littlewood, with 34 full-page illustrations by Gustave Doré. All the original Perrault stories— Cinderella, Sleeping Beauty, Bluebeard, Little Red Riding Hood, Puss in Boots, Tom Thumb, etc.—with their witty verse morals and the magnificent illustrations of Doré. One of the five or six great books of European fairy tales. viii + 117pp. 8⅛ x 11. 22311-6 Paperbound $2.00

OLD HUNGARIAN FAIRY TALES, Baroness Orczy. Favorites translated and adapted by author of the *Scarlet Pimpernel.* Eight fairy tales include "The Suitors of Princess Fire-Fly," "The Twin Hunchbacks," "Mr. Cuttlefish's Love Story," and "The Enchanted Cat." This little volume of magic and adventure will captivate children as it has for generations. 90 drawings by Montagu Barstow. 96pp. 22293-4 Paperbound $1.95

THE RED FAIRY BOOK, Andrew Lang. Lang's color fairy books have long been children's favorites. This volume includes Rapunzel, Jack and the Bean-stalk and 35 other stories, familiar and unfamiliar. 4 plates, 93 illustrations x + 367pp.
21673-X Paperbound $2.50

THE BLUE FAIRY BOOK, Andrew Lang. Lang's tales come from all countries and all times. Here are 37 tales from Grimm, the Arabian Nights, Greek Mythology, and other fascinating sources. 8 plates, 130 illustrations. xi + 390pp.
21437-0 Paperbound $2.50

HOUSEHOLD STORIES BY THE BROTHERS GRIMM. Classic English-language edition of the well-known tales — Rumpelstiltskin, Snow White, Hansel and Gretel, The Twelve Brothers, Faithful John, Rapunzel, Tom Thumb (52 stories in all). Translated into simple, straightforward English by Lucy Crane. Ornamented with headpieces, vignettes, elaborate decorative initials and a dozen full-page illustrations by Walter Crane. x + 269pp.
21080-4 Paperbound $2.00

THE MERRY ADVENTURES OF ROBIN HOOD, Howard Pyle. The finest modern versions of the traditional ballads and tales about the great English outlaw. Howard Pyle's complete prose version, with every word, every illustration of the first edition. Do not confuse this facsimile of the original (1883) with modern editions that change text or illustrations. 23 plates plus many page decorations. xxii + 296pp.
22043-5 Paperbound $2.50

THE STORY OF KING ARTHUR AND HIS KNIGHTS, Howard Pyle. The finest children's version of the life of King Arthur; brilliantly retold by Pyle, with 48 of his most imaginative illustrations. xviii + 313pp. 6⅛ x 9¼.
21445-1 Paperbound $2.50

THE WONDERFUL WIZARD OF OZ, L. Frank Baum. America's finest children's book in facsimile of first edition with all Denslow illustrations in full color. The edition a child should have. Introduction by Martin Gardner. 23 color plates, scores of drawings. iv + 267pp.
20691-2 Paperbound $2.50

THE MARVELOUS LAND OF OZ, L. Frank Baum. The second Oz book, every bit as imaginative as the Wizard. The hero is a boy named Tip, but the Scarecrow and the Tin Woodman are back, as is the Oz magic. 16 color plates, 120 drawings by John R. Neill. 287pp.
20692-0 Paperbound $2.50

THE MAGICAL MONARCH OF MO, L. Frank Baum. Remarkable adventures in a land even stranger than Oz. The best of Baum's books not in the Oz series. 15 color plates and dozens of drawings by Frank Verbeck. xviii + 237pp.
21892-9 Paperbound $2.25

THE BAD CHILD'S BOOK OF BEASTS, MORE BEASTS FOR WORSE CHILDREN, A MORAL ALPHABET, Hilaire Belloc. Three complete humor classics in one volume. Be kind to the frog, and do not call him names . . . and 28 other whimsical animals. Familiar favorites and some not so well known. Illustrated by Basil Blackwell. 156pp.
(USO) 20749-8 Paperbound $1.50

EAST O' THE SUN AND WEST O' THE MOON, George W. Dasent. Considered the best of all translations of these Norwegian folk tales, this collection has been enjoyed by generations of children (and folklorists too). Includes True and Untrue, Why the Sea is Salt, East O' the Sun and West O' the Moon, Why the Bear is Stumpy-Tailed, Boots and the Troll, The Cock and the Hen, Rich Peter the Pedlar, and 52 more. The only edition with all 59 tales. 77 illustrations by Erik Werenskiold and Theodor Kittelsen. xv + 418pp. 22521-6 Paperbound $3.50

GOOPS AND HOW TO BE THEM, Gelett Burgess. Classic of tongue-in-cheek humor, masquerading as etiquette book. 87 verses, twice as many cartoons, show mischievous Goops as they demonstrate to children virtues of table manners, neatness, courtesy, etc. Favorite for generations. viii + 88pp. $6\frac{1}{2}$ x $9\frac{1}{4}$. 22233-0 Paperbound $1.25

ALICE'S ADVENTURES UNDER GROUND, Lewis Carroll. The first version, quite different from the final *Alice in Wonderland,* printed out by Carroll himself with his own illustrations. Complete facsimile of the "million dollar" manuscript Carroll gave to Alice Liddell in 1864. Introduction by Martin Gardner. viii + 96pp. Title and dedication pages in color. 21482-6 Paperbound $1.25

THE BROWNIES, THEIR BOOK, Palmer Cox. Small as mice, cunning as foxes, exuberant and full of mischief, the Brownies go to the zoo, toy shop, seashore, circus, etc., in 24 verse adventures and 266 illustrations. Long a favorite, since their first appearance in St. Nicholas Magazine. xi + 144pp. $6\frac{5}{8}$ x $9\frac{1}{4}$. 21265-3 Paperbound $1.75

SONGS OF CHILDHOOD, Walter De La Mare. Published (under the pseudonym Walter Ramal) when De La Mare was only 29, this charming collection has long been a favorite children's book. A facsimile of the first edition in paper, the 47 poems capture the simplicity of the nursery rhyme and the ballad, including such lyrics as I Met Eve, Tartary, The Silver Penny. vii + 106pp. (USO) 21972-0 Paperbound $1.25

THE COMPLETE NONSENSE OF EDWARD LEAR, Edward Lear. The finest 19th-century humorist-cartoonist in full: all nonsense limericks, zany alphabets, Owl and Pussycat, songs, nonsense botany, and more than 500 illustrations by Lear himself. Edited by Holbrook Jackson. xxix + 287pp. (USO) 20167-8 Paperbound $2.00

BILLY WHISKERS: THE AUTOBIOGRAPHY OF A GOAT, Frances Trego Montgomery. A favorite of children since the early 20th century, here are the escapades of that rambunctious, irresistible and mischievous goat—Billy Whiskers. Much in the spirit of *Peck's Bad Boy,* this is a book that children never tire of reading or hearing. All the original familiar illustrations by W. H. Fry are included: 6 color plates, 18 black and white drawings. 159pp. 22345-0 Paperbound $2.00

MOTHER GOOSE MELODIES. Faithful republication of the fabulously rare Munroe and Francis "copyright 1833" Boston edition—the most important Mother Goose collection, usually referred to as the "original." Familiar rhymes plus many rare ones, with wonderful old woodcut illustrations. Edited by E. F. Bleiler. 128pp. $4\frac{1}{2}$ x $6\frac{3}{8}$. 22577-1 Paperbound $1.00

TWO LITTLE SAVAGES; BEING THE ADVENTURES OF TWO BOYS WHO LIVED AS INDIANS AND WHAT THEY LEARNED, Ernest Thompson Seton. Great classic of nature and boyhood provides a vast range of woodlore in most palatable form, a genuinely entertaining story. Two farm boys build a teepee in woods and live in it for a month, working out Indian solutions to living problems, star lore, birds and animals, plants, etc. 293 illustrations. vii + 286pp.

20985-7 Paperbound $2.50

PETER PIPER'S PRACTICAL PRINCIPLES OF PLAIN & PERFECT PRONUNCIATION. Alliterative jingles and tongue-twisters of surprising charm, that made their first appearance in America about 1830. Republished in full with the spirited woodcut illustrations from this earliest American edition. 32pp. 4½ x 6⅜.

22560-7 Paperbound $1.00

SCIENCE EXPERIMENTS AND AMUSEMENTS FOR CHILDREN, Charles Vivian. 73 easy experiments, requiring only materials found at home or easily available, such as candles, coins, steel wool, etc.; illustrate basic phenomena like vacuum, simple chemical reaction, etc. All safe. Modern, well-planned. Formerly *Science Games for Children*. 102 photos, numerous drawings. 96pp. 6⅛ x 9¼.

21856-2 Paperbound $1.25

AN INTRODUCTION TO CHESS MOVES AND TACTICS SIMPLY EXPLAINED, Leonard Barden. Informal intermediate introduction, quite strong in explaining reasons for moves. Covers basic material, tactics, important openings, traps, positional play in middle game, end game. Attempts to isolate patterns and recurrent configurations. Formerly *Chess*. 58 figures. 102pp.   (USO) 21210-6 Paperbound $1.25

LASKER'S MANUAL OF CHESS, Dr. Emanuel Lasker. Lasker was not only one of the five great World Champions, he was also one of the ablest expositors, theorists, and analysts. In many ways, his Manual, permeated with his philosophy of battle, filled with keen insights, is one of the greatest works ever written on chess. Filled with analyzed games by the great players. A single-volume library that will profit almost any chess player, beginner or master. 308 diagrams. xli x 349pp.

20640-8 Paperbound $2.75

THE MASTER BOOK OF MATHEMATICAL RECREATIONS, Fred Schuh. In opinion of many the finest work ever prepared on mathematical puzzles, stunts, recreations; exhaustively thorough explanations of mathematics involved, analysis of effects, citation of puzzles and games. Mathematics involved is elementary. Translated by F. Göbel. 194 figures. xxiv + 430pp.   22134-2 Paperbound $3.00

MATHEMATICS, MAGIC AND MYSTERY, Martin Gardner. Puzzle editor for Scientific American explains mathematics behind various mystifying tricks: card tricks, stage "mind reading," coin and match tricks, counting out games, geometric dissections, etc. Probability sets, theory of numbers clearly explained. Also provides more than 400 tricks, guaranteed to work, that you can do. 135 illustrations. xii + 176pp.

20335-2 Paperbound $1.50

MATHEMATICAL PUZZLES FOR BEGINNERS AND ENTHUSIASTS, Geoffrey Mott-Smith. 189 puzzles from easy to difficult—involving arithmetic, logic, algebra, properties of digits, probability, etc.—for enjoyment and mental stimulus. Explanation of mathematical principles behind the puzzles. 135 illustrations. viii + 248pp.

20198-8 Paperbound $1.75

PAPER FOLDING FOR BEGINNERS, William D. Murray and Francis J. Rigney. Easiest book on the market, clearest instructions on making interesting, beautiful origami. Sail boats, cups, roosters, frogs that move legs, bonbon boxes, standing birds, etc. 40 projects; more than 275 diagrams and photographs. 94pp.

20713-7 Paperbound $1.00

TRICKS AND GAMES ON THE POOL TABLE, Fred Herrmann. 79 tricks and games—some solitaires, some for two or more players, some competitive games—to entertain you between formal games. Mystifying shots and throws, unusual caroms, tricks involving such props as cork, coins, a hat, etc. Formerly *Fun on the Pool Table*. 77 figures. 95pp.

21814-7 Paperbound $1.00

HAND SHADOWS TO BE THROWN UPON THE WALL: A SERIES OF NOVEL AND AMUSING FIGURES FORMED BY THE HAND, Henry Bursill. Delightful picturebook from great-grandfather's day shows how to make 18 different hand shadows: a bird that flies, duck that quacks, dog that wags his tail, camel, goose, deer, boy, turtle, etc. Only book of its sort. vi + 33pp. 6½ x 9¼.   21779-5 Paperbound $1.00

WHITTLING AND WOODCARVING, E. J. Tangerman. 18th printing of best book on market. "If you can cut a potato you can carve" toys and puzzles, chains, chessmen, caricatures, masks, frames, woodcut blocks, surface patterns, much more. Information on tools, woods, techniques. Also goes into serious wood sculpture from Middle Ages to present, East and West. 464 photos, figures. x + 293pp.

20965-2 Paperbound $2.00

HISTORY OF PHILOSOPHY, Julián Marias. Possibly the clearest, most easily followed, best planned, most useful one-volume history of philosophy on the market; neither skimpy nor overfull. Full details on system of every major philosopher and dozens of less important thinkers from pre-Socratics up to Existentialism and later. Strong on many European figures usually omitted. Has gone through dozens of editions in Europe. 1966 edition, translated by Stanley Appelbaum and Clarence Strowbridge. viii + 505pp. 21739-6 Paperbound $3.50

YOGA: A SCIENTIFIC EVALUATION, Kovoor T. Behanan. Scientific but non-technical study of physiological results of yoga exercises; done under auspices of Yale U. Relations to Indian thought, to psychoanalysis, etc. 16 photos. xxiii + 270pp.

20505-3 Paperbound $2.50

Prices subject to change without notice.

Available at your book dealer or write for free catalogue to Dept. GI, Dover Publications, Inc., 180 Varick St., N. Y., N. Y. 10014. Dover publishes more than 150 books each year on science, elementary and advanced mathematics, biology, music, art, literary history, social sciences and other areas.

COPPER SUN

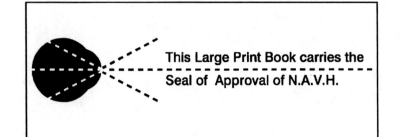

This Large Print Book carries the
Seal of Approval of N.A.V.H.

COPPER SUN

SHARON M. DRAPER

THORNDIKE PRESS

An imprint of Thomson Gale, a part of The Thomson Corporation

Detroit • New York • San Francisco • New Haven, Conn. • Waterville, Maine • London • Munich

Thorndike Press® Large Print The Literacy Bridge Young Adult.

The text of this Large Print edition is unabridged.

Other aspects of the book may vary from the original edition.

Set in 16 pt. Plantin.

LIBRARY OF CONGRESS CATALOGING-IN-PUBLICATION DATA

Draper, Sharon M. (Sharon Mills)
  Copper sun / by Sharon Draper. — Large print ed.
    p. cm.
    Summary: Two fifteen-year-old girls — one a slave and the other an indentured servant — escape their Carolina plantation and try to make their way to Fort Moses, Florida, a Spanish colony that gives sanctuary to slaves.
    ISBN 0-7862-8948-1 (hardcover : alk. paper)
    1. Large type books. [1. Slavery — Fiction. 2. Indentured servants — Fiction. 3. South Carolina — History — Colonial period, ca. 1600–1775 — Fiction. 4. Florida — History — Spanish colony, 1565–1763 — Fiction. 5. African Americans — Fiction. 6. Large type books.] I. Title.
PZ7.D78325Cop 2006b
[Fic]—dc22   2006018615

Published in 2006 by arrangement with Simon & Schuster Children's Publishing Division, Inc.

Printed in the United States of America on permanent paper.
10 9 8 7 6 5 4 3

AUTHOR'S NOTE

I am the granddaughter of a slave.

My grandfather — not my great-great-grandfather or some long-distant relative — was born a slave in the year 1860 on a farm in North Carolina. He did not become free until the end of the Civil War, when he was five years old.

Hugh Mills lived a very long life, married four times, and fathered twenty-one children. The last child to be born was my father. Hugh was sixty-four years old when my father was born in 1924.

I dedicate this book to him, and to my grandmother Estelle, who, even though she was not allowed to finish school, kept a written journal of her life. It is one of my greatest treasures. One day I hope to write her story.

I also dedicate this to all those who came before me — the untold multitudes who were taken as slaves and brought to this country, the millions who died during that process, as well as those who lived, suffered, and endured.

Amari carries their spirit. She carries mine as well.

HERITAGE

BY COUNTEE CULLEN

What is Africa to me:
Copper sun or scarlet sea,
Jungle star or jungle track,
Strong bronzed men, or regal black
Women from whose loins I sprang
When the birds of Eden sang?
One three centuries removed
From the scenes his fathers loved,
Spicy grove, cinnamon tree,
What is Africa to me?

In spite of the heat, Amari trembled. The buyers of slaves had arrived. She and the other women were stripped naked. Amari bit her lip, determined not to cry. But she couldn't stop herself from screaming out as her arms were wrenched behind her back and tied. A searing pain shot up through her shoulders. A white man clamped shackles on her ankles, rubbing his hands up her legs as he did. Amari tensed and tried to jerk away, but the chains were too tight. She could not hold back the tears. It was the summer of her fifteenth year, and this day she wanted to die.

Amari shuffled in the dirt as she was led into the yard and up onto a raised wooden table, which she realized gave the people in the yard a perfect view of the women who were to be sold. She looked at the faces in the sea of pink-skinned people who stood around pointing at the captives and jabbering in their language as each of the slaves was described.

She looked for pity or even understanding but found nothing except cool stares. They looked at her as if she were a cow for sale. She saw a few white women fanning themselves and whispering in the ears of well-dressed men — their husbands, she supposed. Most of the people in the crowd were men; however, she did see a poorly dressed white girl about her own age standing near a wagon. The girl had a sullen look on her face, and she seemed to be the only person not interested in what was going on at the slave sale.

Amari looked up at a seabird flying above and remembered her little brother. I wish he could have flown that night, Amari thought sadly. I wish I could have flown away as well.

■ ■ ■ ■

PART ONE
AMARI

■ ■ ■ ■

1. Amari and Besa

"What are you doing up there, Kwasi?" Amari asked her eight-year-old brother with a laugh. He had his legs wrapped around the trunk of the top of a coconut tree.

"For once I want to look a giraffe in the eye!" he shouted. "I wish to ask her what she has seen in her travels."

"What kind of warrior speaks to giraffes?" Amari teased. She loved listening to her brother's tales — everything was an adventure to him.

"A wise one," he replied mysteriously, "one who can see who is coming down the path to our village."

"Well, you look like a little monkey. Since you're up there, grab a coconut for Mother, but come down before you hurt yourself."

Kwasi scrambled down and tossed the coconut at his sister. "You should thank me, Amari, for my treetop adventure!" He grinned mischievously.

13

"Why?" she asked.

"I saw Besa walking through the forest, heading this way! I have seen how you tremble like a dove when he is near."

"You are the one who will be trembling if you do not get that coconut to Mother right away! And take her a few papayas and a pineapple as well. It will please her, and we shall have a delicious treat tonight." Amari could still smell the sweetness of the pineapple her mother had cut from its rough skin and sliced for the breakfast meal that morning.

Kwasi snatched back the coconut and ran off then, laughing and making kissing noises as he chanted, "Besa my love, Besa my love, Besa my love!" Amari pretended to chase him, but as soon as he was out of sight, she reached down into the small stream that flowed near Kwasi's tree and splashed water on her face.

Her village, Ziavi, lay just beyond the red dirt path down which Kwasi had disappeared. She headed there, walking leisurely, with just the slightest awareness of a certain new roundness to her hips and smoothness to her gait as she waited for Besa to catch up with her.

Amari loved the rusty brown dirt of Ziavi. The path, hard-packed from thousands of bare feet that had trod on it for decades, was flanked on both sides by fat, fruit-laden mango trees, the sweet smell of which always seemed to welcome her home. Ahead she could see the thatched roofs of the homes of her people, smoky cooking fires, and a chicken or two, scratching in the dirt.

She chuckled as she watched Tirza, a young woman about her own age, chasing one of her family's goats once again. That goat hated to be milked and always found a way to run off right at milking time. Tirza's mother had threatened several times to make stew of the hardheaded animal. Tirza waved at Amari, then dove after the goat, who had galloped into the undergrowth. Several of the old women, sitting in front of their huts soaking up sunshine, cackled with amusement.

To the left and apart from the other shelters in the village stood the home of the chief elder. It was larger than most, made of sturdy wood and bamboo, with thick thatch made from palm leaves making up the roof. The chief elder's two wives chattered cheerfully together as they pounded cassava fufu for his evening meal. Amari called out to them as she passed and bowed with respect.

She knew that she and her mother would soon be preparing the fufu for their own

15

meal. She looked forward to the task — they would take turns pounding the vegetable into a wooden bowl with a stick almost as tall as Amari. Most of the time they got into such a good rhythm that her mother started tapping her feet and doing little dance steps as they worked. That always made Amari laugh.

Although Amari knew Besa was approaching, she pretended not to see him until he touched her shoulder. She turned quickly and, acting surprised, called out his name. "Besa!" Just seeing his face made her grin. He was much taller than she was, and she had to stand on tiptoe to look into his face. He had an odd little birthmark on his cheek — right at the place where his face dimpled into a smile. She thought it looked a little like a pineapple, but it disappeared as he smiled widely at the sight of her. He took her small brown hands into his large ones, and she felt as delicate as one of the little birds that Kwasi liked to catch and release.

"My lovely Amari," he greeted her. "How goes your day?" His deep voice made her tremble.

"Better, now that you are here," she replied. Amari and Besa had been formally betrothed to each other last year. They would be allowed to marry in another year.

For now they simply enjoyed the mystery and pleasure of stolen moments such as this.

"I cannot stay and talk with you right now," Besa told her. "I have seen strangers in the forest, and I must tell the council of elders right away."

Amari looked intently at his face and realized he was worried. "What tribe are they from?" she asked with concern.

"I do not think the Creator made a tribe such as these creatures. They have skin the color of goat's milk." Besa frowned and ran to find the chief.

As she watched Besa rush off, an uncomfortable feeling filled Amari. The sunny pleasantness of the afternoon had suddenly turned dark. She hurried home to tell her family what she had learned. Her mother and Esi, a recently married friend, sat on the ground, spinning cotton threads for yarn. Their fingers flew as they chatted together, the pale fibers stretching and uncurling into threads for what would become kente cloth. Amari loved her tribe's design of animal figures and bold shapes. Tomorrow the women would dye the yarn, and when it was ready, her father, a master weaver, would create the strips of treasured fabric on his loom. Amari never tired of watching the magical rhythm of movement and color. Amari's mother looked up at her daughter warmly.

"You should be helping us make this yarn, my daughter," her mother chided gently.

"I'm sorry, Mother, it's just that I'd so much rather weave like father. Spinning makes my fingertips hurt." Amari had often imagined new patterns for the cloth, and longed to join the men at the long looms, but girls were forbidden to do so.

Her mother looked aghast. "Be content with woman's work, child. It is enough."

"I will help you with the dyes tomorrow," Amari promised halfheartedly. She avoided her mother's look of mild disapproval. "Besides, I was helping Kwasi gather fruit," Amari said, changing the subject.

Kwasi, sitting in the dirt trying to catch a grasshopper, looked up and said with a smirk, "I think she was more interested in making love-dove faces with Besa than making yarn with you!" When Amari reached out to grab him, he darted out of her reach, giggling.

"Your sister, even though she avoids the work, is a skilled spinner and will be a skilled wife. She needs practice in learning both, my son," their mother said with a smile. "Now disappear into the dust for a moment!" Kwasi ran off then, laughing as

18

he chased the grasshopper, his bare feet barely skimming the dusty ground.

Amari knew her mother could tell by just the tilt of her smile or a fraction of a frown how she was feeling. "And how goes it with young Besa?" her mother asked quietly.

"Besa said that a band of unusual-looking strangers are coming this way, Mother," Amari informed her. "He seemed uneasy and went to tell the village elders."

"We must welcome our guests, then, Amari. We would never judge people simply by how they looked — that would be uncivilized," her mother told her. "Let us prepare for a celebration." Esi picked up her basket of cotton and, with a quick wave, headed home to make her own preparations.

Amari knew her mother was right and began to help her make plans for the arrival of the guests. They pounded fufu, made garden egg stew from eggplant and dried fish, and gathered more bananas, mangoes, and papayas.

"Will we have a dance and celebration for the guests, Mother?" she asked hopefully. "And Father's storytelling?"

"Your father and the rest of the elders will decide, but I'm sure the visit of such strangers will be cause for much festivity." Amari smiled with anticipation, for her mother was known as one of the most talented dancers in the Ewe tribe. Her mother continued, "Your father loves to have tales to tell and new stories to gather — this night will provide both."

Amari and her mother scurried around their small dwelling, rolling up the sleeping mats and sweeping the dirt floor with a broom made of branches. Throughout the village, the pungent smells of goat stew and peanut soup, along with waves of papaya and honeysuckle that wafted through the air, made Amari feel hungry as well as excited. The air was fragrant with hope and possibility.

2. Strangers and Death

The strangers whom Besa had spoken of arrived about an hour later. Everyone in the village came out of their houses to see the astonishing sight — pale, unhealthy-looking men who carried large bundles and unusual-looking sticks as they marched into the center of the village. In spite of the welcoming greetings and looks of excitement on the faces of the villagers, the strangers did not smile. They smelled of danger, Amari thought as one of them looked at her. He had eyes the color of the sky. She shuddered.

However, the unusual-looking men were accompanied by warriors from the Ashanti tribe, men of her own land, men her people had known and traded with, so even if the village elders were concerned, it would be unacceptable not to show hospitality. Surely the Ashanti would explain. But good manners came first.

Any occasion for visitors was a cause for excitement, so after the initial amazement and curiosity at the strange men, the village bubbled with anticipation as preparations were made for a formal welcoming ceremony. Amari stayed in the shadows, watching it all, uneasy, but not sure why.

Their chief, or *Awoamefia,* who could be spoken to only through a member of the council of elders, invited the guests to sit, and they were formally welcomed with wine and prayers. The chief and the council of elders, made up of both men and women, were always chosen for their wisdom and made all the important decisions. Amari was proud that her father, Komla, was one of the elders. He was also the village storyteller, and she loved to watch the expressions on his face as he acted out the stories she had heard since childhood.

"We welcome you," the chief began. "Let your yes be yes and your no be no. May you be protected from evil, and may you live to a ripe old age. If you come in peace, we receive you in peace. Heroism is the dignity of our ancestors, and, in their name, we welcome you." He passed the wine, made from palm tree leaves, to Amari's father, then to the other elders, and finally to the strangers.

The men with skin like the milk of goats and their Ashanti companions drank the palm wine from hand-carved gourds that had been decorated with ceremonial tribal designs. The newcomers then offered gifts to the chief: small ropes of sparkling beads unlike anything Amari had ever seen, casks of wine, and lengths of fine cloth — so shiny and smooth that Amari marveled. She knew no human could have woven it.

No real explanations for their presence had been given yet, but with the exchange of gifts, the feeling of unease began to lessen and everyone knew that the dancing and drumming would soon begin. Ceremony was important. Business matters always followed proper celebration. It was not yet the time for questions. First came the stories, Amari reminded herself, starting to feel excited.

As chief storyteller, Amari's father was highly respected. Komla knew every story, every proverb, every bit of tribal history ever told or sung or drummed by her people. He spoke at each birth, funeral, and wedding, as well as at unexpected special occasions like this. The villagers crowded around him in anticipation, although even the youngest child knew by heart every story he would tell. The strangers sat politely and waited.

"Let me tell you of the wickedness of Chief Agokoli," her father began. "He was a wicked, wicked man."

"Wicked," the people responded with enthusiasm.

"He would give the Ewe people impossible jobs — like weaving baskets out of sand."

"Impossible!" the villagers responded almost in unison.

"The Ewe people finally found a means to escape from the wicked ruler," Komla recounted. "The people crept out through a hole in the wall and fooled the soldiers of Chief Agokoli. And how did they do that?" he asked the crowd, who, of course, knew the question was coming, as well as the answer.

"They walked backward in the dirt!" the people responded enthusiastically.

"And so they did," Komla said, ending his tale with a tapping on his drum. "They walked backward on the dirt path so their footprints looked like the prints of someone arriving into the village, not departing!" He looked over at Amari as he finished the tale with a wink he saved for her alone.

Everyone in the small community, including Amari, laughed and clapped their hands at the familiar story. Amari loved her father's stories, and the sound of his deep, gravelly voice had always made her feel safe, whether he was whispering silly noises in her ear, speaking formally in a meeting of the elders, or chatting with affection with her mother.

To the family's great amusement, Komla would sometimes sing to them in their small hut after the evening meal. "You sound like a monkey in pain," Amari's mother would tell her husband fondly. But when he was telling stories, his voice was magical; Amari could listen to him all night.

The feeling of tension faded. The drumming would come next, and, after the storytelling, this was Amari's favorite part of her village's celebrations.

Amari looked around for Besa. He was the assistant to the village master arts man, the one responsible for the creation of all the dances and drum rhythms. She knew Besa would be anxious to show off his skill on the drum he had carved and painted himself. Amari was proud of how devoted Besa was to learning the rhythms. He'd told her once, "You know, Amari, the drums are not just noise — they are language; they are the pattern of the rhythm of our lives."

He had no need to look at his hands to produce the drum sounds that lived within him. She loved to watch Besa stare into space, smiling as he drummed, lost in the rhythms he created.

As soon as the master drummers started playing, everyone in her village felt the call. The younger boys, whose fingers itched to show their skills, grabbed their own small drums and joined the beat. Villagers began to get up and move to the rhythms. Besa played with the confidence and skill he always did. Amari's eyes were on only him; her heart beat faster as Besa's fingers caressed the sounds out of his skin-covered drum.

Drumbeats echoed in the approaching darkness. The fire in the center of the assembly area glowed on the faces of the dancers, mostly younger children and women at first, but soon nearly everyone in the village joined in, even the old ones whose toothless grins spoke their happiness. All spoke to the spirits with their joyous movements. Their bodies swayed, their hands clapped, their feet stomped in a glorious frenzy, all to the rhythm of the drums.

Ba ba la ba do ga we do
the words are sounds are words from deep
* within*
from a place that was lost now found
sobo hee we do so ma da ma da so so

sound is self is you is we sound is past is
* now is so*
sobo hee we do so ma da ma da so so
from remembered past to forgotten tomor-
* row*
drum talk throbs breathes life speaks
* song sings words*
Ba ba la ba do ga we do
warriors pulse maidens sway elders
* children rejoice*
thrum to the heartbeat thrum to the heart-
* beat*
ba ba la ba ba ba la ba ga we do

Kwasi, as round and brown as a Kola nut, danced with the rest of the children, gleefully spinning in the dust. Amari watched him and remembered how he once had captured a small bird and copied its movements, flapping his arms like wings, telling her, with much laughter, that he intended to learn how to fly. And as Kwasi stomped and glided through the dust that evening, it seemed to Amari that he really *was* flying.

He ran over to Amari then, breathing hard with excitement. "Come," he said, grasping her arm and trying to pull her into the dancing. "Why do you hide in the shadows? Come dance for the strangers!"

She pushed Kwasi away gently, reminding

27

him she was no longer a child. She was to be married soon, and she preferred peeking at Besa, who stood behind his waist-high drum on the other side of the fire, watching her as well.

The drumbeats rippled in the darkness, the dancers swayed and stomped on the hard-packed earth, and Amari's people clapped and laughed as the firelight glimmered in the night.

The first explosion came from the end of one of the unusual weapon sticks the strangers carried. Louder than any beat of even the largest drum, it was followed by a cry of horror. The chief had fallen off his seat, a huge red bleeding hole in the center of his chest. More explosions followed in rapid succession, then everyone was screaming. Confusion and dust swirled throughout the village. Amari watched, aghast, as a mother with her baby wrapped on her back tried to flee, but both mother and child were clubbed down into the dirt by one of the Ashanti warriors. An Ashanti! How could this be? Villagers ran blindly into the fire, trying to escape and screaming for mercy, only to be felled by the terrible fire weapons of the strangely pale men.

Amari knew she should run; she knew she should try to escape into the forest, but her feet would not move. She could only stare in horror. She gasped as she watched an Ashanti grab her mother and try to put thick iron cuffs on her mother's wrists. She turned her head and followed, in slow motion it seemed, her father's bellows of rage as he leaped toward her mother to rescue her. But before he even reached her, one of the milk-faced men thrust a knife into his stomach, and Komla fell silently to the earth. Amari's mother screamed in anguish and bit her captor's hand. Enraged, he hurled her to the ground. Amari watched, unable to breathe or move, as her mother's head smashed upon a rock. Amari wanted to scream, *Mother, get up, oh, please, get up,* but she was unable to say a word. Her mother did not move. Amari needed her parents to come get her, to tell her not to be afraid, to run with her into the underbrush for safety. But they just lay there, their blood beginning to stain the dust. Amari doubled over in agony. Her parents were dead.

She looked frantically for Besa and Kwasi, but all was smoke and screams and death. Finally, she saw Kwasi running toward her, screaming, "Run, Amari, run!" Her feet loosened then as he reached her. She grabbed his hand, and they ran wildly out

29

of the village into what they hoped was the safety of the darkness. Sharp branches cut Amari's face as she plunged through a thick tangle of trees. The smell of sharp, acrid smoke, not of gentle hearth fires, but of the flames of destruction, followed them. Birds and monkeys above them cried out in alarm, but their noise could not cover the screams of the slaughter of her people.

Suddenly, Amari heard fast-moving, thudding footsteps behind them and the whirr of a spear. Kwasi held her hand tighter and they ran even faster, Amari trying in vain to be as invisible and swift as the wind. *Fly, my baby brother,* she thought desperately. *Fly away!* One moment they were leaping over a fallen log, and the next moment she heard Kwasi moan softly, then his hand slipped slowly from hers. He slumped to the ground, a look of soft surprise on his small face. A spear had sliced though his whole little body. Amari sank down beside him and held him to her. He died in her arms.

She lay there in the darkness, cuddling his small, lifeless body, unable to weep, unable to run any longer. She hardly cared when she was grabbed by one of the strangers. Her arms were wrenched behind her, and iron shackles with heavy, rusty chains between them were snapped onto her wrists, holding them there. Amari was marched back to where the burning village had once stood so happily, grabbed by her hair, and shoved into a pile of other survivors from the village.

No one spoke. No one wept. They were defeated.

3. SORROW AND SHACKLES

When the sun rose the next morning, Amari looked with horror at what was once her tribe's village. All of the homes had been burned, their roofs of thatch and walls of reeds consumed by the fire. The charred and bloodied bodies of relatives remained where they had fallen, with no one to perform proper rites for burials, no one to say the prayers for the dead. Amari knew that the pale strangers probably did not know their customs, could not understand the seriousness of the proper burial procedures, but the Ashanti were people of her own land, supposedly brothers in spirit with Amari's people. *How could they do this and face their own future?* she wondered in horrible confusion. It was just one of many questions for which she had no answer. *Where did these strangers come from? Why do they want to hurt us? How can I continue to live without my family?* It took all of her

32

strength not to look at the bodies of her parents. Amari's heart hurt in a way she could never have imagined.

Twenty-four of the villagers had survived the slaughter. She glanced around the group and realized that most of them were around her age — young and fairly healthy. None of the elders had been spared, none of the children. Esi and her new husband, Makafui, huddled together, even though they had been shackled apart. Amari knew that Esi was carrying her first child, for she had announced it with joy just two days before. Amari also had seen that the parents of both Makafui and Esi were included among the dead. Kwadzo, a young man known in the village as a fierce hunter, pulled angrily at his shackles, his wrists already bleeding as he fought their restraint. A huge gash on his head had stopped bleeding but was open and untreated. He needed the medicine woman to wrap it in healing leaves, but no one seemed concerned about his injury. All of the young male captives had sustained some type of injury.

Finally, at the far end of the huddled circle of captives, Amari spotted Besa. He looked at her with glazed, saddened eyes. In the distance, where such a short time ago he had played with such power and joy, she spotted his beloved drum, crushed and in splinters in the dirt. Amari wished she could smile at Besa to give him hope, but she had no hope to offer. He looked away.

Suddenly, one of the pale-faced men with the death sticks came over to them, shouting in a language she did not understand. He made it clear, however, that they were to get up from the ground immediately. Most of their captors, both black and white, carried both whips and fire sticks. Amari looked around in fear and tried to ask what was happening, but all she received in response was a vicious slice of a whip across her arms and neck. She cried out as she arched her back in pain, but she hurried to her feet and asked no more questions. She glanced at Besa. His face was distorted with anger.

One of the pale men then brought out objects that she would not have used even on animals. They were similar to the iron bands on her wrists, except these fit around their necks! A length of iron chain connected each neck band, so each was linked to the next in a single file of chains and captivity.

As the iron band was placed around her neck, Amari felt as if she would choke. It was cold and heavy and cut into her shoulders. The chain was then pulled sharply as the next person in line was shackled behind her. Amari could not turn and see who it was. She could see only the back of the person in front of her. It was Tirza, the young woman who just hours before had been chasing that runaway goat. Tirza could not stop shaking with fright.

The pale-faced men fastened similar irons on their ankles, with a short length of chain between them, and a longer chain linking each person in the coffle together, thus making it impossible for them to run away or even walk very fast. Fastened together in groups of six, the wrists, ankles, and necks of each captive were painfully connected to the person on either side. Once the villagers were all linked, a white face pulled the first person with a rope, and those linked to him lurched forward as well. Amari stumbled, but the neck iron stopped her fall. She choked and tried to grab her throat, but her arms were shackled as well. Gasping, she fell into step with the others, who, with heads bowed, shuffled together toward they knew not what.

Besa, Amari noticed, was in the front of his coffle of captives. He would not look at her, glancing away whenever she tried to catch his eye. She realized he must be feeling terrible shame — shame that he could not rescue himself, or Amari, or change any of what was happening to them.

If one in their group stumbled, all of them stumbled or sometimes even fell, choking as the chains pulled them down together. Beaten with whips if they fell, beaten if they failed to keep the pace, they headed slowly away from everything they had once known. The bright red pain across Amari's back and on her wrists and ankles made her whole body tremble. She felt as if she might pass out. The heat of the sun showed no mercy, and she couldn't even wipe away the sweat that burned her eyes as it ran down her face.

Her tongue felt thick — she was so thirsty, and she couldn't remember the last time she had eaten. As she walked, she tried but couldn't comprehend the incredible cruelty of the men who had done this. Nothing made any sense. Her stomach knotted up every time she thought of her last glimpse of her mother and father — dead, unburied, and covered with flies. And little Kwasi — he was just a small boy who had never even hurt a grasshopper. How could he be dead? Amari felt dizzy, but she dared not stop or stumble.

The first path they traveled was the long

road that led from their village to the big river several miles away. It seemed as if even the trees bowed their heads as they passed. The birds, normally full of chatter, were silent as the group marched past them for the last time.

Day after day the captives walked, saying very little to one another or to their captors. One afternoon Amari heard Kwadzo try to speak to one of the Ashanti who guarded them.

"Why do you do this, my brother?" he whispered when out of earshot of the white soldiers.

"Our tribes have been at war before," the Ashanti responded, a defensiveness in his guarded tone. "This time, however, I shall be greatly rewarded." He strode ahead then and said no more. Amari wondered what he meant.

The wound on Kwadzo's head grew swollen and purple, and Amari could tell he was in pain, but he continued on, as they all did, one foot after the other, mile after mile. His face was one of anger and hatred. Besa's face, when she got a chance to glimpse it, had become a mask.

The captives were never unshackled. Each set of six ate together, slept together, and had to urinate and defecate together. They were given just a little food each morning and very little water. Each group was forced into a rhythm, keeping a pace that was difficult for the slowest and weakest of them as they marched. In Amari's group it was Tirza who seemed to have given up. She walked slowly and stumbled often. Her back was soon a patchwork of welts from being whipped when she could not keep up with the rest. One night she whispered, "I cannot live like this, Amari. My parents, my sisters — all whom I love — are dead. I would rather die than be enslaved like this."

"Tirza, stop talking like that!" Amari whispered back. "We must live!"

"Why?" she asked dully.

"Because as long as we have life, we have hope!" Amari said fervently.

"Hope of what?"

"Escape, perhaps."

"You are a dreamer, Amari," Tirza told her quietly. "I have no dreams left."

And the next morning Tirza was dead. She had simply ceased breathing during the night. The leader of their captors looked at her lifeless body and cursed. He unshackled her, tossed her body to the side of the road, and spat upon it. The rest of them were told to get up and move on. Amari was surprised and saddened to realize that the travel in their chained coffle, now five instead of six, was lighter and easier without Tirza. Her heart, however, seemed to beat more slowly and heavily. None of them wept for Tirza or even looked her way as they passed.

4. DEATH MARCH TO CAPE COAST

Amari lost count of the days they walked. Her neck, bruised and scarred from the iron brace around it, could barely hold her head up any longer. Her wrists and ankles were raw where the skin had been worn away, and insects swarmed around the oozing wounds. Her bare feet left bloody footprints upon the path — sliced by every stone and sharp stick she stumbled over. At first these difficulties bothered her. But gradually, she simply felt numb.

Kwadzo died one morning, probably from his untreated wound, Amari thought, or maybe from his untreated sorrow, but she could not mourn his loss. She actually envied him. Seven others died during their long journey. Esi, the young wife of Makafui, first lost her baby, then her own life. Amari was sure she bled to death. Unable to control his grief, Makafui grabbed one of the leaders of the march and tried to strangle him with his wrist chains. How he managed to get his hands in front of him, Amari did not know, but before Makafui had a chance to succeed in killing the man, one of the others calmly picked up his fire stick and shot him. He was left on the side of the road for the hyenas, as the others had been.

Amari had no idea where they were being taken or why. They just marched, prisoners in a land so full of beauty and harmony that Amari could not bear to watch the golden sun rising in the east or the freely running giraffes and elephants in the distance.

Occasionally, other coffles of slaves would join their group. They looked with dead eyes at Amari and her sad little procession. No one spoke. Eventually, all of the prisoners were herded together, moving slowly down a path that was becoming increasingly wider and more well traveled. The dirt was packed hard by the feet of those who had passed that way before. Amari wondered if they, too, had been coffled and shackled.

Finally one day they arrived in a city — so much larger than what Amari had ever known that she stared in wonder at the huge buildings made of stone. The variety of noises — screeching monkeys in cages and vendors loudly proclaiming their goods

41

from the side of the road — made her head throb. She marveled at the people who lived there — people with dark and pale and even honey-colored skins. Black men and women who walked freely and laughed loudly, speaking in languages she did not know. White men walking arm in arm with black men, with no chains on either of them. Amari was amazed and understood none of it. Some of the people looked at the group of enslaved captives with pity as they were marched through the center of town, but no one made any move to help them. In fact, Amari noticed that most turned away as if the miserable group were invisible.

The air smelled salty and felt wet upon her skin. The little river in Amari's village had smelled of mud and of the animals that used it as a gathering place to drink the water. But here she could smell a larger body of water — something huge and foreign and frightening.

Although Amari could not understand the language of the white men, she soon began to recognize words they repeated often, such as "slave" and "price." Once they entered the city, she kept hearing them say, "Cape Coast, Cape Coast," with great excitement. *What is this place?* she thought to herself. *Why are we here? And how will we ever find our way back home?* Then she gasped. There *was* no more home. She had no more family. And, for the first time, she began to weep.

Amari and the rest of the captives were guided to a huge white building made of bricks and stone, larger than any Amari had ever seen or even imagined. The leader of the pale warriors barked orders to someone in a colorful uniform at a gate. Huge doors opened and they were led inside. The bright sunlight was suddenly gone, and she had to adjust her eyes to the gloom inside the structure. It smelled of blood and death. She could hear terrifying wails that seemed to be coming from the walls of the place. Amari was filled with dread.

The men were then separated from the women, and Amari's neck irons and leg irons were finally removed. She rubbed her wrists and couldn't help but breathe with relief. Nothing could be worse than what they'd already gone through, she thought.

She was wrong. A huge stone door with iron bars slid open,and Amari was shoved inside a room with the rest of the women who had survived their journey. She thought she was blinded at first because the darkness was so total and sudden. The smell engulfed her next — the odor of sweat and fear, of body wastes and hopelessness. As her eyes slowly adjusted, she could see women — dozens of them — lying on the floor, huddled against the walls, curled into balls. Some of them looked up when the newcomers were tossed into the cell, but most did not bother to acknowledge their presence. Amari trembled with fear and disgust, afraid she would become like they were, afraid she already was.

Amari found an unoccupied place by the wall and sat down on the floor, which was wet and slimy. The room had no window, just a large hole near the ceiling for a little bit of air to circulate. No one spoke to her. Those who were talking among themselves spoke in dialects she could not understand. Only a few could she decipher. Amari surmised that women from many different tribes and countries were imprisoned here — Ibo, Ga, and Mandinka. She was amazed at the thoroughness of their captors, how they had managed to capture so many of them. Had they murdered the families and destroyed the villages of everyone here as well? The thought of so many dead seemed to crush her. She covered her head with her arms and barely stifled a scream. No one listened.

Amari gradually grew accustomed to the

dim light and looked around the room. She spotted a woman in a corner who was rocking a child who was not there. She sang to it and caressed it gently, but her arms were empty. The woman's sorrow was raw and palpable, like spoiled meat.

Amari's stomach growled. She could not remember the last time she had eaten, so when the guards tossed some chunks of bread through the opening, she was grateful. But by the time she got up to get some of the food off the floor, the previously quiet women had already rushed past her and savagely fought over every scrap of bread. She ended up with nothing. Amari dropped to the cold wet floor, bowed her head, and wept.

A large woman came and sat down next to her and offered her a small piece of her own portion. Amari took it gratefully.

"Crying won't help, child," she told her. "This place is slimy with tears."

Amari was surprised to hear the woman speak in her own Ewe language. She wiped her eyes and said in barely a whisper, "I feel like a broken drum — hollow, crushed, unable to make a sound."

"You must learn to make music once more."

Amari was miserable. "I don't understand," she told her.

"In time, you will."

Amari pondered this for a moment while she nibbled at the bread to make it last longer.

"Where is this place?" Amari asked her.

"Cape Coast Castle. It is a prison for our people. We will be held here until they have captured enough of us, then we will be sold and sent into the sea." She breathed deeply.

"Sold? I do not understand."

"You were chosen because you are young and strong. You survived the long journey here. You will fetch a great price."

"From whom? For what?" Amari asked in confusion. "Who would want to sell me or buy me? I am just a girl who has seen barely fifteen summers. I have no skills."

"There are white men who will buy you to work for them by day and amuse them by night."

Amari looked up, her eyes wide with disbelief. "How do you know this?"

"I have been sold before," she replied quietly. "My master, a fat white man from this city, grew tired of me and sold me to buyers who brought me here."

"Have you been here long?" Amari asked.

"Long enough to see one group sold and sent away. We were marched into the courtyard, and white men bargained for us. One by one they were taken through a small door. I could see the white sand and the blue of the sea beyond it, but no more. All I know is they never returned."

"Do you think they were killed?"

"No. They had value. They did not die. At least not physically," she added.

"Why were you not sold?" Amari asked her.

"I caught the attention of the leader of the guards." She paused. "He sends for me to come to him at night."

At first Amari didn't understand, but suddenly she realized what the woman meant. Amari looked at her in horror. "You mean he . . . ?"

"Yes, child. It is terrible. But I am allowed to bathe. I get extra food rations. I do not allow myself to think while I am with him. I hate him. But I will live. My spirit is too strong to die in a place like this."

Amari looked at this woman, at her strong body and kindly face, and began to cry once more, huge racking sobs of despair. The woman took Amari in her arms and let her cry, the only comfort she had known since that horrible night in the village.

5. THE DOOR OF NO RETURN

Once a day Amari and the other women were taken from the cell in small groups. Cold water from large wooden buckets was tossed upon them. Their clothes, what little that remained, were torn and barely covered their bodies. The soldiers who guarded them liked to rip the tops of the women's garments so their breasts were exposed. Amari learned to swallow her shame.

The woman who had befriended her was called Afi. She made sure Amari had food each day and protected her from some of the other women who had grown fierce and violent from their captivity. She showed Amari how to walk with a limp and look with a vacant, stupid stare to make sure the soldiers would pass her by when they looked for women to come to their rooms. She also showed Amari how to exercise inside the cell, to stay strong and ready for whatever may come next. At night she crooned soft songs similar to the ones Amari's mother had once sang to her as a child. Afi told Amari that her husband and a daughter about Amari's age had died two years before. Amari figured that Afi needed her as much as she needed Afi.

"Do you think the ancestors can speak to us in this place?" Amari asked Afi one hot night. The air was thick with the stench of excrement.

"I don't know, child," she replied, trying to cool Amari by fanning her with her hand. "I know they see us, however. And they weep for us. I can feel it."

"We need more than weeping, Afi," Amari said quietly. "We need an army of warriors to come and unfasten the locks, kill our captors, return us to our homes, and bring our families and friends back to us, alive and smiling."

"You know that is not to be, my child," Afi replied gently. "We are caught in a place where there is no hope, no escape from the misery of the present or the memories of the past." They were silent then, for there was nothing more to say.

One day, without warning, Amari and the rest of the women were brought into the center of the prison by the white soldiers, who chained their hands behind them and shackled their feet as well. Then strange white men, one of them so tall and thin that he seemed to sway when he walked, looked over each of the women as if inspecting goats for slaughter.

The thin man came up to Amari and lifted her upper lip, pinching the flesh with his long, bony fingers. He smelled unwashed. Amari whipped her head away from him, her eyes dark with anger. Glaring at her, he slapped her face so hard, she almost fell to the ground. Then he yanked her back up, grabbed her chin, and held it tightly while he pulled at her lip again.

"Open your mouth!" Afi hissed at her.

Terrified, Amari did so. The tall man took his time inspecting the inside of her mouth. He ran his fingers along her teeth and gums, mumbling to himself as he did so. When he was satisfied with his inspection of her, he moved on to the next woman.

Amari stood close to Afi, shivering with fear and disgust as the rough hands of each of the white men examined and prodded her arms, thighs, calves, and breasts.

The men yelled and spoke very fast in their strange language. Amari heard the word "price" many times. Finally, they seemed to come to a settlement. Cowrie

50

shells were counted and passed from the trader with the willowy body to the men who had captured them. Amari saw cloth also being exchanged and jewelry and gold. They had very little need for gold in her village, but she knew what it was. She knew it held the value of her life.

One by one the women were taken through the door that Afi had spoken of earlier. Some screamed; some fought back and had to be pushed. The door was narrow and very low to the ground. No one could stand upright and pass through it; the only way to go through that passageway was to crawl.

A soldier grabbed Amari roughly and pushed her toward that door. He forced her to the ground and then kicked her in the direction of the passageway. She had no choice but to proceed. It was difficult with the chains on, but she managed to crawl, painfully and slowly. The walls were smooth and worn, as if many bodies had passed through that narrow, low tunnel.

At the end of the passage a pair of hands pulled her up, and she had to close her eyes to the brightness of the sun. When she could finally open them, she saw that beautiful white sand lay in front of her. The salty smell that she had grown accustomed to was now overwhelming. As her eyes adjusted to the light, Amari cast her eyes for the first time upon the ocean. Travelers had occasionally come to her village, so she had heard tales of the blueness and vastness of the ocean. But nothing could have prepared her for water so blue, so beautiful, so never ending.

After so many days of the darkness of her cell, the glory of that view was powerful — and very, very frightening. Would she be thrown into the sea? And what was that strange house in the distance that seemed to rest on the surface of the water? It could not be a boat — boats were small and held one or two people. Boats were used for fishing or visiting family members downriver. This was huge, with white fabric dancing from it. That could not be a boat, Amari decided. It must be a place of the dead.

Before she had a chance to absorb it all, a man dragged her to what looked like a goat pen. A fire burned brightly in the center of it, even though the day was very warm, and the man was steering her toward it, Amari realized with fear. *Am I going to be cooked and eaten now? Why couldn't I have died with my family?* she thought wildly. Panicked, she tried to pull away from the man, but his grip only tightened.

A black man who spoke the language of the white men pushed her roughly down into the sand and held her firmly so she could not move. Amari could see only the feet of the second man, but he moved toward the fire, leaned down to pick something up, then walked purposefully toward her.

Intense, fiery pain pierced the sweaty softness of the skin above her left shoulder. Amari could hear her flesh sizzle, and she nearly fainted as she realized she was being branded. Like a wounded animal, Amari screamed and screamed. *Why?* was the only thought in her head. Someone then pulled her away from the fire, smeared a horrible-smelling salve on her wound, and yanked her over to another holding pen full of prisoners like her, all dazed from the pain of the hot branding iron. Many of them sat hunched over, trying to nurse their wounds. A few stared at the pale blue sky, the deep blue of the unbelievable expanse of water, and the death house that tossed on the waves in the distance.

The salve must have been effective, for the intense pain gradually subsided and was replaced by a duller throbbing that would not go away. Amari saw then that Afi had emerged from the prison as well. When she was branded, she did not cry out. Amari could see the pain on her face and the tears roll down her cheeks, but Afi did not utter a sound.

Afi was thrown into the holding pen soon after that, and they hugged each other gently, avoiding the fiery sores on their shoulders. "What happens now?" Amari whispered.

"Child, I've heard stories, but I've never seen the ocean before. I have heard that the water spills over the edge of the world and that only death is found there."

"There has to be something on the other side of the great water," Amari reasoned. "The white soldiers had to come from whatever that place is."

"It must be a place of death, for sure," Afi replied, agreeing with Amari. "For only such a horrible place could create such creatures who could burn a person with a flaming hot iron."

Amari started to remind her that they had been held down by people of their own land — people who looked just like them. But at that moment several men were shoved into the holding cell. Three of them were some of the very same Ashanti warriors who had helped to capture the people from her village. They looked stunned at their sudden change in status. Another new captive, who looked positively irate, was the black man who had just held Amari down on the sand while she was branded. He held his freshly branded shoulder and called out in the language of the whites, but they ignored him. The last man to be tossed into the pen was Besa.

The men had been kept from the women, housed in a separate section of the prison. Amari had not seen Besa since they had arrived. He was thin and filthy and looked absolutely beautiful to her. She wanted to call out his name, run to him, and hug him, but she found she could say nothing as he was taken to the far corner of the holding pen and chained there.

Besa looked up and gazed directly at Amari for just a moment. His face, once so proud and happy, showed only defeat. She understood.

The pen offered no shelter from the intense heat of the day. No water was offered to them. Men in uniform and men with obvious power and authority strode across the sand all afternoon, clearly preparing for something. *But what?* Amari wondered.

Then several of them climbed into a small boat that rocked and tossed in the waves of the large water, and they rowed out to the floating house in the distance. The boat returned with more men in uniform and a load of heavy chains. Amari knew they were for them.

The sunset that evening was unlike any Amari had ever seen. The spirit of the copper sun seemed to bleed for them as it glowed bright red against the deepening blue of the great water. It sank slowly, as if saying farewell. The shadows deepened and darkness covered the beach.

As night fell, the leader of the captors ordered small fires to be made on the beach, and Amari soon smelled the welcome odor of food cooking. It had been a long time since they had been given anything to eat, and she was amazed when the holding pen was opened and generous portions of water and food — fresh fruit, boiled cassava, and some kind of fish stew — were distributed to them. Nobody questioned the offering, and the food was consumed greedily and quickly.

Licking her fingers, she asked Afi, "Why do they feed us so well tonight?"

"To prepare us for the journey, I believe."

"What journey?"

Afi hesitated.

"Tell me," Amari urged.

"We will be taken to the boat of death on the horizon, and we will never see this place again." Her voice chilled Amari even more than the brisk wind that blew off the ocean.

"I do not understand."

"We are slaves, Amari. Slaves."

"I know this." Amari knew, of course, what slaves were — some of the wealthier elders in her own village had a few slaves. They had been won in battle or traded in negotiations between villages and tribes. They were usually respected and sometimes even adopted as extended members of a family.

"But this is not like anything we've ever known, is it?" Amari asked her. She braced herself for Afi's answer.

"No, child. Horrors unimagined, I feel, will assault us."

Amari thought back to the night she was captured and the journey to this place. Her mind could not imagine worse. She shivered in the night air, the brand on her shoulder throbbing. She thought of Kwasi, the little bird who would never fly again, but, in a way, she was glad he would not have to endure any of these horrors. Finally, leaning against the pole she was tied to, she managed to fall asleep.

6. From Sand to Ship

Amari awoke stiff, sore, and very cold the next morning. Small, beach-living insects had feasted on her skin overnight, and she scratched at the red bites that covered her legs and arms. She looked around in alarm, because the dark wall of Cape Coast Castle, which had surrounded her every night since coming to this place, had disappeared. Then she remembered the small door, the bright sand, the blue water, and the fiery burn on her shoulder.

Afi, already awake, looked at her without smiling. "Today is the day, Amari." Amari did not need to ask her for what.

They were all fed generously once again, and more salve was applied to their wounds. The men were then kicked and yelled at, shackled back together, and marched out of the pen. Besa was the last in line. He turned and glanced back at Amari with a look that said, *I would have been a good husband,*

Amari. I would have loved you more with every sunrise and sunset. Then he was gone. Amari pulled her shackled hands up to her face. The chains rattled in rhythm to her sobs.

"You knew him?" Afi asked her.

"Yes, he is from my village. We were captured on the same day."

"He is special to you, am I right?"

"Oh, yes!" Amari told her, a small smile breaking through her tears. "We were to be married." Her smiled faded then.

"You must forget him," Afi told her harshly.

"But —," Amari protested.

"He is dead to you now. Just as your parents and your brother and my family are dead — gone to be with the ancestors."

"But why, Afi? Why must I let go of the only link to who I truly am?"

"What you are is a slave," Afi told her, her voice cold and firm. "You have been bought by men who will sell your body and will do with it what they want. You can be beaten and raped and killed, and your young man can do nothing about it."

"You are cruel!" Amari cried, shaking with anger.

"I am honest," she replied sadly.

"So why should I endure this? Why did

you not let me just die in there?" Amari cried out.

"Because I see a power in you." Afi lifted her shackled wrist and reached over to touch Amari. "You know, certain people are chosen to survive. I don't know why, but you are one of those who must remember the past and tell those yet unborn. You must live."

"But why?"

"Because your mother would want you to. Because the sun continues to shine. I don't know, but you must." She said nothing else, just sat down and began tracing pictures in the sand with her finger.

Amari had little time to mourn Besa's removal or her own past or future, however. The soldiers came for the women next. They were herded together, then lined up and shackled, two by two. Afi was chained to Amari, to her great relief.

She tried to stay calm, but it was impossible. It was terrifying, not to be able to understand what was happening and not to know what was to come. She saw she wasn't the only one — some of the other women screamed and tried to grab handfuls of sand as they were forced out of the holding pen.

Led across the sand, Amari found it surprisingly hard to walk. Her feet sank with every step. As they got closer to the edge of the beach, Amari noticed that the water never stopped moving, sending huge waves of itself against the sand — first blue, then white, then blue again. Bubbling, churning, even leaping onto the land, it seemed to Amari that the ocean was reaching out to grab and devour her. Many of the women backed away from the surf and were promptly lashed. Amari was frightened, but she knew the water would not kill her. Not today.

She watched as the last of the men were loaded into small rowboats, which rocked wildly on the waves. Some of the men cried out in terror. The boats became smaller as they got closer to the death house in the distance. Then Amari could see them no more.

A set of empty rowboats, much larger than Amari had first thought, awaited the next group of captives. The women were pushed from the soft warmth of the sand to the water-soaked beach, and Amari very quickly found herself standing in water up to her knees. She screamed in spite of herself at the sudden coldness of the water and its constant movement against her legs. It crashed against her as if it were angry and seemed to be trying to pull Amari away from the land. Her feet could not find a safe place — the sand beneath the water kept shifting. The water splashed onto her face, and she discovered with surprise that it was salty — like tears.

Afi, sloshing in the shallows just ahead of Amari, was knocked sideways by a wave and fell, taking Amari with her. They both struggled to raise their heads above the water, but the weight of their leg and neck irons pulled them down. Water seeped into Amari's mouth and nose. She could not even scream.

Their captors cursed and hauled Afi and Amari up, then shoved them into the small rowboat. Afi breathed hard and tried not to show how frightened she was. Amari felt no need to hide her fear. She gripped the side of the boat fiercely and shrieked with every swell of the water, with every spray of water in her face. As the captives were loaded into the boat, it rocked and tilted as if it were about to toss them into the water once more.

And then the boat left the shore. Forty terrified women and girls howled as the boat began to float upon the sea. The soldiers on shore laughed at their fright, and the sailors on board beat them with their whips. Amari's arms and face were lashed and sliced as she huddled with Afi in the bottom of the boat, trying to get away from the sailors' ferocity. *Why do they beat us?* Amari thought wildly. *To silence us? To stop our fear?* Nothing made sense.

The screaming gradually subsided into deep, burning groans, which no salve could soften. Amari lifted her head and looked around. The land was quickly disappearing, the soldiers looking like miniatures of themselves as they dragged another coffle of slaves into another small boat. She could hear the cries of the seabirds above and the rhythmic splash of the oars as the rowers carried them away from her land and closer to the huge ship waiting for them. She looked back with longing at the land of her birth.

Amari knew that she would never see this place again.

7. Ship of Death

The water, which never stopped rocking the small boat, carried them swiftly to the side of the huge ship. As they got closer, she knew she had been right: It was a place of death. Amari could not see the top of it. It rested upon the great water like a beast, ready to swallow them all up, she felt. Two of the captives who had been yoked together grew hysterical as they approached the looming structure and leaped without warning into the sea. The slave women gasped as one. Amari did not know the language of her captors, but she could tell they cursed as nets were cast overboard for the escaped slaves.

Amari and the other prisoners in her boat watched, however, in horrid fascination as the two women — a mother and daughter — tried in vain to swim back to shore. The mother struggled to keep her daughter afloat, but the chains were heavy and they were weak from hunger and captivity. Suddenly, the mother disappeared from sight for a moment, only to reemerge screaming in agony. The ocean bled bright red. Two huge gray fish with fins of silver surfaced for just a moment, their backs gleaming in the sunlight. One of them clenched a brown arm in its teeth. Then both mother and daughter disappeared. Amari stared at the spot, waiting for them to reappear. They didn't. She had held her breath through the whole thing. She was so stunned, she could not even pray.

The sailors were now even angrier than before. The whips slashed across the backs of the remaining slaves once more, as if those still alive had to pay for the loss of the two who had died. No one else tried to jump.

A rough plank had been rigged for them to climb from the small boat to the ship. It was narrow and shaky, but the sailors made sure the women had no opportunity to escape into the sea, should they dare. When she got to the deck, Amari stood amazed — it was like a small city made of wood. Poles taller than any tree reached to the sky. Loud, flapping pieces of cloth, larger than a hut, were attached to the poles by ropes, some of which were thicker than her whole body. Barrels and boxes littered the area, and dozens of men ran around shouting at one another and clapping one another on the back. They were laughing and cheerful, but Amari noticed that everyone seemed to carry a weapon — a gun, a sword, a knife. Confused and frightened, she didn't know what to think.

Amari had very little time to think, anyway. A whip lashed across her shoulder as she gazed around the ship, and she was quickly jolted back to reality. She jumped and yelped at the sudden pain. She and the other women were herded to one side of the deck, where a hole in the floor awaited. They were pushed into that hole and slid down into what Amari knew just had to be the underworld.

She wished that she had breathed more of the fresh air on the deck and in the boat, for the air in this place seemed to have been sucked out and replaced with the smells of sweat and vomit and urine. The male slaves had all been loaded before them, and she looked in disbelief at the sight before her. On narrow shelves made of wood, hundreds of naked men and boys lay chained together, wrists, necks, and legs held tightly by iron shackles. Only a few inches separated one man from another.

Each man had about six inches of head-room, not even enough to sit up. Under the upper level of boards a second level had been constructed, and under that, a third. Each row of shelves held men — human beings — chained like animals and stacked like logs for the fire, row after row, shelf after shelf.

The first row seemed to have more head-room and breathing area, but the second and third rows beneath them were already slimy with waste. The men on the bottom were splattered with the blood of the men who had been beaten, as well as the vomit and urine and feces that the men chained above them had no choice but to eliminate where they lay.

A large rat ran across Amari's feet as they were marched past the men. She felt faint — surely this could not be real. Some of the women cried out as they found a man they knew. Amari did not want to see Besa tied like an animal. She turned her head and moved on.

The area for the women was in a separate location. Their feet were locked in leg irons and they had only the rough boards to lie upon, but Amari noticed that they had more room and that the air was a bit fresher. Nor were they stacked the way the men were.

Amari was surprised to notice a number of children in their area. The men who had captured her group had killed all of the children — she had supposed because they were too much trouble to take care of. But the captives on this ship, as she found out later on the journey, came from all over Africa and by many different ways. Amari saw a small boy who huddled near his mother; he was about the same age as Kwasi had been. She wished for a moment that he had lived so that she could hold him and comfort him. Then she shook that thought free; she would never want him to know these horrors.

The ship of death was surprisingly very much alive. It inhaled and exhaled the foul air of where they lay chained, and it rolled with the rhythm of the water. Loud noises echoed down to them — pounding, clanging, and screeching. And it seemed the white men were always shouting. She also heard laughter above. No one in the hidden, dark area beneath the ship laughed. All were silent with fear.

Eventually, the activity above seemed to slow down. Amari felt a sense of anticipation, as if something was about to happen. Perhaps it was night. She could not tell. Afi, still chained next to her, quietly began to hum an old Ewe song. It was the lament sung at a funeral — a death song. She sang to the ancestors and to the other slaves. Gradually, even those not of that tribe joined in. Close to a hundred women softly sang with her. It was the saddest sound Amari had ever heard.

8. Toward the Edge
of the World

Hours passed — it was impossible to tell if it was day or night. Amari was unbelievably hungry and had to relieve herself. She was still chained and had no idea what she should do. She nudged Afi, who, as usual, was watchful and awake.

"Feel the motion of this ship of death," Afi whispered.

Amari could feel a gentle rocking, rhythmic and constant. "It feels different somehow," she told her.

"We float on the face of the sea," Afi murmured. "And we travel toward the edge of the world."

Amari started to ask her how she knew, but then she decided to trust Afi's instincts. "There is no escape?" Amari asked, even though she was certain of the answer.

"Not only is there no escape, there is no land to escape to. They have stolen that as well."

Amari did not understand. She had no time to ask her, for at that moment several sailors, with cloths tied around their faces, came down, unchained the feet of the women, and led them up out of the hold. After climbing the ladder up to the deck, Amari gasped with astonishment. Afi was right.

The land had indeed disappeared. Bright blue water surrounded them. The beach, the fort, the small boats — everything had vanished. One woman lurched at the sight, grabbed Amari's arm, and squeezed it so tightly that she left marks. She mumbled words in a language Amari did not understand. Another woman fainted. Some covered their eyes from the sudden brightness; others cried out fearfully. Afi said nothing. She had known.

The sailors began throwing salt water on the women from buckets on the deck. The water stung Amari's wounds and coated her with brine. Other women twitched and howled as the water hit them, and the sailors laughed at their discomfort. A barrel had been set on one side of the deck for the women to relieve themselves, and they were given food — some kind of beans mixed with an oily substance that Amari could not identify. It was horrible, and she gagged as she swallowed it, but she ate it all.

A sailor spoke sharply to the women, and they all stared at him blankly. He repeated himself again and again. "Now you dance! Dance! Dance, you monkeys, dance!" None of them had any idea what he meant. Finally, a young white man who looked to be about Amari's age brought out a small drum and began pounding a beat. It was just a simple, basic rhythm — *DRUM-dum, RUM-dum, DRUM-bop-bop; DRUM-dum, RUM-dum, DRUM-bop-bop* — over and over again. The women looked around in confusion. The dull beat made by that foreign drum carried no message and certainly offered no cause for celebration. *It has none of the life and voice our drummers were able to coax from a drum,* Amari thought.

A whiplash stung Amari's face and she jumped. The sailor holding the whip nodded, pointed to her, and jabbered some words as he hopped up and down. Amari then realized what the men wanted them to do. *They expect us to dance, or at least jump, to this horrible rhythm!* Amari thought incredulously. Slowly, reluctantly, the women began to jump.

Amari supposed it was for exercise. But it was also for another purpose, she noticed with a sickening realization. Most of the female captives had on very little clothing. Their clothes had been ripped and torn and stripped from them since they had been taken from their homes. The sailors, all carrying knives or guns, walked among the women as they danced. They watched the women closely, sometimes touching their bodies. The women knew what the men were looking for.

One of them, a huge man with bright orange hair, kept watching Amari. She had never seen a person with hair that color before, and he frightened as well as fascinated her. He never touched her, but while the women danced, she noticed he kept his eyes on her face rather than on the rest of her body.

At the end of the dance, instead of being taken back down to the hold where they had been chained all night, the women were tied to the sides of the deck. The children were untied and allowed to run free.

"Keep your child close to you," Afi told one mother. "Who knows what these strange men like to eat!" The mother nodded and grabbed the boy.

It wasn't exactly pleasant on the deck of the ship — it was dreadfully hot, and the constant salty wind on her face only increased her thirst. They had been given no fresh water to drink since that first meal of the morning — but Amari was glad to be away from the stench of the bottom of the ship.

"They will come for us tonight," Afi whispered to Amari, jarring her thoughts back to a harsh reality. "They treat us like animals, but tonight we will be forced to be their women."

"But, but . . . I do not know what to do!" Amari wailed, thinking with embarrassment of her dreams of lying in Besa's arms after they were married.

"Submit in silence. If you fight back, it will go worse for you," Afi said sadly.

"Perhaps it is better to die," Amari told her sharply.

Afi sighed. "If you die, they win. We cannot let that happen."

"They have already taken everyone I loved," Amari replied, ashamed to look at Afi in the face. "And tonight they take the only thing I have left that is truly mine. Death would be a relief."

"You will live because you must," Afi said sternly. "I should welcome death, but I cannot — not yet. And neither can you." She turned away from Amari and looked out at the sea.

Amari did not know how to reply. She

trembled violently at the thought of one of these strange, smelly, milk-faced men taking her against her will. *Shall I throw myself overboard?* she thought. *It would be so much easier to give up and die.* Yet she could not do that. And she didn't know why.

The male captives were brought to the deck next, a few at a time. They also screamed as the salt water was thrown on them, and then they were forced to perform the same horrible dance. Amari listened to the thunder that their feet made and thought ruefully, *The feet of my people bring forth rhythm even when the noise of the white men can produce none.*

Afi nudged Amari and whispered, "Death has come for some of us."

Amari stared as several bodies, stiff and lifeless, were pulled from the decks below. The sailors, again with cloths tied around their mouths and noses, unceremoniously tossed the dead men overboard. Amari was too numb to even remember the words of a prayer.

The male slaves, unlike the women, were not allowed to stay on the deck after they had been fed and made to dance. They were whipped and chained and led back to the fetid dungeon where they had been all night. Every hour a few more were brought up and put through the same routine, until at last there were no more.

The sailors cleaned up the deck and whistled cheerfully. Night was approaching. Amari looked at the sun as it disappeared into the sea; it burned coppery bright and beautiful. She tried to sear that beautiful sight on her memory as a shield to the ugliness that she now knew was about to happen.

9. Lessons Painful

When night finally enveloped the ship and only a wisp of the moon shone dimly, the deck was dark except for the light from the torches the sailors used. Like pigs in heat, they came for the women. One by one the women were unchained and dragged, screaming and kicking, to a distant area of the ship or a corner of the deck. Amari heard them plead for mercy, for understanding, but no one listened. Two men grabbed Afi and led her away. She lowered her head and did not cry out or try to fight them.

Amari huddled in a corner, trying to make herself look like one of the children, trying to look lame or stupid or unappealing. But then someone grabbed her arm. She looked up. It was the sailor with bright reddish hair. She moaned.

He pulled Amari to a small room that held nothing but a box made of wood and a sleeping area that seemed to be elevated off the floor somehow. *These men don't even sleep on mats on the ground?* she thought briefly, but then the horror of what was about to happen overwhelmed her and she looked around wildly for a means of escape.

The man closed the door, and the room was suddenly very small. His large body took up most of the area and completely blocked the door. He pushed Amari roughly onto the floor. She could hear the cries and screams of other women as they were being attacked.

"Scream!" he yelled at her harshly.

Amari did not know what he meant, so she just sat there, about to faint from fright.

"Scream!" the redheaded sailor yelled again, and this time he raised his huge, hairy arm as if to hit her.

Amari screamed.

He mumbled some words and seemed to be pleased. Then he put his finger to his lips and whispered, "Shhh." It was the same sound Amari used to make for Kwasi when she wanted him to be quiet. Her whole body shook with dread and fear. The sailor spoke more words, but to Amari they sounded like wooden buckets clattering together. She could make no sense of any of it.

His voice sank to just above a whisper, and he put his huge hand across Amari's mouth so she could not make a sound. She could barely breathe.

He's going to kill me! she thought with terror.

But he removed his hand and signaled for her to remain silent. She did.

He spoke more words that she could not understand, rattling on as if she understood. Amari had no idea what he was talking about, but he did not seem to be in a hurry to rape her, so she relaxed a little.

He grabbed a pouch around his neck, and Amari tensed, ready to cry out again. Slowly, he pulled an object from the pouch and handed it to Amari. At first she was afraid to take it, fearing it might be a means to poison her or put a spell on her. But he smiled as he handed it to her, so she took it hesitantly.

It was small, not much bigger than the palm of her hand, and made of wood. It was a carving of a child, a white child with long strands of hair. Amari looked at it in wonder, thinking it must be some kind of talisman. The sailor pointed to the carving and then pointed to himself several times. Then he took the small carving away from Amari, kissed it gently, and pretended to rock it. *Either this is a madman or that is a likeness of his child,* Amari thought.

"Child," the sailor said.

Amari said nothing.

"My child," the sailor repeated.

Confused, Amari had no idea what he was saying. She coughed a little.

He pointed to a bucket of water on the floor and made sipping motions as he lifted a dipper.

She nodded slightly, and very gently, considering the size of the man, he gave her a dipper of water. It was cool and fresh, and she drank it thirstily.

"Water," he said, pointing to it.

Amari wasn't sure what he meant.

"Water," he said again. "Water, water, water, water." He kept repeating the word and pointing to the liquid.

"Wa-ta," she said slowly.

The large sailor slapped his thigh and laughed.

Amari looked at him cautiously, not sure what to say or do next.

"Water," he said once more.

"Wa-ta," Amari repeated.

"Bucket!" he said, kicking the bucket with his foot.

Amari thought once more that surely this man must be mad. Why would he do such a thing?

"Bucket!" he repeated, pointing to the

wooden object now lying on its side.

"Buh-ka," Amari repeated quickly, suddenly understanding. He was teaching her the language of the white skins! "Buh-ka," she said again, more clearly this time. If he was going to teach her, she fully intended to learn it. She hated not knowing what the sailors were saying.

Amari thought briefly of her father, who loved meeting men of other tribes and learning their languages. Then she inhaled sharply and squeezed her arms around her body, the painful reality hitting her that her father would never again discover a new word or idea to share with her.

The sailor looked at her with what looked like concern and jumbled out words that seemed to be a question, but Amari just shook her head. She felt that her father's spirit was there with her and that somehow he had protected her this night from the certainty of rape.

Hesitantly, Amari pointed to the door of the small cabin. He told her the word was "door." She repeated it over and over until she could remember it.

The strange, redheaded sailor taught Amari the words "ocean" and "ship" and "man" and "floor" and "wall," as well as many other simple words and phrases. She also asked him, through pointing and signs, to tell her the words for "chain" and "whip" and "shackle." He frowned, but he told her.

Knowledge of the language of the white men was a powerful weapon that she could possibly use one day to her advantage. Coldly and thoughtfully, she listened and learned. After a couple of hours, when most of the screams of anguish from the women had long since ceased, he opened the door of the small room and led Amari back to the deck.

He made sure she had fresh water, let her relieve herself, and tied her gently to the deck pole, which he told her was called a "mast." Then he disappeared.

Most of the women back on deck were curled into balls, shivering in the chill night air. Some rocked back and forth, trying to erase the terrible memories of the past few hours. Afi, wide awake as usual, waited for Amari. Her face was bruised, her upper lip bleeding.

"He did not take you?"

Amari shook her head no, almost ashamed that she had escaped the fate of most of the women.

"He was kind to you?"

Amari thought about it and realized that what had happened to her really was one drop of kindness in this huge sea of evil that surrounded them. She nodded her head yes. She was afraid to look Afi in the eye.

"Good. You were lucky . . . this night. But prepare yourself, child. One of them — probably many of them before this journey is over — will take you."

Amari gasped. "How much longer can this journey be?" she asked Afi, suddenly very frightened again. "Surely the next day will bring us to our destination — wherever that might be."

In spite of her injuries, Afi managed to twist her lips into a rueful laugh. "No, child. This is just the beginning of many nights of horrible humiliation. I feel that this journey will be very long."

Amari touched Afi gently.

"Many will die," Afi said quietly. "Some will live but will die inside. Others will pray for death and be forced to live. But we all will be changed forever." She did not cry or wail as some of the other women did, but Afi's face was covered in tears, which mixed with the blood on her face and lips.

"What shall we do?" Amari said finally, burrowing into Afi's arms — as much as their chains would allow.

"Find strength from within," Afi told her, stroking her head.

"How do I do that?" Amari whimpered.

"It is there. You will know when it is time to use that strength as your shield from what they will do to you."

Amari suddenly felt overwhelmed with powerlessness. "I want it to be like it was," she sobbed. "I want my mother."

"Oh, child," Afi whispered gently. "I know you do."

"It's not fair," Amari cried.

"Nobody promised us happiness or fairness, child. I have known much happiness in my life — the love of a good man, children, a village of friends and loved ones — and much sorrow as well. You have yet to find that, my child. Your destiny lies beyond."

"Beyond what?" Amari asked.

"I do not know. Some things the spirits keep secret." She chuckled, in spite of everything, and hugged Amari once more.

10. THE MIDDLE PASSAGE

Afi was right. The next night the kindly redheaded sailor was nowhere to be seen. Amari was taken to a filthy corner of the ship by a dark-haired, skinny sailor who used her, hurt her, and tossed her back on the deck, bruised and bleeding, all of her dreams finally and forever destroyed. Afi said nothing but held Amari and rocked her until her tears stopped flowing.

The following night Amari was taken by two sailors. They took turns. She wanted to die.

The morning after that brutal assault Amari spotted Besa in a group of men who were brought on deck. It was the first time she'd seen him since they had been on the ship. He had lost weight, as most of them had, and his body was covered with welts and sores. He made brief eye contact with Amari, a flicker of hope in his eyes for a moment. The pineapple birthmark looked distorted and shrunken. But she could not face him, for she was no longer the innocent girl he had once loved. She no longer felt worthy of his admiration or even his friendship. Amari turned away from him in shame.

The routine of the ship took on a horrible monotony. The everlasting indigo blue of the ocean surrounded them day after day. The copper sun and the piercing paleness of the sky, which were so welcome in the captives' homeland, imprisoned them each hour. Every morning the women were fed, doused with salt water, and made to dance. Oh, how Amari hated that drum! The men were then pulled from the hold, squinting in the bright sunlight — filthy, weak, and almost crippled from being tied down for almost twenty hours each day. More and more bodies were tossed overboard, where the huge gray fish waited hungrily for their meal.

Every evening the sailors prepared greedily for their night of pleasure. Sometimes Amari was rescued by the redheaded sailor, but on most nights she was just another female body to be used by one of the forty or so sailors on board that awful ship. A couple of times she had seen the large redhead climbing up the mast to do the night watch, so she figured that perhaps he did not always have the opportunity to save her from a night of defilement. Or, she thought, perhaps he just did not care that much.

Amari no longer smiled — ever. She learned to harden herself from feelings and emotion, as well as from physical pain. She was, however, grateful for any evening of escape from the other men and for the large redheaded man's attempts to teach her their language.

She learned his name, which was Bill, and how to say "yes" and "no" and quite a few conversational phrases. He showed her how to count using the fingers of her hands. She learned the words "hungry" and "eat," even though hunger was a constant and the food she was given was barely life-sustaining, as well as verbs like "try" and "cry" and "die."

The language of the white skins was strange and fell heavily on her tongue, but she continued eagerly. She gathered words as weapons to be used later.

"What that?" she asked Bill one rainy night as she pointed to the rain slicker he wore. He told her the name for it, as well as the names of other articles of clothing. He taught her the names of the parts of the body, words for weather, and words for food. She pointed, he named it, she repeated it. He showed her how words connected into phrases. Verbs were difficult for her.

"I am Bill," he explained.

"You am Bill," she repeated.

"No, you say, 'You *are* Bill.' "

"I not Bill. I are Amari." She was often confused, but slowly, it made sense. Amari found that she could understand more than she could say, which she knew was an advantage. Sometimes she repeated words and phrases to herself as the men made her dance or while she was tied up for hours on the deck of the endlessly rocking ship. It kept her from going mad.

When Amari awoke one morning, the sky was thick with dark, ominous clouds. Cold winds blasted the deck. The ship rocked violently as waves splashed high over the roping on the sides. The women, drenched and terrified, were flung wildly about, held only by the ropes that tied them to the masts.

One woman, whose name was Mosi, screamed with desperation as her daughter, who was about four years old, was torn from her arms. At that instant another huge, foaming wave washed over the deck, and the child disappeared with it as it fell back into the ocean. Mosi pulled at her ropes like a crazed animal, broke free, and ran across the deck to the place where her child had disappeared. She looked over the side of the boat and, pointing to a spot some distance away in the water, yelled to the women, "I see her! I see her. Oh, my baby!" Amari pulled at her ropes, but she could do nothing.

A sailor had spotted Mosi and headed toward her. She took one look at him, one final look at the women — as if to say farewell — and leaped gracefully into the sea. Amari watched frantically, waiting for someone to rescue them, but the sailors, too busy with the sudden storm, never even bothered to glance overboard to see the fate of the mother and child. They were simply two more dead slaves.

They did, however, untie the women then and lead them to the lower deck. It had been many days, perhaps weeks, since they had been in this area of the ship — Amari had lost all count of days and time. The stench, which had been unbearable at the beginning of the voyage, was now almost unbreathable. It seemed that no one had bothered to clean out the lower deck since the voyage began. The men, tied there for over twenty hours a day, had no choice but to lie in the filth.

Many of the bottom levels of the shelving

were empty, Amari noticed. That was the result of the constant stream of stiff, dead bodies that were tossed overboard each morning, she realized.

Amari and the other women splashed slowly though the slime of urine and feces and vomit that covered the floor. Rats, now grown huge and healthy, chewed on the emaciated bodies of some of the men chained there. Too weak or too tightly chained to shake them off, the men suffered in silent agony.

The women were chained to what the sailors called the "tween" deck. The door of the hold was closed behind them. Amari vomited, unable to fight the nausea. So did many others.

Hour after hour the ship bucked through the storm. Children clutched their mothers, women moaned, everyone prayed. At first Amari prayed for the storm to stop. Soon she simply wished that the ship would be taken by the storm and sunk to the bottom of the ocean.

But no relief was to come that night, nor the next day. The winds kept roaring, the ship rolled, and the slaves chained beneath the decks suffered endlessly.

Finally, finally, Amari realized that the movement of the ship had slowed. She could no longer hear the wind. Too weak to move, she lay huddled in a ball, bemoaning the fact that she was still alive.

She heard the sound of a door opening. The sailors who entered began to curse at the sight before them. They unchained the women and led them to the deck. They did not bother to tie them, for they were too weak to even stand. Of the ninety women left on board, sixteen had died during that storm. Ten of the children had died as well. The women watched with empty eyes as the bodies were tossed overboard. Amari wished that she had been one of them.

11. Land Ho

Many of the sails and several of the mast poles had been damaged in the storm. Crew members scurried about making repairs. If she listened carefully, Amari could figure out bits and pieces of the conversation between the captain and his crew.

"Can you tell what they say?" Afi asked Amari.

"Not exactly," Amari whispered back. "But they seem to be worried that the ship is damaged."

"That I can see," Afi said with a chuckle. "Perhaps destruction is the only thing these barbarians understand."

"They are headed to something called Carolina," Amari told Afi later that day. "What do you think that means for us?"

"It means that place is where your destiny lies, my child," Afi said with assurance.

"And yours as well," Amari added, almost as a question.

Afi gazed out upon the ocean.

"Afi! Your destiny is with me, is it not?" Amari pleaded desperately. Afi did not look at Amari. "When I have an answer for you, I will tell you," she said finally.

Amari stopped asking, but her heart was heavy.

For the next few days the slaves were treated a little differently. The men were brought up on deck more often and allowed to stay for longer periods. They all started receiving larger food portions and generous rations of water. The ship's doctor checked each one of them carefully, applying salves to their many wounds and giving medicine to those who appeared to be sickly. The sailors were no longer allowed to molest the women at night. All activity seemed to indicate the end of their journey — crates and cartons were packed, sails were sewn and repaired, and sailors whistled as they shaved their beards.

"Huh! The sailors seem to be excited to return to their own women," Afi said bitterly as she and Amari sat quietly on the deck watching the activity.

"What will happen when we arrive in their land?" Amari asked.

"We will be sold once more — perhaps many times. We no longer belong to ourselves, Amari."

"What do you think it is like there?"

"The same sun shines upon their land. The moon and the stars glow each night. Trees grow green and tall in the sunlight. But I have a feeling it will be as different from our land as life is from death."

"I'm afraid, Afi," Amari admitted.

"So am I, child. So am I."

Amari had very little time to worry about the future, however, for she heard Bill, the redheaded sailor, who was working on the tallest sail of the ship, suddenly shout, "Land ho!"

She wasn't sure what the words meant, but by the loud, boisterous reaction of the sailors, who whooped in celebration, she knew it could mean only one thing. This part of their journey was almost over.

Amari could see seabirds flying overhead, and she looked with the rest of the women at the faint hint of green in the distance. She did not share in the joy of the sailors, however. Amari was overcome by fear.

12. Welcome to Sullivan's Island

Ka-boom! The ship's cannon fired suddenly, sending the slave women on deck scurrying for cover. Amari cowered close to Afi, sure that her life was about to end. The sailors, however, seemed unconcerned, even cheerful, as they steered the ship toward its destination. Some of them whistled, a sound that Amari found to be particularly distasteful. She peeked over the edge of the ship, and suddenly, green and golden beyond the blue of the sea, the land appeared from the distant mists. Amari had had no idea what to imagine, but the land she saw was surprisingly beautiful, with lush green trees growing quite close to a long, sandy beach.

"Afi," she whispered, "the land is lovely. I thought it must surely be an ugly place."

"Yes, it is beautiful to look at. Remember that when the ugliness overtakes you," Afi told her. "Find beauty wherever you can, child. It will keep you alive."

"I could not have survived without you, Afi," Amari told her, giving the older woman a clumsy hug.

"And you have been a gift to me as well, Amari. I'm glad we were together for this horrible journey."

"What happens now?" Amari asked.

Afi had no time to answer, for a small boat came up close to the ship, and a balding white man climbed on board. He wore a cloth tied across his face. The captain of their ship laughed and welcomed him aboard.

The first thing Amari noticed was that the newcomer was clean, smelling strongly of the scent of too many flowers. He coughed and choked as if the very air of the slave ship would infect him with illness. It was clear he was reacting to a terrible odor.

Amari could make out only a few of the words between them. She could figure out the words "stink" and "slave" and "cargo" and that the man who had come on board was some sort of official from the land they were heading toward. Amari realized as she listened intently to their conversation that she and her fellow slaves were the cargo. Then she saw the captain hand something to the man. It was a small leather pouch that bulged with silver objects. The man took it greedily and stuffed it into his shirt.

The captain then laughed again and pointed to Afi and Amari and the other women on the deck. The man walked over to the slave women and rubbed his hands together. With a look that seemed to Amari to combine disgust as well as desire, he proceeded to examine each of the women slaves very carefully.

Afi was called first. Like the rest of the women, she was just about naked. He checked every bone and muscle of her body by running his hands over her, noting flaws or bruises. Afi's back showed many scars, and he frowned with displeasure. He looked inside her mouth and checked her teeth. He checked her genitals. She kept her eyes closed. Amari knew that Afi's mind was in another place.

"Good breeder," she heard the man say as he smacked Afi on the buttocks. Amari did not know what that meant.

Afi was sent back to her place on the deck, and Amari was called next. Using Afi's strength as an example, Amari stood quietly as she was touched and examined and fondled. Her impulse was to jerk away from him, but she forced herself to stand silently.

The rest of the women were checked next, then the men, who had been brought up on deck, were examined as well. The man scribbled some marks on a flat sheet he carried and gave it to the captain. Amari listened carefully to his words, and even though she did not fully understand their meaning, she knew that her life was about to change again. "Your cargo is approved to land, Captain. Welcome to Sullivan's Island."

13. THE SLAVE AUCTION

The next day the slaves were taken in groups from the ship. The women were placed in small boats similar to the ones that had taken them away from their home-land; fewer boats were needed to unload the surviving slaves than when they had started out.

As he helped her from the ship into one of the small boats, Bill refused to look at Amari directly. He mumbled into her ear, "Be brave, child. God have mercy on you." Amari glanced back to see him, but he was gone.

The rowers were swift and the journey was short. It took only a few minutes to reach the beach on the place they called Sullivan's Island. Chained and pushed, Amari was unloaded with the others. She tried to walk, but she kept falling onto the sand. Her legs felt like they were made of mashed fufu. She glanced around and saw that most of the slaves, and some of the sailors as well, had difficulty adjusting to land after such a long time journeying on the ocean.

A long, well-trodden path lay in front of them. Tall grasses grew in abundance on either side of it. Three solemn seabirds flew overhead. All was unusually silent.

When most of the slaves were able to walk, they were led to a large building about half a mile from the beach. It was made of wood and stone — a smaller version of the prison at Cape Coast. None of their captors spoke to them, except to yell or curse, nor did they try to explain what was happening. Talk surrounded them, however, as one slave was pointed to with great interest or another was laughed at.

The slaves were fed, given water, and even supplied with extra water in small basins with which to bathe. Their wounds were patched or covered, and they were oiled and prepared for whatever was to come next. The whole area was full of nervous tension.

A tall black man entered the room. He limped noticeably, and he was dressed in a ragged version of the clothing of the whites. He looked at them, shook his head sadly, then addressed the slaves in the white language, seemingly giving instructions. They gazed at him blankly.

Finally, as soon as all of the white men had stepped outside of the building, the black man switched to the Ashanti language, speaking quickly and softly. "Listen, my brothers. I know not all of you can understand me, but I can see that some of you are Ashanti and Ewe. I will be whipped if they catch me 'talking African,' as they call it, but I must tell you some things. You must learn their language quickly — it is called English — but try not to forget your own. Submit and obey if you want to live. You are at a place called Sullivan's Island, where you will be kept for ten days, until they are sure you have no disease. Smallpox is the worst. Then you will be taken to a place called Charles Town, where you will be sold to the highest bidder." A white soldier reentered the building, and the black man smoothly switched back to the language of the whites.

The black man, whom the soldiers called Tybee, passed out some rough garments for them to wear — a simple smock for the women, a shirt and trousers for the men. He told them the names of each item in English as he gave it to them — "shirt," "shift," "apron" — then pointed out other words they would need, like "massa," "yes'm," and "yessir." Amari was surprised and pleased that she was able to understand quite a few of the words he said.

They stayed there on the island for several days, waiting for the unknown. During the day the slaves were fed and their wounds were treated, but at night fear was the blanket that covered each of them.

Amari lay on the ground one particularly hot night, trying to escape into sleep. She curled herself into a ball, but as she closed her eyes, memories assaulted her, so she sat back up, leaning against the rough wooden wall. She looked over and was surprised to see Besa, who had worked his way as close to her as he could in spite of his chains. She quickly lowered her head.

"My lovely Amari," he greeted her quietly in their language, as if hope still shone in their sky. "How goes your day?"

"Better, now that you are here," she said, remembering sadly that day that seemed so long ago. "But I am no longer lovely, and my days will never be happy again." She tried not to cry.

"When you look at the sun and the stars," he whispered, "I want you to remember me and smile. I want you to know that you will always be my lovely Amari."

One of the guards noticed them talking then and slashed at Besa with his whip. Besa glared at him, but he understood the danger of retaliation. He allowed himself to be led back to the far side of the men's area, where the guard kicked him fiercely. Amari had to look away.

Early the next morning the slaves were once again shackled and packed into boats. Looking healthier and feeling stronger than they had in a very long time, they were ready for sale.

The shoreline, Amari noticed as they were unloaded at the place her captors called Charles Town, was rocky and harsh rather than soft beach.

Amari looked then at an amazing sight. Tall buildings and people, seemingly everywhere, crowded the area. *What has happened to the trees?* she thought. *And what are all these structures? Surely these white people must have great magic to make such buildings! And there are so many of them!*

"Afi," Amari whispered. "The faces of brown and black that I see — are they slaves?"

"I cannot tell for sure, but I think so," Afi whispered back. "Most of them do not seem to walk with authority."

"I think we have arrived in a backward world — where black skins are few and not respected and pale skins seem to rule,"

Amari commented quietly.

They were taken to a place that Amari heard them call the "customhouse." It was a big drafty building with a large door. Pushed into a small shed next to it, the slaves waited in silence on the dirt floor. The sun rose, the room began to get unbearably hot, the hours passed, and the sun set again. They were given food and water at the end of the day, then locked back in the shed for the night.

Amari, hot and sweaty, whispered to Afi, "What are they waiting for?"

"Buyers," Afi declared. Amari's stomach clenched with fear.

Early the next morning white men lined up the slaves, sloshed cold water on them, and had other slaves rub oil all over their bodies. The oil stank, and Amari coughed at the odor.

"Now it begins," Afi said sadly.

By the time the sun had begun to shine brightly, the sale had started. Besa and a coffle of men were taken as the first to be auctioned off. As he and the others were led from the holding area, a great cry of enthusiasm could be heard from the crowd outside. Amari could hear loud, excited words tossed back and forth, much like the tones of bargaining her mother had used on market days. She heard someone say the word "Sold!" and she knew she would never see Besa again.

The rest of the men, some in sets of two or three, some singly, were sold as the morning went on. By midday it was time for the women.

In spite of the heat, Amari trembled. She gazed out of the shed's single window at the sun, which glistened bright and harsh. No warmth. No soft shadows to hide her embarrassment. No hope. She wondered how the sun could shine so brightly on this land of evil people. Nothing made sense to her any longer — not days or nights, not past or present.

This was the summer of her fifteenth year, and this day she wanted to die.

More buyers had arrived. Afi and Amari and the other women were stripped naked. Amari bit her lip, determined not to cry. But she couldn't stop herself from screaming out as her arms were wrenched behind her back and tied. A searing pain shot up through her shoulders. A white man clamped shackles on her ankles, rubbing his hands up and down her legs as he did. Amari tensed and tried to jerk away, but the chains were too tight. She could not hold back the tears.

Amari shuffled in the dirt as she was led into the yard and up onto a raised wooden table, which she realized gave the people in the yard a perfect view of the women who were to be sold. She looked at the faces in the sea of pink-skinned people who stood around pointing at the captives and jabbering in their language as each of the slaves was described. She looked for pity or even understanding but found nothing except cool stares. They looked at her as if she were a cow for sale. She saw a few white women fanning themselves and whispering in the ears of well-dressed men — their husbands, she supposed. Most of the people in the crowd were men; however, she did see a poorly dressed white girl about her own age standing near a wagon. The girl had a sullen look on her face, and she seemed to be the only person not interested in what was going on at the slave sale.

Amari looked up at a seabird flying above and remembered her little brother. *I wish he could have flown that night,* Amari thought sadly. *I wish I could have flown away as well.*

■ ■ ■ ■

PART TWO
POLLY

■ ■ ■ ■

14. THE SLAVE SALE

Polly really didn't like Negroes. As far as she was concerned, they should all get shipped back to Africa or wherever it was they came from. They talked funny, they smelled bad, and they were ugly. *How could the good Lord have made such creatures?* Polly wondered as she glanced with boredom at the slave sale. Dark skin, big lips, and hair the texture of a briar bush — they were just plain unpleasant to deal with. Besides, Negroes made it difficult for regular folks like herself to get work. Who could compete with somebody who worked for free?

She scratched an insect bite on her arm, unrolled a sheaf of paper, and leaned against the wooden wagon of Mr. Percival Derby, owner of Derbyshire Farms. Proud of the fact that she could read, Polly looked over her certificate of indenture one more time.

She mumbled and moved her lips as she

read, " 'His Majesty King George the Second, in the Year of Our Lord One Thousand Seven Hundred and Thirty-Eight, on this, the second day of June, in the city of Charles Town, colony of South Carolina, hereby sets the indenture of one Polly Elizabeth Pritchard, age fifteen years, to Mr. Percival Derby, for a period not to exceed fourteen years.' "

Polly frowned. She'd not been able to shorten the fourteen-year term. A normal indenture was seven years, but she had to pay off the debts of her parents, and the only way she was allowed to do that was to sign up for a double indenture. She'd have to work for Mr. Derby until she was an old woman — almost twenty-nine — but she was determined that long before that time she would have figured out a way to get out of the contract.

She looked back at the slave sale. The women were wailing and acting as if something terrible was happening to them. Polly snorted and turned away. Living here in the colonies had to be better than living like a savage in the jungle. *They ought to be grateful,* she thought. She thought of the Negroes she'd known as a child — well-fed and happy slaves, with no worries about finding employment. No, she had no sympathy.

The sale was getting boisterous. Polly looked up. "Fresh from Africa," the auctioneer told the crowd. "Mold 'em into what you want 'em to be. Look at 'em! All of them healthy and ready for childbearin'! Come on up and take a look! Feel free to inspect the merchandise."

An unbelievably large white man who smelled of strong wine and an even stronger body odor waddled past Polly and up to the auction area. She covered her nose and laughed behind her hand. He seemed to have difficulty breathing. He climbed onto the riser where the Negro women stood and headed directly to the youngest one there — a girl about her own age. He opened the girl's mouth and put his fingers inside.

Polly grimaced, not because she felt sorry for the girl, but because the man was so repulsive. Then the fat man touched the girl's breasts and ran his hands down her legs. "Nice," Polly heard him rasp. "I'll give ten pounds for the girl," he said to the auctioneer, wheezing between his words. He ignored the woman standing next to the girl.

"Do I hear more than ten pounds for this fine example of African womanhood? Hardly a scratch on her. Bright enough to be taught simple commands, like 'Come here' and 'Lie down'!" The crowd laughed

111

at that, but Polly didn't.

"Twenty pounds!" called a voice from the back of the crowd.

The fat man looked up in astonishment. "Thirty!" he responded loudly. He sat down on the edge of the wooden platform and pulled out a filthy handkerchief. He wiped his face, which was sweating profusely.

"Forty pounds!" called the voice from the back again. People turned to see who was outbidding the large man in the front.

"She's not worth forty-five!" the big man yelled to the crowd.

"Is that your bid?" the auctioneer asked.

The fat man hesitated. "Yes," he said then. "I want her!"

"I hear forty-five. Do I hear fifty?" The crowd waited in anticipation.

"Sixty pounds for the African girl," the voice cried out at last. "I want her for my son. Today is his sixteenth birthday!" The crowd cheered. No one seemed to want the large man to win this one.

The auctioneer looked at the large man, who was still wiping his brow. "He can have her," the big man said finally. "I'll get me a young gal another day."

"Sold," the auctioneer said loudly, "for sixty pounds to Mr. Percival Derby of Derbyshire Farms." Polly looked up with surprise. She hadn't known who was doing the bidding. Then she shrugged. She just hoped Mr. Derby's new purchase would get put out in the fields where she belonged.

"Will you be wantin' her mama, sir?" the auctioneer said to Mr. Derby. "I offer her to you first, out of respect, you see."

Polly watched as Mr. Derby, who had walked up to the stage to claim his property, glanced at the older woman standing next to the slave girl, then said, "No, Horace, but thanks for the offer. Family ties only confuse the poor creatures. They'll forget each other as soon as the sun sets. Trust me."

Mr. Derby grabbed the arm of his new slave and attempted to lead her off the stage, but for some reason she just went wild. Polly watched, fascinated, as the girl squirmed and screeched and babbled incoherently. Polly wondered if Negroes from Africa had feelings and intelligent thoughts or if that gibberish they spoke was more like the screaming of monkeys or the barking of dogs.

When she was five or six years old, back in Beaufort, where she'd been born, she'd played with Negro children sometimes, running through the tobacco fields, playing hide-and-seek. But her father had frowned on such and would call Polly inside their small house. He'd say, "The company you keep will rub off on you, Polly-girl. Don't get your hands dirty by dealin' with dark-kies."

Her mother would shake her head at her husband, then pull Polly close to her. "I want you to grow up to be a fine lady, my pretty Polly. I don't want you to have to do laundry like I do. So let the slave children tend to their work in the field, and I will read to you from the Bible." Polly would snuggle on her mother's lap and fall asleep listening to the rhythm of her voice as she read.

Turning her attention back to the sale, Polly realized that the girl they were dragging off the auction block now was weeping real tears and seemed to be genuinely attached to that older female African whose shackled hand she wouldn't let go of.

Mr. Derby slapped the girl across the face, but she continued to pull and buck on the chains. She lurched toward the woman, but her leg chains got twisted and she stumbled. She fell hard, landing at the woman's chained feet. The older woman, who was also crying, leaned down and quickly whispered something in the girl's ear.

The girl was then pulled with difficulty

114

from the stage, dragged across the dirt courtyard, and forced into the back of the wagon that Polly leaned on. The people in the crowd cheered at the spectacle, but Mr. Derby did not seem to be amused. He glared at Polly, who stepped quickly out of his way. He turned on his heel then and went to pay for his purchase.

Polly watched him coolly as he strode away, his shiny black boots getting dusty as he walked. She knew he wouldn't leave right away. His son, who he had sent to pick up supplies from the wharf, had not yet returned. The bidding continued as the last of the women were sold. It seemed to Polly that the slave girl curled in a corner of the wagon would never stop crying.

15. POLLY AND CLAY

Polly, with hair the color of dried grass and eyes the color of a stormy sky, understood tears. She also knew that tears fixed nothing. As far as she was concerned, crying showed weakness and was simply a waste of time. Tears had not kept her father out of prison, nor had crying made a difference when he'd died of smallpox. She'd wept bitterly when her mother had died of the disease as well, but not one tear had given her a bite to eat or a place to stay. So she did her best to ignore the slave girl who hiccuped and shook with sobs.

Mr. Derby's son, presumably the young man with the birthday and the tearful gift in the back of the wagon, arrived then with a smartly dressed black man who struggled under the weight of several bags of supplies. "Hurry up, Noah. Get these loaded," the boy yelled to the black man. The young Master Derby carried a small whip, and he used it liberally to make Noah work faster. Polly noticed that the slave breathed slowly and loudly, as if he was tense, but he made no attempt to stop the young man from hitting him. She was always amazed at how much abuse slaves took without it seeming to bother them. Perhaps they didn't feel pain the way others did — she wasn't sure.

"Yassuh, Massa." Noah, dressed in clothing almost as elegant as a white slave owner's, bowed, then continued to load the wagon.

"Do you dress all your slaves as fine as King George?" Polly asked.

Clay turned slowly. "How dare you speak to me!" he responded furiously. "If you're the gal whose indenture my father just bought, you best learn your place around here."

Unintimidated, Polly gazed directly into his angry gray eyes and replied, "The slave owners I've encountered seem to clothe their slaves in just enough to allow for decency — certainly never in finery. Do you dress them all like that one?"

Clay burst into laughter. "They could all run around naked as far as I'm concerned, but when Daddy comes to market, he likes to arrive with his driver dressed with style," he explained.

"So why do you hit him?" Polly asked. She didn't like Negroes particularly, but she saw no reason why they should always be beaten.

"They expect to be disciplined," Clay explained. "It shows them that I care enough to make sure they do their tasks correctly. That's what my father always taught me. And what business is it of yours, anyway?"

"Just curious."

"Curiosity can get a gal like you in a heap of trouble. You best learn to keep your mouth shut," Clay warned.

"I've seen a heap of trouble," Polly replied. "I'm not afraid of you." But her heart fluttered under her smock.

Clay raised his arm as if to strike her, then lowered it as the anger on his face eased into a smile. "You're a saucy young thing," he said finally. He spat into the dirt.

Polly just looked at him with a cool stare.

"Was that your indenture I saw you looking at?" he asked. "You can read?"

Polly was not sure how to answer him, but she nodded as she quickly folded the paper and tucked it into a pocket of her apron.

"Let me warn you, girl. Women don't need to be reading, so just keep that ability to yourself. And don't ever get it in your mind to teach a slave to read! My father would have you whipped for such."

Polly inhaled sharply but did not answer him. She thought only slaves could be whipped. She noticed that Noah was gently picking up the trembling slave girl, moving her to the other side of the wagon and placing her on a blanket that lay wrinkled on the rough floorboard. The slave girl never opened her eyes; she just curled herself into a ball and huddled in that corner of the wagon.

Clay Derby mirrored his father in looks: dark, thick eyebrows that left his eyes in shadow, long fingers, and broad shoulders. His father, walking with swift authority, approached the wagon. People moved out of his way as he walked.

Clay seemed a little less sure of himself in the presence of his father, Polly thought. He pulled on his doublet, flicked some dirt from his boots, and smoothed his stockings. "Come," Clay said to Polly, taking her arm roughly, "I can see that Father has paid for my gift and is about ready to go. Whenever you speak to him, be sure to show proper respect. He hates women who don't know their place."

"Yes, sir," Polly mumbled sullenly.

"Did you enjoy the slave auction?" Mr. Derby asked Polly as he returned to the wagon and began to check on his goods.

Evading the question, Polly replied, "It was like nothing I have ever seen, sir." She looked at the ground.

"Speak up, girl," Mr. Derby commanded. "Look at me when you address me!"

Polly looked up at him, her blue eyes bright with a bit of defiance. "Yes, sir!" she said clearly. Mr. Derby opened his mouth as if to respond, then seemed to think better of it, for he turned to his duties instead.

The African girl, her hands tied in front of her with a rope, was still sniffling quietly. She was dressed in a thin shift made of a burlap seed bag. Her slender brown shoulders heaved.

"Quit that sniveling!" Mr. Derby yelled at her suddenly. He leaned over the side of the wagon and slapped her sharply across her face.

The girl, seemingly surprised, looked up and gulped back her tears. Polly noticed a brief smoldering anger on the girl's face, then it dissolved into a look of resigned submission.

"Noah, hurry and finish loading," Mr. Derby commanded the slave. "We have a long journey ahead of us." He did not use the whip as his son had. Noah packed up the rest of the supplies — farm tools, several bags of seed, and some rolls of cloth — and tied them down carefully. There would be barely enough room for Polly to squeeze in.

"Polly, you get in the back there," Mr. Derby ordered when Noah finished.

"Yes, sir," Polly muttered as she climbed into the wagon. She sat as far away as she could from the African slave girl, making sure the bundles separated them. The girl had covered her head with her hands.

"Polly Pritchard, my indentured girl, meet my new little savage. From my inspection of her, I figure the two of you are about the same age." Mr. Derby choked out a laugh.

Polly didn't see what was funny.

"And I know you have met my son, Clay," Mr. Derby said. Mr. Derby looked at his son with pride, but the young man had his dark eyes on the terrified African girl.

Mr. Derby climbed onto the seat of the wagon, indicated to Clay to join him, then gave the signal to Noah to begin the journey. Noah made a chucking sound to the horse, and the wagon lurched onto the dirt road.

Polly could feel each bump and jolt of the road beneath her as the wooden wheels lurched over each uneven place in the dirt or gouged hole left by other wagons. After one particularly deep dip in the road Polly was tossed across the bags of seed, landing

121

hard against the slave girl, who opened her eyes and looked around frantically. Polly scrambled quickly back to the other side of the wagon.

The two girls eyed each other carefully. Polly had always prided herself on her looks. When she got the chance to glance in a mirror, she was always pleased at the peachy paleness of her face, which bore, thankfully, no scars from smallpox like many women she knew, and the blue-green clarity of her eyes. Unconsciously, she touched her hair, which her mother had loved to brush. It grew thick and straight — she remembered her father used to call it "golden flax." She knew the African girl was probably admiring her. Polly looked at the large brown eyes, the short-cropped hair, and the ebony-colored skin of the slave and saw nothing worthy of admiration. She sniffed. The girl even smelled bad.

The journey seemed to last forever as the wagon rumbled down the road. The sun, wickedly hot, seared Polly's fair skin. She longed for just a dipper of water.

Polly turned her attention to Clay. Sitting in a slouch, he kept spitting off the side of the wagon at regular intervals. Mr. Derby sat next to the driver, continually checking his fingernails and picking specks of dirt off his boots.

They had been traveling for almost two hours when Mr. Derby announced, "Well, Clay, what shall we call our latest acquisition? Since the new slave is to be yours, I shall let you name her."

Before Clay could speak, however, Polly spoke up quietly, "She probably already has a name, sir." Clay spun around and glared at Polly, as if to remind her of his warning about women staying in their place.

"Nonsense!" Mr. Derby replied, irritation in his voice. "Those jungle words have no meaning to civilized humans. I suggest you keep your opinions to yourself!" Polly said nothing more, but she looked long and hard at the slave girl's face.

Clay did the same thing. Finally, he said to his father. "I shall name her Myna, because she is mine!" He cleared his throat and spat once more.

Polly thought she had never met anyone with such an enlarged impression of himself.

Mr. Derby snorted. "It will do as well as any other."

"She is a most excellent birthday present, Father," Clay said as he glanced once more at the girl who huddled in the corner. He grinned and rubbed his hands together.

Mr. Derby looked at his son indulgently. "A boy turns sixteen only once! So I decided that just as my father provided a slave girl for me when I got old enough, I would do the same for you. I imagine one day you'll do the same for your son," he added.

Polly listened in amazement. She'd had very little experience with wealthy people, but she had never met anyone with attitudes like the Derby men seemed to have. She glanced at the African girl, who surely had no idea what her future held. She found herself feeling sorry for this new slave who huddled in the wagon, glistening with sweat.

"Black women are different, you know, Clay," Mr. Derby continued. "They like it when you pick them out for special favors at night. It keeps them happy, and . . ." He paused to flick a speck off his waistcoat. "And it reminds them in a very special way who is the master and who is the slave." He took a deep breath of the summer air.

"I will take good care of her, Father," Clay replied, pleasant anticipation in his voice. The wagon suddenly lurched to one side, the horse snorting and neighing as it pulled at the reins. Mr. Derby and Clay were tossed on the wagon seat.

"Can't you handle that animal?" Clay shouted at Noah.

"Yassuh," Noah replied, pulling the animal into a more controlled gait. "Musta been a bug or a 'skeeter that spooked him, suh."

Polly had a feeling Noah knew exactly what that horse was doing every moment. She also decided she didn't like this young man with the dark eyebrows, the sneering smile, and the repulsive need to spit so often.

Clay and his father continued their conversation as if Polly and the slave sitting next to her did not exist. "White women, like my Isabelle and your mother before her, are to be respected and treated like fine china," Mr. Derby told his son. "It's not often a man finds true love twice in his lifetime," he said with a lilt in his voice. "I wish you'd try harder to warm up to your stepmother, Clay."

"You should never have married her," Clay replied sullenly. "She's far too young for you, and she wears that vacant smile all the time. She reminds me of a sheep." He spat off the side of the coach once more, then shifted on his seat. "Why did you decide to purchase the girl's indenture?" he asked, glancing back at Polly.

"The little white girl comes to us with an indenture as long as my arm — there's no way she can pay it off in less than fourteen years. I figure she will be a good investment. She's from Beaufort, south of here. Both her parents are dead."

Clay turned to look at her. "Don't worry, Polly-girl. You'll like it at Derbyshire Farms. Lots of sheep, slaves, and chickens. And rice. Lots of work to do." He gave a small laugh.

Polly bristled. "Polly-girl" had been her father's pet name for her, and it angered her to hear it pour so carelessly from the mouth of this unpleasant young man.

A faint breeze moved the hot air as they traveled. No other wagons or people were to be seen. Huge live oak trees lined each side of the road, with dangling beards of Spanish moss hanging from each branch. Polly thought the trees looked like old men, bent over and exhausted from the heat. Perhaps they watched over all who lived here, she thought briefly. It had been a long time since someone had cared for her.

After the deaths of her parents she'd lived almost like a prisoner in the rat-infested attic of a dirt farmer named Jeremy Carton. He rarely spoke to her except to give her orders. He had a wife and a daughter, both of them thick of mind and body, who'd ignored her as well, except when the pigsty had to be cleaned or the manure from the horses needed to be collected for fertilizer. Polly longed for a kind word, a loving touch, but she kept a stony distance from everyone. The Carton family never saw her cry, not even when her parents died, never heard a word of complaint from her. She knew they thought her to be cold and unfeeling.

This is going to be my chance to make something of myself, she vowed. *I shall not let anything or anyone get in my way. I intend to make myself necessary to the Derby family, while learning how the upper class lives.* It pleased her to imagine her grand goals, but she was deadly serious about working her way up to be the fine lady her mother had dreamed she would be.

The oppressive heat and constant rhythm of the wagon wheels finally made Polly sleepy, and she dozed uncomfortably for a couple of hours. When she was startled awake by a deep rut in the road, she could see the fiery redness of the sun above the trees in the distance.

The wagon pulled into a narrow lane then, and Polly could see the two-story brick manor house ahead. It was almost blindingly white in the late afternoon sun; it looked as if it had been whitewashed several times for the brick to be so completely covered, Polly surmised. Its red-gabled roof, nestled between two huge stone chimneys, also carried an aura of perfection. It was surrounded by a carpet of lush grass, kept short, she found out later, by the many sheep that grazed upon it. On her far right were green fields, and behind them dark woods grew full and deep. Far to her left many black faces labored in a large field near a river. They seemed to be standing in water.

"Welcome to Derbyshire Farms, Miss Polly," Clay said, making a sweeping movement with his arm. "The river you see yonder is the Ashley."

Polly didn't know what to say. Everywhere she glanced, she saw perfection. Not a stone was out of place on the path they drove on, not a flower in the garden seemed to be wilted. *Oh, to own such a glorious property!* she thought with an intake of breath. She noticed Mr. Derby looking carefully at his domain, as if checking to make sure everything was as it should be. Several slaves rushed out to meet the wagon. One carried a broom and began sweeping the path behind them. Another carried a tray of cold drinks for Mr. Derby and Clay. No one spoke to the master or his son.

Mr. Derby ignored the slaves and ordered Noah to turn to the right. They continued down a rutted lane, then stopped in front of a small shack made of wood. Polly noticed several other similar huts in the area, but she had no time to wonder about them, because just then Mr. Derby ordered them out of the wagon.

Polly nodded and climbed stiffly down. She motioned to the African girl to do the same. Mr. Derby pointed to the shack. "Here is where you will live. This slave is your responsibility for now. I can't spare any field hands to break in a new African, and I certainly won't have anyone of my household doing such a task."

"But . . ." Polly looked at him with a surprised frown on her face and started to object. Then she suddenly realized with dismay what he meant. She was not to be installed in his household, where she could observe and absorb fine living, but would be forced to live with this slave girl instead. How humiliating!

"I could be of great help to you, sir, as part of your household staff," she offered.

"This *is* how you will assist me," Mr. Derby replied, his face showing impatience. "I need for her to act like a human instead of a monkey. Do you think you can tame a savage?"

"Yes, sir. I can do anything I put my mind

to," Polly replied haughtily. But she hated the thought that she would have to deal with the black girl on a regular basis.

Mr. Derby looked at Polly carefully. His voice was like a sharp stone. "Don't underestimate me, child. I will not tolerate insubordination. Do I make myself clear?"

What was clear to Polly was that Mr. Derby was used to having his way. "I'm grateful for the opportunity, sir," Polly said with as much meekness as she could muster. "I will serve you well."

Mr. Derby folded his arms across his chest, then continued. "Your job is to teach her a little of the King's English, to teach her how civilized people live and act, and most importantly, to teach her absolute obedience. She belongs to my son, and when he needs her, it is your job to make sure she is delivered to him. Understood?"

"Yes, sir," Polly said quietly. Clay stood behind his father, chewing on a blade of grass, grinning.

"Both of you are to assist Teenie and not get in her way. I demand perfection, and I expect my servants to be useful and occupied at every moment of the day. In addition, I will not tolerate the questioning of any orders I give — ever!"

"Teenie, sir?" Polly asked, a frightened

question mark in her voice.

"Do you have a problem with any of this, young lady? Because I can take you right back to where I found you — working for common scum like Jeremy Carton as a scullery maid. I have given you a home, a job, and an opportunity to better your life — much more than you deserve! Now get on with you before I change my mind!"

Mr. Derby ordered Noah to take the wagon back up to the main house. He motioned to Clay, and the two walked away. Polly breathed a loud sigh of relief as they left. The slave girl did the same, almost at the same moment. They looked at each other tentatively, but neither girl smiled.

16. TEENIE AND TIDBIT

Polly entered the shack, not knowing what to expect. The slave girl, who was about the same height as Polly, followed hesitantly behind her. As her eyes adjusted to the dim light, she looked around. It was just one room, barely large enough to turn around in, made of rough wooden planks. It held a small wooden table, a chair, one bed, and a straw mat on the dirt floor. It smelled faintly of sweat.

"I've lived in places much worse," Polly said to the slave girl, who had already sunk to the floor and curled her arms tightly around herself. She thought back to the damp and moldy shack she'd shared with her mother while her father was in prison, and the attic room at Jeremy Carton's place.

The slave girl whispered words that Polly could not decipher.

"You'd better quit talking that jungle talk," Polly admonished. "I'm pretty sure that would be frowned upon in this place." She scowled as she looked at the confused expression on the girl's dark face. "I don't know what Mr. Derby is thinking. How am I supposed to make you civilized?"

Polly looked closely at the slave. Her cheeks were sunken into her thin face, which made her eyes seem very large, like a deer's. When the two girls exchanged glances, Polly could see bitterness flash in the slave girl's eyes for a moment. Her lips were full, but her nose was tiny, almost like Polly's own. Polly was unaccustomed to being this close to a Negro, and she marveled at how dark and mysterious the girl's face looked. A thin sheen of sweat covered the slave's slim body. Her hair, thick and matted, obviously had not been brushed in a long time. Welts and bruises, some of them quite recent, covered her arms and legs.

Polly's stomach suddenly growled, and she pressed her hands against it. When had she last eaten?

The slave girl watched Polly carefully, then grabbed her own stomach.

"Well, I suppose you're hungry too," Polly said. "You have no idea what I'm saying, do you?"

The girl just stared at her.

"This is impossible!" Polly shouted, and

the slave cringed. "What am I doing out here in a shack taking care of some . . . some . . . savage!" Furious with frustration, she pummeled the lumpy straw mattress with her fists until she was out of breath. "What am I supposed to do with you?"

The girl shrugged as if she understood.

Polly sat down heavily in the wobbly wooden chair and ran her fingers through her own uncombed hair. Her stomach growled again. "I suppose we must start somewhere," she said with a sigh. "Hungry," she said, rubbing her own stomach. "Hungry." Polly put her fingers to her mouth and moved her lips as if she were eating. "Hungry. Eat," she said, not expecting a response.

The slave girl looked around cautiously, then, to Polly's utter surprise, said, quite clearly, "Hun-gree. Eeet."

Polly looked at her suspiciously. "Either I'm a very good teacher or you are not as stupid as you look. Eat food," Polly said, adding a new word. The slave girl repeated the phrase easily.

"Well," Polly said with a look of amazement on her face. "I'm just going to talk to you as if you understand and teach you new words as we get to them. I imagine the sooner I complete this task, the sooner I can be assigned some more respectable duties, like sewing or serving the lady of the house."

The slave girl stared up at her.

"From what Mr. Derby told me, this place is called Derbyshire Farms," Polly began. "It is a rice plantation. Can you say 'plantation'?" Polly repeated the last word slowly. "Plan-ta-shun."

"Plan-ta-shun," the girl repeated. Although she certainly hadn't expected this, Polly refused to show the girl any encouragement.

"I am Polly, and I work for Mr. Derby just like you." She hesitated, then added, "Well, not exactly just like you. You're a slave, which means you belong to him."

"Slave," the girl said clearly. Her eyes narrowed and her lips drew back fiercely over her teeth as she said the word. *She knows exactly what that word means,* Polly thought.

"Let's do something easier, like introductions," Polly said, trying to change the subject. "I am Polly," she said, pointing to herself. "Pol-lee."

"Pol-lee."

"Yes," Polly said, allowing herself a smile, "and you are Myna. Can you say Myna? It's your new name." She pointed to the girl on the floor. "Myna."

The slave girl shook her head. "Amari,"

she said with pride, pointing to herself.

"I warned you about talking those African words," Polly reminded the girl. "You are Myna. My-na." She said it clearly several times.

"No Myna." The slave girl frowned and shook her head forcefully. "Amari!" She said it again slowly. "Ah-mar-ee."

Polly sighed and said, "Ah-mar-ee."

Amari smiled at her for the first time. "Amari!" she said again.

"Well, Amari, the master and his son say your name is Myna, so you better learn that one since it looks as though there's not much chance you'll ever get back to Africa. Just like I'll probably never get back to Beaufort," she added, almost to herself, "not that I'd want to."

The door of the cabin burst open then, and the shortest, skinniest black woman Polly had ever seen pushed her way through the door. She barely came to Polly's shoulder, but she carried herself with the dignity of a giant. Hiding behind her skirts was a very small boy — about three or four years old — who clung to her leg like a little insect. "Well, ain't this the berries! What we got here?" she boomed, even though the two girls were sitting right in front of her.

Finally, Polly said timidly, "How do you

136

do? I'm Polly, and this here is Myna."

"I knows who you is," the little woman said with a smile. "I knows everything. Hiding stuff from me is like tryin' to put socks on a rooster! You want to know the dirt goin' on roun' here, just ask old Teenie. Tiny little Teenie." Then she erupted into a full, hearty laugh that didn't seem possible to Polly, considering how small the woman was. "And this here is my boy, Tidbit." The child retreated farther behind his mother, but he peeked out to see the new faces.

"Pleased to meet you, Miss Teenie," Polly said with difficulty. She didn't think a Negro deserved the title of "Miss," but somehow this woman seemed to require it. Her father had taught her to disrespect Negroes, but her mother had taught her to respect her elders.

"Don't be callin' me Miss Teenie lessen you want to get us both in trouble, gal. Just Teenie be fine. Y'all hungry?" she asked with a broad grin that showed she had almost no teeth. "Y'all both 'bout as thin as a bat's ear."

"Hun-gree," Amari whispered.

"Well, butter my butt and call me a biscuit! The little African can speak a little English, huh? Don't let the massa know, gal. Play dumb as long as you can." With that, she turned and headed out of the door, her child right behind her. "Come on to the kitchen. I'll set you up with some vittles. Lordy me," she said, "now we's got a African and a 'dentured gal to keep track of."

She walked toward a small building just off the big white house so quickly that Amari and Polly had to trot to keep up with her. The child Tidbit scurried next to his mother, and a small brown dog scampered up to join them. Smoke snaked from the chimney of the cookhouse, and the smells of stewing pork and fresh bread wafted from its narrow door.

Enticed by the smells, Polly eagerly entered the room. A stone hearth made up the entire back wall. A huge pot hung over the fire, which held a delicious-smelling sauce bubbling within it. *How did this tiny little woman lift that heavy kettle?* Polly couldn't help but wonder. Cooking pans and long utensils that she had never seen before hung from spikes nailed into the wall. She saw jugs and pointed sticks and even some utensils made from gourds. The floor was hard-packed dirt.

In a matter of minutes Teenie had two steaming bowls prepared for the two girls. Polly took a seat at a bench and motioned to Amari to do the same. Polly picked up her spoon and noted with disgust that Amari put her hand into the bowl and greedily scooped the food into her mouth. *Table manners,* she mentally added to the long list of impossible tasks ahead of her.

Tidbit sat with them, eyes large with questions. His bare feet swung beneath him. The dog curled quietly under the table. Polly smelled the food, then tasted it. *Brown peas, flavored with salt pork, maybe? Mashed with onions into yellow rice,* Polly thought. *Looks bad, tastes wonderful.* "This is very good," Polly said to Teenie between mouthfuls. "What is it called?"

"What's that you say, gal? You never had no Hoppin' John? Ain't you got rice and peas and salt pork where you come from?"

"Not like this," Polly admitted. "My mother wasn't much of a cook."

"The old folks say that iffen you eat black-eyed peas on New Year's, it s'posed to make you rich for the new year," Teenie said. Then she added ruefully, "Never worked for me, though!" She laughed and scooped more into Polly's bowl.

As Polly ate, she thought with a smile of her mother, who always managed to either undercook the spoonbread, burn the occasional rabbit or squirrel her father brought home, or forget to add spice to the stew. They ate lots of fried catfish — some of it quite raw and some of it crispy black. When her mother had fixed Hopping John, it was crunchy and gritty — obviously not cooked as long or as well as Teenie's meal. Polly glanced at the girl who insisted her name was Amari and saw that her thoughts were far from this warm kitchen as well.

Tidbit watched every move the girls made. He giggled every time Amari stuffed her fingers into the bowl.

"What's the dog's name?" Polly asked Tidbit.

"Hushpuppy," the boy replied cheerfully as he reached down to hand the dog a scrap of bread. "He know how to hush and hide," the boy said proudly.

"I'm gonna give you two gals a couple of days to learn your way round here 'fore I put you to work," Teenie told them as they finished eating. "And, Tidbit, I done told you to keep that raggedy old dog outta my kitchen!" The boy just laughed and disappeared under the table with the dog.

"Come by here tomorrow and watch me work," Teenie continued. "That's the best way to learn. Just stay outta my way, 'cause I be busier than a stump-tailed cow in fly time. I fixes all the meals round here."

Before Polly could respond, Teenie added, "Your job, Miz Polly, is to explain everything you see to this here African gal. Teach her the words, 'cause Massa ain't gonna wait no long time 'fore he be expectin' her to hold her own. And Miz Africa, learn what words you can, but learn to keep your mouf shut, 'cause Clay, that hellhound, got less patience than his daddy!" She grunted with distaste. "That boy got a thumpin' gizzard for a heart!"

"Yes'm," Polly mumbled.

"Gal, where you from? I done told you 'bout callin' me 'ma'am' and 'miss.' Your mama done raised you right," she said with a grin. Tidbit giggled from under the table.

"I'm from Beaufort, in the low country," Polly explained. "Nothing much there but bugs and gators and a few folks scraping the dirt to make do. My mother is dead. My father as well." She swallowed hard.

"Oh, chile, how they die?" Teenie's face grew tender.

Polly looked at her and saw that Teenie really wanted to know. "My father was born in England, and he was a good-looking man," she began. She smiled as she thought of his charming grin. "He told me ladies used to follow him home from the pubs every night. He would buy them fine wine and expensive gifts and tell them the lies they wanted to hear. He lived a grand life until he ran out of money." She paused. "He was thrown in jail like a common criminal just because he couldn't pay his debts."

Teenie sucked in her breath but made no comment.

"He had friends in the court system, however, and he was given the chance to start over in the colonies as an indentured servant. He came here on a prison ship — a frightful experience, he said. Eventually, his indenture was sold to a man named Jeremy Carton in Beaufort, right here in Carolina Colony. That's where he met my mother, who put an end to his fondness for other ladies, but not, however, his affection for ale and wine. I was born there."

The slave girl gently petted the dog under the table, looking as if she was trying to follow the conversation.

Polly continued, "My father worked like an ordinary slave on a tobacco farm." She looked up to see if Teenie had reacted to that, but Teenie simply continued to stir the food in the pot over the fire. She used a whisk that looked like it was made from the twig of a tree. "He worked hard, but he could never make enough to pay off his debt. My daddy was a good man but not real careful with what little money he got. He drank too much sometimes. . . ." Polly shifted on the bench a little.

"What about your mama?" Teenie asked gently.

"My mother came up rough — she was an orphan. She was shuffled from family to family most of her childhood. She learned to make do for herself most of her life. She worked as a maid when she could, as a beggar when she couldn't."

"Well, pick my peas! A white woman as a maid and a beggar! Must not be no slaves from where she come from," Teenie commented.

"Not all white people are rich landowners," Polly said, almost coldly. "Most white folks I know scuffle for every scrap of food they get."

"But they ain't slaves," Teenie reminded her quietly. "Go on, chile."

Polly thought for a moment and continued. "My father kept getting in trouble, spending months in jail, and was unable to pay back his indenture. My mother tried her best to keep us together as a family, even signing on with Mr. Carton as an indenture herself, but there was never enough work or money or food, even though she offered to do other people's laundry after her work

143

was done for Carton. Nobody would hire a white woman because folks knew they could get slaves to do the work for free!" Polly tensed as she thought of the unfairness.

Teenie took that moment to cut each girl a large slice of pumpkin pie. She cut a tiny piece for Tidbit, who stuffed most of it into his mouth in one bite, then grinned a large orange smile. The rest he gave to the dog.

"Well, the sun don't shine on the same dog's tail all the time," Teenie said philosophically. "Everybody got hard times at one time or t'other."

"I suppose," Polly began again, this time speaking very slowly. "But then, three months ago, my parents came down with smallpox." Teenie stopped chopping the onions for a moment. "Daddy died first, then three days later, my mother. I nursed them both, and I never got as much as a pimple." She paused, stood up, and walked outside of the hot cookhouse, taking deep breaths. "I am *not* going to cry!" she sternly told herself. When she felt she could continue, she went back into the kitchen.

"So how you end up here, gal?" Teenie rattled a stack of tin plates.

"Mr. Jeremy Carton decided that I must sign on to pay back what my parents owed him, and I had no choice but to do it. His is just a small dirt farm, so, I suppose to prevent me from running off — and I would have, too — he took me with him to Charles Town to get supplies yesterday. But then he met Mr. Derby in a tavern, and he somehow sold my indenture to him. I'm not sure how or why. So here I am."

"Seven years to pay back yo' indenture ain't bad," Teenie pointed out. "You is young and got plenty o' time to make you a place in this here world. White women with indentures got it easy — eventually, you can fit in." Polly glanced over at Teenie, surprised at the emotion in her voice. Teenie poked furiously at the coals in the hearth.

"I must pay back fourteen years," Polly told her. "I must pay my own plus what was left of my parents' indentures. Mr. Derby says I should be glad he was willing to take on all that debt. I suppose I should be thankful. But I'm fifteen years old. By the time I pay him back, I'll be almost thirty — a wrinkled, old woman." She stared for a long time at the blazing embers in Teenie's fireplace.

"Thirty ain't so old," Teenie said quietly. "That's close to how old I be, far as I can tell." She gazed out the door of the small kitchen house and looked dreamily down the path that led away from the plantation.

Polly watched as Amari moved close to Teenie and touched her hand. Something seemed to pass between them — a look of understanding, perhaps. Amari whispered a few words in her own language.

Teenie moved away abruptly and returned to her brisk command of the room. "Go on now, you two gals get outta here. It be almost dark, and I 'spect you both at dawn. Tidbit, go fetch me some wood for my fire! And take that dog with you," she yelled, although she didn't seem angry. The boy disappeared into the yard.

Amari and Polly headed slowly back to the little cabin. Polly watched, amazed, as Amari rushed to grab the mat on the floor, shook it out, then curled up on it quickly.

"Why are you laying on the floor?"

Amari covered her head with her arms.

"You don't want to sleep in the bed?"

Again the slave girl ignored her.

Polly shrugged and climbed onto the narrow cot. The straw-filled mattress was lumpy and smelled of moldy vegetables, but it was better than anything she had felt in a long time. She slept.

The knock on the door startled Polly awake. It was Tidbit, looking like a tiny night spirit. He was shivering, and so was his dog. "Massa Clay say he want his birth-

146

day present now. I'm to take her there."

Polly gasped with realization and reached over to shake Amari awake. Amari sat up and looked from Polly to the trembling child. Her face was a question. Polly said slowly and with genuine sorrow, "You must go with Tidbit. Master Clay is asking for you."

Amari looked at Polly, then the child, and suddenly seeming to understand, she groaned. "No! No! No!" she begged.

Polly touched her arm but couldn't think how to help her.

Tidbit stood silently, shifting from foot to foot, looking very uncomfortable.

Amari finally took a deep breath, stood up without a word, and followed the child out of the door. The night was very dark.

■ ■ ■ ■

PART THREE
AMARI

■ ■ ■ ■

17. Amari and Adjustments

The next three months were hot, confusing, and miserable as Amari tried to assimilate into the culture of plantation life. Dawn always came too quickly, and she woke each morning with a start as she heard the roosters announce the day.

Amari and Polly chopped and gathered wood for Teenie's fire, learned to set it, stoke it, and keep it blazing, and were taught how to hang the heavy pots so food would cook as Teenie commanded. Teenie showed them the stones that had been dug into the side of the fireplace where bread was baked and the iron grills where food was fried.

Amari still wasn't sure of how she felt about Polly, who at first seemed to be indignant that she wasn't working in the big house. Amari snorted with disdain at Polly's resentment. The white girl, she gradually learned, had the chance to be free one day. Amari knew too well that *she* would never taste freedom again.

Gradually, as they fell into a daily routine, Polly seemed to relax, but Amari could see she still felt somewhat superior to the slaves around her. She wouldn't touch any of them, not even to give Tidbit a hug. And she looked with longing at the main house all the time. Amari figured she was waiting for her opportunity to work there instead of in the kitchen with the slaves. The two girls merely tolerated each other.

Tidbit scurried everywhere with Amari and Polly, showing them how to turn the meat on the spit, the secrets of gathering eggs from the chickens without getting pecked, and what ingredients were needed to make the dough for the bread. For such a small child, he knew as much about the running of the kitchen as his mother, Amari thought, impressed. She thought sadly of how she used to try to avoid chores. How she wished she could help her mother once more!

Amari slowly learned how to cook and eat foods she never could have imagined. Sometimes they had squirrel or venison, which Amari learned was the meat of one of the many deer she saw around the place. The animal would be skinned and gutted, then the flesh was cut into long strips and hung in the smokehouse to dry over hot, smoked wood. Hams, mutton, even wild turkey hung there in the darkness of the smokehouse, waiting to be used in the winter, when food was not so plentiful. Teenie told Amari that it was the only building on the plantation that was kept locked at all times. Not even Teenie had a key.

Fresh fish was brought in by slaves every day, and Teenie taught both Amari and Polly how to clean it and fry it. Amari also showed Teenie how to make fish stew like her mother had made. It was on those days that she closed her eyes and dreamily imagined herself back, just for a moment, in the smoky hut of her parents.

One day, when Teenie brought in a basket of yams from the garden, Amari babbled in excitement — half in English, half in her native language — unable to make Teenie understand at first that Amari's mother had grown yams just like these in her own garden.

"You talkin' 'bout how yams grow in Africa?" Teenie finally asked when Amari had calmed down.

Amari took a deep breath and grabbed a yam from Teenie's basket. "My mama," she began, then tears filled her eyes and she gave up trying to explain. She closed her eyes and sniffed it. She could almost smell her mother's boiled chicken and yams.

"You know, my mama come from Africa too," Teenie told her. "She teached me what she knew 'bout Africa food. Long as you remember, chile, it ain't never gone."

Amari nodded in appreciation.

Tidbit's constant laughter made the long workdays seem a bit easier. He laughed when Amari dropped food in the fire and when the rooster chased Polly and pecked her arm. Hushpuppy shadowed the child's every move, running with Tidbit in the sunshine, and Amari knew the dog slept curled up with him at night.

Tidbit jabbered all the time, asking questions, making little jokes, playing tricks on his mother and the two girls. Amari learned quite a bit of English from the boy, who seemed to know intuitively what she needed to know. She also liked the way Polly talked to her constantly, making sure she knew the words for each food or task they encountered. Although she was proud that her command of the language was growing, it bothered Amari that she still spoke it so poorly. She knew she sounded stupid, and she didn't like it. She got mixed up on verbs like "come" and "came," as well as on plurals of words like "house" and "mouse." Why would these people say "houses" but not "mouses"? Why "mice" and not "hice"?

Amari understood much more than she let anyone know, however. Most of what was said around her she could figure out, but she knew the value of keeping her mouth shut and acting ignorant. An occasional slight nod from Teenie told her she was doing the right thing.

In the evening both she and Polly fell asleep exhausted, with Amari praying that she would not be called to the big house. But at least twice a week Tidbit stole quietly through the darkness to fetch Amari to come to the bedroom of Clay Derby. Each time, she forced her mind to go back to the dust of her childhood, to soft rain showers, to warm sunshine over her village — anything to help her endure, to help her forget his smell, his greasy hair, his damp hands.

But the worst was when he felt like talking — these were times she really hated because she was forced to stay in his room much longer.

"You ever talk to that cow my father married?" Clay asked her one night.

"Oh, no, suh," Amari had replied quickly. "I have no call to speak to the missus."

"She doesn't belong here," Clay said

angrily, almost to himself. "And now she's having a child, and my father acts as if it is the next Messiah!" He ground his fist into the sheet.

Amari had no answer; she just wanted him to say she could leave.

He lifted his head off his pillow then and spoke directly in her face. His breath smelled of spoiled food, and Amari had to force herself not to gag. "You like me, don't you?" The question was sudden and abrupt.

Shocked at the question, Amari swallowed hard. If she said no, he might get angry. If she said yes, he might manage to misunderstand her hatred of him. So she pretended she didn't know what he meant.

"I asked you a question. I know you understand much more than you let on. You *do* like me, don't you?" he implored quietly. To Amari, his voice sounded a little plaintive, almost as if he *needed* her to say she liked him.

"Yassuh," Amari whispered, cringing.

Amari was amazed to hear him breathe a sigh of relief. "I had a feeling you cared about me," Clay said, assurance creeping back into his voice. "Did Teenie give you the extra blanket I left for you?" he asked, sounding concerned.

"Yassuh. Thank you, suh." What she didn't

tell him was that she couldn't bear to touch the thing, so she had given the blanket to Sara Jane, a slave who had recently given birth.

"I think I'll let you come back tomorrow night," Clay said to Amari through the darkness. "I'm looking forward to it. Go on back to your place now."

"Thank you, suh," Amari whispered miserably. She crept out of his bed, down the back steps, and over the path through the darkness back to her cabin. She shivered uncontrollably and could not sleep. Morning always came harshly.

18. Roots and Dirt

One afternoon while Polly and Tidbit had gone to pick berries for a pie, Amari and Teenie were in a small garden Teenie had planted behind the kitchen.

"If you dig this yellow root here — it be called fever grass — then boil it," Teenie was telling her, "you can get rid of stomach cramps. And tea made from the bark of that tree yonder will stop a headache."

Ordinarily, Amari enjoyed these sessions with Teenie. It reminded her of times her mother had tried to teach her about herbs and roots and teas, but she had been too full of herself to pay much attention. But this day Amari was unusually quiet, having been compelled to spend the previous night with Clay, and he had forced her to do things that made her shiver with shame.

"The old folks calls this purple blossom buzzard root — it be good for female problems," Teenie told Amari quietly. When

Amari didn't answer, Teenie looked into her face. "You look as low as a toad in a dry well, chile."

"You got root that kill?" Amari asked glumly.

To Amari's surprise, Teenie replied quietly, "Yes, chile, I reckon I do. But death is not for me to give." She continued to dig furiously, her head down.

"Show me!" Amari implored, her heart beating faster.

"Not today," Teenie answered with a firm shake of her head. "Ain't nothin' you can do right now, chile." Teenie paused, then said, "For me, it was the overseer, Willie Badgett. Eventually, they gets tired of you and moves on — but the terribleness of it just goes to another slave woman." She reached over and touched Amari on the shoulder. She left her hand there a long time.

Grateful for the touch, Amari told Teenie, "I want die." She blinked back tears.

"No, chile, you was brought here for some reason — Lawd knows what it is, though." Teenie's voice was so sympathetic, Amari pressed her head into Teenie's chest.

"How long you be this place?" Amari asked after a moment, pulling away from her.

"I was borned here, chile. I tolt you my mama was a African like you be, but they sold her off when I was 'bout your age."

"Oh no — so very, very bad." Amari knew how deeply that must hurt.

Teenie's facial expression softened. "My mama be a strong Africa lady — Ashanti, she told me. She tell me how the thunder of the drums be echoin' 'cross the valleys, how the sun look at sunset — like a big old copper pot hangin' in the sky — and stories 'bout the antelope and the giraffe, 'bout the monkey and the spider. I tells Tidbit all I can remember."

"You telled me once that long as you 'member, nothin' ain't really gone," Amari reminded Teenie.

"I remembers it all," Teenie said softly. She reached into a pocket of her apron then and pulled out a small, faded scrap of multicolored fabric. Amari put her hand to her mouth with wonder. It was a tiny piece of woven kente cloth.

"Oh!" Amari whispered. It took her back to her father's loom.

"My mama give me this," Teenie explained. "When they snatched her away screaming from her mother, she grabbed on to her mother's head wrap. It ripped, and this little piece of it came off in her hand.

She clutched it all the way 'cross the big water, even kept it in her mouth when she had to. When she got to this place, she buried it not far from that tree yonder, just to keep it safe. Just before they sold her, she give it to me, and she whisper to me that I never forget." Teenie sighed. "This be my little piece of my mother, my little breath of Africa. It's all I got." She carefully tucked it back into her pocket.

The two said nothing for a few moments while they let the memories come in. Teenie cleared her throat then, looked up at the sky, and said, "Prob'ly be rain tomorrow."

"S'pose so," Amari muttered. Needing to change the subject, she asked, "How you get to be cook here?"

"'Fore she died, the first Miz Derby put me in charge of the kitchen. That was right after Daisy the cook got sold because she tried to poison Massa Derby. Not too many folks willin' to challenge what old Miz Derby say. I been cookin' ever since."

Amari looked up with surprise at the mention of a first wife of Mr. Derby. "Other Miz Derby be dead?"

"Yeah, chile, she died givin' birth to that suck-egg mule, Clay. Maybe that why he be so evil — he ain't never had no mama to love him."

Amari thought about that for a moment and wondered how his first wife's death had affected the master of the house. But she didn't have all the words she needed to express it. So she asked, "Massa Derby miss first wife?"

"I 'spect so. She was shapely, black-haired, and good-looking for a white woman, plus she kept his house perfect, and he loved that. He used to act all addlepated when he was round her, like she was honey and he was the buzzin' bee. But she had a sharp tongue and would beat a slave for next to nothin'."

"What Massa Derby do when she die?" Amari asked.

"Massa like to die hisself — couldn't eat nor sleep. He wouldn't even look at that baby. Paid no 'tention at all to that chile till he be 'bout six year old. Clay grewed up alone in that big house with a bunch of nannies from 'cross the water."

"Why Massa marry up with Miz Isabelle?" Amari ventured.

"Why do white folks do anything?" Teenie answered with a laugh, holding her arms up to the sky. "All's I know is she had to come here to a cold ol' fish like Massa Derby, put up with his awful son and paintings of the dead wife, and be cut off from all her friends and family."

Teenie went back to digging for roots and plucking tomatoes then, not willing to discuss it any further. Amari returned to the kitchen. She picked up a broom made of branches and began to sweep the dusty floor. The harder she swept, the thicker the dust became — dirt swirled everywhere. She saw nothing but dirt in her own future.

19. Peaches and Memories

One dusty afternoon about a week later Teenie called to Tidbit, "Go fetch me some peaches for my pie, boy. And take these two gals with you. Y'all look like you could use some fresh air."

Tidbit jumped at the opportunity to stop shelling peas and motioned to the girls to hurry before Teenie changed her mind. Apples, peaches, and plums grew abundantly on the plantation, as well as dozens of vegetables that Amari had never seen. Amari followed the boy down the path, looked up at the same coppery hot sun that used to warm her in her homeland, and breathed in the fresh air thankfully.

Tidbit climbed high into the branches of the first peach tree he came to. It was thick with sweet fruit. His job was to toss the fruit down to Amari and Polly, who carried baskets. But instead of gently handing it down, he laughed and threw the peaches like weapons, smashing the soft fruit against their heads. Hushpuppy barked crazily at the bottom of the tree, chasing the peaches and even eating some of them.

"Stop, Tidbit!" Polly cried with laughter. "Your mama's gonna get you for wasting food."

"Polly, Polly Peach Pie!" Tidbit chanted from the tree.

Amari had grown to love having the boy around. It was almost like Kwasi's spirit had found her in this strange new world. "Climb down from the tall tree, my little one," she said in her own language.

Tidbit shimmied to the ground, a peach in each hand, and looked at her strangely. "That Africa talk?" he asked.

Amari nodded.

"My mama be tellin' me stories 'bout Africa all the time, but she do it when ain't nobody else listenin'. Where Africa be?" the boy wanted to know.

"Far away. Over ocean. Under sky," she replied in English.

"What does it look like?" Polly asked.

"It look like bright colors, like happy. Sunshine. Family. Chickens and goats. Not need much." Amari smiled softly, thinking back to the green seas of grass that she and Tirza ran through as girls, the red and green screaming jacana birds that awakened her, the annoying little monkey that would whisk into the village and steal papayas when her mother turned her back, the smell of the wood fire in front of their hut. She wanted to explain how *right* everything felt in a place where she was surrounded by mischievous children, overbearing cousins, and doddering elders who were all a part of her. The storytellers who had absorbed her history, the villagers who breathed the same air and dreamed the same memories — all of them were black. She did not have the words to express the depth of her loss. "Everybody black. Feel good," was all she said.

Amari remembered the utter safety she felt as a child in her village, knowing that if she fell down and skinned her knee, any woman close by would dry her tears, put a little mud on the wound, and send her on her way with a hug.

"Little boys like me be there?" Tidbit asked with genuine curiosity.

"I had a brother," she said slowly. "Little older than you be. Happy boy with laugh like gold." She had to close her eyes at the thought of Kwasi.

"Where he be now?" Tidbit asked innocently.

Amari's face crumpled. "Dead," she said. Tidbit looked at her and nodded with a look of almost adult understanding. The three of them were silent for a few minutes, the only sound being the trilling of warblers and swallows.

Tidbit then asked Polly, "Where you was 'fore you come here?"

Polly looked thoughtful. "I grew up not far from here — in the low country. I remember moving from place to place and never having enough money, but that never bothered my parents. They doted on each other, but I was their shining star." Amari was thankful Polly spoke slowly so she could follow along.

"What that mean?" Tidbit asked.

"You know how your mama looks at you just before you go to sleep? That worried look when you stay out with Hushpuppy too long?" The boy nodded. "That's how my mama and daddy loved me."

Amari understood as well, but it surprised her. She'd never really thought about Polly's loss or grief. She just figured that because Polly was a white girl, her life just had to have been easier.

Polly looked into the distance and kicked at the tree trunk. "My mother told me once that she wanted to be a lady — somebody who wore lace and rode in a fancy carriage. But it never happened," she mumbled. "So she wished it for me."

Amari wasn't sure of every single word, but she knew Polly missed her mother. She reached over and touched Polly's hand. She was surprised that Polly didn't jerk away.

"You ever goin' back to Africa?" Tidbit asked Amari.

"No," Amari replied quietly and sadly, and she knew that it was forever true. Tidbit nestled against her, as if he understood her sorrow.

The two girls, accompanied by an unusually quiet Tidbit, walked back to Teenie's kitchen in silence. They delivered the peaches to Teenie and returned to their chores without comment.

20. ISABELLE DERBY

In spite of Teenie's diminutive size, Amari noticed that no one ever questioned her authority in the kitchen, not even the white people who lived in the main house. For a slave, that was power.

Isabelle Derby, the current mistress of the house, turned out to be surprisingly motherly and caring. Amari had heard whispers and rumors about her from some of the house slaves who stopped by Teenie's kitchen. Her husband controlled her every move and kept her away from everyone she had once known, they said. Amari noticed also that the household servants obeyed her without question — maybe because she was the only white person they knew who looked at them with a smile.

All the slaves also whispered about the fact that she was pregnant.

Each morning Mrs. Derby, dressed in white, as she usually was, came to Teenie's kitchen, greeted everyone with a cheerful hello, and planned the meals for the day. She would sometimes unlock the smoke-house so Teenie could choose a smoked meat if nothing fresh was available. Amari knew that Teenie would fix what she wanted to in spite of what Mrs. Derby suggested, but they had this conversation every morning anyway.

"It's a lovely day, Teenie," she'd always begin. She would always glance out of the narrow door and toward the horizon as she said that. It seemed to Amari that she wished she could be in another place.

"Yes'm. Gonna be hot again — hotter than buzzard's breath." A look of wistful sorrow crossed Mrs. Derby's face.

"Perhaps some iced tea for Master Derby at dinner would be refreshing." Mrs. Derby always frowned as she spoke of her husband.

"Yes'm. I be fixin' fresh chicken and snow peas and hush puppies. Anything else you be wantin' today?"

"Maybe some of your delicious peach pie?"

"Already done started it, ma'am. Be real good for you and that chile you carryin'. You need a little meat on them bones."

Mrs. Derby looked down at her swollen belly. "I pray for this child, Teenie," she said quietly. Amari watched as the woman gently rubbed her stomach.

"Yes'm. Maybe that chile make you happy for shure."

"Perhaps," Mrs. Derby replied, the wistful look returning.

Amari was fascinated with this white woman who seemed to be so pleasant and gentle. She tried to be in the kitchen area whenever Mrs. Derby came around, because the mistress of the house had a kind word for everyone and always smelled like flowers. Amari liked the fact that she didn't look at her as if she were ugly or an animal or a piece of flesh to be used. Mrs. Derby smiled at her with genuine compassion.

One early morning when the grass was still wet with dew, Amari was returning to the kitchen with a bucket of water for Teenie. She didn't often get time alone, so she walked slowly, savoring each solitary moment, even though she knew Teenie would scold her for being late.

She looked up with surprise as she almost collided with Mrs. Derby, who was walking alone on the path that led to the woods. Dressed in a long billowing gown that accentuated her pregnancy and a white hooded shawl, she looked almost like a spirit to Amari.

"You are Myna, am I correct?" Mrs. Derby asked her, to Amari's surprise. Her voice sounded whispery.

Nervously, Amari replied, "Yes'm." She stared down at her own bare, dirty feet, which stood so close to the fancy white shoes of the mistress. Teenie had told her never to look the masters directly in their eyes, but Amari had stolen looks at Mrs. Derby as often as she had been able to.

"Are you adjusting to your life here?" the woman asked kindly.

Again Amari simply replied, "Yes'm." How could she tell this woman of the horrors of her forced nights with Clay or her gut-wrenching longing for her mother?

"It must be very difficult for you, dear," Mrs. Derby said, as if she had read Amari's mind. "I know what it is like to be unhappy."

Surprised, Amari looked up. This white woman was admitting a weakness to her — a slave? Mrs. Derby smiled and reached out to touch Amari's shoulder. Amari, startled by her kind touch, gazed into eyes so green, they looked unreal. She had never encountered anyone with eyes that color. Amari also noticed what might have been tears on Mrs. Derby's face, but perhaps it was just her imagination.

Mrs. Derby hesitated, then said, "I know

about you and Clay."

Amari stepped back, her heart beating fast. What did she mean, "you and Clay"? Did this woman think she went to his room *voluntarily?* Amari didn't know what to say, didn't know *how* to say all the jumbled thoughts in her head.

"It is an unfortunate situation," Mrs. Derby said with feeling. "But I have no control over what he does. To tell you the truth, I have very little power over anything around here," she said morosely. "I just want to let you know I sympathize. I hope it ends soon."

Amari, whose face was hot with embarrassment, managed to mumble, "Thank you, ma'am."

"I must go now," Mrs. Derby said suddenly, looking nervously toward the manor house. She gave Amari one last look, then turned and hurried back to the house, her body a silhouette against the morning sun.

Later that afternoon Amari, peeling potatoes in the corner of the kitchen, listened as Lena, one of the house slaves, gossiped with Teenie. Grasping on to every word, Amari did her best to figure out the conversation. "Miz Isabelle be carryin' that baby real high, Teenie. I figger it's a boy."

"No, gal," Teenie commented. "It's a girl

for shure. Miz Isabelle deserve a purty little girl to keep her company in that big ol' house. I feels sorry for her."

"How you feel sorry for a rich white woman?" Lena asked harshly.

"Money ain't everything, chile. And ain't none of his money belong to her — she got 'bout as much chance to use his money as you do."

"Yeah, but she ain't no slave," Lena insisted.

"Pretty close to it," Teenie said. "He decide where she go, who she talk to, what she wear — everything. She just sleep in a better bed than you do!"

Lena continued, "And Noah, that slave she brought with her, I heard tell she got legal papers all writ up for him, so when she die, he be free."

"Do say, now," Teenie replied, but she made no real comment. Lena had ambled out of the kitchen then, to tend to other chores.

Intrigued, Amari wanted to know more. "How old she be — Miz Derby?" Amari asked Teenie.

Teenie counted on her fingers. "Maybe round 'bout eighteen. She jest a young thing. She came to that marriage with her slave Noah, lots of land, and piles of money, which is what ol' Massa wanted." Teenie glanced at Amari, a look of warning on her face. "Now, don't you be mindin' white folks' business, you hear me, gal? Just get them 'taters peeled right quickly."

Amari nodded and tried to focus on the mountain of potatoes in front of her.

Several evenings later, just before darkness completely obscured the path, Amari, exhausted from the labors of the day, hurried to finish gathering kindling to stoke Teenie's fire during the night. Suddenly, she stiffened, for just off the path she heard soft voices — a deep male voice, speaking in hushed tones, then a female's whispered reply. The woman seemed to be upset or crying.

"Who there?" Amari asked, not sure what she was interrupting. She recognized most of the slaves on the place by now and knew they posed no threat to her. But she feared running into Clay.

She heard a rustling in the bushes, then footsteps retreating. Amari listened for a moment or two, but all was silent, so she hurried back to Teenie's kitchen. She had learned, in her short time on the plantation, never to ask too many questions. Some things were best left unsaid, so she did not mention the incident to Teenie or Polly.

At the end of each day Amari collapsed, exhausted, on the floor mat in their small cabin. At first she thought she was being selfish, taking the sleeping mat from Polly, but Polly actually seemed to prefer that lumpy, smelly mattress. Gradually, Amari had figured out that not everyone slept as she had back in her village.

Clay, for example, slept on a soft, clean feather mattress, with perfumed sheets and silken curtains around the four-poster bed. But the curtains hid his vile habits, the smell of the perfume made her gag, and the clean sheets stank of his sweat by the time he was done with her. Oh, how she hated the smells of that bed!

Amari didn't know how the other slaves managed, for after their day's labor, they returned to their huts to care for their children, tend their small gardens, and prepare their own meals for the next day. Sometimes she heard bits of their conversations and voices singing late into the midnight hours.

"Why do you think they sing?" Polly whispered one hot, humid night as they listened to the somber songs drift through the window.

"Songs float up to sky — fly free," Amari had replied simply. She sadly thought back to the music of her mother's voice. She fell asleep, and thankfully, on that night, she was not awakened by Tidbit.

■ ■ ■ ■

Part Four
POLLY

■ ■ ■ ■

21. Rice and Snakes

Polly was determined to get a position in the big house. The slave girl was adjusting, Teenie didn't really need her, and Polly was tired of working like a common slave. She waited for her opportunity, praying for a moment alone with Mrs. Derby to ask for a more suitable position in her household. But Teenie kept her busy from dawn to dusk doing what Polly considered to be slave labor — peeling potatoes, shelling peas, shucking corn, and carrying heavy stacks of kindling for the fire.

Lots of corn grew on the land, and Polly was consistently impressed by Teenie, who seemed to know thousands of things she could make from it, but Derbyshire Farms was actually a rice plantation. Rice was everywhere. Rice ruled.

"Do you think Mr. Derby gets his wealth from the rice?" she asked Teenie one humid afternoon.

"Lawd, chile, what you care about Massa Derby's money? All I knows is every year Massa Derby go to market and buy big strong male slaves directly from Africa, for to work in the rice fields," she explained. "I was surprised at first when he brung Myna here — little biddy girl thing — she ain't no bigger than a rock-eatin' chicken. For shure she ain't strong enough to work the fields." She sighed. "But then I figgered out the reason why. I'm sorry, chile," she said to Amari.

Amari simply shrugged. "Why he buy Africa men?" she asked Teenie.

"They knows the rice 'cause they work it in their own country. They the brains of the whole project here. Massa won't admit it, but he need them men to keep this place goin'. They is what's makin' him rich."

Polly pondered this a moment, trying to find any opportunity to move from the kitchen to the house. "Perhaps Mr. Derby could use an assistant to help him keep his books. I can read and cipher, you know," she added with a bit of pride.

Teenie snorted. "Ain't much call for none of that round here. That's enough o' talkin' about the massa's money. I want y'all to head over to the rice fields and take this here water to the workers. Tote a little corn bread for 'em too. Lawd knows when they gonna git the time to eat or drink, though." She prepared a large wooden bucket for each girl to carry.

Polly groaned inwardly as once again she was given what she considered to be slave duties. *What is the advantage of being white if I have to work like I'm black every day?* she thought with consternation. *Mama would die if she saw me here!*

Teenie motioned to the boy. "Tidbit, you and that dog of yourn go with them and show them the way. But you stay outta that water, you hear? Gators get you!" Teenie wiped the sweat from her face.

"Yes, Teenie," Polly replied with resignation. She grabbed one of the buckets.

"Leave everything with Cato — if he ain't dead yet. He so old, he couldn't cut hot butter with a knife!" She laughed at her own joke. "And don't be all day down there — y'all got work to do back here."

Polly gritted her teeth, slowly repeated everything Teenie had said to Amari, even though she figured the girl had already understood most of it, and headed out of the kitchen and down to the river.

As they were walking down the path, Polly heard Teenie call out one final warning: "Y'all be careful of snakes, now!" Tidbit laughed, dropped to the ground, and pretended to slither like a snake. Hushpuppy, always ready for a new game, cavorted around Tidbit, barking wildly.

"Get up, silly boy," Polly said, her grim mood fading. "Your mama will get us if you get any dirtier." The boy got up, but he darted along the path like a little insect, picking up bugs and rocks along the road and tossing sticks for Hushpuppy to chase.

"I hate the heat of late summer," Polly remarked, her hair sticking to her face in the humidity. Amari didn't respond, but she seemed to be enjoying the warmth of the sunshine.

Polly had never been this far from the big house. She had heard of the rice fields, but she stood amazed at what she saw. Two dozen black men and women, knee-deep in thick mud, bent over the delicate-looking rice plants. There was no shade anywhere, and Polly could see thick rivulets of sweat running down their faces. They moved slowly, joylessly. *How can people live like this?* Polly thought.

"What y'all want?" a wrinkled, skinny slave sitting on the bank of the river asked. His hair, what was left of it, dotted his head like tiny clouds. "Hey, Tidbit! How be the little man and his dog?"

Tidbit bounded over to the old man and gave him a big hug. "Hey, Cato."

"Teenie sent corn pone and water for the rice workers," Polly told him.

"Hopes they get to eat 'em 'fore the bugs do!" He cackled, then almost choked in a spasm of coughing. "So how it be fer the new 'dentured gal?" he asked Polly when he got his breath. "That sunshine-colored hair of yourn gonna get you out of your indenture right quick," he predicted. "Alls you need is a lonely little white boy!" He laughed at his own comments, then coughed even harder.

Polly touched her hair but did not answer him directly.

Amari asked him, "You work hard today, Cato?" Polly had learned that Cato, the oldest slave on the plantation, always seemed to know everything that went on while managing to do very little work at all.

"They ain't got much choice but to let me do pretty much what I wants to nowadays, since they done 'bout worked me dry," he said, chuckling. "Right now I'm workin' at watchin' this here grass grow!" He laughed and coughed deeply.

Cato looked up at Polly then. "You two still workin' in the kitchen?" he asked.

Polly nodded.

"Not fer long, chile. You'se a white gal — soon they gonna have you sewing fer Miz Isabelle." Polly thrilled at the possibility. "But Miz Africa here gonna be down here in the swamps with us — soon as Massa Clay get tired of her." Amari let out a soft moan.

"How do you know this?" Polly asked.

"I ain't the oldest slave on the place fer nothin'. I hears things and sees things."

"Maybe it is too soon for her," Polly said, frowning.

Amari looked at Polly, a look of surprise on her face.

"You don't have to convince ol' Cato. I'm just tellin' you what I knows. Massa love to see the Africans workin' the rice."

"You ever hear tell of anybody goin' back to Africa?" Tidbit asked.

Cato replied seriously, "No, little one. Don't nobody go back to Africa. When they put you in the rice fields, you'll be dead in five years, so don't matter no how."

"Five years? Why?" Polly asked, sounding genuinely shocked.

"Let me 'splain," Cato replied. "I spent eighteen years out there — some kinda record they tells me. Every day the rice hands be exposed to the burnin' sun. Sometime it seem like the very air we be breathin' is hotter than human blood. Then there's the malaria, and the new-monia and the snakes, plus the mosquitoes and the flies and their maggots — all joinin' us to keep us company while we sweat. Pregnant women be havin' stillbirths, and the babies that end up bein' born die young — like they sickly or somethin'. That's why Massa keepa bringin' in new Africans — they knows the rice, and they strong."

Amari inhaled deeply and looked at Cato, her eyes wide.

"Hey, boy!" Cato called to Tidbit as he heard the dog bark with alarm. "Get away from that water! You want a gator to eat you?"

"Gator can't catch me!" Tidbit replied, but he ran back up on the grass.

"You know how rice be planted?" Cato asked the girls as he continued. They shook their heads. "One seed at a time."

"But rice be so small!" Amari remarked.

"Yep, that it is. You makes a hole in the mud with your toe. You drops the one tiny little rice seed in the hole. Then you closes the hole with the heel of your foot. Toe. Plant. Heel. All day long. Bendin' over. Knee-deep in swamp water." Cato coughed once more and looked down at the ground.

"And that's just the first part. Then you

gotta tend to the plants and flood the fields and cut the stacks and thresh the seeds — seem like it go on forever. That's what be in your future, Miz Africa. And when he get old enough, this here boy's future too."

Polly looked at Cato in disbelief. "They'd put Tidbit out there?" she asked, horrified. The thought of little Tidbit sweating and working in the dangerous swampy water made Polly feel ill.

Amari put her hand to her mouth, barely holding back a sob. "What to do?" she finally asked.

Cato shrugged. "It might help if Miz Isabelle like you, but she ain't got no say-so over much round here. I s'pose you gotta keep on makin' yourself useful in Massa Clay's bedroom — that be all any slave woman can do," Cato explained sadly, "lessen she run away."

At that moment they heard a bloodcurdling scream coming from one of the slaves in the rice field. Cato moved astonishingly quickly for an old man, and he hurried down to see what happened. Polly, Amari, and Tidbit followed.

"Oh, my Lawd! Copperhead!" a slave named Jacob cried hoarsely. "My Hildy been snake-bit!"

Polly watched, horrified, as Jacob emerged

from the swampy mud, carrying Hildy's limp body to the shore. He laid her gently on the grass. Polly could barely see the two small wounds on her leg; there was very little blood. Some of the slave women quickly daubed her leg with mud and wrapped it tightly with strips of cloth ripped from their own dresses. The woman's eyelids fluttered, she called for her husband, then she arched her back and was still.

"She be dead?" Amari asked, her voice barely a whisper. Tidbit, for once, was still and quiet.

"Not yet," Cato replied quietly. "Just passed out. But the poison likely to kill her by sunset. Copperhead don't play." Cato looked directly at Amari as he spoke again. "Two dead of snakebite this season. Two more died of the malaria. One gator bite. One drownt. Do whatever you can to stay outta this here place, gal. Ya hear?"

Amari looked terrified, Polly thought, and rightfully so.

As they left the rice fields, Polly could hear the workers being called back to work — no free time just because of a little snakebite.

22. LASHED WITH A WHIP

When Polly and Amari returned to Teenie's kitchen, both of them clearly upset, Teenie didn't seem the least bit surprised. "How's Hildy?" she asked as she pulled Tidbit close to her.

"Cato told us she might die," Polly reported, tucking her shaking hands under her arms. Then she asked, "How'd you know?"

"I declare, chile. You oughta know by now that it don't take long for news to travel round here," Teenie said. "So, did Cato also scare you 'bout how gals like Myna here be endin' up in rice fields?"

Polly nodded, then frowned. This time last year, when she was back in Beaufort with her folks, she wouldn't have given a second thought to a slave going to work in the rice fields. That's what a slave was *supposed* to do. Who cared about the feelings of an ignorant slave, anyway? But this was someone she knew, maybe even felt sorry for. Somehow that made a difference.

"Cato speaks true," Teenie said solemnly. "But I got an idea. Let's see what we can do. The two of you go out back and wash yourself. Get back in here real quicklike."

The two girls returned with clean faces and hands, and Teenie handed them each an outfit worn by the house serving maids. "Flora, one of the serving gals, is Hildy's daughter. She done run down there to see to her mama," Teenie explained. "Massa don't allow such behavior, but he don't know yet. So you two gonna take her place at supper." Polly and Amari exchanged looks of surprise.

"Polly, you just do what Lena, the head serving gal, tells you to do. Say nothing except for 'yes, sir' and 'yes, ma'am.' Myna, you copy everything they do and act like you know what you doin'! You understandin' all this, gal?"

Polly was pleased that Amari replied as she had been taught, "Yes, Teenie." But she was thrilled about the chance to go work in the big house. Finally!

Teenie looked worried, however. "Don't you drop nothin', you hear! Now git!" she told them.

Polly changed quickly into the stiff black

uniform, inwardly praying that perhaps this would be the start of her move up to the main house and out of the kitchen with the slaves. She then helped Amari tie the sash on her apron. Tidbit laughed out loud when he saw the two girls dressed as maids.

Polly shooed him away. "Have you seen Mr. Derby since the first day we arrived here?" she asked Amari as they prepared to take the food to the main house.

Amari shook her head. "Not see, which be good."

"Have you ever been inside the main house?" Polly asked. Then she gasped as she realized what Amari's answer would be.

"Only nighttime," Amari replied harshly.

"Oh, Myna, I forgot."

"I not forget," Amari stated, her voice sharp as broken glass.

"Do you think Mrs. Derby knows what Clay is doing?"

"She know," Amari said angrily.

"Maybe she can help you," Polly offered tentatively. "She seems to be very pleasant."

"She need help herself," Amari replied sharply.

Polly tried to understand, but she couldn't truly fathom the depths of Myna's apparent distress. Slave women were always called to the bedrooms of their masters — it was

simply a fact of life. Myna should understand that by now and be getting used to it.
But she let the subject drop as they prepared
to carry the food.

Amari took a platter of venison, while
Polly carried a huge, glistening corn pone
on another large platter. They walked carefully up the path from the kitchen to the big
house and entered through the back door.

Lena took one look at the two girls and
rolled her eyes up to the ceiling. "Lawd have
mercy, we gonna get in trouble for shure!
Tell Teenie if I gets a beatin' over this, I
ain't never forgivin' her. Now go on back
and bring the rest of the food."

Polly and Amari dashed back several more
times to get the rest of the food for supper
for Mr. Derby and his wife. All of it was
laid out on a sideboard, to be served as
Lena directed.

Polly looked around the room in rapt
curiosity. *Now, this is where I belong,* she
thought with a smile, taking in the dark
green curtains covering the windows to keep
out the afternoon heat, the fine, pale green,
embroidered carpet decorating each floor,
and the pictures of ancient Derby relatives
lining the walls. Fancy silver eating and
drinking utensils lay in a huge cupboard on
the other side of the room. Polly had never

seen such finery. *Oh, how Mama would have loved this!* she thought.

Polly tiptoed to peek into the adjoining room, which was obviously Mr. Derby's study. She inhaled with pleasure. Shelves of leather-bound books filled one wall. She'd give anything to simply touch them; to have access to them would be heaven. Her mother had taught her to read using the Bible and occasional pieces of newsprint that came their way, but Polly longed for books of her own. *If I could get assigned to the main house,* she thought, *I would sneak into this room during every free moment.* She sighed and returned to the dining area.

Standing silently near the door of the dining room, almost like a statue, was the coachman who had driven the two girls here from the market just a few months ago. Once again he was dressed in an elegant coat and a shirt with lace cuffs. "This here is Noah," Lena explained. Noah nodded slightly but continued to stand stiffly and formally. "He's the coachman, the butler, Miz Isabelle's bodyguard, and prob'ly the fanciest house slave we got round here — best lookin', too!" Lena laughed. "Massa trusts him, and" — she lowered her voice to a whisper — "word is that Miz Isabelle done taught him how to read! He —"

Suddenly, Lena cleared her throat and snapped to attention. Polly and Amari did the same. Mr. Derby, dressed in a red velvet suit, escorted his now very pregnant wife into the room. Clay sauntered in behind them, gave a look of undisguised disgust to his stepmother, and sat as far away from her as he could. He seemed to be trying to get Amari's attention, Polly thought, but Amari had dropped her head and refused to look at him.

"Where's Flora?" Mr. Derby demanded as soon as he had helped his wife be seated.

"Her mama got snake-bit today, sir. Real bad. She done run to the quarters to see her," Lena explained quickly. "But we got something special for your supper today, yes we do. Polly, pour the wine like I showed you." Polly hurried to obey.

"Well, I hope she's not too badly injured," Mr. Derby said irritably. "I hate it when my workers are laid up."

Mrs. Derby spoke up, although barely audibly. "Shall I check on her tomorrow, Percival?"

"No, my dear. I really disapprove of you dealing with the servants. It's not wise in your condition, you know."

"She might need medical attention," Mrs. Derby suggested softly.

"I'm sure she'll be fine," her husband said. "It is *you* I worry about, Isabelle. Right now the most important things on my mind are your happiness and comfort," he said firmly, "and the safety of our child. I could never forgive myself if anything happened to that baby. I have not been this excited, or this happy, in many years." He took her hand in his. It seemed to Polly that he gazed at his wife with genuine concern.

Mrs. Derby smiled at him, touched her belly, and let the matter drop.

Turning to Clay, Mr. Derby said, "Son, run down to the quarters tomorrow and get one of the slaves from the fishing gang to take her place."

"It will be my pleasure, Father," the young man replied lazily, "but why not just send Noah? He's able-bodied. Perfectly good waste of a strong worker, seems to me." Polly saw Clay look at his stepmother with a wicked grin.

Isabelle Derby inhaled, then looked at her husband in alarm. "You promised, Percival. You promised when we married that I could keep my bodyguard."

Mr. Derby's face softened as he put his arm around his wife's shoulders and gave her what seemed to be a reassuring hug. "I think Clay is merely teasing you, my dear. I wouldn't think of upsetting you by doing such a thing. All I care about right now is your health and your happiness." To Clay he said, "Try to be kinder, son. You'll have a brother or sister soon."

Clay rolled his eyes, looked at Mrs. Derby with disdain, and drank another glass of wine. It was clear to Polly that he truly disliked his stepmother.

As they continued to serve the food, Amari looked nervous, so Polly tried to help whenever she thought Amari might not understand a command. She wasn't going to let Amari spoil her chance to impress the Derbys. Noah continued to stand like a sentry at the door, never moving, never displaying any emotion.

Mrs. Derby drank very little of the white wine that Amari had carefully poured for her. She had given Amari a pleasant smile, however, and had thanked her as Amari deftly slipped a white linen napkin onto Mrs. Derby's lap.

"You must eat more, my dear Isabelle," Mr. Derby said to his wife. "You want our child to be healthy, don't you?"

She looked up nervously. "Yes, of course you are right, Percival," she replied. She motioned to Polly to put a little more corn pone on her plate, but Polly noticed she only nibbled at it. "Please tell Teenie the supper is delicious," Mrs. Derby said to Lena.

"Now, don't compliment the slaves on doing their jobs, my dear. Your kindness only makes them weak and careless." It sounded to Polly that Mr. Derby admonished his wife almost as if he were speaking to a child, but he also seemed to dote on her. He touched her constantly, fixing a ringlet of hair that had fallen into her face, brushing a speck from her shawl, and patting her left hand with his right.

As Lena skillfully served the stew, venison, corn, and beans to the Derby family, Amari and Polly were kept busy taking plates back to the kitchen, bringing up steaming baskets of bread, and, finally, a fresh-baked blackberry pie.

Mrs. Derby continued to pick at her food, and her husband sometimes stopped his conversation with Clay to cut a small piece of meat for his wife so she would eat it. "Now, don't you feel better?" he would say after she had swallowed it. She would smile wanly in agreement. It seemed to Polly that he treated his wife more like a delicate possession than a real person. Any genuine conversation he seemed to save for his son.

"I'm thinking we can bring in a few more

slaves," he told Clay. "The rice crop will do well this year, and the market has gone up. Let's plan on making a bigger harvest next season."

Clay nodded, casting another glance at Amari. "That means expanding the fields by the river. We'll need fresh Africans for that — they know rice so well."

"How many, do you think?" his father asked.

"Three or four, at least," Clay replied. "They don't seem to last long out there."

"Well, I'll keep my eyes open the next time I go to market," Mr. Derby said. "We best be getting them soon, so they can be broken in by planting time."

They speak about buying slaves the same way they discuss the purchase of cattle or supplies, Polly noticed, surprised at how uncomfortable that made her feel. *When I am the mistress of such a place, will I discuss the purchase of people as they do?* She was not sure of the answer.

"Do you think we'll need to sell any slaves to get money for next year's supplies?" Clay asked his father.

"Not this season, son. I've monitored the books quite closely, and I think this year we will make quite a profit without selling any property." He seemed pleased.

Property. They call the slaves property. Polly thought about the slaves she had come to know since she had come to the plantation. The thought of one of them being sold distressed her in a way she had not thought possible. *Without Amari and Teenie and Tidbit, how awful it would be here,* Polly suddenly realized.

Clay stopped to scratch his head, then said to his father, "I hear talk in town of folks in the North starting to speak about ending slavery."

Mr. Derby, sipping his third glass of wine, snorted, "That will never happen. Those Northerners. They can't even *grow* the rice they love so much. They know nothing about how a business is run. Rice, tobacco, corn — where do they think it comes from?"

Clay, who had had even more wine than his father, leaned back on the two back legs of his chair carelessly. "Slavery just makes good sense to me. Anyway, our slaves are better off here than in some jungle eating bugs and slugs like savages."

"Of course they are. They need us, son."

Mr. Derby is right, isn't he? Living here has got to be better than a jungle, right? Polly wasn't sure anymore. She could see Lena grinding her teeth in anger. She glanced over at Amari to see her reaction, but Amari stared straight ahead.

Isabelle Derby sat pale and quiet, her eyes cast down through most of the meal. It was as if she were one of the many room decorations. Unhappiness seemed to ooze from her like perspiration on a humid day. Polly shook her head as she realized that being a fine lady didn't necessarily mean finding joy. Clay's antagonism toward Mrs. Derby was almost palpable — he glared at her every time she picked up a spoon or wiped her lips with a linen napkin.

Finally, the meal was over, and the last of the dishes were being removed. Polly, relieved that neither she nor Amari had done anything to call negative attention to themselves, congratulated herself on a successful evening. *I'm going to speak to Mrs. Derby right after dinner,* Polly vowed bravely. *This might be my only chance. I will offer my services as her personal assistant. Surely, with the new baby, she will need someone to help her.*

Mr. Derby finished a last glass of wine, then lit his pipe and stretched his long legs out from his chair just as Amari was walking by with the final platter of leftover blackberry pie. Amari, looking at Polly rather than the floor, tripped over his legs and fell. *No! No!* Polly breathed as the platter flipped and the pie careened to the floor. Purple-red berries splattered onto the pale carpet. There was a moment of absolute silence.

Amari cowered on the floor in obvious terror. Polly, too afraid to breathe, waited for the thunderous voice of the master.

"You stupid black wench!" he roared. "Lena, go get my whip!" Polly gasped at the same moment as Amari did. Polly knew Lena had no choice but to obey. She returned quickly and handed it to Mr. Derby, never looking at him directly. Coiled like a snake, the whip was made of leather. The tip of the lash was laced with wire.

Polly inhaled and held her breath.

Mr. Derby grasped the handle, drew his arm back, and fiercely brought the braided lash of it across Amari's back. She screamed, twisting with pain at his feet. Again he beat her. And again. Seven times he thrashed her. Ten. Twelve. The back of her new housemaid uniform was ripped to shreds, stained with her blood.

Polly clenched her hands into fists, furious at being so helpless and angry at her own selfishness as well. Because even though she flinched every time Amari was hit, she couldn't help but realize that this incident would forever ruin her chances of working in the main house.

Lena quietly murmured words of prayer. Horror distorted Mrs. Derby's face. Clay looked surprisingly uncomfortable and agitated. Only Noah never changed his stance or facial expression.

Finally, Isabelle Derby got up from the table and walked over to her husband. Noticeably trembling, she grabbed his hand as he lifted it to strike Amari again. "Enough," she said quietly. "The girl has learned her lesson. Make her clean up the mess and let her be. It is distressing to me to see such a scene. It might mar our child."

Mr. Derby, as if returning from another place, shook his head and coiled the whip. "You are right, my dear," he told his wife. He took a deep breath. To Polly he said, "I put you in charge of this ignorant African. You have failed me. It is your fault she made such a fool of herself tonight. Clean the floor, then tend to her wounds. As soon as she's healed, she goes to the rice fields to replace Hildy."

Polly bowed her head and murmured apologies that she knew Mr. Derby would not hear. She dared to look at Amari, who lay deathly still, and at the carpet, stained with both blood and pie. Polly wasn't sure what to do first. She had never been so scared in her life.

Mr. Derby escorted his wife out of the room then. Clay, looking quite distressed, gazed at the bleeding and unconscious Amari for a long time before following after them.

Noah slowly left the room as well, as his job was protector of the master and his wife. "Vinegar," he whispered as he headed out of the door. "Vinegar will remove the stains from the carpet."

■ ■ ■ ■

Part Five
AMARI

■ ■ ■ ■

23. Fiery Pain and Healing Hands

Her back was on fire. Amari didn't remember being brought back to the cabin, didn't hear Teenie's shouts or see Polly's tears. All she knew was that every breath made the pain intensify, every movement made her gasp and scream. She was dimly aware of voices above her, of hands carefully washing the bleeding, sliced skin on her back, of cooling salves being applied. Then, mercifully, she slept.

For three days she hovered between the darkness and the light. She dreamed of her parents, of her little brother, of the belly of the slave ship. And of the flames that devoured her flesh. On the third morning Amari felt gentle hands and cool water on her face. She opened her eyes and saw Polly.

"Welcome back," Polly said softly.

"Water," Amari whispered. Polly lifted Amari's head and gave her small sips of water from a cup.

"Hurt so bad," Amari said next. She groaned as she tried to move.

"Yes, I know. Let me put some more of Teenie's salve on your back. I don't know what's in it, but already the welts are starting to heal a little. At least the bleeding has stopped."

"So sorry," Amari said.

"Don't apologize. It's not your fault. Mr. Derby needs to have somebody give *him* a stiff lashing to let him know how it feels!" She stomped back and forth in their cabin. Amari, even in her dazed state, could feel that Polly's anger was too big for the small room.

"It be better soon," Amari said, trying to calm Polly a bit.

Polly picked up an empty wooden bucket and threw it across the floor. "Mr. Derby is horribly cruel. He probably tripped you on purpose! How could he beat you like that? It was just a spilled pie!"

"Must clean stain," Amari whispered, trying to move.

Polly placed her hand on Amari's arm. "Be still. Me and Lena cleaned it up so you would never know it was there. His precious carpet is unharmed."

"Thank you," Amari breathed out.

"All you have to worry about is getting

better. I never thought I'd say this, but I miss having you around."

Amari blinked with surprise. She knew how much Polly yearned to escape from the kitchen — her desire to move on and her distaste for the work of slaves were very apparent. Amari grimaced as she moved her head. She looked at Polly with remorse. "Now you never get chance to go to big house. So sorry."

Polly placed another cool rag on Amari's head. "You continue to surprise me, Amari. I had no idea my desires were so obvious. You watch and you learn. That is very wise."

Amari tried to nod her head, but it hurt too much. After a few moments she asked with a slight smile, "Teenie work you too much?"

Polly replied. "All I have to help me is Tidbit, and that's about as much help as a rabbit in the rice field!"

"You sound like Teenie," Amari remarked quietly.

At that Polly almost laughed out loud.

Amari was remembering what Mr. Derby had threatened, however. "Rice," she said bleakly. "He gonna send me to rice field." She couldn't stop the tears that began to trickle down her face.

Polly's face fell. "Yes, he threatened to

send you to the rice fields. We just have to think of something to get him to change his mind. In the meantime, he won't do anything until you are well, so let's make sure your recovery is very, very slow!"

Amari knew, however, that it was just a matter of time before she would be toiling in the hot sun, up to her knees in water, planting the rice, one kernel after another. "Rice field come soon," she mumbled.

"I have to get up to the kitchen to help Teenie. I'll be back to check on you. You'll be all right for now?" Polly asked Amari, real concern in her voice.

Polly's voice faded as Amari drifted in and out of reality. Dreams of sunny days with Besa and the fiery sun over the rice fields floated above her. In her haze her mother was alive and laughing, dancing in front of her cooking fire. And, strangely, she dreamed of Mrs. Derby, whose face sometimes replaced her mother's in her dreams.

When she awoke, it was dark outside and Amari could smell a hint of a pleasant, flowery scent. "Try to sip this tea, child," Mrs. Derby's voice whispered.

Startled, Amari almost knocked the cup over as she felt her head being lifted. *What is Mrs. Derby doing here?* Amari wondered. She felt instantly embarrassed because she hadn't bathed in days, she knew her wounds and salves probably stank, and she had proved herself incapable in the master's home. The tea, which tasted faintly like peppermint, she sipped slowly. "So sorry," Amari whispered.

"No, dear. I am the one who must apologize. I am so full of remorse for how badly my husband hurt you," Mrs. Derby replied. She continued to help Amari drink the tea until Amari felt herself drifting back to sleep.

Slowly, Amari returned to the world, sipping mugs of hot liquid, eating a little of the special foods that Teenie made for her, and staying awake for several hours at a time. Tidbit hovered, trying to make Amari feel better by making little jokes and silly faces.

One evening during the second week following the beating, after an exhausted Polly had returned to their cabin, Amari felt well enough to sit up. She did not let her back touch anything, but it felt good to breathe deeply and not lie prone for the moment. She tried to stand up next, but she found she wasn't quite strong enough yet. She groaned softly as she sat back down.

"Is the pain very bad?" Polly asked gently.

"Hurt much. Big much," Amari admitted. "But it be better."

"Is there anything you want me to do?" Polly asked.

Amari shook her head. There was nothing that anyone could do.

"You know Mrs. Derby came to see you every day, don't you?"

Amari nodded. "She smell like flowers."

"She always looks so sad," Polly commented.

"Baby come soon and she be happy," Amari said.

Polly smiled. "She deserves someone to love."

The wounds on Amari's back healed slowly, with the help of Teenie's ointment and Mrs. Derby's tea. Within another week, Amari was back to work with Polly in the kitchen. They had heard nothing more about Amari being transferred to the rice fields, so she worked as hard as she could and tried to make herself invisible to anyone in authority.

Clay had not called for her since the beating, and for that she was grateful. He had, however, ordered Tidbit to deliver a bag of sweets to Amari. They had obviously been purchased in town. *Why would he do this?* she asked herself with a shudder. She gave the treats to Tidbit, who ate them with delight.

"You feelin' all right today?" Teenie asked her one morning. "You still lookin' like a bird that done fell out the nest."

"Some better today." Amari lifted her arm up and touched one of the welts on her back. She winced. "Hurt to touch," she said.

"The pain gonna go after 'while, but them scars gonna be there forever," Teenie told her honestly.

Amari took a deep breath. "I know," she replied.

Teenie touched Amari gently on her head. "You got a strong spirit, Myna."

Amari just shrugged. She could see no reason for having such a strong spirit, nor could she see any hope in her future. She just survived each day. However, she couldn't help but think of Afi, who kept her alive during the horrors of the voyage to this place by telling her the same thing.

"Sometimes spirit die," Amari replied quietly while she stirred the pot on the fire.

24. Gator Bait

Clay sauntered unannounced into Teenie's kitchen one hot afternoon. Teenie, making crust for a pie, was shuttling back and forth, carefully watching over Polly, who was peeling apples, and Amari, who was stirring a mixture of apple juice and brown sugar over the fire. Tidbit sat on the floor, tracing the path of an ant in the dust of the floor with his finger. Hushpuppy growled softly and everyone looked up.

Amari cringed when she saw who had entered, the barely healed lashes on her back suddenly aching, but Clay did not even look at her.

"Y'all better keep that vermin dog out of the kitchen where my food is prepared," he said without warning.

"Yassuh," Teenie mumbled without question. "I told you to get that dog outta here," she said softly to Tidbit. "Take him out to the barn, you hear?"

"Yes'm," the boy replied obediently as he hurried to the door with the dog. Just as Tidbit got to the doorway, Clay grabbed the child, picked him up, and slung him over his shoulder.

Tidbit screamed with fear, while Hushpuppy barked fiercely. With one swift movement, Clay raised one heavy boot and kicked Hushpuppy, propelling the dog out the door of the kitchen and into the yard. The dog yelped and limped away.

"What you gonna do with my boy, sir?" Teenie asked fearfully. To Tidbit she said, "Hush now, chile. Massa Clay ain't gonna hurt you. He just need your help." Her face showed she didn't believe a word she said, but Amari knew she had to calm the child so as not to provoke Clay's anger.

Clay grinned. "I have some friends visiting from Charles Town. We've decided to go alligator hunting this afternoon, and we need some gator bait!"

Teenie clasped her hand to her mouth. Amari saw desperation in her eyes. Finally, Teenie said, her voice full of pleading, "He be too young for such, suh!"

"He's just the right size," Clay replied, patting the boy on his backside.

"He can't swim, suh," she implored.

"Then he'll learn today," Clay replied. He

glanced at Amari then. "Hey, Myna, you ever seen a gator hunt?"

Amari glanced at Teenie before saying, "No, sir."

"Then come and watch. I want my friends to see what I got for my birthday. Besides, I have missed your company," Clay said boldly.

Amari wasn't sure what was happening or what she should do, so she looked at Teenie again. The look on Teenie's face truly frightened Amari, because for the first time since she had arrived at the plantation, Teenie looked terrified.

"Go, chile," Teenie urged her. "I pray you bring my boy back alive."

"You never know," Clay said merrily. "Sometimes the gators are fast and sometimes they are slow."

Teenie wiped her hands on her apron over and over. "Please, suh, not my baby, suh."

Clay ignored her. "Myna will return in a couple of hours with either a boy who's ripe to be gator bait again next week or a few of his fingers and toes left over to bury." Then he turned on his heel, and with Tidbit still over his shoulder like a sack of flour, he headed across the yard. Amari followed, wondering what new cruelty Clay had in store.

Tidbit was only four, but he knew when to keep his mouth shut. He stopped struggling and crying out, although Amari knew he had to be petrified. His eyes searched for Hushpuppy, who lay in the yard licking his hindquarters where he had been kicked. When Tidbit saw the dog was all right, he kept his eyes on Amari as she hurried behind Clay.

Clay headed down to the river, whistling and stopping occasionally to spit. Amari had always hated that particular habit. Standing near the shore of the Ashley River ahead of them, Amari could see three young men about the same age as Clay. One, dressed all in leather, stood next to a handsome black horse that stamped its hooves on the soft grass. Another, who wore an elaborate lace collar and cuffs, looked overdressed even to Amari, who had no knowledge of the fashion of rich white youth. He gazed serenely at the water. The other young man, dressed more casually, had curly red hair like the sailor who had taught her words. He tossed rocks into the water as they waited for Clay. All four of them gave off an air of superiority and power that frightened Amari. Their presence made her even more wary of what might happen.

The young man with the ruffled collar

held about a hundred-foot length of rope in his hands. Four muskets leaned against a tree, the branches of which hung over the water. Two other horses grazed nearby.

Clay called out to his friends as he got close, "Hullo! Feeling like a little gator stew tonight?"

"If we're lucky!" one of them replied. Evidently, the three young men thought that was so funny, they laughed uproariously. Amari understood enough English to know that Tidbit was in real trouble.

"I told you I knew where to find the best gator bait in the world!" he boasted as he lowered Tidbit to the ground. It seemed to Amari that Clay was trying a little too hard, talking a little too loudly, showing off for his friends.

"Just the right size," the owner of the black horse said as he poked Tidbit with his toe. Tidbit cringed. Amari wanted to reach out and comfort Tidbit, but she dared not.

The boy looked from Clay to each of the young men, and though his little body shook with fear, he didn't make a sound.

Taking the rope from his overdressed friend, Clay gave it to Amari and ordered, "Tie the rope around him, Myna."

"So who is this delicious slice of slave girl?" asked the young man dressed in

218

leather. He reached over and patted Amari on her backside.

With sudden fierceness, Clay jumped between Amari and the young man who had touched her. "Keep your hands off her!" he snarled. "She is *mine!* That is why I named her Myna."

Amari was so surprised, she dropped the rope. The leather-clad friend backed away and held up his hand. "I have the pick of the women on my father's plantation," he said. "I was just asking who this one was."

Clay, seemingly calmer, replied, "She was my birthday gift this year. I wanted the three of you to see her." Again Amari couldn't understand why Clay acted as if he was proud of her, showing her off to his friends. She felt like an animal on display, almost as bad as the day she was sold at the market. She hung her head and wished she could disappear into the waters of that river.

To Amari, Clay repeated, "Tie the boy with the rope. Make sure it is secure."

Amari nodded and hugged the trembling child as she knotted the rope. She whispered into Tidbit's ear, "Be brave, little one, and hold your breath." She stood up and reluctantly handed the rope to Clay.

In control of the situation once more, Clay stooped down and said to Tidbit. "All you must do is swim, little nigger. You hear? If you can swim faster than those gators, you get to go home to your mama, understand?"

Tidbit quivered and nodded. He looked at Amari one last time before Clay picked him up and abruptly tossed him into the river. Clay held the rope while his friends laughed and cheered as the little boy swam for his life.

"Now, would you look at that," the tallest one called out, pointing to Tidbit struggling in the water. "The little nigger boy *can* swim!" Tidbit thrashed about hysterically, his tiny face wild with fear.

"I've never seen anyone move his arms and legs so fast!" Clay said, laughing.

"All that splashing ought to attract a gator soon," another one remarked.

As Amari watched Tidbit bobble in the water, for the first time since she had been captured, she felt angry enough to lash out and kill. She was sick of tears, of submission, of putting up with inhumane treatment. She knew if she couldn't do something to save Tidbit, she might explode. Finally, she could hold it in no longer. *"Stop!"* she cried hysterically. *"Please stop!* Bring Tidbit back. Please." She broke down, sobbing.

Clay's three friends stopped their cheering and stared in astonishment at this slave girl who had nerve enough to try to interrupt an afternoon's sport. Clay, with surprising calm, told Amari, "If you don't let us continue, your little friend is likely to get eaten. Now shut up!" He did not hit her as she expected him to.

Amari, defeated, looked from Clay to his friends in utter disbelief. This was beyond her grasp, to torture a child like this. *What kind of people are they?* And then she saw it — the dark figure of an alligator appeared in the water near Tidbit's splashing feet. She held her breath.

"Oh, look, here comes the first gator!" called out Clay's friend with the red curly hair. Instantly, their attention turned from Amari to the river again. In one smooth motion the lace-collared fellow snatched up his musket, cocked it, and fired.

Ka-boom! The musket shot sounded like an explosion as it was fired at the alligator. The water turned bright red as the animal rolled over in the water. The startled horses reared and pulled at the ropes that tied them to the trees.

"You got him, Conrad!" Clay shouted to his friend.

Amari could see only bloody water and foam in the distance. She couldn't tell if

Tidbit had been shot or bit or had survived. She didn't know what she would do if she had to return to Teenie without the boy.

"Good shot!" one of the others called out.

"Pull the boy in and let him catch his breath," Clay ordered. "The next gator will be mine," he said as he checked his gun.

Conrad hauled Tidbit in. The boy, dripping with blood and water, scrambled up the muddy shore next to them. He was shivering uncontrollably, but he seemed unhurt.

Amari ran to him, knelt down on the muddy riverbank, and hugged him tightly. As she felt his narrow shoulders shake, the fury she had felt earlier began to build once more. She wasn't sure how much more of this she could take. She whispered, in her native language, the same words of comfort that Afi had once told her: "In spite of all you must endure, my little Tidbit, the flame of your life spirit will not leave you." Then, because she knew he would not understand what she was saying, she told him, in English, "You will live. You are strong. Do you understand?" Tidbit nodded miserably.

"Enough of that!" Clay shouted. He pulled Tidbit away from Amari, made sure the rope was still secure, and pitched the boy back into the water. This time two alligators surfaced. Amari wanted to scream out once more, but she realized she couldn't distract the hunters. They *had* to shoot or Tidbit would be attacked. She wished she could run and snatch Tidbit out of the water and just disappear. Tidbit paddled furiously as the alligators circled him. Two shots exploded in the afternoon sunshine as both Clay and one of his friends fired at the huge reptiles.

Amari wondered for how much longer the child could be tortured so.

Twice more Tidbit was tossed into the bloody water, and twice more he barely escaped the jaws of the hungry alligators. It seemed to Amari that the young men always waited until the last possible moment to fire.

Tidbit almost seemed to be in shock by the time they finally decided their afternoon of enjoyment was over. He could barely walk. Amari ran and picked him up.

"It is getting late," Clay said to his friends as he untied the rope from around Tidbit's waist, "and this game is beginning to bore me. Let us retire to the house for supper, but I fear I no longer have a taste for gator stew!" The other three young men reacted with loud laughter as they readied their horses. The one who rode the black horse reached down and hoisted Clay up so he could ride with him.

Clay looked down at Amari and smiled as she tried to comfort Tidbit. "We'll have to do this again sometime. I had fun. Didn't you?"

"Yassuh," Amari mumbled. Her fists were tight as she held Tidbit.

"And, Myna?" he said, his tone changing from warm to cold in an instant. She looked at him in fearful expectation. "Don't you *ever* raise your voice to me again!"

"No, sir. Yassuh," Amari stuttered. She knew she had escaped another beating — or worse.

With that, Clay and his friends headed toward the north fields, where the corn was grown, whooping like children as they galloped off.

Amari and Tidbit headed slowly back to the house. Neither of them spoke. Halfway there Hushpuppy met them, limping a little, but wagging his tail energetically. Tidbit fell to the ground and buried his head in the dog's soft fur.

■ ■ ■ ■

PART SIX
POLLY

■ ■ ■ ■

25. Birth of the Baby

Early one morning, about two weeks later, the doorway of the kitchen was suddenly darkened by the unexpected shadow of Mr. Derby. He looked surprisingly agitated. Polly dropped the spoon she had in her hand. She watched as Amari moved swiftly to the back of the small room to try to make herself invisible. Tidbit ran behind his mother. Even the dog hid in a corner.

"Where's Lena?" Mr. Derby roared.

Teenie looked around in confusion. "She ain't here, Massa. I ain't seen Lena since last night," Teenie said truthfully.

"And what about Flora? I swear I'll kill her if she's not back at the house when I return!"

"I ain't seen her, neither, Massa," Teenie said as she stirred the kettle wildly. "I been cookin' all de mornin'."

"Why is it that when I need a slave, they all disappear?" He strode across the kitchen and swept plates and platters to the floor in a fury. He stopped directly in front of Amari, who cowered at his feet. "Why aren't you in the rice fields like I ordered?" he demanded.

Polly could see that Amari had no answer. She knew that Amari had learned that, when not given a direct order, a slave's best bet was to say nothing.

Mr. Derby looked at Polly. "Does the African understand English yet?"

"Yes, sir, a little, sir," Polly replied. *What is he going to do?* she wondered, her fear growing.

"Do you know anything about childbirth?" he asked Polly suddenly.

"Sir?" Polly asked, confused. Then she realized Mrs. Derby must be in labor.

Mr. Derby with concern edging his voice, said, "Isabelle is about to have the child. I have sent Noah to Charles Town for the doctor, but it will be several hours before they return." He wrung his hands. Polly had *never* seen him look helpless or afraid. "She's in a lot of pain. Can you help her?"

"Yes, sir. Of course, sir." Polly breathed with relief, for herself and for Amari as well. Amari would not to be taken to the rice swamps — at least not today.

"And you," he said, pointing to Amari,

"get up and help her! Hurry! I'll ride to the next plantation for more help." He stormed out of the kitchen, leaving behind sudden sighs of relief.

"You ever helped birth a baby, chile?" Teenie asked Polly.

"Never," Polly replied frantically.

"What 'bout you?" Teenie asked Amari.

"Yes, many, many," Amari replied quickly.

"Both of you get up there and see to Miz Isabelle. Here's boiled water. Hurry!"

Amari and Polly rushed out of the kitchen and up to the big house — their first trip back since the night of the spilled pie. They climbed the stairs as quickly as they could without splashing the hot water and tiptoed down the highly polished wood floor of the upstairs hallway, searching for Mrs. Derby's room. Ordinarily, several slaves would be in the house, cleaning or washing, but today, oddly, there were none. Clay was nowhere to be seen either.

"Oh, Lord in heaven!" they heard Mrs. Derby cry out from the first room on the right. She lay in her bed, which was surrounded on all four sides with thin linen curtains. Huge pillows surrounded her pale face. She moaned in pain as Amari and Polly entered the room and pulled back the curtains. She looked at the two girls and tried to smile weakly. "You must help me," she said, desperation in her voice, "if the baby is, if the baby is . . ." She could not finish the sentence.

"Yes, ma'am," Polly replied. "We will make sure you and your baby will be just fine." Polly had never been so close to a woman who was about to have a baby, and she was more than a little frightened. The smell of sweat and body fluids was overpowering.

"You don't understand," Mrs. Derby said as another labor pain gripped her. "You must help my baby."

"Baby good thing," Amari said, trying to reassure her.

Mrs. Derby inhaled sharply, cried out once more, and tightly grabbed a handful of the sheet. When the contraction passed, she said urgently, "I will die, but you must save my baby."

"You not die, Missus," Amari said in her most soothing voice. "Babies be born every day."

"She's talking out of her head," Polly said to Amari. "Let's help her get more comfortable." They adjusted her blankets, set up clean cloths and towels close by, and made sure the hot water was ready in the basin. Polly hoped Amari knew what to do.

Amari touched Mrs. Derby's bulging belly and declared, "Baby come quick — very soon." The labor pains rolled faster and stronger with each contraction. Mrs. Derby was turning red with exertion and pain.

The girls massaged her hands, washed her face with cool water, and helped her through each contraction by talking to her gently and quietly. Soon it was apparent that the baby had no intention of waiting for a doctor or Mr. Derby or anyone else. Mrs. Derby arched her back, screamed, and passed out.

Polly lifted the blankets and saw the baby's head. She motioned to Amari, who gently eased the baby out. The infant cried — lusty, loud, and healthy.

Amari held the child with a look of wonder on her face. "Beautiful baby," Polly heard her whisper.

Polly brought Amari some wet towels to clean the baby off. It was a little girl, with bright green eyes like her mother and curly dark hair. Then she froze, her hand still extended.

"Oh, my Lord!" Polly exclaimed. "The child is black!"

26. Facing Mr. Derby

"Black baby. White mama. Big trouble!" Amari said with fear tightening her voice as she carefully washed the child and wrapped her in the blanket.

Polly's jumbled thoughts careened from how this could have happened (rape, perhaps?) to how Mr. Derby would react (uncontrollable rage, to be sure) to how she felt about a proper white woman producing a black baby (mild disgust, at the very least). "What should we do?" Polly asked, almost panicked. "Tell Mr. Derby?"

"No!" Amari cried, alarm in her voice. "Get Teenie. Hurry, hurry."

Polly rushed out of the room, praying she would not encounter Clay or Mr. Derby as she ran to the kitchen. "Teenie!" she screamed when she got there. "Come quickly! We don't know what to do!"

"Is the chile borned yet?" Teenie asked as she ran with Polly back to the house.

"Yes, the baby is fine and healthy," Polly said, panting. "It's a little girl."

"Do it look like Mrs. Derby — all pink and perfect?"

"The child is not what anyone expected, Teenie."

"What you mean, chile? Is Miz Isabelle ailin'?"

"No, she's sleeping. She doesn't know yet."

"Know what? You ain't makin' no sense, Polly!"

By that time they had reached Miss Isabelle's room. Amari was sitting in a chair with the baby in her arms, cuddling it close to her. Teenie stared at the baby in shock.

"Oh, Lawd, Lawd, Lawd!" Teenie exclaimed as she sucked in her breath. "It be Noah," she announced with finality. "No wonder everybody be scarce as hen's teeth today."

Noah? Polly thought. *Noah! Of course! It all makes sense now. But how could she? Why would she?* Polly's stomach churned as she tried to figure out the magnitude of this problem.

At that moment Mrs. Derby opened her eyes. She looked around in fear. "My baby?" she asked desperately.

"You got a purty little girl child, Miz Isabelle. But you got a big problem, ma'am," Teenie told her with concern in her voice.

"May I see her?"

Amari placed the sleeping baby in her mother's arms. Mrs. Derby gazed down at the child, her eyes brimming with tears. "My beautiful baby," she murmured over and over. Finally calmer, she looked up at Teenie and the girls. "I must explain," she whispered, "before I die."

"You ain't gonna die, Miz Isabelle," Teenie assured her. "You is fit and fine. Everybody feels a little poorly after havin' a baby."

Tenderly, Mrs. Derby touched the infant's velvety brown face. "You don't understand. My husband will kill me," she said with certainty.

"He adore you, ma'am," Teenie said reasonably. "Anybody who look at him can see that. He ain't gonna hurt you."

Mrs. Derby blinked back tears. "Even though he married me for my money, I know he really has come to feel real affection for me. But I love Noah — I have for many years. And he loves me. But now Noah will die, and so will I. My husband is going to kill us both — and our baby."

"He would never do such a thing!" But Teenie knew that Mr. Derby was probably quite capable of murder and would be within the limits of social acceptability to do so for this impropriety. Her mind was reeling.

"What to do?" Amari asked in a whisper.

"What should we tell him, ma'am?" Polly asked.

Mrs. Derby pushed herself up into a sitting position. She suddenly looked excited. "Tell him the baby died! Tell him it was a stillbirth! You must take my baby away to safety. Here, take her," she urged them. She lifted the baby up, but when Amari reached for the child, Mrs. Derby drew the child to her chest once more.

"He gonna want to see the baby's body, ma'am," Teenie tried to reason.

"Tell him it was deformed — a monster! Tell him anything! Just keep my baby safe!" She kissed her daughter gently and snuggled her closer.

"We best get you cleaned up 'fore the massa get back. He only went to the next plantation," Teenie declared. "I got a bad feelin' 'bout this. We all gonna hang 'fore nightfall!" she muttered. "Lawd, Lawd, Lawd. What we gonna do? We done fell out the trouble tree and hit every branch on the way down!"

Polly, Amari, and Teenie moved quickly to help Mrs. Derby get cleaned up and ready to face her husband. The baby nursed peacefully at her mother's breast, her cocoa brown skin a sharp contrast to Mrs. Derby's pinkness.

Mrs. Derby patted the baby, held her close as she slept, and brushed away tears. Finally, she handed the infant to Amari. "Protect her," she said simply.

Amari blinked to keep away her own tears and took the baby with great seriousness. Polly watched as Amari held the perfect little infant close to her breast.

"We must go now, Missus," Teenie said with quiet alarm. Mrs. Derby nodded with sad resignation as Polly, Amari, and Teenie left with the baby.

As they crept down the steps, Teenie whispered to Amari, "Sara Jane just borned a baby 'bout three months ago. She got lotsa milk. That's where we'll hide her for now." They tiptoed down the hall.

Only Polly noticed Clay through a window as he approached the other side of the house. She signaled for Amari and Teenie to be still. He seemed to be looking in the other direction. She prayed he had just arrived back home and had not seen anything. When they heard him enter the back of the house, they exited quickly through the front.

"Tidbit!" Teenie called as they reached

the kitchen. The sleepy boy and his dog jumped up from the pallet they shared near the fireplace. "Take Myna and Polly down to the quarters to Jubal and Sara Jane's place. And don't ask no questions!" The child looked at his mother's frightened face and seemed to realize this was no time for foolishness.

Teenie told Polly, "Don't tell her nothin' except this baby's mama is dead and she gotta nurse it. Of course, don't take no genius to figger out whose baby this be. Lawd, what a mess! Hurry!"

Amari and Polly dashed out after Tidbit, Amari clutching the child close to her.

"Baby be safe with Sara Jane?" she asked Polly.

"We have no choice. The baby's life is at stake," Polly replied, trying to sound hopeful.

Sara Jane's large, loving arms took the baby girl with no questions. "She be fine, chile," Sara Jane said to Amari. "Sara Jane will keep this little one safe. Now y'all get on back to the kitchen. Tonight be full of danger."

Polly shivered as they hurried to Teenie's kitchen. *Will this work?*

As soon as they got back, Teenie told her, "Get on up to the house and see to Miz

Isabelle, Polly. Amari, you stay here with me. I still got supper to fix." She began pulling down pots noisily, mumbling, maybe praying, to herself, Polly figured. She hurried off to the main house.

Polly had just made sure that Mrs. Derby's hair was brushed and that she had on a fresh dressing gown when Mr. Derby returned. Polly heard him rush up the stairs. She braced herself. He burst into the room, where he found his wife fast asleep. Polly, sitting in a chair next to her, pretended to be weeping. Her heart thudded in her chest. She prayed she could convince him.

"Where is the baby?" Mr. Derby demanded. He looked around in confusion.

Polly, eyes full of honest fear, told him sadly, "The baby was stillborn, sir. I'm so sorry. But your wife is fine," she added.

"What?" He took a few steps back. "It died?" He raked his fingers through his hair. His face seemed to crumple. "Was it a boy or girl?" he asked, barely able to choke out the words.

"A girl, sir."

"I want to see her. I want to see my baby." His voice broke.

"You don't want to do that, sir," Polly said, stammering a little. "The child was, uh, not normal. It is better to bury it quickly."

Anguish ripped Mr. Derby's face. "Don't you try to tell me what I want to do! Bring me the body of my daughter." He blinked furiously, but Polly could see the tears in his eyes.

She didn't know what to do. At that moment his wife's eyes fluttered open. She looked around, confused for a moment. When she saw her husband, she said with a sob, "The baby never took a breath, Percival. I'm so sorry."

"Are you all right, my darling?" Mr. Derby asked her gently as he leaned over her.

She reached up and touched his face. "I am fine."

"Did you see her — our daughter?" he asked.

Mrs. Derby hesitated. "Yes, I did. She was . . . she was . . . deformed." She took a deep breath and closed her eyes. Polly was impressed with how effective she was.

Mr. Derby narrowed his eyes. "Something doesn't make sense here," he said suspiciously. He paced the room and looked at Polly sharply.

"I prayed every day for this baby," Mrs. Derby whispered.

That much Polly knew was very true.

"I could not have fathered an imperfect child," Mr. Derby declared. He seemed agitated. "I must see her — if nothing else, to say good-bye."

Mrs. Derby spoke up frantically. "I instructed the servants to wrap her and bury her far away from our home."

"Nonsense! Our daughter, regardless of any infirmity, must be buried with honor in our family plot," he told her. "How dare you discard my child like that?" he scolded, anger and sorrow lacing his voice. Polly found herself feeling sorry for the man.

"I'm so sorry, Percival," Mrs. Derby whispered again. "Please do not bring her into my presence again. Just thinking of her is more than I can bear." Polly thought she looked more terrified than sorrowful.

He leaned over and kissed his wife on her forehead. "I share your grief, my dear," he said to her. "You just rest for now, and I will take care of these unpleasant details." As he was leaving the room, he said to Polly, "Bring me the body of my daughter. When the doctor gets here with Noah, he will want to examine her." Polly curtsied, and he slammed the door behind him.

Mrs. Derby whispered to Polly, "Is my baby safe?"

"Yes, ma'am," Polly replied. "For now. But

when the doctor gets here, we have to show him something."

"Perhaps the doctor can be delayed," Mrs. Derby suggested. "Can you get word to Noah before they return?"

"I'm not sure, ma'am. Will you be all right for a while? I must check with Teenie and see what can be done."

"Yes, of course. Please go and do what you must. You move beyond kindness to help us. I shall forever be grateful." Polly hurried down the stairs and out to the kitchen, desperate to avert a tragedy. *How has it come to this?* she thought. She realized then how deeply her life was entangled with those of the slaves she had once so despised.

27. DEATH IN THE DUST

Amari was waiting for Polly in the kitchen. "Is the baby safe?" Polly asked her.

Amari nodded, then asked, "What Massa say?"

Polly looked at her and said, "It's very bad. Mr. Derby wants the doctor to see the body of the child."

"What we do?" Amari asked, turning to ask Teenie for advice.

"We must stop the wagon with Noah and the doctor before it gets here," Polly declared.

"Ain't no 'we' about it," Teenie replied as she shucked a basket of corn. "You a white gal. You the only one that be allowed on the road after dark."

Polly took a deep breath. "All right, I'll go. Tell me what to do."

"Whatever it take to turn that wagon round!" Teenie said without conviction. "Ain't gonna be easy."

Dusk had fallen. Polly left the kitchen and headed down to the main road, the road that had brought her to this place with Amari. *So much has changed since then,* she thought. She half walked, half jogged about a mile, the darkness so thick that it seemed to smother her, when she heard the wagon approaching. As it got close to her, she ran toward it, startling the horses.

"Please, sir," Polly began. "Are you Dr. Hoskins?" She did not look at Noah, although she had a feeling he knew what was going on.

"Yes, I am. Is Mrs. Derby all right?"

"Oh, yes, sir. She's just fine — and the baby, too — crying and nursing and being sweet like newborns always are, sir." Polly knew she was babbling, but she couldn't find the words to make him turn around. "That's why I came out to meet you, sir — to tell you that the baby has been born with no complications, Mrs. Derby is fit and fine, and your services are no longer needed. Mr. Derby wanted to save you an unnecessary house call." She spoke very quickly, glad that it was dark and that they couldn't see how scared she was.

Noah seemed to understand immediately that it was not a good idea for the doctor to make it to the plantation, for he spoke up to say, "I'll be glad to drives you back to Charles Town, suh. No trouble at all, suh."

"Nonsense!" the doctor replied gruffly. "No, you will not drive me back — it took us four hours to get here! I shall see to my patient and her infant, I shall eat a fine meal prepared by Derby's servants, and I shall spend the night here and return refreshed to Charles Town in the morning. We shall proceed to Derbyshire Farms!"

"But, sir —," Polly tried weakly.

"Who are you, my dear, and why are you out here on the road after dark?" He offered Polly his hand and helped her up onto the wagon. "It is not safe, you know — highwaymen will slice your throat in a heartbeat."

Defeated, Polly replied, "My name is Polly Pritchard. I work for Mr. Derby."

"Did he send you out here to send me back?" Dr. Hoskins asked.

Polly wasn't sure whether to lie or tell the truth. So she said nothing in reply. The wagon moved slowly toward the house. Polly prayed, silently fingering the tie strings on her bonnet.

Mr. Derby waited near the big circular pillars at the front of the house. He looked grief-stricken. "Thank you for making this long drive, Hoskins," he said to the doctor as he stiffly stepped down from the wagon, "but I'm afraid your trip was in vain. Isabelle is fine, but the baby was stillborn." He choked on the words.

Dr. Hoskins looked confused. "Stillborn? This young woman here told me the baby was fine and healthy. What's going on?"

Polly tried to jump down from the wagon, but Mr. Derby grabbed her arm, the anguish on his face turning to anger. "What is going on here? I told you I would never allow any insubordination in my household. You explain what is going on this instant!"

Polly's heart pounded. She opened her mouth to speak just as she heard Lena's voice behind her, yelling from an upstairs window. "Oh, Massa, come quick! Miz Isabelle done fainted!"

Mr. Derby released Polly and ran with the doctor into the house. Polly collapsed on the ground with relief. *This night is not going to end well,* she thought fearfully.

Amari ran out of the kitchen as soon as the two men had disappeared. She looked directly at Noah, who was staring toward Mrs. Derby's window with concern. "Baby is black," Amari told him bluntly. "Pretty girl child."

Noah groaned and covered his head with his hands. "Is Isabelle all right? The baby is alive?" Polly was surprised by the seeming depth of his anguish.

Teenie had come out of the kitchen to join them. She wiped her hands on her apron. "Yeah, they both alive for now. But it won't take long for Massa to figger out what really happened. We's all in big trouble, tryin' to cover up yo' mess." Tidbit ran from the kitchen and toward his mother. She yelled at the child fiercely, "You go git in the kindlin' box and hide there, you hear? Don't you come out till I come git you!" The boy took a long look at her face and hightailed it back to the kitchen.

Noah sat on the ground in the dirt. It seemed to Polly he was overwhelmed by the evening's events. "We growed up as children together," he explained. "She was the mistress, of course, and I be the slave, but that didn't make us no matter at all. We'd go fishin' and runnin' through the woods — just likin' each other, you know?"

Teenie grunted and kept glancing at the window to the upstairs room where Lena and Miss Isabelle were trying to stall the doctor and Mr. Derby.

"What was you thinkin'?" Teenie asked finally, annoyance and amazement in her voice. "Just 'cause a chicken got wings don't mean it oughta fly. Y'all shoulda known better!"

"As she got older," Noah continued, ignoring Teenie, "she turned down every good-lookin' boy who come to court her. Her daddy finally put a stop to that young-girl foolishness and married her off to Massa Derby. She cried for days before the weddin'." Noah stopped. His shoulders drooped.

"When Massa Derby move her here, she insist I come with her. Her daddy didn't see no harm, so she and me was real happy. When she found out she was with child, we figgered the baby belonged to Massa Derby. At least that what we was hopin'."

Mistress and slave — falling in love! Polly realized with a start. *I didn't think such a thing was even possible.* "Has something like this ever happened before?" Polly asked.

Noah shook his head. "I don't know, missy. No one's done lived to tell 'bout it."

"You got to run away, Noah," Teenie told him clearly. "Massa gonna kill you for shure."

"I ain't runnin. I love her," he replied simply.

Teenie snorted. "Love don't mean pig spit round here." She had no more time to argue with him, for at that moment Mr. Derby

247

emerged from the front door of the house, angrily holding up a weak and sobbing Mrs. Derby. In his right hand he held a gun. The doctor, noticeably, had remained inside.

Polly, Teenie, and Amari drew back at the fury on Mr. Derby's face. Noah stood slowly and with dignity. He looked at Isabelle Derby with a look of absolute love on his face. She seemed to relax as she gazed at Noah. She smiled at him, then reached out to him with her free hand. Her husband slapped her arm down. "Isabelle!" he barked, his voice tight with fury.

Coming from the opposite direction, from the slave quarters, the sharp wailing cry of a newborn could be heard. As they all turned in that direction, they could see Clay Derby strolling toward them, carrying the baby girl. The infant had been stripped of her blanket, and she protested loudly in the chill night air.

Polly was having difficulty finding each new breath. She had to force herself not to reach out and grab the baby from Clay.

"Looking for something, Father?" he asked with a grin. "I found this baby down at Sara Jane's place. She swears it's her baby, but it looks to be newborn, and her little picaninny must be about three months old. Seems a bit impossible, don't you think?" Polly could tell that Clay was actually enjoying this!

She and Amari watched, horrified, as Clay lay the naked, screaming baby on the dirt in front of his father. Polly grabbed Amari's hand and squeezed it. She wanted to run to the child and pick her up, but she dared not move.

A look of revulsion crossed Mr. Derby's face as he stared at the perfect brown features of the infant. Isabelle Derby cried out, "My baby!" and reached for the child on the ground in front of her, but her husband held her firmly. Noah, impassive once more, showed no outward emotion, but tears slipped down his face.

Mr. Derby, his voice full of self-control, spoke calmly and clearly to his wife. "I loved you," he said, almost plaintively. "You were so young and beautiful — like springtime all year long. I just knew you would erase all the sorrows from my past."

Mrs. Derby shuddered, her head hung low.

"But you chose to betray me," her husband said, venom returning to his voice. "You are not even worthy of my vomit." He inhaled. "But I shall not kill you," he continued in a low, eerily controlled voice. She looked at him in surprise. "Instead, I shall refuse to let you die."

Polly was confused. She did not understand what he meant, but soon it became terribly apparent.

Mr. Derby pulled his wife over to where Noah stood. Then, with one hand, he cocked the musket and aimed it at Noah's broad chest. He spat at Noah, then glanced at his wife. He made sure she was watching. Then he fired.

Noah's blood splattered them all as he fell to the ground not far from his child. Polly screamed, Amari cried out, and Teenie fell to her knees mumbling, "Oh, sweet Jesus!"

The noise of the gunshot startled the baby, who cried even louder from where she lay on the ground. Mrs. Derby, shrieking and twisting like a madwoman, fought to get free of her husband's grip. Mr. Derby suddenly released her in a heap on the ground as he calmly but swiftly reloaded the gun.

Sobbing hysterically, Isabelle Derby scrambled in the dirt toward her baby. She had almost reached the infant when another gunshot exploded in the darkness. The baby was suddenly silent.

28. Punishment

Not since the day her mother died had Polly felt such agony. She gasped in disbelief, unable to catch her breath. Head spinning, she clung to Amari, who was choking on her sobs. Mrs. Derby threw herself onto her child, then fainted, this time for real.

Mr. Derby dropped the gun, then looked at his hands. He seemed stunned. He turned to Clay and said quietly, "Go tell old Jubal to get up here and take care of . . . of all this." He would not look at the bodies. "And make sure Sara Jane gets punished," he added without emotion. Polly watched Clay disappear into the darkness with a look of satisfaction on his face.

Dr. Hoskins peered out of the door then, unsure of what he might encounter. "Come get my wife, Doctor," Mr. Derby called. "I believe she's fainted again. Unfortunately, she had to witness the disciplining of some unruly slaves, and it proved a bit much for her. See to her, will you, old fellow?" Mr. Derby took a deep breath and smoothed his doublet.

The doctor crept slowly to the bloody scene, observed it all, but made no comment. He picked up Mrs. Derby in his arms and carried her back to the house. Lena waited at the door to assist him, her eyes bright with fear.

Then Mr. Derby turned his attention to Teenie, Polly, and Amari, who huddled together. "Follow me," he told them curtly.

He led them down the familiar path to Teenie's kitchen, where he stopped. "Where is the boy Tidbit?" he asked Teenie.

She hesitated. "I don't rightly know, suh. He done heard all the noise, and I guess it scared him. Maybe he run off to the woods."

"Call to him. You better hope he answers."

Polly could see that Teenie was not sure what to do. "Tidbit," Teenie whispered softly.

"Call him so he hears you!" Mr. Derby demanded.

"Tidbit, honey, you in there?" Teenie called, her voice quavering.

A faint rustling could be heard coming from the kindling box. Mr. Derby marched over, tossed aside the small pieces of firewood, and pulled the boy out of the box by one arm. The dog growled softly. "Mama?" Tidbit called out.

When Mr. Derby dropped the boy to the ground, Tidbit ran quickly to the skirts of his mother. She picked him up and held him close to her body.

Mr. Derby spoke then. Polly sensed he was just barely in control of himself. "Follow me," he demanded once more, and he led them a few paces from the kitchen to the smokehouse. He pulled out a key, unlocked the door, and turned to look at the frightened group in front of him.

"You," he said, pointing at Polly, "are a liar! I will not have such a person in my household!"

Polly cowered before him, her hands held up in front of her face. "Have mercy, sir," she whispered. He ignored her.

"And you," he said to Amari with consternation, "have been trouble since I was kind enough to bring you here." Amari looked frightened, Polly thought, but furious at him as well. That gave Polly courage to stand a little straighter in spite of Mr. Derby's fury.

"And finally you," he said fiercely to Teenie, "I trusted to obey me. Your responsibility was to me and you failed."

"I so sorry, suh," Teenie mumbled.

"Too late," he said harshly. He thought

for a moment. "When Dr. Hoskins leaves in the morning, he will have three passengers. I'll send Clay with him to make sure there are no more problems. If it were not for my son, I might never have discovered the whole truth."

Polly searched for the words that might calm him down or change his mind. "Sir," she began.

But Mr. Derby ignored her as he firmly pushed each of them into the dark, windowless smokehouse.

Polly, Amari, and Teenie looked at one another but did not fight him or object — they did not want to do anything to further incur his anger. Mr. Derby slowly closed the door, then opened it again.

"Tomorrow is a market day in Charles Town," he said. "Polly, I plan to sell your indenture to a whorehouse in New Orleans. You'll bring a pretty penny. They like them young down there." He uttered a short, harsh laugh.

Tears welled up in Polly's eyes, but she shook her head and refused to cry. Anger began to replace her misery as she looked at Mr. Derby with steely-eyed fury.

"And, Myna, I can find another toy for my son to play with. I'm sure I can get more than I paid for you — a broken-in African is highly sought after."

Amari looked devastated, but she, too, seemed to have run out of tears. She faced Mr. Derby with quiet resolve. The two girls stood there, stony and silent.

"You'll leave at first light." They heard the lock fasten firmly in the latch and his footsteps as he headed back to the house.

"What 'bout me, suh?" Teenie called out through one of the wooden slats of the smokehouse. "Who gonna cook yo' food if you sells me?"

The sound of his boots stopped. "Oh, Teenie," he called back, "I'd never sell you. You're much too valuable."

Teenie breathed a small sigh of relief. She clung to Tidbit fiercely in the darkness. "Oh, thank you, suh," she whispered.

"I'm selling Tidbit instead," Mr. Derby's voice said clearly. The sound of his boots on the hard dirt disappeared as he headed back to the big house.

Teenie's wails echoed in the darkness.

29. LOCKED IN THE SMOKEHOUSE

"Oh, Lawd, what we gonna do?" Teenie moaned miserably. She sat on the dirt floor, holding Tidbit close to her. "He be my onliest chile. My baby boy," she whispered into his hair. "My baby boy."

Polly could hear Tidbit whimpering, "Whassa matter, Mama?" She knew he couldn't possibly comprehend the enormity of what was about to happen to him.

"Is there any way out of here?" Polly looked around, but the smokehouse was so dark that she could distinguish only the shadowy figures of a couple of hams hanging from hooks.

"No, chile. The smokehouse was built secure so can't nobody come in here and get free meat. And ain't but two keys — Massa got one and Miz Isabelle got the other." Teenie continued to rock Tidbit on her lap.

Amari, who sat on the floor near the door,

suddenly asked, "Slaves ever run off?"

"Shure, they runs off — any chance they get," Teenie replied. "But mostly they gets brought back. They got dogs that can smell a person in the woods and folks whose job it is just to catch runaways and bring 'em back."

"Has anybody ever succeeded?" Polly asked.

"Yes, chile. Far as I knows. They mighta got killed on their journey, but they never came back here, so in my mind, they got to the North safely."

"What is North?" Amari wanted to know.

"North is where freedom lives, chile. They got slaves there, too, but I've heard tell of black folk livin' up North with jobs they gets paid for and houses that belong to them, and don't nobody own them at all!"

"So why don't more slaves run away?" Polly asked.

"It's hard to hide when yo' skin is black and everybody else got white skin," Teenie explained. "Now you, chile, could run off and fit right in. You could leave Myna and my Tidbit here and have you a chance to be free."

"I'd never leave them!" Polly blurted before she could even think about it. Yet, once she said it, she knew it was true.

"Easy to say while we's all locked up," Teenie commented quietly.

"Do they chase runaway indentured servants as well?" Polly asked her.

"Couple of years back, Massa had a 'dentured boy who run off. Massa brung him back after a few days, and he put a iron collar round the boy's neck so folks would know he was a runaway and not free to be on the roads."

"Where this boy now?" Amari asked quietly, touching her neck, which still held the scars from her own iron chains.

"He drowned that summer — I believe he let that iron collar just take him on down," Teenie told her.

"North," Polly mused. "We could all be free." She wondered what freedom would mean to Amari, who could never get back to what she had lost.

"Shhh, what that noise?" Amari suddenly whispered. They all heard it — a faint scratching on the back wall of the smokehouse. They all moved quietly to the back of the small room.

They heard the scratching again, then Cato's whispered voice. "Y'all all right?" Polly smiled as she heard him clear his throat and cough.

"If they catch you here, they kill you for

shure," Teenie whispered to Cato.

"If they kill me, at least I be free at last. I ain't worried 'bout it." Cato laughed quietly. His voice got serious then. "Teenie, you got to let the boy go with them purty lil gals. Yo' boy got a chance to be free."

"How you figger?" Teenie asked, skepticism in her voice.

"Doc Hoskins don't believe in no slavery."

"How you knows this?" Teenie asked suspiciously.

"How many times I gotta tell you that I just knows stuff? Lissen, Doc Hoskins ain't got it in him to sell nobody."

"But Clay is going with us!" Polly exclaimed. "I think it would give him pleasure to see us sold."

Teenie shifted her weight and handed Tidbit to Amari. "Hold him for a hot minute, chile. I got an idea." To Cato she whispered, "Go to my kitchen. Look out back under that big rock by the persimmon tree. You'll find a rag with a passel of seeds in it. Put just two seeds in Massa Clay's midnight wine." She was silent a moment. "Maybe three."

Polly heard Cato grunt. "I hear you. You jest leave Clay up to ol' Cato. Last I heard, he was down in the quarters beatin' the sweet Jesus outta Sara Jane. I best hurry if

I'm to fix him his usual bedtime glass o' wine. Get the boy ready, Teenie," he told her.

"I ain't partin' with my baby!" Teenie said emphatically.

"You wants that boy to be a slave like you? You wants to see him be gator bait again?"

Teenie groaned. Polly could almost touch the anguish in her voice. "I wants a better life for him, that's for shure."

"You gotta trust these gals and trust the good Lord and trust the spirits of hope," Cato said philosophically, still whispering through the wall. "You gotta let him go. You gotta give the boy the chance to be free."

"Cato," Teenie called out in a strained voice.

"I be here," Cato replied.

"Be real careful with them seeds. I'm gonna need a big pile of 'em soon. Yassuh, Massa Derby gonna have himself a right good meal pretty soon. I got a mind to fix him a stew he ain't never gonna forget — ain't ever gonna remember."

Polly wasn't exactly sure what she meant, but Cato whispered in reply. "I hears you."

Teenie took the sleeping child from Amari and held him closely.

Polly still could not see how leaving with the doctor in the morning, heading to the slave market, would lead to a chance for freedom.

Amari asked through the wall, "Where be North, Cato? Where is free?"

Cato answered clearly. "Do not go north. That's where they be lookin' for you."

"That makes no sense," Polly interjected. "What do you mean, don't go north? If we go south, we get deeper and deeper into slave territory. Our only chance for freedom *must* be in the North!" Surely he could see that.

Cato repeated, "Do not go north. Tracker dogs search the roads headin' north. Runaway papers be posted in the North." He coughed again.

"Where we go?" Amari asked.

"Head south. Find a place called Fort Mose. It be in Spanish Florida. I hear tell it be a place of golden streets and fine wine. Spaniard folk run it, and any slave who get there be set free!"

" 'Dentured gals, too?" Amari asked.

"The ways I hears it, the folks at Fort Mose got open arms to slaves, 'dentured folk, even Injuns!" Cato told them.

"It sounds too good to be true," Polly commented.

"Ain't nothing gooder than freedom," Cato replied, almost too softly to be heard.

"Much danger?" Amari asked.

"Yes, chile, much danger. Swamps and alligators and bears and bugs to start, plus not knowin' how to get there, plus the fear. It be a long, hard trip."

"How we not get lost?" Amari asked, her voice trembling.

"Follow the river south, then leave it. All rivers run to sea, and you must travel by land. Stay way inland from the ocean. Else you have too many rivers to cross. That's all I knows to tell you. When you find them streets of gold, think of ol' Cato." His footsteps and his cough disappeared into the night.

Polly leaned against the wall, trying to think. *None of this makes any sense. Trying to escape by running south? Rivers? Bears? Swamps? Impossible!* She wished desperately that she could ask her mother for advice or just curl up in her arms and not have to worry about difficult decisions.

But she sat on the dirt floor of a smokehouse, surrounded by the dried carcasses of two pigs, a cow, and a deer, feeling scared and powerless. She glanced at Amari, a girl who just a few months ago had seemed dirty and disgusting. Now they were caught up together in a situation that was so awful, she had to grab her head to erase the bloody images from her mind. *Mr. Derby murdered a baby! What kind of man could do such a thing?*

Polly watched as Amari, wrapped in her own private thoughts, finally slept. Teenie cradled her son, whispering to him, singing to him, telling him stories. She heard Teenie murmur over and over, "Long as you remember, chile, nothin' ain't really ever gone."

Polly thought with compassion of Teenie's sorrow and the anguish Mrs. Derby must be enduring right now — it was enough to drive someone mad. She wondered what the morning would bring.

30. TIDBIT'S
FAREWELL

Polly shook herself awake as she heard voices outside the smokehouse. Sunlight filtered through the slats of the wooden structure.

"Isabelle will recover quickly from the trauma of having a stillborn baby," she heard Mr. Derby say. "Already she speaks of us having another child."

The doctor's voice sounded unconvinced. "Yes, of course. Make sure she gets plenty of rest."

"I intend to keep a close eye on her," Mr. Derby replied, his voice laced with barbs.

Polly poked Amari, who was still asleep on Teenie's shoulder. Startled, Amari looked around in fear. Teenie, who perhaps had not slept at all, was whispering to Tidbit.

"You remember all them stories I tolt you 'bout my mother and the Ashanti and the monkey and spider stories?" she asked the boy, desperation in her voice.

"Yes'm," the boy replied, sounding as if he wasn't sure why his mother was telling him all this now.

"You remember the drums that talked like thunder? And the sun that shone like copper over the valley? You remember what I tolt you 'bout my mama and how she grabbed a piece of her own mother to take with her?" Polly heard Teenie saying.

"Yes, Mama, I remembers," Tidbit said, a whispering dread in his voice.

"You takes this piece of cloth, you hear, boy? Keep it safe, 'cause all my memories be tucked in it. You promise me you will never forget?" she asked him plaintively as she hugged him close to her. Polly watched her tie a leather string around the boy's neck. A tiny leather pouch hung from it. Teenie tucked a colored piece of fabric into the packet and closed it tightly with a draw-string.

"I remembers it all, Mama," Tidbit said, his voice sounding truly frightened now.

"You gonna grow to be a man — a free man."

"I don't wanna be no man," Tidbit protested. "I just wants to be yo' lil boy."

"You gonna always be my baby boy," Teenie said, though her voice was thick with grief. "Always."

Polly thought back painfully to the night her mother died, how she had whispered to Polly with her last bit of strength, "You make yourself a lady, you hear, my darling? I will always be with you." Polly knew that Teenie's heart felt as if it were being slashed into pieces.

"You goin' with us, Mama?" the child asked.

"I'll be along directly," Teenie lied. "You stay close to Myna and Polly till I gits there, you hear?" The boy agreed quietly, but he seemed to sense that something was wrong because he started crying. "You mind them and do what they says, you hear?"

"Yes'm," Tidbit replied in a small voice.

They all heard the lock removed, and the bright sun shone in like a harsh surprise after the darkness of the smokehouse all night. Mr. Derby stood outside the door and called to them, "Come on out of there now. You have a long journey ahead of you, and, Teenie, I expect to have breakfast on the table in half an hour!"

"Yes, suh," she replied sullenly as she emerged from the small room. Teenie squeezed Tidbit's small hand tightly into hers. Amari and Polly came out next, blinking in the bright sunlight. When Amari reached for Polly's hand, Polly took it.

The wagon stood hitched and ready. Dr. Hoskins sat on the seat, looking straight ahead, not at the hapless group standing near the wagon. Clay was nowhere to be seen.

"My son is ill," Mr. Derby said to the doctor, "so I'll entrust to you the transactions for the sale of these three." The doctor nodded silently.

Polly and Amari exchanged looks. Evidently, Teenie's seeds had been effective.

"Would you like me to check young Clay before I leave?" Dr. Hoskins asked halfheartedly.

"No, I believe he simply drank too much wine. He will sleep it off."

Dr. Hoskins looked relieved. "I will make sure your money from the sale of these three is safely delivered to you by a courier from Charles Town. He will return with your wagon."

"It's good riddance to the lot of them," Mr. Derby replied, a look of disgust on his face. To the frightened group in front of him he yelled, "Get in the wagon — and be quick about it!"

Polly climbed in first. "Yes, sir," she whispered. It was the same wagon that she and Amari had arrived in. Amari climbed in behind her.

"Myna, take this child," Mr. Derby commanded. He grabbed Tidbit from Teenie and slung the boy onto the wagon behind Amari.

Teenie exploded in grief. "Don't take my baby! He my onliest child! Oh, Lawd, please don't take my baby from me!" Tidbit, seeing his mother so upset, began to wail, reaching for her and trying to squirm out of Amari's arms. Hushpuppy barked frantically, adding to the uproar.

Mr. Derby, his face red, slashed at the dog with his whip. It ran yelping toward the rice fields. Mr. Derby then stung Teenie with the whip as well. "Get to your kitchen and to your duties. You have no more business here!" He pushed her in the direction of the kitchen, but she continued to scream in protest, inconsolable.

Polly huddled in the wagon, wishing she knew a way to vent the anger that she needed to expel. But she was as helpless as the others.

"I believe it best if I leave quickly," Dr. Hoskins said over the noise.

"I agree," Mr. Derby replied. He smacked the horse on the rump. It whinnied, then began to amble on its way. The doctor directed the wagon toward the road. Tidbit shrieked as he realized that he was really being taken away from his mother. Teenie fell to the ground, yelling her grief to the sky. Mr. Derby whipped her again and pulled her to her feet. He half dragged, half walked her back to the kitchen. Hushpuppy continued to bark frantically in the distance.

"Mama!" Tidbit screamed hysterically. "Mama!"

They turned past a bend in the road, and although she could still hear Teenie's anguished cries, Polly could see her no more. Amari held Tidbit, trying to soothe him, but Polly knew that nothing she could say or do would make the child feel better.

■ ■ ■ ■

PART SEVEN
AMARI

■ ■ ■ ■

31. THE DOCTOR'S CHOICE

The wagon lumbered slowly down the road. Most of the leaves of the trees, Amari noticed, were turning golden and copper with rusty hues. The sun shone brightly over, the wind blew gently from the east, but a storm of turmoil hovered over the small wagon in which they rode. Polly sat with her arms wrapped tightly around her body. Tidbit still cried for his mother, burying himself in Amari's arms. Amari, feeling bereft and empty inside, held the child and stared at the thick woods on either side of the road.

I'm to be sold once more? Is this the way it will be forever? To be passed from one owner to another like a cow? Afi had constantly talked about her bright spirit and her future. But Amari could see nothing but the darkness; she found she did not have Afi's strength.

After an hour or so Dr. Hoskins, who so

far had said nothing at all to the passengers in the back of the wagon, slowly pulled over to the side of the road. The horse snorted and grabbed mouthfuls of soft grass.

The doctor was silent for a moment, then he turned around to look at his three passengers. He took a deep breath, then said quietly, "I am ashamed to be a human being this morning. I witnessed not just murder last night, but violence and cruelty and vicious hatred. By saying nothing, I feel I am as responsible as my so-called friend who pulled the trigger."

Amari and Polly exchanged stunned looks.

Dr. Hoskins continued. "I am just one man. I don't know how to fight everything that is happening around me. I don't understand how one man can own another. And I don't know how to stop it." He looked around at the deep woods and the darkness within them. "But I can help the three of you."

"How, sir?" Polly asked immediately.

"I plan to give you at least a fighting chance." He kept looking around him, as if someone would come down the road and discover what he was doing. "I have a little money and some food that Lena made up for our journey this morning." He pointed to a small bundle beneath the seat of the wagon.

"You not take us to town to be sold?" Amari asked, her voice hopeful.

"No, child. I'm not."

"What do we do, sir?" Polly asked.

"The Ashley River runs parallel to this road," he said, pointing to the west. "Find the river and follow it north. You will have to stay hidden during the day and travel only at night. Can you do that?"

"Oh, yes, sir!" Polly replied with enthusiasm.

"You'll have at least a day before they discover you're missing. I'll wait until tomorrow evening before I will be forced to report your 'escape' to Mr. Derby. If I could come up with the money to pay the purchase price for the three of you, I'd do it gladly," he said, "but unfortunately, I have no such means. All I can give you is time."

Amari frowned as she tried to make sense of the doctor's words. He spoke very fast, and she had to take her time to make sure she understood.

"How we gonna 'scape?" she asked, still unsure of the doctor's plan.

"I am setting you free," the doctor replied.

"We be free?" Amari asked, hardly daring to believe it. The word itself stunned her.

The doctor replied, "Well, I'm going to try to give you one small chance to be free. It's up to you and to the spirits of hope and possibility."

That much of the conversation Amari understood clearly. She thought of Afi and her unfailing faith in the future.

"We are so grateful for this opportunity, sir," Polly said, her voice breaking. "You are saving our lives!"

"This could just as easily destroy your lives," he warned. "There will be patrols out and documents posted for your arrest and dogs following your trail."

"How do we hide from dogs?" Amari asked.

"You can't. Dogs are trained to trace your smell and attack you when they find you. I'm not going to try to sugarcoat the danger."

"What happen to you when Massa Derby know you help us?" Amari asked.

"Me? I'll tell him we were attacked by highwaymen. I'll fake an injury to make it seem real. Don't worry about me — I'll be fine." Amari stared intently at the kindly, silver-haired doctor; she never would have imagined a white man willing to help her.

"You gonna tell Teenie her chile not get

sold?" Amari asked as she held Tidbit's hand.

"Of course. But it won't be soon," he warned. Amari breathed a sigh of relief. She couldn't bear to think of Teenie's misery.

The doctor looked sadly at the three young people in the wagon. "You're just children," he mused, shaking his head. He reached under the seat and pulled out an old feed sack. From it he took a small bundle of food, a couple of coins, and a flintlock musket. Amari gasped at the sight of the gun.

"Use this only to save your life — not for hunting. You do not want to draw attention to yourself."

"How it work?" Amari asked.

Polly spoke up quietly. "I know how to use it — my father taught me. You half cock the hammer, pour in the gunpowder, wrap the lead ball, then stuff it into the barrel and fire." Amari was impressed.

The doctor nodded with approval. "Are you a good shot?" he asked.

Polly looked away. "No, sir, not very. My father tried to teach me, but I could not shoot straight."

The doctor shook his head. He gave Polly a small pouch that held the ammunition, as well as the sack. "You have enough gunpowder for only one shot. Make it count."

"Yes, sir, I will. Thank you, sir." She carefully replaced the gun into the bag and hoisted the sack over her shoulder.

"Hurry," the doctor said, glancing around worriedly. "Get out of the wagon and as deeply as you can into the woods."

Amari looked up at him and smiled as she and Polly climbed out of the wagon. They both helped Tidbit jump down. "Thank you, sir," Amari said. She never thought she'd be thanking a white man!

"May God have mercy on all of you," the doctor replied. The wagon disappeared into the distance. The three children stood wordlessly for a moment, watching it, then, realizing their danger, darted into the darkness of the woods.

32. The Journey Begins

Amari, Polly, and Tidbit moved slowly but steadily through the woods, as if they knew where they were going. Although the road had been brightly lit with the sunshine of the morning, the woods were shadowy and dim under the thick canopy of trees. Amari, somehow feeling very much at home among this greenery, led them deeper and deeper until they reached a point where no path was apparent, and the trees and bushes grew so closely together that not even Tidbit could squeeze between the thick green growth.

"Myna, let's stop for a bit and get our bearings," Polly suggested.

Amari nodded in agreement, and they all sat down on the ground and caught their breath. Finches and swallows chirped high above them, but otherwise the forest was surprisingly silent. Polly closed her eyes and leaned against an oak tree.

Tidbit whispered, "Myna, I got to pee!"

Amari looked at the boy fondly. "Go quick — behind that tree." The boy ran and returned shortly to the security of Amari's arms. Amari gave him a reassuring hug, then she looked at Polly, who sat next to her, scratching the mosquito bites on her arm. "My name be Amari," she informed the two of them.

Polly opened her eyes and looked at Amari with a slight frown. "What's wrong with the name they gave you?" she asked. "We're used to it now."

Amari took a deep breath of the woodsy air. "Not Myna no more. Amari." She spoke with clarity and certainty.

"If you say so," Polly said with a shrug. "I suppose it is a good name for a free woman."

"Free!" Amari exclaimed in quiet exultation. She had no intention of ever using that slave name again.

"I want my mama," Tidbit whimpered. He fingered the pouch that hung around his neck.

"You be free too, small one," Amari whispered to him. "You make your mama proud, you hear?" The boy just buried his head in Amari's arms.

"Which way do we go now, Amari?" Polly

280

asked. "It's so easy to get turned around. I think the river is that way," she said, pointing to her left.

"No, river that way," Amari replied, pointing to her right. "I be smellin' muddy water."

Polly sighed. "How will we ever get to the North if we can't even find the river?"

"We not go north — we go south," Amari said defiantly.

"But Dr. Hoskins said to follow the river to the North. That's where we have a better chance at freedom," Polly insisted. "He's a doctor — he's got to know what's best for us."

"Cato say go south," Amari insisted.

"And he also said the streets were paved with gold. I think Cato's story is just an old slave's tale about a place that doesn't even exist!"

"I believe Cato!" Amari said emphatically. Her heart pounded — she had no intention of giving in to this white girl. "He be right about Massa Clay. He be right about doctor." She crossed her arms across her chest.

"But he *knew* them," Polly insisted. "This place he called Fort Mose is just a pretend place he's heard of — like the Promised Land — a place you go when you die. And I don't want to die — not yet!" Her face reddened in anger.

"We die if we go north," Amari said quietly.

"You will forever be a slave if we go south," Polly insisted.

"You want go north? Go alone," Amari said with a fierceness she hoped she had the courage to back up.

Polly inhaled sharply. After a long pause she replied, "We would all die if we split up."

"Choice up to you. Me and Tidbit goin' south. You come if you want." Amari bent down and picked up the small bundle of food. She hoped that Polly wouldn't go off on her own, but she just knew she had to go south.

"Slavery's not so bad up north," Polly said slowly. "I hear tell that lots of black folk are free up there."

"I free here. I free now," Amari replied, digging her toe into the dirt. Then, without looking at Polly, she added, "You white gal. You not need us." She knew that Polly could make it alone and would certainly find refuge quicker without the presence of two runaway slaves.

"I think we need each other," Polly said with quiet resolution.

Amari started to reply, but a noise from

behind them made her pause. A twig broke. Then another. Amari held Tidbit tightly and held her breath. None of them moved. Someone was approaching. She motioned for them to be absolutely silent.

Suddenly, emerging triumphantly from the trees, lunged a dirty and burr-covered Hushpuppy. The dog rushed to Tidbit, licking his face and yelping with obvious joy. "Hushpuppy!" the boy exclaimed with happiness as he hugged his dog. "You found me!" The dog flopped down at the boy's feet and began to lick them, too.

Perhaps this was a sign of good fortune for their journey, Amari thought. And Polly must have thought the same thing, because she looked at Amari and smiled.

"Do you truly believe there is a place called Fort Mose?" Polly asked her.

Amari nodded. "I feel it — here," she said, pointing to her heart. "It be place where, if you get there, you be free inside and outside."

"I hope Cato is right," Polly said slowly. "But going south makes no sense to me."

"Patrols be lookin' north," Amari reminded her.

"How will we ever find our way to a place we are not even sure exists?" Polly asked.

"Spirits will lead us."

"I don't believe in all that spirit talk," Polly said quietly. "And it is such a long way."

"Long walk anyhow," Amari replied. Then she asked, "You not trust Amari?"

Polly looked at her for several moments, as if she were weighing her decision. "Well," she said finally, "we should get started."

Amari nodded in approval. "No talk," she reminded Tidbit. "We must move quiet like snakes."

"Silent snakes," the boy whispered back.

The three of them picked their way through the forest for the rest of the afternoon, stopping only to drink from the streams they crossed. Amari led them slowly and carefully through a maze of oak and elm and maple trees. Rabbits darted across their path, and deer looked at them with large, surprised eyes. But no voices followed them and no people approached. The dog, as if he knew silence was important, did not bark once.

For the first time since her capture in Africa, Amari relaxed. Even though her feet were bare and the ground was covered with sticks and pine needles, she felt no pain, for this walk was leading her, perhaps, to that destiny that Afi kept speaking of.

As dusk approached, Amari signaled for

them to stop. "River be very close," she whispered. "We follow water in dark time."

"Tidbit tired," the boy whined quietly. "I wanna go back to my mama!" He rubbed his eyes and sat down with a thud. "I don't wanna walk no more!"

Amari knew she had to let him rest. "We stop here," she said. "Sleep some, for we walk much soon." She gave him a small piece of meat from Lena's bundle, and he promptly fell off to sleep, his head resting on Hushpuppy.

The girls could see the river in the distance and smell its earthy, wet shoreline as they hid in the darkness of the trees. Amari could hear laughter of men on boats and slow, sad chants of slaves working in the rice fields nearby, finishing up their labors for the day.

"We got to leave river," Amari whispered to Polly.

"Why?" Polly asked. "I thought the plan was to follow the river."

"All rivers run to sea," Amari explained, remembering what Cato had said. "We gotta go by land."

"How will we know which way is which?" Polly asked, looking perplexed.

"Moss grow on north side of trees," Amari explained, trying to remember exactly what Teenie had once told her. "So we follow other side of tree!"

"We can't see moss at night," Polly said reasonably.

"Stars lead us," Amari replied with confidence.

Polly shook her head, but she stopped arguing. The two girls rested their heads gratefully on twin tree trunks, but only for a short time. Amari knew they needed to travel in the safety of darkness. Tidbit fussed when she awakened him, but he soon rubbed his little eyes bravely and marched with them into the darkness without much complaint.

Fireflies blinked in the thick saw grass near the edge of the river. Bullfrogs erupted with tuneless burps. Mosquitoes swarmed in full force, and the three travelers swatted them constantly, their arms and bodies becoming covered with itching bites. A nightingale called far in the distance.

Amari lifted her head to the night sky. Bright stars decorated the darkness above, and she wondered if they were the same stars that had winked at her so far away in her homeland.

33. Deep in the Forest

Morning dawned slowly, brightening the forest. Amari, unusually weary but not willing to admit it, was glad when Polly suggested they find a thicket of trees to rest in. The girls had taken turns carrying Tidbit during the last hours of the night, and he was much heavier than he looked. Even Hushpuppy seemed tired.

Amari led them to the darkest part of the forest — a place where three huge trees had fallen together, and the hollow beneath them was just big enough for the three tired travelers.

"I hope the foxes or deer that usually rest in this spot won't be offended," Polly said gratefully, and she snuggled into the narrow indentation.

"Might come back," Amari suggested nervously as she nestled in next to Polly.

"Tidbit too tired to care," he said as he

and Hushpuppy squeezed in next to the girls.

As the day grew brighter and warmer, the hidden children tried to sleep, but ants and mosquitoes feasted on their bodies while the growing heat of the day made them damp with sweat. Near nightfall, they shared the last of the corn bread and ventured to the river to gather some water.

"One day free," Amari announced as she scratched the numerous bites on her body.

"How far freedom be, Amari?" Tidbit asked fretfully.

"Many, many days, little one," she told him gently.

He squirmed. "What this freedom we runnin' to, Polly?" he then asked. It was clear to Amari that he didn't understand such a grown-up concept.

Polly pulled a leaf from an oak tree. "Freedom is a delicate idea, like a pretty leaf in the air: It's hard to catch and may not be what you thought when you get it," she observed quietly.

Amari replied with a nod, not exactly understanding what Polly had said but comprehending the idea. It seemed to go over the boy's head.

Tidbit put his small fists to his eyes. "I just be wantin' to see my mama," he said, pulling his dog closer. "I know she be missin' me right 'bout now."

"Your mother is very proud of you, Tidbit," Polly told him. "You don't want to disappoint her, do you?"

"I don't care. I wanna go back to my mama's kitchen!" Tidbit cried loudly. "I be hungry and hot, and I don't like it here!" He plopped down on the ground.

"Shhh," Amari said, trying to soothe him. "Gotta stay quiet, little one. You want bad mens to catch us?"

Tidbit, looking miserable, shook his head.

"You gotta protect Hushpuppy," Polly told him. "Can you do that?"

The boy looked glum, but he stood up, stroked the dog, and scratched his legs.

Polly and Amari looked at Tidbit with concern, but they had no choice but to move on. They covered their tracks with leaves and headed into the darkness once more.

By the fifth day of their journey they were all tired and hungry, and their feet, scratched and swollen, cried out for relief. Occasionally, Amari suffered mild bouts of dizziness, and she had to ask the others to stop so she could clear her head and catch her breath.

"Hunger make me little bit weak," she said with embarrassment one morning.

"You're not completely recovered from that beating," Polly reminded her. "Take your time."

"No time to go slow," Amari replied. "Must get far, far away."

"You be all right, Amari?" Tidbit asked.

"I can still beat *you* running!" Amari told him with a laugh as she got up to chase him. He giggled and darted off.

Now and then they found nuts and berries in the forest, but hunger lived with them every day. Amari's mother had taught her a few things about gathering food, and Amari wished she had listened better. But she *had* listened to Teenie, and one evening she left Polly and Tidbit for an hour and brought back a pouch full of nuts and berries that she had gathered — walnuts, pecans, and boysenberries — as well as roots and herbs she had dug. "Good to eat. Give us strength," she told the others.

"How do you know which roots to pick, which herbs are safe?" Polly asked as she nibbled on the fruit of a mayapple, which looked a little like a lime. "I remember seeing these bloom in the spring back in Beaufort. But I don't recall ever eating one."

"My mother teach me," Amari replied

simply, "and Teenie, too. But I not sure about plants grow here. Some I never see before." Amari picked those plants she recognized and others that just looked tasty, but she was very aware that some berries, like the ones Teenie kept hidden in her garden, could be lovely to look at but very dangerous to eat.

"This one taste funny," Tidbit commented, but he ate the mayapple hungrily. When he was done, he asked, "Why you not bring more?"

"Never take all," Amari explained. "You dig one plant, leave two plant; dig one, leave two. So plant come back next season. And ask plant permission."

"Ask permission?" Polly asked. "Why?"

Amari wondered how she could explain the need to work in harmony with the natural world. She tried to find the words. "Plant die. People live. Hunter ask animal before kill it. Then give thanks. Animal die so village live."

"So it is like showing respect for nature?" Polly asked, a look of approval and understanding on her face.

Amari nodded.

"I still hungry!" Tidbit exclaimed softly, pulling on Polly's arm.

"We'll find some good food soon," Polly

told him. "Maybe beyond those next trees on that hill," she said, vaguely pointing to some trees in the distance.

He looked in that direction, but he clearly did not believe her. He whimpered and dragged the rest of the night, often having to be carried. Amari's arms ached from carrying him.

A couple of hours later Tidbit said, "I don't feel so good." He bent over and held his stomach, then ran off behind a tree.

Amari, who also had been feeling quite nauseous, looked at Polly. "You feel sick too?"

At that moment Polly doubled over and ran to find another tree.

Amari threw up. Even though she felt hot, when she touched her face it felt clammy and damp. She made her way to a pile of soft branches and lay there, her stomach cramping terribly. Tidbit came back and lay down near her. "I sick, Amari." She rubbed his little stomach; it felt tight and hard against her hand.

Polly took in deep breaths and asked heatedly, "What did we eat that made us sick? I thought you Africans knew all about plants and herbs!"

Amari tried to think, but her head was spinning. She felt terrible that she had made them all sick, but Polly's accusations made her angry. *She* certainly had not made any efforts to find food. Amari opened her mouth to retort but grabbed her stomach in pain instead. "I so sorry. I not sure — I bring back many kinds." She was going to apologize again, but she had to run to another tree to throw up once more.

The three of them spent a day and a night in that area, trying to regain their strength after numerous bouts of diarrhea and vomiting. Tidbit didn't seem to blame Amari, but Polly remained furious. "It's bad enough I'm lost in the forest with a couple of runaway slaves!" she told Amari. "But now you go and nearly kill us!"

In spite of her weakness, Amari tensed with anger. "I knows you ain't no slave. You free, Polly," Amari told her coolly. "Free to leave us when you wants to. Free to go back to Massa Derby. He say he sell you to be whore," she added sharply. She turned away from Polly.

Polly hung her head. "We're in this together, Amari," she answered softly.

Amari knew it was hunger, illness, and fatigue that made Polly so upset, but she also knew that Polly spoke what was truly on her mind. All of them needed proper food, and soon.

"We gotta eat," Amari announced later that night. She looked around the forest floor until she found what she needed — a sturdy stick that was pointed at the end and a sharp stone. She slowly sharpened the stick until the point gleamed in the moonlight. "I go to river to find food maybe. You be here when I get back?"

"I'll be here," Polly replied quietly.

"I be back soon," Amari said without acknowledging Polly's reply.

Amari disappeared into the darkness.

When Amari returned a couple of hours later, her feet were covered with mud. In her hands, however, she triumphantly held up three large, shimmering catfish.

"I don't believe it!" Polly exclaimed. "How did you do it?"

"Fish fast. I be faster!" Amari replied with a chuckle.

"But how will we cook them?" Polly asked. "If we make a fire, someone may see us."

"We eat raw," Amari said with authority.

"Raw?" Polly asked. "But won't that make us sick again?"

"Raw." Amari took the sharp stone and cut each fish open from tip to tail. She deftly removed the bones, then cut the fish into bite-sized pieces. The heads and tails she tossed to Hushpuppy, who gobbled them greedily.

Polly made such a face that Amari had to laugh. But she picked up her portion and bit into it. "Not as bad as I thought," she said as she swallowed carefully.

Amari bit into her own portion. She chewed slowly and deliberately. Amari woke Tidbit, who tried to turn up his nose at the idea of eating the raw and bloody fish, but his hunger took over and he gobbled his piece, even licking his fingers when he finished. Then he made a face. "You ask permission of this fish?" he asked.

"Fish happy to die for you this night," Amari answered with a smile. "He tired of swimming."

"Let's see if we can get moving again," Polly suggested.

"I got power of fish in me — feel more better," Amari said as she tried to stand up. She was genuinely surprised when Polly reached out and grabbed her hand to help. The two girls looked at each other with renewed understanding.

Amari and Tidbit helped to bury the fish bones, and the three of them prepared, with fresh determination, to continue in the darkness.

34. Lost Hushpuppy

As days went by, Amari had no further luck at catching more fish. She was starting to feel overwhelmed with exhaustion. Her head hurt all the time, and even though the others seemed to have recuperated from the mayapple incident, she didn't want to tell them that she still felt dizzy and nauseous.

The forest had thinned, and hiding places were getting harder to find. Occasionally, Amari heard wagons on the road to the east of them and the sounds of farmers or their slaves working nearby, so the trio moved only in the darkest of night and thus made very poor time as they traveled.

Amari didn't try to find any more berries or fruit, worried that she would make them all sick again. Instead of eating, hunger ate at them. One evening, just before sunset, Amari stumbled over a fallen log and toppled to the ground in a heap. "Ow!" she cried as she rubbed her foot.

"Are you hurt?" Polly asked, concern in her voice.

"No, feet just be tired of walkin'," Amari replied with a short laugh. She leaned against the log, planning to get back to her feet, when something made her decide to look underneath it. Dozens of insects, worms, and grubs squirmed in the un-accustomed light. Amari took a deep breath and grabbed a handful of white, soft grubs. "Safe to eat," she said, "I think." She closed her eyes, put some in her mouth, and chewed slowly. "Taste like chicken," she said, trying to make Tidbit smile.

She offered Tidbit and Polly some grubs as well, and surprisingly, they ate them without complaint, as well as some of the earthworms. It was a matter of survival.

Night after night they walked, afraid of every hoot of the owl and howl of the coyote. Some nights they crossed small streams, which gave them a chance to refresh themselves, quench their thirst, and soothe their aching feet. Sometimes they found small water creatures like crabs or clams to eat. By day they tried to sleep — under logs, in caves, in thickets. Their faces, arms, and legs became hardened with insect bites and scratches. Amazingly, however, they had heard no voices, met no other humans in the woods, nor were chased by patrollers who were looking for runaways. Perhaps Cato had been right, Amari thought.

One morning, just as dawn broke and they hurried to find a hiding place for the day, Tidbit cried out in alarm. "Where is Hush-puppy?"

Most of the time Amari scarcely noticed the dog — he rarely strayed far from Tidbit.

"Hushpuppy must be looking for a mouse for his dinner," Polly said to Tidbit.

"Can I call him?" Tidbit asked tearfully. "Maybe he be lost."

"No, child. You can make no noise. Too dangerous," Amari told him. "Hushpuppy come back."

Polly tried to console him as well. "A dog can always find the boy he loves. He'll be back."

But the dog did not return that morning, or by that afternoon or that evening. At that point Tidbit began to cry. He refused to get up and prepare for the night's travel.

"Hushpuppy will find us," Polly tried to tell him. "He found us all the way from Mr. Derby's house, didn't he?"

"I ain't goin' without Hushpuppy." Tidbit spoke to the dirt he dug his fingers into.

"Tidbit, we gotta go now," Amari said a

little impatiently as she lifted the child to his feet. "Hushpuppy gonna come back." They headed out once more, but Tidbit dragged his feet and kept turning around to look for the dog.

The nights had grown more difficult lately, for the warmth of the sun during the day barely lasted past dark, leaving the nights cold and clammy. "Rain soon," Amari commented as she clutched Tidbit's hand, almost dragging him along. In her other hand she carried the sharpened stick, which she used as a walking staff.

"Rain will feel good," Polly said tiredly. "I don't think I've ever been so dirty!"

"Hushpuppy never find me now," Tidbit wailed miserably.

Amari leaned down and picked Tidbit up, wrapping his legs around her waist, and they headed south into the wet, damp night. Amari began to wonder if she was doing the right thing. It had been her decision to come south, and she was feeling increasingly responsible for them all. What if they were simply going in circles? What if Fort Mose didn't even exist? And she was tired, so very tired.

She also didn't know how to console Tidbit, who was crying softly and begging for his mother and his dog. Finally, when she feared she could not take one more step, they came to a small cave. Amari looked at it as if it were a castle.

"Do you think it's safe to build a fire?" Polly asked. Polly, too, was trembling with cold.

"Think so," Amari replied.

"Do you know how to start a fire?" Polly asked then.

Amari looked around the floor of the cave. "Not sure. Not like home."

Polly grew thoughtful. "My father used to boast he could start a fire with just a stick, a leaf, and a shiny bug!"

"Sound like tall tale," Amari said with a smile.

"Well, we have to try something," Polly said as she began to gather dry twigs from the back of the cave, looking hopeful. Amari found a big branch and dragged it to the center.

With lightning quickness, Amari began rubbing her sharp stick between her hands, twirling it in the center of a larger branch, the way she remembered her mother doing it. But nothing happened. Her fingertips, numb from the damp, chilly air, weren't able to twist the stick fast enough. In her homeland she had started many fires, but usually with a burning stick from someone's cooking fire. Even Teenie's kitchen had a fire that never went out — those hot coals had been carefully tended at night.

Still, she rubbed and rubbed. Polly and Tidbit hovered close. After what seemed to be a very long time, a faint whisper of smoke snaked up from the twigs and leaves. Amari blew on it gently, and soon a small flame flickered in the darkness.

"Fire," Amari said quietly.

"Glory be," Polly whispered. She slowly fed the flames leaves and small sticks until it became large enough to ease their shakes and shivers.

Amari gloried in its warmth, for her head felt thick, like it had been packed with straw. She felt weak and dizzy. She knew she had to find them some real food soon.

"Maybe we use gun to get food?" she asked Polly tentatively.

"We only have one shot," Polly reminded her. "Suppose we miss or someone hears it and finds us?"

Amari nodded reluctantly.

"Do any animals live here, do you think?" Polly asked as they stared into the flames.

"Maybe animal share with us this night," Amari said with a half smile.

Tidbit fell into a fitful sleep in Amari's arms, his face drawn.

Amari sat close to Polly for warmth and companionship, looking at the fire, thinking not of the horrendous fire that had destroyed her village, but of the smoky cooking fires that decorated the front of each household as the women prepared the evening meal. If she closed her eyes, she could almost smell the pungent fish stew.

Suddenly, Amari could hear the footsteps of an animal pacing outside of the cave. She grabbed Polly's arm, and they peered into the darkness. They could get only glimpses of the creature, but it seemed to have a huge, furry head. And it seemed to be looking for a way to get past the fire. It smelled of wet fur and fresh blood.

"Fox?" Amari whispered.

"Foxes have small heads; this one is huge, whatever it is," Polly whispered back anxiously.

"Could be bobcat," Amari guessed.

"Maybe we are in its home," Polly offered. "I don't think it wants us here."

Amari looked around nervously. "We got 'nuff wood to keep fire going?"

"Not much," Polly replied softly. "Where is your stick?"

Amari looked stricken. "In fire. What if it be bear?"

The animal continued to pace. As the fire

dwindled, the two girls huddled even closer together. The animal edged forward. Amari barely breathed. The scraping and sniffing and growling sounds were right at the entrance now.

Suddenly, the creature bounded over the fire. The girls screamed.

Tidbit startled awake and shouted with joy, "Hushpuppy!" The dog dropped what it had been carrying and leaped joyfully on the boy.

Amari, so relieved that it wasn't a bear, started laughing. "I never be so glad to see a dog!"

"Where you been?" Tidbit asked the excited dog. He ran over to the thing Hushpuppy had been carrying and dragged it over to the girls. It was the biggest, fattest rabbit any of them had ever seen.

"So that's why we didn't recognize him!" Polly commented. "He looked so much bigger carrying that."

"And he smell like blood," Amari said as she examined the rabbit.

"We gonna eat it raw like the fish?" Tidbit asked with a grimace.

The thought of another meal of raw meat made Amari feel utterly queasy. "No, little one. We cook. We be safe in cave for now."

Polly and Tidbit ran out of the cave and

searched under logs for dry twigs to feed the fire. Amari found a sharp rock and was able to skin the rabbit, careful to save any part of it that might be helpful on their journey. The skin would make a good pouch, and she remembered her mother once saying that the entrails could be dried and used as string. Hushpuppy was given a huge pile of the leftover parts, which he ate with gusto.

Amari carefully pierced the meat with a stick Tidbit had triumphantly brought her, and after the fire had been built up again, each girl took turns slowly turning it until it was cooked to perfection. Even the drippings were saved. They ate well for the first time since they had begun their journey.

Licking his fingers, Tidbit said softly, "I miss my mama."

Amari pulled him close. A sudden image of her own mother and all that she had lost overpowered Amari for a moment. Tonight, however, she reminded herself, she must concentrate not on what was lost, but on what must be found.

35. Dirt and Clay

The next evening, feeling full of energy, the three young travelers headed out with renewed enthusiasm. The forest had turned to deep pine, the tall evergreens casting thin shadows from the moonlight. In the distance lights from farmhouses flickered.

"Hushpuppy seems to know he is the hero of the moment," Polly said with a smile as the dog bounded after every unfortunate rabbit or squirrel that crossed their path. "But he's too full to catch much now."

Amari laughed softly. Tidbit chased the dog merrily, his high spirits returned, and they all seemed to relax as they made their way slowly through the cool, dark night. They crossed another shallow waterway, where the soft river mud soothed their tired feet.

For four more nights they traveled smoothly, heading ever farther away from the plantation of Percival Derby. They had no more huge feasts, but the leftover pieces of the cooked rabbit lasted a few days, and roots and tubers were plentiful every time they reached a river. Amari was glad that it was not the rainy season — the small streams they crossed would have been roaring rivers. In addition, Amari figured out a way to catch crayfish in the shallows, the tangy flesh a delicious treat as they began their seemingly unending nighttime treks.

But she was tired — tired of walking, of being uncertain, and of feeling sick all the time. Every muscle in her body cried out for rest. The night was unusually warm, and Amari had broken out in a sweat. She didn't think she could keep this up much longer. She had no way of knowing how far they had gone or how much farther they still had to travel. She had nothing to grab on to for support. It reminded her of being on the ship, where it was impossible to determine time or place — just the endless sea.

She was fearful also, but she did not want to share her worries with the others. What would happen if they were found? She wiped her brow and tried to think positively, showing brave smiles to Polly and Tidbit. Just as she let herself relax, however, her worst fears became reality.

As they walked on, Amari could see nothing but shadows — some lighter than others. The trees — long, slim silhouettes — seemed to guide them most of the time, but sometimes the branches looked like arms with hands of many fingers, ready to attack.

And then, suddenly, the branches of a short, sturdy tree moved. Just as Amari jumped, one branch grabbed her wrist. She cried out and tried to pull her arm free. Polly instantly grasped Tidbit's hand and pulled him into the darkness.

Amari screamed again and tried to turn, but she couldn't get free. Then she heard a voice full of venom and danger.

"Where do you think you're going?" As Amari twisted to escape, she found herself face-to-face with Clay Derby.

"Let me go!" Amari exploded, but Clay held her arm as firmly as the shackles she had once worn as he pulled her close to the trunk of the tree.

"I been looking for you and that white girl you run off with for a long time now," Clay drawled. "My father would have been proud of me, God rest his soul."

"How you find?" Amari asked in furious frustration.

"Wasn't hard. You leave footprints the size of a horse." He laughed with disdain, spat on the ground, and pulled a rope from his doublet. He first tied Amari's arms together, then tied her to the tree, pressing himself against her to keep her still.

"How you know where to look?" she wanted to know.

"Oh, the doctor made up that cock-and-bull story about highwaymen and seeing you all head north. But he is a poor excuse for a liar. Everybody went north looking for you, but I figured you might try something stupid like running south."

"Why you care?" Amari asked with quiet anger.

"You are mine, gal." His leer turned into a confused scowl. "I have missed you, Myna," he admitted. "Didn't you miss me a little? I thought you liked me." He touched her face gently.

In spite of her fury, Amari was amazed at the plaintive tone in his voice. "Why you not just let me be?" she asked angrily.

Clay leaned over very close to her face. "Because I aim to reclaim what's mine. You hear me, Myna?"

Amari took a deep breath, closed her eyes, and this time it was her turn to spit. She spat directly in his face. Clay roared and slapped her so hard that her head bounced back against the tree trunk. She felt herself fading into a faint, but she felt victorious.

Clay slapped her again, bringing her back to full consciousness. Amari glared at him.

From the shadows, Amari heard Hush-puppy growl.

"Where is the child?" Clay asked Amari as he looked around.

Amari looked at him with narrowed eyes. "Dead," she said emphatically.

"I don't think so," Clay replied calmly. "That would save me the trouble of dashing his head against a tree. I followed your footprints, remember?"

Amari struggled against the ropes. She had never been so angry. If he hurt Tidbit, she would kill him, she vowed.

"And where is the white girl?" Clay asked as he watched her struggle. He seemed to be amused.

"She leave us — go north," Amari lied.

"You know, you're as poor a liar as the doctor," Clay told her as he ran his hand down her arm. "I shall enjoy punishing you when we return to Derbyshire Farms. I am master there now, you know. My father died suddenly — not long after you ran off."

"Massa Derby dead?" Amari asked with surprise. She wondered if Mrs. Derby had breathed a sigh of relief. Amari lowered her head. *Is it wrong to be glad that someone is dead?* she thought.

"Yes, the doctor said it was his heart, but I believe he was poisoned," Clay said ominously.

Amari peered into the darkness and prayed that Polly and Tidbit would not try to save her and get caught themselves. Again she heard Hushpuppy growl from the darkness of the woods, quietly but with menace.

"What happen when we go back?" Amari asked, trying to keep Clay talking.

"Oh, you'll be punished severely — perhaps a brand on your face or maybe the removal of a finger or toe. I have not yet decided."

Amari felt her heart quicken, but she refused to let Clay see that she was scared.

"I fully intend to teach you the folly of trying to run away from me. But tonight," he said, his voice dropping low, "I intend to make up for lost time. I really have missed you, gal." He stroked her leg, and Amari kicked at him.

Undeterred, Clay put his hand on Amari's other leg. A dusty blond shadow erupted from the woods at that moment, both hands shakily holding the musket. Polly closed her eyes and squeezed the trigger. The sound was deafening. Amari screamed. Clay sank to the ground with a moan.

"He be dead?" Amari asked fearfully as

they crept close to him.

Polly, her face showing both terror and surprise, dropped the gun, then fell to her knees and turned Clay over. "No, he is not dead," she declared with relief. "It's a good thing I am such a poor shot. I didn't want to hurt him, just frighten him away!"

Clay's eyes fluttered and he groaned softly.

"The bullet barely grazed the side of his head. He will be fully conscious soon. We must hurry." She tore at the knots that held Amari.

Amari looked at Polly with gratitude, amazement, and new respect. "I not know you so wild!"

Polly grinned. "I didn't know it either. I just knew I had to do something quick and sudden." Then she got down to business. "It is *his* turn to be tied," she suggested.

"He get loose soon, yes?" Amari asked.

"Probably," Polly replied. "We don't have much rope. I suppose he will be able to undo the knots eventually. But at least we will have some time to get away."

"He should die," Amari declared, no regret in her voice.

"Maybe so, but it is not for us to do," Polly replied.

They pulled Clay over to the tree and bound him as tightly as they could. "We must get out of here quickly," Polly said. "Someone may have heard the gunfire."

As they backed away from him, he began to stir. "He be wakin' up," Amari whispered frantically.

Polly grabbed Clay's knapsack and tossed the gun inside it. "We must flee! If he gets loose, he will surely find us and kill us."

"Maybe not," Amari replied. She pointed to a spot just beyond Clay's thigh where a large rattlesnake slithered toward him.

"What should we do?" Polly whispered.

"Nothing," Amari replied quietly.

Clay opened his eyes and focused slowly on Amari, Polly, and Tidbit sitting a few feet away from him. A trickle of blood oozed from the wound on his head. He pulled at his restraints. "How dare you?" he roared as he became more aware of what they had done. He yanked at the ropes. "I'll kill you for this!"

"I don't think so," Polly replied.

"Mark my words, you'll pay for this!" he warned viciously as he tugged at the ropes some more. "When we get back, I'll throw that boy in his mother's cooking pot and make her watch him die!"

"We not go back," Amari told him clearly.

"Oh, yes, you are," Clay swore as he continued to struggle with the ropes. "You can't even tie a decent knot," he crowed triumphantly, freeing one arm. "Even if you run, I will find you and catch you, and I plan to spend the rest of my life making you suffer."

"Rest of life might not be long," Amari observed quietly. The snake, unmoving, coiled tensed and ready only inches from Clay's leg.

Clay looked directly at Amari, his face a mask of rage and confusion. "I tried to be kind to you," he told her. "How can you repay me like this?"

She looked at him with pity. "You just not understand."

Angrily, Clay continued to wiggle and struggle with the ropes that held him. Then he turned his head and spotted the snake. He froze. The snake was motionless as well.

Amari looked at Polly. Polly looked at Tidbit. They all looked toward the woods. In silent agreement they hurried away from Clay.

■ ■ ■ ■

PART EIGHT
POLLY

■ ■ ■ ■

36. Should We Trust Him?

They ran. Faster than Polly thought possible, they jumped over logs and under low-hanging branches, the only thought being to put miles between them and Clay Derby. Her left side cramped and ached, but they dared not stop. With great urgency, they hurried through the darkness, Amari clutching one of Tidbit's arms, Polly the other. His little feet barely touched the ground. Sweat poured down Polly's face. Finally, after what seemed like miles of frantic running, they stopped by a shallow river to rest.

Amari was breathing so hard, she threw up. Tidbit collapsed by the stream and then crawled into the water to cool off. Slowly, her pounding heart slowed, but Polly knew they were probably still in grave danger.

"Do you think the snake got him?" Polly asked.

"Maybe snake not mad enough to bite," Amari said as she worked to catch her breath. "Maybe Massa Clay got loose and kill the snake," she added fearfully.

Tidbit emerged from the water, dripping wet. "If Massa Clay find us again, he gonna take me to my mama?"

Polly clasped her hand to her mouth, shocked and saddened at the child's question. Polly looked at Amari, then told Tidbit carefully, "Tidbit, if Clay comes back, he will try to hurt us. So we have to keep running and stay very quiet. Do you understand?"

Tidbit shifted from one foot to another, looking surprisingly mature. "I don't care if he beat me. I just wanna see my mama." He was blinking back tears.

Amari grabbed him then and pulled him to her. "I know, little one. I know."

Polly sat down with them, and the two girls tried their best to comfort the little boy. Through it all, she listened to the night sounds but could hear no approaching footsteps. "Do you think we did wrong to leave him like that?" she whispered to Amari.

"Massa Clay not in our hands no more," Amari replied.

Reluctantly, Polly picked up Clay's knapsack and looked through it. In it was a hunk of dried salt pork, a few apples, some wrapped cheese, and several hard biscuits. She gave one to Tidbit.

"My mama made this bread," he said, first sniffing it, then holding it close to his body. "I wanna go see my mama!" He began to cry.

Amari looked at the boy sadly. "We come too far to go back," she said. " 'Sides, if I goes back, I be a slave again. And I ain't never bein' no slave ever no more." Polly nodded thoughtfully and stood back up. Amari picked up Tidbit, and they headed south once again.

They did not stop for two days, moving even during the day, staying well away from the roads as they did. They saw people only in the distance. Tidbit's little legs struggled to keep up. Many times he had to be carried or cajoled into continuing the journey. There was no sign of Clay, but they never stopped looking over their shoulders.

"We should have tried to find Clay's horse," Polly said wearily one evening.

"No," Amari replied. "Better this way."

One evening, bone-weary and dragging through the red-clay mud of still another shallow river they had to cross, they paused to search for crayfish or clams. "I found five!" Tidbit whispered excitedly. Even he knew to be ever vigilant and quiet.

Then Polly saw him: a boy about their age, sitting on a rock overlooking the river. He was hunched over a fishing pole and did not appear to notice them.

Polly motioned to Amari and Tidbit to get back into the darkness of the pine trees. Hushpuppy also silently disappeared. But just as Polly stepped backward, the boy looked up.

He had dirty reddish hair, a torn shirt, and wore no shoes. He gazed at Polly without much surprise. "Who are you?" he asked bluntly.

"I suppose I could ask you the same thing," she retorted, hands on her hips. She wanted to show him how bold and unafraid she was, but her heart quaked.

"What are you doing out here in the middle of the night?" he countered.

Polly raked her fingers through her hair and brushed a twig off her dress. She couldn't believe she was worrying about how she *looked!* "Getting some fresh air. And who goes fishing after dark?"

"I do."

"You catch anything?" she asked.

"No. Too dark," he admitted. He looked at her closely in the moonlight. "I never seen you round these parts before."

Polly replied saucily, "There's probably a

lot you've never seen."

"What's your name?" the boy asked.

"Polly." She immediately gasped and put her hand to her mouth. She should have told him Sarah or Sally or anything other than her real name!

"So, Miss Polly, you look like you got a lot to hide. You're dirty, you look hungry, and you look lost."

"I know exactly where I am. I am speaking to a young man who does not have the good manners to be polite to a lady!" She tried to speak to him with dignity, but it was hard with muddy feet.

He laughed. "My name is Nathan. I live in that little house through those trees there. We ain't got much — just a house, a barn, some chickens, and a couple of skinny cows and pigs. But we got a little land, and it's ours, and we make do. My daddy drinks at night, so I go fishing. And you are probably right about my manners — my mama would have taught me, but she died." He tossed a stone into the water. "But I do know a pretty girl when I see one — even if she is muddy-footed and saucy-mouthed."

Polly was surprised to find herself blushing. Her whole face and neck felt like hot, stinging needles. She'd never felt like this before. She cleared her throat. "I must be on my way," she said as she tried to go around the rock on which he sat.

"Do you know where you are?" he asked.

"Of course," she replied.

"Where?" he challenged her.

"I don't have to tell you anything," she said with a boldness she did not feel. She glanced nervously in the direction of the forest where Amari and Tidbit hid.

He gazed at her curiously. "You're not far from Savannah, Georgia." He paused. "Is that where you want to be?"

"Exactly," Polly said with annoyance.

"What about the others?" he asked quietly.

"What others?" Polly said, trying to bluff. "I am alone."

"The slave girl. The little boy. The dog." He continued to gaze at her with a half smile. "I spotted you yesterday, and I been following you."

Polly's eyes went wide. "You've been . . . Why?" Polly asked nervously. "Do you work for Clay Derby?"

"Never heard of him," Nathan replied. "I just figure you must be runaways, but I never seen such a raggedy bunch before."

"We are on a mission of mercy," Polly began desperately. "I am mistress of —"

"Of mud?" The boy interrupted her and laughed out loud. "Y'all look like you need some mercy yourselves. You are obviously nobody's mistress — I figure an unhappy indenture. The two little Negroes are runaways for sure." He paused and gazed at Polly long enough to make her feel uncomfortable. Then he said slowly, "I figure that your little 'mission of mercy' is worth a bucket of reward money."

Polly backed away from him slowly. "You mustn't tell," she whispered, pleading. "We have come so far, and our journey has not been easy."

Nathan grinned. "I can see that." Then he pointed to the woods where the others were hiding. "Tell your friends to come out. Maybe I can help."

Polly hesitated, unsure of what to do. She knew Amari and Tidbit had heard everything.

"Go on, Polly-girl," Nathan said gently. "Call them. You can trust me."

Again her father's special name for her was spouting from the mouth of a cocky young man. This time, however, she almost liked the way Nathan said it, with just a hint of a Georgia twang. She opened her mouth to call the others, but before Polly could speak, Amari stepped quietly out of the darkness of the trees. She held Tidbit on her hip. Hushpuppy, hovering close, growled quietly.

Nathan looked at them for a moment, then asked, "Are you all hungry?"

Polly nodded stiffly, still uncertain.

Nathan jumped down from the rock and stood face-to-face with the dirty, tired group. "Look, I got to tell you, my daddy would turn y'all in, get the reward money, and have it drunk away by Sunday next. But me, I think slavery is stupid. I figure anybody ought to be free enough to go fishing at midnight if he wants to." He grinned again. "It is a big country, with room enough for the Indians, for black folk to find their own place, and for pretty little white girls with dirty feet!"

Polly was sure her furious blushes were evident even in the moonlight. She'd never met anyone who made her feel so fluttery.

Amari coughed. "You got food?" she asked quietly.

"Not much," Nathan replied. "Follow me." They trailed the boy through the forest, which thinned gradually to a clearing where a small garden and a larger field of crops could be seen. Two small buildings — a house and a barn made of rough wood and logs — stood nearby. "I'm going to hide y'all in the barn. I do most of the work around the place, so Daddy is not likely to find you if you stay quiet." He led them through a small door, pulled fresh hay for pallets for them, and told them he'd return in a moment.

Amari looked around nervously. "This be a trap?" she asked.

"I hope not," Polly replied. "He had an honest face."

Amari smiled at her. "I think his face make you happy."

Polly blushed again. "Nonsense," she said quietly. She didn't want to admit that Amari was right.

Nathan was back a few minutes later with bread, cheese, dried venison, and apples. "This is all I could find, and my daddy is going to wonder why I got so hungry, but I'll just tell him I been out all day hunting. Eat," he urged them.

The hungry group of travelers took the food gratefully. Tidbit even ate the apple cores and promptly fell asleep on the nearest pile of straw.

"Where y'all headed?" Nathan asked the girls.

"South," Amari replied.

Nathan looked confused. "Don't most runaways head north?"

Amari glanced at Polly, who lowered her

voice and asked Nathan, "Have you ever heard of a place called Fort Mose?"

Nathan looked up in surprise. "That's down in Spanish territory. Far south."

"It be real?" Amari asked.

"Of course it's real. You been heading toward a place that you didn't even know for sure existed?" he asked, scratching his head.

"Amari always believed in it," Polly explained.

"My father does some trading — much of it illegal, I'm sure — and you'd be surprised who shows up here from time to time. I've met French beaver trappers, English gun sellers, and Dutchmen who sell indentures."

Polly tensed.

"Last month," Nathan continued, "a Spanish priest from this place called Fort Mose came through here, trying to teach my daddy the 'one true faith.' Daddy just laughed at the man and told him to get out. Unless a man has a plan where my daddy can make money, he's not interested."

"What man say 'bout Fort Mose?" Amari asked. "Streets of gold?"

"Streets of mud would be my guess," Nathan replied. "It is a small place but different from most. From what I could tell, it is run by Spanish soldiers and priests.

Runaways are welcome and given their freedom, as long as they promise to swear allegiance to the Spanish king."

"Freedom to do what?" Polly asked.

"Freedom to stay there, I suppose," Nathan told her. "If you leave, you lose Spanish protection and are subject to the laws of the colonies."

Polly and Amari exchanged looks.

"No whippings?" Amari asked, unconsciously touching her scarred back.

"I would think not," Nathan said, sympathy showing on his face. "How far have you come from?"

"Charles Town. South Carolina Colony."

Nathan looked impressed. "That's an awfully long walk." He was quiet for a moment. "Can you tell me what you were running away from?"

Polly thought for a moment. "A very bad situation," was all she would say. "Do you know the woods around here quite well?"

"For sure," Nathan replied proudly. "I know every rock and holler and tree within a hundred miles. Squirrel and deer see me coming and tremble, 'cause they know they could be my dinner!" He laughed.

Polly felt relaxed with this pleasant young man. She had a feeling that her father would have liked Nathan — taking him fishing and telling him tall tales. She wished she could talk to her father just one more time — ask his advice or listen to him laugh uproariously at his own jokes after dinner. "It is so very kind of you to help us," she told Nathan. She felt herself reddening again.

Nathan looked directly into her eyes. She had to look away. "I will show you the safest path through the forest after you have rested," he said. "Remember to stay very quiet. My father is just plain mean."

The three travelers nodded and snuggled into the clean straw. Polly dreamed of her father for the first time since his death — his bawdy jokes, his weakness for ale, and the soft grin on his face whenever he looked at her. "My princess. My Polly-girl," he would say when he kissed her good night. She slept soundly for the first time in many days.

But the next morning she was awakened suddenly by a red-faced man who held a pitchfork in his hand. He towered over the three children. "What this we got here in my barn? Two niggers? And a dirty little white gal who must be poor white trash if she be sleepin' with 'em!"

Amari jumped back, pulling Tidbit behind her.

"Please, sir," Polly began to say.

Then Nathan appeared in the doorway, his face showing both agony and apology as he looked at Polly. "What you got here, Daddy?"

"You hear anything creeping around last night, boy?"

"No, sir," Nathan said. His voice cracked as he spoke.

"Didn't I tell you about locking the barn door to keep out animals? Never figured I'd have to lock out the likes of this here. 'Course, they ain't much better than animals." He laughed roughly.

"I'm sorry, sir. I thought it was locked." The look on Nathan's face pleaded with Polly to understand — or to forgive.

Polly wasn't sure if she should believe his looks of apology or not. She looked at Nathan with great disappointment. "Let me explain, sir," she began, trying to appease Nathan's father.

"Shut up, gal!" the man roared. He leaned in close to Polly's face. "Trespassers! I'll have the lot of you hanged, lessen there be a reward out for you. If that be the case, I will get my money, *then* see you hanged!"

Polly was terrified, but she continued. "There is a large reward, sir, for the return of these slaves," she said slowly. "I am in the process of bringing them to Savannah.

My mother is sick, and we need the reward money." She managed to make a teardrop fall, although he could not know it came from fear rather than sorrow.

The man hesitated. He looked at her closely, tightening his grip on the pitchfork. "Do say, now."

"Sir, can you help me get home to my mother?" Polly begged. "You can have the reward money. I just want to get home to my family."

"You look to me like you be lying, gal. If I find you been lying to me, I swear I'll kill you all. Nathan!" he called suddenly. "Get in here, boy!"

"Yes, sir?"

"Lock the barn tight this time. You hear me, son?"

"Yes, sir."

"After I eat and you feed the animals, we'll take them down to Savannah. I'm going to make me some money on this motley lot one way or another." He strode out of the barn, tossing the key at Nathan.

Nathan turned to Polly as soon as his father was out of earshot. "You must believe me, I did not betray you."

Polly did not reply right away. She stared at him, then, realizing they didn't have much choice but to trust him, she shrugged her shoulders. "Can you get us out of here? We don't have much time!"

Nathan nodded. "If you head due west, you will run into a swamp. It's not pleasant, but he's not likely to pursue you there. Hide for a day or two, then head south."

Polly gave him a small smile.

"How we get out from here?" Amari asked, bringing the subject back to the immediate problem.

"Hit me," Nathan told them.

"What?" Polly and Amari said at the same time.

"Use the handle of the pitchfork. Knock me down. Hit me in the head. Then run for the swamp!"

"I cannot hit you!" Polly exclaimed.

"Give me it," Amari said, picking up the pitchfork. She looked at Nathan and smiled. "You be good person. I hit you not with hate, but with much thank."

Nathan nodded as Amari raised the handle of the pitchfork in her hand.

"Wait!" Polly cried.

Amari lowered her arm.

"Will we ever see you again?" she asked Nathan softly.

"Probably not. My father will beat me for sure when he figures out what has happened. But remember me, will you?" He grinned briefly, looked at Polly for a long moment, then said to Amari, "Do it! Hurry."

Amari swung firmly. The handle struck Nathan's head with a sickening thud, and he crumpled into the straw.

"Is he dead?" Tidbit asked. It was the first thing he had said all morning.

"No," Amari replied as she touched Nathan gently on the neck. "He be fine. Let us flee!" She grabbed Tidbit's hand and dashed out of the barn. Polly took one last glance at Nathan lying there, then followed them.

They hurried across the field, past the sharp edges of the palmetto palms, and deep into the darkness of the woods. Amari led them, as if by instinct, it seemed to Polly, due west, far away from their usual southern route. They dared not stop, but they slowed to catch their breath.

Exhaling with difficulty, Amari said softly, "Follow me." She led them quickly to an area where the ground they walked on was soft and squishy; water oozed between their toes as they walked. "Swamp," she told them.

"Snakes," Polly added, thinking of the slaves in the rice fields.

"Gators," Tidbit whispered fearfully.

"Safety," Amari told them all. "Nobody

find us here." They held hands and slowly marched into the sucking ooze. The mud, covered by a shallow layer of liquid slime, seemed to try to grab them and pull them down with each step. Deeper and deeper they ventured into the swamp; soon the muck was to their knees. Thick mud covered their thighs, then their waists.

Amari had to lift Tidbit onto her hip as it became impossible for him to wade through it any longer. Finally, as deep into the swamp as they dared to go, under the shade of a huge mimosa tree with branches that were covered with hanging moss, they stopped. Birds called shrilly above. Something slithered past Polly's leg. She gasped but did not cry out.

They waited. The mud turned cold.

■ ■ ■ ■

PART NINE
AMARI

■ ■ ■ ■

37. LOST AND FOUND AND LOST

They stayed in the swamp until well after dark. No one pursued them. After listening carefully for the sound of dogs or hunters and hearing nothing but the burping of bullfrogs, Amari signaled that they should ease out of the mire. Slowly, the children made their way to the edge of the swampand collapsed on the relatively solid ground. Thick, black mud covered them completely — it was even inside their ears.

"Nathan must have told his father we went in another direction," Polly whispered.

"He good man," Amari said in agreement.

"Amari, we gotta wash!" Tidbit piped up as he tried to scrape the mud off of his arms.

Amari smiled at the muddy boy. "You look like little dirt ball," she teased. "But rain be washin' you soon. Just wait."

The rain began about an hour later, gentle at first, then hard enough to rinse off the

337

mud and chill the children as well. It rained all night.

"I be so tired," Amari said, shivering, as they stopped to eat some of the food Nathan had given them. She looked at her swollen feet and her insect-bitten legs. The others looked just as weary. "But we gotta use the dark to move."

No one spoke much. Amari walked slowly and without much energy. Just before dawn they reached the outskirts of Savannah, but they made a wide detour to avoid the populated areas. The rain finally stopped, and the warmth in the air felt wonderful.

"Do you think Nathan's father will look for us near Savannah?" Polly asked.

"You wonder about Nathan or his father?" Amari responded with a small smile.

"I don't think he betrayed us," Polly replied. "He is not like his father."

"He be son of evil man," Amari told her. But then she added, "Evil man be father of good man."

Polly looked thoughtful, then voiced the fear they all had been holding. "What about Clay?" she whispered.

No one had an answer.

As daylight approached, they looked for a place to rest for the day. Hushpuppy had a knack for finding huge overturned logs or shallow caves or even abandoned shacks for them each day. He led them this morning to a small wooden shack, not much bigger than an outhouse, hidden in a thicket of trees. Its door, dangling on one hinge, had blown open, so the earthen floor was covered with leaves and animal droppings.

"It looks like it might have been a hunter's shelter," Polly observed.

Amari looked carefully inside and outside the small building. It was clear that no one had been there for a long time. "Safe for now," she stated.

It was so small, the three could barely sit down together, but they were grateful for shelter and a place to sleep, even if they had to do it sitting up. They shared some of the nuts and berries and tried to sleep. Hushpuppy curled up under a tree not far away.

Amari dozed, then was startled awake by the rustling of leaves and the snapping of branches. Something or someone was approaching fast, and there was no time to hide.

A furious-sounding voice bellowed, "Patrick! I know you're in there, man. You can't hide from your responsibilities out here anymore! You're as useful as a lighthouse in a bog! If you don't get home and take care of your family, I swear I'll —"

Tidbit shrieked in alarm as the door flew open and a woman, dressed, amazingly, all in buckskin, stared openmouthed at the three children. Equally astonished, they stared right back. She was a large woman, with ruddy cheeks and stony blue eyes. Thick ringlets of dark hair escaped her bonnet, which also seemed to be made of buckskin.

"What is this? Who be ye? What you done with my Patrick?"

Polly spoke up. "We have not seen anyone, ma'am." She could not think of anything else to say. Amari and Tidbit cowered beneath the woman's gaze.

"Where y'all come from?" the woman asked suspiciously.

"Savannah, ma'am." Amari hoped the woman couldn't sense Polly's lie.

"What y'all doing in Patrick's shed?"

"Sleeping, ma'am," Polly answered, truthfully this time.

The woman stared at them with eyes of thunder for a moment or two, then she sat down heavily on the ground and doubled over with gales of laughter. "Well, I'll be gob-smacked," she said between laughs. " 'Sleeping, ma'am,' " she said in a tiny little voice, mimicking Polly. "Y'all must be on the ockie — runaways for sure — am I right?"

Amari could see that Polly was unsure of what to say.

"What we got here? Two slaves and a . . . What be ye, gal?"

"Indentured servant, ma'am," Polly said quietly.

"Hmmm," the woman replied. "You ever see a pothook, lass?"

"By the hearth?" Polly asked, confused.

"No, around your neck," the woman said. "That be the punishment round these parts for runaway indentured gals. An iron collar with hooks on it."

"Oh, please, no, ma'am," Polly pleaded. "Please, not that."

The woman laughed again. "You've no call to be askert of Fiona, child. I ain't going to turn y'all in. I'm just telling you what the punishment be for runaway indentures. Punishment for runaway slaves be a lot worse, now," she said, looking at Amari and Tidbit.

Amari spoke softly. "Who you be, ma'am?"

"Me? I am Fiona O'Reilly. My pa brought me to this place from Ireland when I was just a wee snip of a thing — 'bout the age of that cub you be holdin' on to. He be yours?"

Amari started to say no but thought better of it. "Yes, ma'am. He be mine." She pulled Tidbit close.

"Well, you can't stay here, none of you. My Patrick is a good man but a hard man — a mite lazy, mind you, one who would rather be a-hunting than clearing the fields for harvest, which I guess explains my clothes. He brings me skins, and I make my clothes! I can sew a garment from anything!" She looked down and laughed at her buckskins.

Tidbit could not stop staring at the large, unusual woman. "Your man kill many deer to make that dress for you," he said solemnly.

Fiona erupted in laughter once more, smacking her large thighs with her hand as she chortled, "Little one speaks true, but there be no telling what my Patrick might do if he finds you here. For sure he won't be a-laughing."

"Well, we'll just be on our way, then, ma'am," Polly said as she motioned to the others to gather their belongings to leave. "We don't need any more trouble. It has been a long, hard journey."

"Savannah's only half a day's walk from here," Fiona said quietly. "Methinks you not speak true before."

Polly bowed her head and glanced at Amari. Her look seemed to say, *Trust her.*

"We could use some help, ma'am," Polly admitted. Amari hoped they were doing the right thing.

Fiona seemed to think for a minute, then said firmly, "You're coming with me. Be quick about you, now!" She picked up the edge of her heavy skirt and hurried through the woods.

Amari, Polly, and Tidbit had no choice but to follow the woman, who in spite of her size moved nimbly through the woods. Hushpuppy dashed after them.

Fiona's home, larger than the cabin that Nathan and his father shared, sat neatly between several rows of corn and beans. Amari noticed small shacks off to the right — slave quarters, she knew.

Fiona led them to the barn, which held two wagons, three horses, and numerous pieces of farm equipment. "Climb into the back of that one and hide," she commanded, pointing to the smaller of the two wagons, "until I think of what to do with you."

"You keep slaves here, Missus?" Amari asked meekly as Fiona bustled around the barn, muttering to herself.

"Of course, child. Everybody has slaves. How do you think we handle this land? But my Patrick is a good man and does not mistreat his property. Our slaves like it here." Amari couldn't understand how the woman could see no wrong in owning slaves as long as they were well treated.

"Then why are you helping us?" Polly asked.

Fiona looked at her carefully and thought a moment. "It's like this: If my Patrick brings home a new slave like he did last week, for example, that's his right as master and man of this house, and I dare not interfere. As a woman, I ain't got muckle to say about those kind of decisions. But when I got the chance to decide for myself, I find it gives me pleasure to choose to help you be free. That's the truth, and I did not know it until I spoke the words." Fiona looked immensely pleased with herself.

"Thank you," Amari murmured as she helped Tidbit climb into the back of the wagon.

"Wait here," Fiona told them. "I will send someone in here to hitch up the wagon." She hurried out of the barn.

Amari nervously looked around the barn. "She be good woman?" Amari whispered to Polly.

"Yes, but she is afraid," Polly replied. "I do not think she has ever made her own decision before. I hope her husband does not return soon."

The barn door opened then, and a thin, stooped black man limped over to them. "I'm to harness the wagon," he mumbled, not even glancing at Amari and Polly.

Amari jerked her head suddenly. She knew that voice! "What be your name?" she asked.

"Buck," he answered slowly as he led the large brown horse to the wagon. "They calls me Buck."

Amari knew the perfect modulation of that voice, the deep bass edged with gold. Her mind ran quickly back to the reddish dust of the road that led to Ziavi, the shrieking of the blue turaco birds at dawn, the taste of her mother's groundnut stew. She shook her head to hold back the tears. "Are you my Besa?" she asked in Ewe.

The man looked up quickly. On his face was a small, faded birthmark, shaped a little like a pineapple. "Amari?" he said softly.

"My Besa, my love, I have found you. It is I, Amari!" Her heart thudded as she allowed all her memories to come rushing back. She jumped from the wagon and ran to him.

But just as she reached him and was about to embrace him, he held his hand out and stopped her. "No, don't!" he pleaded.

"Besa!" she cried with urgency. But then

345

she saw — the Besa she had known no longer existed. His right eye was missing. His face, deeply scarred on that side, looked like old leather. Half of his teeth seemed to be missing as well.

"Oh, Besa, what has happened to you?" she asked him, finally touching his arm softly.

"I have had five owners since I saw you last, Amari. Owners!" He spat on the ground in disgust. "To even say the word makes me hate them more!"

"We are alive," she said gently.

"I'd rather be dead!" Besa replied bitterly, glaring at her. "You have been treated well, then?"

She bowed her head. "No. I have not. I have been raped. I have been beaten. I have been made to feel like I am nothing. But I live."

"My spirit is dead," he said, his voice empty. "They beat it out of me with their whips, cut it out of me with their knives, shot it out of me with their guns. I can barely see, and every step causes me pain."

Her stomach churned as she listened to his ordeal. "Come with us!" Amari cried suddenly. "We have run away — all the way from Charles Town. We are heading to Fort Mose, a place where everyone can be free."

Besa looked at her as if she were crazed. "There is no such thing as freedom, Amari. I tried to escape several times. Each time I was caught by their dogs, beaten, and then sold. You will be caught as well."

"We will *not* be caught," Amari insisted. "We have already come this far. Give yourself a chance to believe once more," she pleaded. "Please come with us, Besa." Amari reached out to him again, but he jerked back. She felt her heart turn inside out.

"I no longer believe in anything," Besa told her harshly.

Amari inhaled sharply. *What have they done to you?*

Besa looked up at the faces of Polly and Tidbit, who were peering over the side of the wagon. "You travel with a white girl?" he asked with surprise. "First chance she gets, the white one will turn on you. Trust no one."

"She is my friend," Amari told him stiffly, realizing, as she said it, that it was true. She softened then. "Please, my Besa. You are my past. Come be my future as well."

"No," he said with finality. "I will take no more risks. I have found a woman here — a good woman. She keeps me warm at night, and she carries no dreams in her heart. She is safe." He turned slowly from Amari and finished harnessing the horse to the wagon.

She stood there in the dust, one hand reaching toward Besa, but the distance between them had become so vast that she knew she could never touch him again.

Fiona returned to the barn then, full of orders. "Put fresh hay in the back of the wagon, Buck," she commanded.

"Yes'm," he said, lapsing back into lazy English.

"You're to say nothing of this to the master when he returns, you understand?" Fiona said to him.

"Oh, no, ma'am. I knows how to keep my mouf shut."

"Well, get on with you, then. I thank you for your help, Buck."

Besa turned and gazed at Amari, a mask of resignation on his face. He limped slowly out of the barn. He did not look back.

Polly touched Amari on her shoulder. Amari covered her face with her hands. Her shoulders heaved; she could barely contain her grief and her anger. *It's not fair!* she screamed to herself. *Look what they have done to him! I hate the whites! I hate them!*

"What is the problem, lass?" Fiona asked with concern. "You know that God prefers prayers to tears."

Amari glanced up at the large woman and shook her head ruefully. *Prayers? What good have they done?* Then she pulled herself back to the reality that faced her. It was hard to hate what the whites had done and be thankful to Polly and this white woman in the same moment. "I be grateful for your help, ma'am," Amari managed to say. "Your kindness make me much happy."

Visibly pleased, Fiona showed them the bundles she had brought from the house. The first was a pile of clothes. "My Peggy, God rest her soul, left this world one year past. She died of the fever. About the age of you gals, she was." She paused.

"I'm sorry, ma'am," Polly said. "You must miss her. We have all lost loved ones as well."

"Yes, I suppose you have," Fiona replied. "Well, you need fresh clothes — those you have on are filthy and torn. Put these on."

Fiona gave the girls two simple dresses, one of blue calico and the other of brown flannel. Each dress was well worn. She had also brought bonnets, aprons, and shoes. Polly changed quickly.

Amari took her time. She slowly peeled off the ragged shift she wore. Fiona gasped as she saw the ugly welts on Amari's back.

"Oh my goodness, child. What happened to your back?"

"Whip, ma'am," Amari said simply.

"You must have been extremely disobedient," Fiona exclaimed.

Amari looked up with daggers in her eyes, but she remembered the danger they were in and struggled to make her face emotionless. "My massa thought so, ma'am," she said quietly.

"Is that a *brand* on your back?" Fiona continued. She reached over and touched the raised and blackened letter on Amari's shoulder. Amari flinched. Full of shame, Amari wished the woman would drop the subject. "We brand our cattle, of course, but I've never bothered to check to see if any of our slaves carry brands. Is that a common practice, dearie?"

"Yes'm," Amari mumbled. It was hard not to explode.

"Well, there's nothing so bad that it couldn't be worse," Fiona said philosophically. She glanced one last time at Amari's back before she slipped on the brown dress, then hurried over to Tidbit. Fiona handed him a fresh shirt and a clean pair of breeches.

"What should we do now, Miss Fiona?" Polly asked.

"You running north?" Fiona asked.

"No, ma'am," Amari replied. "South."

"Why?" Fiona asked, looking perplexed.

"Freedom," Amari replied. "Place call Fort Mose."

"That's in Spanish territory," Fiona told them. "Your journey is one I would not take."

"All we know be dead and gone," Amari tried to explain. "Only left be hope and dreams." She thought sadly of Besa and angrily of their dreams.

Fiona nodded. "My father brought us to this country for freedom, but he died doing it. My Patrick works hard for our freedom, and still death found us. Hope and dreams are all any of us have." She wiped away a tear.

Again Amari wondered how a slave owner could speak so strongly about freedom.

"How far to Spanish territory?" Polly asked after a moment's silence.

"I do not rightly know. But it is too far to walk. I'm giving you all this wagon, lass," she said to Polly.

"What will your husband say?" Polly asked in alarm.

"I'll tell him thieves came in and took it while he was out a-hunting!" Fiona replied with a laugh. "Serves him right for staying away for so long. I'll tell him they took off heading north."

"I know the horse is valuable," Polly added. "We are very grateful." She reached into the sack that Dr. Hoskins had given them, looked briefly at Amari as if to make sure she agreed, then offered Fiona the coins.

"Thank you, ma'am. You be so kind," Amari added quietly.

Fiona quickly tucked the coins into one of her large pockets. "Big Brownie is old and 'bout to die. Better to die on a journey than in a barn, I say. He may get you where you need to go."

Tidbit ran to her and hugged her. "You nice like my mama. Soft like my mama."

Fiona nodded and her eyes welled up. "You children get going. May the good Lord take a liking to you, but not too soon! Here's a bit of food — oranges and biscuits and a little salt pork." She lifted the bundle and put it beneath the wagon seat.

"Thank you for everything, Miss Fiona," Polly said. "Should we travel on the main road?"

"You drive the wagon, lass. Can you pretend to be a mistress?"

Polly hesitated. "Yes, ma'am. I think I can do that."

"If anyone stops you, tell them these two are your slaves. If you think there is danger, hide them under the straw."

Polly nodded.

"Travel by night and follow the road south. I've never been that far, but I hear tell that it goes straight through Georgia Colony to the end of the world — Spanish territory."

They climbed into the small wagon — Polly holding the reins of the old horse, Amari sitting next to her on the seat. Tidbit sat in the back on the hay. Dusk was approaching.

"May your feet bring you to where your heart is. Godspeed," Fiona called as they waved. "Godspeed."

Amari looked back once for Besa, but he did not appear. She shed no tears. Besa was now a memory, tucked away with all the rest of the things she had lost.

Hushpuppy bounded into the back of the wagon into Tidbit's arms just as they pulled onto the road. The moon shone brightly that night, and Amari decided it was lighting a path to her future.

■ ■ ■ ■

PART TEN
POLLY

■ ■ ■ ■

38. THE SPANISH SOLDIER

With the wagon, they made remarkable time. What might have taken them three or four days walking, they covered in one evening, rolling not exactly smoothly over the bumpy, rutted road, but thankfully. Old Brownie seemed to have regained a bit of his youthful energy, neighing and shaking his mane at the start of each evening's travel.

Polly chuckled to herself as she remembered a horse her father had once owned. Old Fart, he had called it because the horse had had a terrible problem with flatulence. He eventually sold it to a farmer he didn't like. "One fart deserves another!" her father had joked, making up funny horse stories, complete with vividly descriptive sound effects, all to amuse Polly. Her mother had frowned with mild disapproval at first, but eventually, the three of them ended up laughing uproariously in front of the hearth that whole evening. Those were the times she missed — not the days of hunger or rats or sickness, but the warmth of the fire when her family laughed.

"What do you miss most about your mother, Amari?" she asked as they rumbled down the road in the starlight.

Amari was silent for a moment, then she said, "Seem like no matter what I ask her, she always got the right answer. Sure be nice to talk to her one time."

Polly nodded in understanding. "My father wasn't perfect," she admitted, "but my mother truly loved him. She would light up like a lantern when he walked into a room." She paused. "At the end, she was in severe pain, but she was so brave, never complaining, only worrying about what would happen to me."

Amari pulled the reins so the horse would step around a branch on the road. "I never seen my mama scared, never seen her not know what to do." She breathed deeply of the night air. "Even the night she die, she fight like a lion."

"You know, you're brave as well, Amari. Your mother would be proud of you," Polly said honestly. "Your belief in Fort Mose, along with your strength and courage, is what has brought us this far."

Amari shook her head. "I be scared all the

time," she admitted. "I never be brave as lion like my mama."

Polly looked up at the sparkling night. "I think of my mother at night as we travel," she told Amari. "It helps." Amari glanced at the sky and smiled as if the thought was comforting.

"What about *my* mama?" Tidbit asked then. "I wanna go back home."

Amari and Polly both hugged him. "We gotta find new home," Amari told him. "Your mama want you to be big boy. You know she love you, even if she can't be with you." Tidbit seemed unconvinced. He put his thumb in his mouth and leaned against Amari.

By day they still hid as best they could, sleeping under the wagon and praying they would not be discovered. There had been no sign of Clay.

Polly noticed that Amari seemed to be having trouble sleeping. One afternoon when Amari woke with a start, covered with sweat, Polly told her quietly, "You must think of your young man as dead, Amari. I am so sorry."

Amari nodded her head in agreement. "Maybe been better if I not see Besa like that."

"Maybe it was a good thing," Polly suggested quietly. "Perhaps it will give you strength to go on."

"Make me feel sick inside," Amari told her. "And angry, too."

Polly traced a pattern with her finger in the dirt. "You know, I never really knew any black people before I came to Mr. Derby's place. I mean, everybody had slaves, of course, but I never actually thought about them. And I certainly never had a black friend before," she admitted.

Amari looked away. "Sometime I hate white people," she admitted softly. "I never hate before I be a slave." She stretched her arms. "I never even see white person until they attack my village. It be hard to have hate feeling and like feeling at same time."

Polly said, "I understand, Amari."

Amari looked at Polly and said shyly, "I think now I have friend with pale skin."

Polly replied quietly, "For certain you do."

Amari looked into Polly's eyes. "If we gets to Fort Mose, you gonna stay?"

Polly didn't answer right away. "I don't know. I have not thought about it deeply. I truly have no place else to go."

Amari shrugged. "I never go back to my land," she said, her voice plaintive. "But this be land of white people. Maybe you find a place for you."

"Maybe," Polly replied thoughtfully.

Amari put her head in her hands and rocked. Finally, her voice full of anguish, she revealed her concerns. "Maybe nothing be there, Polly. Maybe it be no good place. Maybe Besa right and we be catched."

"And maybe he is wrong, and you and Tidbit will be forever free!" Polly said firmly. "You told Fiona that Tidbit is yours. He *is* your child now, Amari. He needs you to be strong."

"Maybe I not be strong enough to be a mother," Amari said doubtfully.

Polly smiled and looked at the sleeping child. "You would die for that child."

"Yes, for sure," Amari admitted. "In my village all women be mothers to all the children. Maybe Tidbit belong to both of us," Amari said.

Tidbit opened his eyes and grinned. "Tidbit belong to Tidbit!" he said cheerfully. Amari's sad mood seemed to lift as she and Polly tickled him. Even when they played and laughed, however, they did it quietly, always watchful of footsteps or danger, always fearful of the return of Clay.

The land in southern Georgia lay vastly undeveloped, with fewer and fewer settlements of farmers. Amari did see in the distance, however, occasional garrisons of soldiers the farther south they traveled.

"Those soldiers make me nervous," Polly whispered to Amari, not wanting Tidbit to hear.

"Soldiers carry guns," Amari said, remembering the men who had attacked her village. "That not be good."

"Let's be extra quiet tonight," Polly suggested.

The moon hid behind the clouds, and the night shadows played tricks on Amari's imagination. She kept looking behind her. Nevertheless, they drove their little wagon carefully and slowly down the deserted path that night. It seemed to shout their location as it managed to hit every bump and hollow in the road.

They'd traveled for several hours without saying a word when, without warning, a shadowy body appeared about ten feet in front of them. "Halt, who goes there?" the male voice called out shakily.

Polly thought immediately of Clay — perhaps he had found them once more. Amari clutched Tidbit to her, and Polly grasped her arm. She was not sure if the man had seen them. To get so close and then be captured!

The voice spoke again. "*¡Pare!* Halt! I mean, stop, I mean *¡Pare!*" The footsteps moved unsteadily. "If you mean me harm or if you be *un fantasma* — a ghost — go away!" Whoever had been speaking fell silent.

"What should we do?" whispered Polly.

"Run!" Amari whispered back. "Leave the wagon!"

The two girls climbed down to the road, motioning to Tidbit to jump. But Tidbit, instead of silently slipping from the wagon, shouted, "Who be that, Amari?"

The shadowy voice on the road roared. Tidbit screamed. Polly's heart sank. She knew they were captured. But the person on the road didn't grab either of the girls — he reached out and snatched Tidbit from Amari.

Tidbit protested loudly and wriggled to get free. Then the voice yelped in pain, and suddenly Tidbit was back on the ground. Amari grabbed him back close to her.

"He bit me!" a man's voice whined. Polly relaxed a bit. It wasn't Clay's voice and, when she thought about it, not even a threatening voice.

Polly headed toward the man, then stopped. Hushpuppy barked hysterically. The silence of the night completely destroyed, they all stood there on the road like actors in a play, each waiting for the other's next move.

Polly spoke first. "Are you drunk?" she asked, trying to understand the man's unusual behavior.

"*No estoy borracho* — I am not drunk," the man responded. "I never partake of strong spirits, but it might help, however, in this insect-infested country." He belched. "What I am is afraid of things in the night — wolves and bears and such."

"And children?" Polly asked.

"Why not? It is dark and you surprised me."

"He is soldier," Amari said, her voice low.

"Now, that is a fact," the man replied in agreement as he stumbled on the road. "*Soy un cabo en el ejército del rey* — I am a corporal in the army of His Majesty King Philip V. Of course, I have never met the king, but who am I to question kings and generals?" He burped again. "Greetings to you from *mi país de España* — my beloved home country of Spain."

"You are Spanish?" Polly asked suspiciously. She wished she could speak the language.

"And most proud of it, my dear. And missing my home mightily." He sighed. "I am Domingo Salvador, just another lonely soldier from Madrid."

"So why you grab the child?" Amari asked him angrily.

"The night frightens me. He could have been a bear. *Tuve miedo* — I was afraid," the soldier admitted, seeming to cower from Amari's words.

"I not no bear," Tidbit stated, sounding mildly insulted. Then he giggled.

"What are you children doing out here *a media* — in the middle of the night?" the soldier asked.

Polly replied with another question. "Where are the rest of the soldiers in your company, and why are you out here alone at night?"

"They are asleep, but we patrol the area for English troops and runaways. Me, I would rather be home with my Maria. We had just married when I was called to this service." He swatted at his arm. "All I have for company are *los mosquitos y las memorias.*" He belched once more.

"What do you do with runaways?" Polly asked carefully.

The soldier looked at Polly with bleary eyes. "Officially, runaways do not exist until they leave the colonies. But once they cross *El Río del Santa María* — the St. Marys River — we help them to St. Augustine. King Philip does not believe in slavery of any kind," he told them proudly.

"Which way to this river?" Amari asked warily.

"Just two days' journey down this road," the soldier replied. "Why do you ask? You be *fugitivos,* runaways?"

"Of course not," Polly said. "Maybe you are intoxicated after all. I am returning to my home from a visit to my grandfather's house."

The young soldier replied. "I am sorry to have frightened you."

"Go back to your company, Corporal Salvador," Polly told him, "and I will not tell my father that I saw you on the road."

"Oh, *gracias,* thank you, *señorita,*" the soldier replied as he smoothed out his uniform. "On the morrow I will believe you were all in *mi sueño* — my dream." He then looked at Polly seriously. "Be very careful, *señorita.* The soldiers of the English are cruel and dangerous. The river you need to cross is not far."

"Thank you, sir," Polly said, realizing he was not as simple as he looked.

The Spanish soldier looked at the three children and smiled. "The place you seek, my children, is called Gracia Real de Santa Teresa de Mose. The English call it Fort

Mose. It is two miles north of St. Augustine."

Sounding suspicious, Amari spoke up. "What you know 'bout that place?"

Corporal Salvador sat down in the middle of the road. "It is *muy pequeño* — very small. Only about a hundred people live there — just a few families. But they own the land they work on, and *ellos son libres* — they are free — to do as they please," he added quietly.

"What are the people there like?" Polly asked.

"Mostly freed slaves. Some white folk — mostly Spaniards, *españoles.* Lots of Indians from different tribes — Creek, Seminole, Cherokee — all living together. There is nothing like it *en todo el mundo* — in all the world."

"White soldiers in charge?" Amari asked.

The Spanish soldier laughed. "Actually, no. *El capitán* of the fort is Francisco Menendez, a black man. He was once *un esclavo* — a slave."

Amari looked impressed.

"Of course, I know you are not interested in this place and simply returning home to your father," the soldier continued, "but if you should ever be in that location, you would find churches — Catholic, of course

— shops, gardens, and simple homes. Lots of *niños* — children — as well." He looked at Tidbit, who scooted behind Amari.

"You are right, sir," Polly said, continuing the pretense that none of them knew what they were actually discussing. "My father must be worried by now. I must be on my way."

Corporal Salvador saluted the small group of travelers and told them gently, "*Buena suerte* — good luck, my children. *Vaya con Dios* — may you go with God." With that, he disappeared back off the road and in the direction of his camp.

"It be real!" Amari said with excitement in her voice. "We must hurry."

"No streets of gold, however," Polly warned. "Not that I believed Cato, anyway."

"Streets of free," Amari whispered. "Much more better." She was grinning.

■ ■ ■ ■

PART ELEVEN
AMARI

■ ■ ■ ■

39. CROSSING THE RIVER

The next morning brought the sun, brightly illuminating not only the road, but also Amari's spirits. She could barely contain her nervous anticipation, with images of neatly cobbled streets surrounded by safe stone walls dancing in her head.

"We must be very close to the river," Polly surmised. "I can't wait! Do you think we dare to travel during the day?"

"Yes, we find it now," Amari said as she stretched her arms up to the sun. They hadn't eaten since yesterday morning, and she felt drained and shaky. And in spite of her determination and excitement at being so close to their destination, she couldn't erase the reality that for now the three of them were hungry and thoroughly exhausted. She stumbled as she tried to walk a few paces, then she sat back down on the side of the road.

"Are you are all right, Amari?" Polly asked

with concern. "Get back up on the wagon."

"Just tired," Amari replied, but she climbed up without protest, holding on to Polly's hand for support.

"We gotta find something to eat!" Tidbit reminded them.

Amari rummaged in the wagon to see if any food remained. She found one small pouch full of berries. She gave them all to Tidbit. So, when they came across a grove of wild apple trees, Amari could hardly keep herself from shouting with joy. All of them — even Hushpuppy — filled up on the sweet fruit as they crouched as far from the road as they could.

That evening they finally reached the banks of the St. Marys River. It lay dark and smooth ahead of them. The moon shone brightly, illuminating the scene. Cypress trees decorated the edges, their branches and roots leaning over as though welcoming them. Amari thrilled at the sight; it hardly seemed possible that they could be so close to freedom.

Tidbit looked at the river fearfully. "I scared of gators, Amari," he said, pulling away. "This water be real deep."

"You got good reason," Amari replied, remembering that awful day. "But I take care of you."

"I don't see any alligators," Polly said, "but that doesn't mean they're not there. Lots of snapping turtles, though. Look!" She pointed to the gray-black rocklike creatures that moved lazily in the sandy mud on the bank of the river.

"Too far to swim," Amari admitted.

"It's very wide," Polly agreed. "How will we cross it?"

Amari replied, "We come too far to stop now." She could see flickering lights in the distance, indicating settlements or garrisons of soldiers or, maybe, Fort Mose. Her heartbeat quickened.

"We need a boat," Polly replied.

The horse, which had been eating the soft greens that grew by the riverside, whinnied softly. He shook his thick mane and ventured into the shallows to drink.

"Can horse swim?" Amari asked with sudden inspiration.

Polly looked dubious. "Sure, but the river looks awfully wide."

"Maybe we just wish we be across," Amari countered. "We gotta try." She unharnessed the horse from the wagon.

"We gonna ride across the river on back of Brownie?" Tidbit asked, jumping up and down.

"Suppose we fall off?" Polly wanted to know.

"S'pose gator get me?" Tidbit added.

Amari took a deep breath. "We not gonna give up now," she said. She patted Brownie on his neck, grabbed his mane, and pulled herself slowly to his back. The horse didn't seem to mind.

So Amari then pulled Polly up, who reached down for Tidbit. Polly placed Tidbit snugly between them, hugging him tightly. Even though Amari had never ridden a horse before, she found she was not afraid. Slowly, she nudged the horse to the water's edge, all the while watching for alligators or other predators.

The horse clearly loved being in the water. He pulled with all of his might to get free of the shallows, then he seemed to relax as the water became deep enough for him to swim. Hushpuppy swam deftly beside them.

Amari noticed the horse was moving his legs as if he were galloping, heading confidently to the other side of the river. The three riders were wet up to their waists, but the horse was strong and steady, and they did not slip into the water.

"This be fun!" Tidbit cried exultantly as they moved silently on the dark water. He still peered to each side, however, checking for alligators.

Amari held her breath, the excitement almost more than she could bear. Freedom lay on the distant sandy bank of this river. No one spoke. The moon shone brightly, making everything seem to glow.

Hushpuppy reached the shore first and immediately began shaking water off his fur. When the horse pulled the children up onto the sandy beach, Tidbit jumped off right away and cheerfully ran on the wet sand.

Amari jumped off next, hugging Tidbit with joy. "We be free, little one. Free!" She danced around the beach area, swinging Tidbit in the air.

Polly joined in, and Tidbit giggled with glee. Hushpuppy, however, began whimpering. Then he gave a nervous growl.

Amari paused and looked with concern at the dog. Though she couldn't see what was upsetting Hushpuppy, she instinctively grabbed Tidbit's hand and led him away from the shore. Amari turned to warn Polly when she saw it. "Look out, Polly!" Amari yelled hoarsely. Polly turned her head. "Gator!"

The alligator, close to ten feet long, moved with unbelievable speed, but Polly was even faster. She shrieked and scrambled away up the riverbank. The sound of the alligator's jaws snapping together on nothing but air encouraged all three of them to run wildly into the edge of the woods.

Breathing heavily, Polly asked, "Is it gone?"

"It be gone," Amari said as she looked back to where they had run from and scanned the water's edge. "Gators not go far from water."

"I be so scared, I almost pee!" Tidbit admitted.

Safe and feeling truly free, the three travelers sat down on the ground and laughed and laughed and laughed.

40. TIME TO MEET THE FUTURE

They slept the rest of that night under a tangle of branches that might have been left by a storm. They woke to warblers singing, making melody with a red and black woodpecker that tapped a beat on the trunk of a tree.

Amari stretched, then announced, "Today we go to find Fort Mose. It is time."

"We gonna find food there?" Tidbit asked, rubbing his tummy.

Polly grinned happily. "I expect so! Time to meet the future," she said.

"How long this gonna take?" Tidbit asked.

"Not sure," Amari replied. She knew they were close, but she had no idea whether it would take two days or two weeks to arrive at Fort Mose. Overcome with the enormous thought of finally reaching their destination, Amari felt herself filling up with emotion. She wanted to shout, scream, jump — they had finally arrived!

The three of them climbed back up on the old horse, then headed due south. Amari felt comfortable as the horse ambled slowly through the thick stands of palm trees that shadowed them, for they reminded her of the palm trees in her homeland so far away.

She slid off the horse with Tidbit and walked for a few miles.

"What this place be like, Amari?" Tidbit asked. He alternated between running off to chase the dog and returning to hold her hand.

"Don't know for sure. People be kind, I hope," she replied.

"What if they don't like us?" Tidbit continued as he tossed a stick to Hushpuppy.

"Who not like you?" Amari said to him with a laugh. "You be such a clever little boy."

"Will my mama be there?" Tidbit asked seriously. He had never removed the pouch his mother had placed around his neck.

Amari stopped short. She knelt down on the ground so she was eye to eye with Tidbit. It seemed to Amari that he had grown taller and gained maturity while on this journey. He had seen so much in his few years. "Teenie love you very much, you know that?"

Tidbit nodded, biting his lip.

"She can't be here with you, but she knows you be safe, and that make her happy."

"Is she all right?" Tidbit asked.

"Your mama is glad because she know you be full of joy. That make her smile so big, that smile find you here in this far place." Amari paused, remembering Teenie's lessons and her sacrifice. "Why you think she give you that piece of kente cloth you wear round your neck?" Amari asked him gently.

"So she always be with me," the boy replied. He had begun to tremble.

"What did your mama keep a-tellin' you while you be with her?"

"She tell me stories about Africa and about her own mother, and she tell me, 'Long as you remember, ain't nothin' really gone.' "

Amari, blinking away tears, hugged him. "You gonna always remember?"

"I ain't never gonna forget nothin' she done tell me," the boy said with great seriousness. He squeezed the leather pouch.

Amari raised Tidbit's face so he would look around. "She be in every breeze and cloud, every leaf and flower. She smilin' at you right now."

Tidbit thought about that. Then he asked

her solemnly, "Will you be my mama now, Amari?"

She hugged him tightly. "Oh, yes. Forever I will. You be my little boy. Always."

"Polly be there always too?"

"Always," Amari promised again, even though she knew that keeping promises was sometimes impossible in life.

He hugged her back, then asked quietly, "Is I still a slave, Amari?"

Amari looked at the boy with love. "No, Tidbit, you no slave. You free man, just like your mama dream. You never be slave again."

The boy grinned at that. "You be free too, Amari?"

Amari looked up at the vast, clear sky and exhaled. "Yes, I be free too. Never no slave no more."

Amari thought back, however, to what Polly had said at the start of this journey: "Freedom is a delicate idea, like a pretty leaf in the air: It's hard to catch and may not be what you thought when you get it." Amari wondered if this long and arduous journey would bring her the happiness she dreamed of. Maybe this place would turn out to be a terrible disappointment.

That afternoon they finally saw it — the place they had dreamed of for so long. For a moment they could only stop and stare. *Fort Mose. Fort Mose.* The fort itself was a tiny structure, actually — only about twenty yards square. Surrounded by a wall made of logs covered with earth, it carried no markings to indicate what it was, but Amari knew in an instant that this was the place. Surrounding the walls was a ditch filled with those prickly palmetto palms that had sliced them when they ran from Nathan's house. Soldiers, both black and white, patrolled outside the wall, and she assumed more stood watch inside in the watchtower, which stood higher than the walls.

Outside the walls of the fort, small houses with roofs of thatch dotted the landscape, huddled close together as if for protection. Small gardens grew near each house.

"It be much smaller place than I thought," Amari whispered.

"Nathan was right about the streets of mud," Polly said with a small laugh.

"Freedom not big. Freedom not pretty," Amari declared. "But freedom sure do feel good."

41. FORT MOSE

"What we do now?" Tidbit asked as they peeked at the fort in the distance.

Amari could barely contain her eagerness. "We go in!" she said joyfully.

Tidbit jumped from one foot to the other, and Polly kept covering her mouth to hold back a case of nervous giggles. Then, as if they did this every day, they boldly headed down the road toward the tiny fort. The horse ambled behind them.

Amari grabbed Tidbit by the hand, then reached out to Polly with her other hand. Polly gripped it firmly. The two girls looked at each other and understood all that was not said.

And they began to walk. First slowly. Then faster. Finally, almost trotting in anticipation, they walked down the hill, past the first few houses clustered near the road, and directly to the gate of the fort, about a half mile ahead. One house in particular, a small rounded hut made of rough logs and covered with thatch, stood very close to the road.

"Where y'all goin'?" a woman's voice called out.

Amari tensed, then stopped. The woman, dressed in a simple green calico dress and a bonnet to match, was standing in front of the house and waving to them. Her skin was dusty brown — the color of earth, Amari thought.

A fire burned in front of her house, and the smell of cooked rabbit filled the air.

"Uh, we be heading to the fort," Amari replied cautiously. She held Tidbit's hand tightly, but she released Polly's. Polly stepped back a little.

"Y'all be hungry?" the woman asked.

"Oh, yes'm," Amari replied.

Tidbit crept closer to the woman's woodsy fire. "We be *real* hungry, ma'am!" They all laughed at that, and the woman motioned for them to sit down. Polly tied the horse to a tree.

"How far y'all come?" the woman asked. She spooned three bowls of steaming food for them — corn pudding and roasted rabbit — acting as if greeting strangers was what she did every morning. Perhaps it was, Amari thought. The woman even tossed a bone to Hushpuppy.

"We come from Charles Town, South Carolina Colony," Amari admitted quietly.

The woman whistled through her teeth. "That be a far piece," she said. "You walk all this way, or you come by boat?"

"No boat," Amari replied, thinking how much quicker and easier their journey might have been if they had had a boat. "We walk."

"Hard journey?" the woman asked, glancing at their battered feet.

"Yes'm, very hard," Polly replied.

"Always is," the woman said with resignation.

"This be Fort Mose?" Amari asked, wanting to be absolutely sure they were in the right place.

"Sure is, chile. Gracia Real de Santa Teresa de Mose."

"I done dream of this place," Amari said softly, "for very long time."

"Dreams disappear when you wake up — ever notice that, chile?" the woman asked as she gave Tidbit more food.

Amari looked up in alarm. "Why you say that?"

"Relax, chile. You safe." The woman spooned a plate of food for herself. "My name is Inez. I was a slave in Georgia. Me and my man, Jasper, run away last year and come to this place. We figure we done made it to heaven, then the Spanish soldiers took him away."

"Why?" Amari asked with concern.

"It be like this," Inez said. "The English soldiers control the colonies. The Spanish ain't no saints who think everybody ought to be free. They free the slaves because it makes the English soldiers angry and because England be losin' lotsa money when they lose slaves."

"I don't understand," Polly said, looking confused.

Inez continued. "See, the Spanish own this Florida territory, and it be needin' protection from the English, who they is always fighting with. So they sometimes make the runaways serve in their army before they be truly free. That's where my Jasper is — down in Cuba someplace, serving in the Spanish army."

"But that's not fair!" Polly exclaimed.

"Everything that done happened to you been fair?" Inez asked her.

"No, ma'am," Polly answered quietly.

Amari thought about this, then asked, "You free, Inez?"

Inez smiled. "Yes, chile, I got my papers that says I be free. I be free to work hard, free to be hungry, and free to miss my man.

But yes, chile, I be free. Now, tell me who you are and who this little one be," she asked, nodding her head toward Tidbit.

"My name be Amari, and this be Tidbit — he my son now," Amari said out loud for the first time.

"My real name Timothy," Tidbit said quietly.

Amari looked at him in surprise.

"Mama name me Timothy," the boy said, "but I was real little when I was borned, so everybody call me Tidbit. But Mama always told me when I get to be a man, my name be Timothy."

Amari smiled with pride at the child who would one day be the man named Timothy.

"Well, Mr. Timothy, let me be the first to call you by your free name," Inez said, lightly pinching the boy on his chin. To Polly she said, "So what be your story, chile?"

Polly shifted her weight and finished what she was chewing. "I'm Polly. I was an indentured girl. I ran off with Amari and Tidbit because . . ." She paused. "It was very bad when we left." She bowed her head, as if the memory was too much to recite.

"Troubles never be over, chile," Inez said gently. "But it be good to share them with friends."

Polly looked up. "We could not have made it without each other," she acknowledged, smiling at Amari.

Amari returned the smile as she finished eating.

"Food be good thing too!" Tidbit said, interrupting. "More, please?"

As Inez was refilling Tidbit's bowl, Amari asked, "Who live here in this place?"

"Only about a hundred folk. Mostly runaway slaves who now be free. Some Indians. Some whites — mostly Spanish soldiers. Two priests. Everybody gets along because nobody got much. Everybody know everybody else. Sometimes blacks marry up with Indians, sometimes with whites. It sure ain't like nothing else, I reckon."

"Cato be right — little bit," Amari murmured to Polly.

"A few months back," Inez told them, "we had 'bout twenty escaped slaves come here from Georgia Colony. Their massa traced 'em here."

Amari looked up in alarm and thought of Clay. "They had to go back?" she asked. She wondered if Clay could ever, would ever trace them here.

Inez laughed. "No, chile, them folks just stood there and laughed at him — right in his face. He had no power here, so he had to leave."

"So we're safe now?" Polly asked. "Even if someone from Carolina Colony should find his way here, he could not make us go back?" Amari knew that Polly was worried about Clay as well.

" 'Bout as safe as you gonna be," Inez replied. "You say your name be Polly?" she asked as she looked at Polly closely.

"Yes, ma'am," Polly replied.

"A young feller come through here just a few days ago, lookin' for somebody name of Polly. A redheaded white boy. Could he be the one you worryin' about stealin' you back to Carolina?"

Polly covered her mouth in surprise. "Is he still here?"

"I thinks not. He might be down in St. Augustine, but I don't know for shure. He mighta said somethin' about comin' back this way. I don't rightly remember. He be a friend of yours or a foe?"

"A friend, I think," Polly replied. Her sunburned skin turned a little redder.

Amari turned to Polly and grinned at her. "So what we do next?" Amari asked Inez.

"Y'all need to meet Captain Menendez," Inez suggested. "He be the one who welcome y'all officially, find you place to stay, and get you registered down in St. August-ine."

"What does that mean?" Polly asked.

"Well, you gotta meet with the priests — everybody here be Catholic, you know. And you gotta promise to serve the Spanish king. Personally, I don't see much difference between a Spanish king and a English one. Both of 'em rich. Neither of 'em ever show up here." She chuckled. "But that be what they makes you do when they takes you down to St. Augustine. Everybody got paperwork, chile, but the difference here is it make you free."

Amari grinned at that, excited to start the process. "Free," she whispered.

At that moment Amari looked up as a tall, dark soldier with black and gray curly hair, deep-set dark eyes, and a spotless uniform walked purposefully from the fort toward them. *He reminds me of Father,* Amari thought with a pang.

The man nodded to Inez, looked over the tired and bedraggled new arrivals, and said in an officious tone, "Welcome to Fort Mose. I am Francisco Menendez, captain of this fort and responsible for all who live here."

Amari wasn't sure what to do, so she stood up and bowed. Polly did the same and said, "Thank you, sir." Tidbit, copying the two girls, bowed as well, but he leaned too far and fell over in a heap.

The captain chuckled, picked up Tidbit, then sat him down carefully. "Feel free to sit, my children," he said to Amari and Polly with a pleasant smile. "Please introduce yourselves."

Amari made the introductions, telling him briefly of their adventures on the journey and their desire to stay there as a place of refuge. She was amazed at how easily she was able to convey her thoughts in English.

"You have just learned English since you have been in this country?" he asked.

Embarrassed, Amari was afraid she had said something incorrectly. "Yessir," she replied quietly.

"Then I must compliment you on a re-markable job — to learn so much so quickly. Are you ready to learn Spanish now as well?"

Relieved, Amari grinned at him and nod-ded.

"Life here is not easy," the captain warned.

"Oh, no, sir," Amari said quickly. "We knows hard work. Even Tidbit — I mean, Timothy — is willin' to work."

"I am an escaped slave as well," the captain told them. "I have been recaptured twice and taken back to slavery. But I escaped each time and finally made my way back here. This place is not heaven, but it is so much better than the hell of slavery."

"Yes, sir," Polly whispered.

"How many years left on your indenture?" he asked Polly.

"Fourteen years, sir," Polly told him.

"That's madness!" the captain replied. "This Derby fellow must be out of his mind."

"Yes, sir," Polly said with sorrow. "We saw him kill a slave and a newborn baby the night before we left."

"Well, you will be safe here as long as we have the protection of the Spanish. What skills do the three of you have to offer?" he asked.

Amari thought for a moment. "Before we leave, suh, I feel like I worth nothing. But I knows how to cook and hunt and find herbs. And my mother taught me how to make threads from cotton. My father be a skilled weaver in my village and I watch him as much as he let me. If women be 'lowed to weave here, I got lots abilities," she said proudly.

Inez interrupted quietly, "You got more than that, chile."

"What you mean?" Amari asked.

"Now is not the time," Inez answered cryptically. "Later."

The captain ignored Inez and said to Amari, "Women can do anything they have skills for in this place. Can you build a loom?"

Amari closed her eyes, thinking back to her father's sturdy brown hands and how deftly they had constructed his loom, how nimbly his fingers had danced as he wove, and how magically the designs seemed to appear on the fabric. She wished she had spent more time with her parents when she'd had the chance. "Yessir. I remembers well how my father made it."

He nodded his head with satisfaction. "Good. You can earn good money as a maker of cloth and clothes."

"Money?" Amari asked with surprise. "I be paid for my work?"

"Of course," the captain replied. "Only slaves work for no reward."

Amari looked at Polly and beamed.

To Polly the captain asked, "Now, what can you offer? We all work together here."

Polly, seemingly unsure of herself at first, glanced at Inez, who gave her a nod of encouragement. "I can cook and clean. And," she added as an afterthought, "I can read and write."

Captain Menendez looked up with instant interest. "You are educated?"

Polly looked surprised at the captain's reaction. "Yes, sir. My parents had their troubles, but they taught me to read and write and count."

"There is a profound need for education for the children here," the captain said, his brows furrowed as if he were deep in thought. "Freedom means very little if there is no knowledge to go with it."

"I'd be glad to teach the children, sir," Polly offered.

"We'll start a school!" the captain said with excitement. "Do you think you can do that?" he asked Polly.

"Of course, sir." Polly glanced at Amari and Tidbit, a broad smile on her face.

"Excellent!" the captain said, clapping his hands together. "We have much thirst for learning. I shall have Jesse, our carpenter, make plans to build a small school."

"Can you show me how to make Timothy on paper?" Tidbit asked, obviously impressed with Polly's hidden talent.

"Yes, I can, Timothy," Polly replied. "And much more."

"And you, little man," the captain said, turning to Tidbit, "your job here will be to learn to read and write, but I shall apprentice you to the carpenter, so that you can learn to be a builder as well. Would that suit you?"

"Yassuh," the boy replied. "I be likin' that just fine."

The captain turned to Inez. "Give them the dwelling that had been occupied by Felix and his wife. They have moved down to St. Augustine." Inez nodded.

The captain began to leave, but then he turned back to the new residents of his domain. "Tomorrow we will begin the formalization process. But for now rest, relax, meet the people here. Inez will take good care of you. You are indeed welcome — even your dog," he added with a smile. He saluted and walked away.

Amari was thrilled and her face showed it. It was the first time since she had been taken from her homeland that she had met a black man in a position of authority. "Close your mouth, chile," Inez said with a chuckle. "Round here it ain't unusual to see a black man in charge. He wear his uniform well and be using his power wisely. He been around for a long time. Even the Spanish soldiers don't be messin' with Captain Menendez."

"I like his uniform," Tidbit said as the captain disappeared down the road. "Can I be a soldier?"

"Perhaps one day, when you are all growed up," Amari told him.

"I be fightin' for my freedom," the boy said, pretending to hold a musket.

"All your life, little one," Amari told him. "Take your time."

"I feel good about this place," Polly said with contentment. "I'm so tired of traveling, I could sleep for a week."

"You do that, chile," Inez told her. "Y'all still got a heap of healin' to do. You got family now — folks who will help take care of you. Go on and rest if you've a mind to."

Polly scooted close to the fire and held her hands out to its warmth. Amari knew that Polly had much to ponder as she gazed at the flames. She, too, had found a place of safety, at least for now.

Inez stood up and said to Amari, "Walk with me, chile. I wants to show you where the captain done give you to stay. It be on the far side of the cornfields."

"Timothy, you stay here and take care of Polly, you hear? I be right back," Amari called. Tidbit, who was busy chasing a chicken in Inez's yard, waved good-bye.

"Even the air here smell free," she said to Inez as they walked.

42. Copper Sun

Inez showed Amari the boundaries of the little settlement — a river, a marsh, and the hills they had traversed earlier. The entire community would fit in one tiny corner of Mr. Derby's plantation, Amari observed, as she walked past the small gardens of the people who lived there. Several people waved. To Amari's amazement, Inez pointed out a blended family whose Spanish mother and Negro father sat in front of a fire with their two children, as well as a family of Seminoles, who lived in the house next to them.

"Everybody here come from someplace else — ain't nobody been here very long. Don't nobody know how long they gonna stay. It just be good for right now," Inez explained. Amari understood.

She thought of Cato, who had dreams of streets of gold. "How this place come to be?" Amari asked.

"Folks been livin' here for a long time, but Fort Mose got made official by the king earlier this year of our Lord, seventeen hundred and thirty-eight," Inez explained. "Fort Mose s'posed to be protection for the town of St. Augustine," Inez said. "The Spanish king ain't no fool."

"How this little spot o' land s'posed to do that?" Amari asked.

"When the soldiers come, it be from the way you come — from north of here. St. Augustine be real important to the Spanish, so we out here as the outpost. I 'spect that's what Fort Mose is all about," Inez replied.

As they reached the thatched cottage that would be her new home, Amari thrilled at the sight. Surrounded by a small garden where vegetables were already growing, the dwelling was much larger than the slave shack she had shared with Polly back at Derbyshire Farms. With a window, a back door as well as a front door, and a hearth for cooking, there would be plenty of room for the three of them. It was perfect! But then Amari had a terrible thought.

"You got fightin' here?" Amari asked with alarm.

"Not much yet, but when there do be fightin', our men gonna be the first to die," Inez told her.

"Seem to me it be better to die for freedom than live as a slave," Amari said with feeling. It was hard for her to absorb the fact that she was truly free.

"Yes, chile, it be hard for a woman to be a slave," Inez replied slowly. "I know — I lived it too. Massa be messin' with you in the night." She kept her eyes away from Amari.

Amari bowed her head and looked at the ground. "For me, it be the son. I was his birthday present."

Inez touched Amari's shoulder with understanding. "How long you been on the road, chile?" she asked.

"I think about two month — it be hard to say."

"You been feelin' poorly on your journey?" Inez asked.

"We always hungry," Amari told her. "Never enough to eat. Never enough rest. But, yes, I been feelin' sickly."

"You ain't sick."

"I ain't?" Amari asked hopefully. "But I feels real bad 'most every day."

Inez paused a moment. Then she said gently, "You be with chile, Amari."

Suddenly, it all made sense — the nausea, the dizziness, the feeling of being heavy and lethargic. "Oh no!" Amari cried. She slumped to the floor of the cottage.

Amari thought with revulsion of the hated nights she had been called to Clay's room. The smell of the lantern by his bed. The stench of his sweat. She thought she would vomit.

"This cannot be. Not now. Not when freedom be in my hand," she whispered.

Inez squatted beside her. "You all right, chile?" she implored.

"No, ma'am. I cannot do this. This child make me think about bein' slave." Amari wept.

"Babies don't know nothin' 'bout no slavery. They just knows 'bout love," Inez said gently.

"I hate it!" Amari cried, clutching at her stomach. She could not erase the image of Clay's hateful face from her mind.

"No, chile. You don't hate it. Already you be lovin' it. In your mind you already protectin' it from the bad memories you carry. I sees the struggle on your face."

"No!" Amari cried out.

"Yes," Inez whispered into her ear. "Your heart be sayin' yes."

Amari did not want to admit that Inez might be right. "I be so scared," she whispered to Inez.

"I know, chile, but you ain't the first. You got women here who will help you, women who done gone through the same thing. Like me," Inez offered.

"You?" Amari asked through her tears.

"I had a chile, my massa's chile for shure. She be as pretty as the dawn — blond hair, blue eyes, and skin the color of weak tea."

"What happen to her?" Amari asked.

"Massa's wife hated that chile. Had Massa sell her when she was not much older than your Tidbit — sold her down to New Orleans. Massa sold his own flesh and blood." Inez gave Amari a hug. "I never seen her ever again."

Amari hugged Inez and swallowed her own tears. "I be so sorry about your baby. You must for shure knows how Tidbit's mama must be feelin'. I hope your child be safe and happy like Tidbit is."

"Lord only knows," Inez said as she looked to the sky.

"I feels so stupid," Amari told her. "I shoulda figgered it out."

"You ain't had no mama to see the signs and take care of you," Inez told her softly. "And it probably was best that you didn't figger it out while you was on your journey. You had to focus on survivin'."

"What I do now?" Amari asked her in alarm.

"Relax, chile. Let nature take its course.

You ain't got but a few months to wait."

"My chile be born free?" Amari asked.

"Oh, yes, Amari. Your chile be free."

"Free." The word felt like cool water on Amari's lips.

Inez looked around the cottage. "I'm gonna make y'all a broom for your new place. I'll get Tidbit to help me gather the branches. You stay here and think about your future, chile. It be a good day to spend some silent time. I'll be back directly." She turned and left, heading back to her own place.

Amari placed her hands on her belly, full of wonder and confusion. *I cannot do this!* she thought frantically. She felt like running away from herself, from this new reality. *But I'm so tired — I just can't run anymore. Not from the past. Not from my future.* She closed her eyes and leaned against the wall of the cottage. Distorted images of Clay Derby's face floated into her mind. The most disconcerting image was the look of genuine affection he occasionally showed her. Amari beat her hands on the dirt floor, tears of anger welling in her eyes.

What shall I do? Amari thought helplessly. She willed herself to imagine her mother, who would know what to say and how to comfort her. All of her mother's dreams of growing old and watching her grandchildren play had been brutally dashed into the dust. *This child carries the spirit of my mother,* Amari realized suddenly, as well as the essence of her father, little Kwasi, the murdered people of her village, and the spirits of all of her ancestors.

Amari opened her eyes and glanced out of the small door of the hut to the bright sky above. It was getting close to sunset. She lovingly visualized Afi, who had been the friend and mother she needed during that horrible journey to this land. Afi, who had told her that her destiny lay somewhere beyond those horrors. Amari had understood none of it at the time, but now, perhaps, it was beginning to make just a little sense.

Wiping away a tear, Amari thought painfully of Teenie. "Long as you remember, chile, nothin' ain't really ever gone," she'd said many times. Amari vowed never to forget. She wished with all her heart that Teenie could have come to this place with them. Teenie had also understood that Amari had been brought to this land for a reason, had sensed Amari's strength before Amari knew she had any, and had placed her own child in Amari's care for a chance at freedom.

She inhaled sharply as she thought of Mrs. Derby, of the infant who had been given no chance to live, and of all the other women, both black and white, who continued to suffer as property of others. Amari also said a prayer of thanks for Polly, who was, incredibly, her friend.

Amari refused to think of Clay any longer, for she knew his evil spirit could never touch the love she was already beginning to feel for the child within her. Inez had been right about that as well.

If this child is a boy, Amari thought, *I shall name him Freeman. He will stand tall and proud and be forever free. I shall teach him my native language and tell him of the beauties of my homeland. If it is a girl, I shall name her Afi, after the one who loved me and helped me find my destiny. I will tell this child of her ancestors and her grandparents and tell her the stories my father told me. My child shall never be enslaved,* Amari vowed fiercely.

Amari glanced toward the west and watched the sun set. It glowed a bright metallic copper — the same sun that set each evening upon her homeland. She knew that she had found a home once more.

AFTERWORD

Although this is a work of fiction, the facts of the story are true. Fort Mose (pronounced Mo-ZAY) was a real place. As early as 1670, enslaved Africans began to escape and make their way south, rather than north, down the Atlantic coast to the Spanish settlement at St. Augustine, Florida, where they were offered liberty and religious sanctuary. These runaways eventually established the Gracia Real de Santa Teresa de Mose, the first free black town within the present-day borders of the United States.

Located two miles north of St. Augustine, Fort Mose was a frontier community of homesteaders from diverse cultures — including Caribbean, West African, Native American, and European — creating a complex family network. Their skilled labor, technological ability, art, music, ideas, and traditions served as valuable resources to the area.

In 1738, when this story takes place, the United States did not yet exist. There were a series of loosely connected colonies, most of which were ruled by England. The area known as Florida, however, was controlled by Spain, which made for some lively clashes and political posturing between the two countries. For example, the Spanish promised freedom to any escaped slave who became Catholic and promised to fight with the Spanish against the English.

A West African Mandingo by birth, Francisco Menendez, formerly enslaved in Carolina, arrived in St. Augustine around 1724. He became captain of the black militia of St. Augustine and fought to ensure the promise of the king of Spain. The black militia was well known in the area for their bravery. Captain Menendez was well respected by people in both Fort Mose and in St. Augustine and had a reputation as a fierce fighter.

In 1740, although the black militia fought bravely against General James Oglethorpe of Georgia, who sought to return escaped slaves back to the colonies, Fort Mose was badly damaged. Most of the citizens of Fort Mose, however, had already been safely moved to the protection of St. Augustine. The fort was rebuilt a few years later, larger and stronger, but it was finally abandoned in 1763 when Florida became an English colony.

Designated a National Historic Landmark in 1994, Fort Mose is now an important designation on the Florida black Heritage Trail. Although the actual site is now underwater off the coast of Florida, it remains a tangible reminder of the people who risked and often lost their lives in their struggle to attain freedom.

Note to teachers and students about resources: I did years of research to write this book, using hundreds of sources. It is impossible to include in the story all the information that I learned. If you'd like to learn more about this period in history, the list below contains not all, but some of the best sources that I found. Please do not let this list limit your research. There are many more books and Web sites on the subject of slavery and freedom. I offer this list as a service, just to get you started.

Web Sites
Daily life of slaves:
   http://www.sciway.net/hist/chicora/slavery

18-3.html

Housing: http://www.sciway.net/afam/
slavery/houses.html

Hunger and hardships:
http://www.sciway.net/afam/slavery/
food.html

The work day:
http://www.sciway.net/afam/slavery/
work.html

Slavery time line:
http://www.innercity.org/holt/slavechron.html

*The Middle Passage — the journey of slaves
from Africa to the New World:*
http://www.juneteenth.com/mp2.htm

Runaway slave ads:
http://etext.lib.virginia.edu/etcbin/costa-
browse?id=r38040013
http://etext.lib.virginia.edu/etcbin/costa-
browse?id=r38040015

Maps of the slave trade:
http://www.uwec.edu/geography/Ivogeler/
w111/slaves.htm
http://www.africanculturalcenter.org/

4_5slavery.htm
http://exploringafrica.matrix.msu.edu/
 curriculum/lm15/stu_actone.html

The African/Atlantic slave trade:
http://www.sciway.net/hist/chicora/
 slavery18-2.html
http://www.pbs.org/wgbh/aia/part1/
 1narr4.html
http://exploringafrica.matrix.msu.edu/
 curriculum/lm7/B/stu_7Bactivityone.html

Slavery:
http://www.pbs.org/wnet/slavery/timeline/
 1731.html
http://www.innercity.org/holt/
 slavechron.html
http://www.pbs.org/wnet/slavery/resources/
 index.html
http://hitchcock.itc.virginia.edu/Slavery
http://lcweb2.loc.gov/ammem/snhtml/
http://www.sciway.net/hist/chicora/slavery
 18-2.html

The Middle Passage:
http://exploringafrica.matrix.msu.edu/
 curriculum/lm7/B/stu_7Bactivityone.html
http://www.juneteenth.com/middlep.htm

Fort Mose:

http://library.thinkquest.org/CR0213580/
fortmose1.html

http://www.pbs.org/wgbh/aia/part2/
2h14.html

http://www.oldcity.com/sites/mose/

http://www.archaeology.org/9609/abstracts/
ftmose.html

http://library.thinkquest.org/CR0213580/
fortmose2.html

http://library.thinkquest.org/CR0213580/
fortmose4.html

http://dhr.dos.state.fl.us/services/magazine/
01winter/mose.cfm

Indentured servants:

http://odur.let.rug.nl/~usa/D/1601-1650/
mittelberger/servan.htm

http://www.stratfordhall.org/ed-servants
.html?EDUCATION

Underground Railroad map:

www.cr.nps.gov/nr/travel/underground/
detailedroutes.htm

*National Underground Freedom Center —
Cincinnati, OH:*

www.freedomcenter.org

Underground Railroad resource study:

www.historychannel.com/blackhistory/
  ?page=exhibits2
www.nationalgeographic.com/railroad/
www.undergroundrr.com

Slave narratives:
http://afroamhistory.about.com/od/
  slavenarratives/
http://core.ecu.edu/hist/cecelskid/
  narrative.htm
http://docsouth.unc.edu/neh/texts.html
http://metalab.unc.edu/docsouth/neh/
  neh.html
http://lcweb2.loc.gov/ammen/snhtml/
  snhome.html
http://xroads.virginia.edu/~hyper/wpa/
  index.html

Books

Blassingame, John W. *The Slave Community: Plantation Life in the Antebellum South.* Oxford: Oxford University Press, 1979.

Captive Passage: The Transatlantic Slave Trade and the Making of the Americas. Washington, D.C.: Smithsonian Institution Press, 2002.

Carney, Judith A. *Black Rice: The African Origins of Rice Cultivation in the Americas.* Cambridge, MA: Harvard University Press, 2001.

Clarke, Duncan. *Slaves and Slavery.* London: Grange Books, 1998.

Currie, Stephen. *Life of a Slave on a Southern Plantation.* San Diego: Lucent Books, 2000.

Deagan, Kathleen and Darcie MacMahon. *Fort Mose: Colonial America's Black Fortress of Freedom.* Gainesville, FL: University Press of Florida/Florida Museum of Natural History, 1995.

Dean, Ruth, and Melissa Thomson. *Life in the American Colonies.* San Diego: Lucent Books, 1999.

Everett, Susanne. *History of Slavery.* Edison, NJ: Chartwell Books, 1997.

Franklin, John Hope and Alfred A. Moss, Jr. *From Slavery to Freedom: A History of Negro Americans.* New York: McGraw-Hill, 1998.

Hagedorn, Ann. *Beyond the River: The Untold Story of the Heroes of the Underground Railroad.* New York: Simon & Schuster, 2002.

Harms, Robert. *The* Diligent: *A Voyage through the Worlds of the Slave Trade.* New York: Basic Books, 2002.

Haskins, Jim. *Get on Board: The Story of the Underground Railroad.* New York: Scholastic, 1993.

Hawke, David Freeman. *Everyday Life in Early America*. New York: Harper and Row, 1989.

Howell, Donna, ed. *I Was a Slave. Book 5: The Lives of Slave Children*. Washington, D.C.: American Legacy Books, 1998.

Johnson, Charles and Patricia Smith. *Africans in America: America's Journey Through Slavery*. New York: Harcourt Brace, 1998. (Also available on video)

Kelley, Robin D. G. and Earl Lewis. *To Make Our World Anew: A History of African Americans*. Oxford: Oxford University Press, 2000.

Kleinman, Joseph and Eileen Kurtis-Klienman. *Life on an African Slave Ship*. San Diego: Lucent Books, 2001.

Landers, Jane. *Fort Mose. Gracia Real de Santa Teresa de Mose: A Free Black Town in Spanish Colonial Florida*. St. Augustine, FL: St. Augustine Historical Society, 1992.

Lester, Julius. *To Be a Slave*. New York: Scholastic, 1968.

Rappaport, Doreen. *Escape from Slavery: Five Journeys to Freedom*. New York: Harper Collins, 1991.

Thomas, Velma Maia. *Lest We Forget: The

*Passage from Africa to Slavery and Emanci-
pation.* New York: Crown Publishers, 1997.

ABOUT THE AUTHOR

Sharon M. Draper visited the slave castles in Ghana several years ago. She was so moved, she knew she had to tell the story of one girl who might have made that harrowing journey through "the door of no return." Sharon currently lives in Cincinnati, Ohio, where she writes the stories that teenagers love to read. She's also a popular conference speaker, addressing education and literary groups both nationally and internationally. The recipient of the Coretta Scott King/John Steptoe Award for New Talent for *Tears of a Tiger*, she has also won the Coretta Scott King Award for *Forged by Fire*, and the Coretta Scott King Author Honor for *The Battle of Jericho*. Her other books include *Romiette and Julio*, *Darkness Before Dawn*, and *Double Dutch*. For more information go to www.sharondraper.com.